Pan-Asianism in Modern Japanese History

Regionalism has played an increasingly important role in the changing international relations of East Asia in recent decades, with early signs of integration and growing regional cooperation. This in-depth volume analyzes various historical approaches to the construction of a regional order and a regional identity in East Asia. It explores the ideology of Pan-Asianism as a predecessor to contemporary Asian regionalism, which served as the basis for efforts at regional integration in East Asia, but also as a tool for legitimizing Japanese colonial rule. This mobilization of the Asian peoples occurred through a collective regional identity established from cohesive cultural factors such as language, religion, geography, and race. In discussing Asian identity, the book succeeds in bringing historical perspective to bear on approaches to regional cooperation and integration, as well as analyzing various utilizations and manifestations of the pan-Asian ideology.

Pan-Asianism in Modern Japanese History provides an illuminating and extensive account of the historical backgrounds of current debates surrounding Asian identity and essential information and analyses for anyone with an interest in history as well as Asian and Japanese studies.

Sven Saaler is Associate Professor at the Graduate School of Arts and Sciences, University of Tokyo. He was formerly head of the Humanities Section of the German Institute for Japanese Studies (DIJ) in Tokyo.

J. Victor Koschmann is Professor of History at Cornell University where he has specialized in modern Japan's intellectual and cultural history with reference to political thought.

Asia's Transformations
Edited by Mark Selden
Binghamton and Cornell Universities, USA

The books in this series explore the political, social, economic and cultural consequences of Asia's transformations in the twentieth and twenty-first centuries. The
series emphasizes the tumultuous interplay of local, national, regional and global
forces as Asia bids to become the hub of the world economy. While focusing on the
contemporary, it also looks back to analyze the antecedents of Asia's contested rise.

This series comprises several strands:

Asia's Transformations aims to address the needs of students and teachers, and the titles
will be published in hardback and paperback. Titles include:

Debating Human Rights
Critical essays from the United States and Asia
Edited by Peter Van Ness

Hong Kong's History
State and society under colonial rule
Edited by Tak-Wing Ngo

Japan's Comfort Women
Sexual slavery and prostitution during World War II and the US occupation
Yuki Tanaka

Opium, Empire and the Global Political Economy
Carl A. Trocki

Chinese Society
Change, conflict and resistance
Edited by Elizabeth J. Perry and Mark Selden

Mao's Children in the New China
Voices from the Red Guard generation
Yarong Jiang and David Ashley

Remaking the Chinese State
Strategies, society and security
Edited by Chien-min Chao and Bruce J. Dickson

Korean Society
Civil society, democracy and the state
Edited by Charles K. Armstrong

The Making of Modern Korea
Adrian Buzo

The Resurgence of East Asia
500, 150 and 50 year perspectives
Edited by Giovanni Arrighi, Takeshi Hamashita and Mark Selden

Chinese Society, Second edition
Change, conflict and resistance
Edited by Elizabeth J. Perry and Mark Selden

Ethnicity in Asia
Edited by Colin Mackerras

The Battle for Asia
From decolonization to globalization
Mark T. Berger

State and Society in 21st Century China
Edited by Peter Hays Gries and Stanley Rosen

Japan's Quiet Transformation
Social change and civil society in the 21st century
Jeff Kingston

Confronting the Bush Doctrine
Critical views from the Asia-Pacific
Edited by Mel Gurtov and Peter Van Ness

China in War and Revolution, 1895–1949
Peter Zarrow

The Future of US–Korean Relations
The imbalance of power
Edited by John Feffer

Working in China
Ethnographies of labor and workplace transformations
Edited by Ching Kwan Lee

Korean Society, Second edition
Civil society, democracy and the state
Edited by Charles K. Armstrong

Singapore
The state and the culture of excess
Souchou Yao

Pan-Asianism in Modern Japanese History
Colonialism, regionalism and borders
Edited by Sven Saaler and J. Victor Koschmann

Asia's Great Cities
Each volume aims to capture the heartbeat of the contemporary city from multiple perspectives emblematic of the authors own deep familiarity with the distinctive faces of the city, its history, society, culture, politics and economics, and its evolving position in national, regional and global frameworks. While most volumes emphasize urban developments since the Second World War, some pay close attention to the legacy of the longue durée in shaping the contemporary. Thematic and comparative volumes address such themes as urbanization, economic and financial linkages, architecture and space, wealth and power, gendered relationships, planning and anarchy, and ethnographies in national and regional perspective. Titles include:

Bangkok
Place, practice and representation
Marc Askew

Beijing in the Modern World
David Strand and Madeline Yue Dong

Shanghai
Global city
Jeff Wasserstrom

Hong Kong
Global city
Stephen Chiu and Tai-Lok Lui

Representing Calcutta
Modernity, nationalism and the colonial uncanny
Swati Chattopadhyay

Singapore
Wealth, power and the culture of control
Carl A. Trocki

Asia.com is a series which focuses on the ways in which new information and communication technologies are influencing politics, society and culture in Asia. Titles include:

Japanese Cybercultures
Edited by Mark McLelland and Nanette Gottlieb

Asia.com
Asia encounters the Internet
Edited by K.C. Ho, Randolph Kluver and Kenneth C.C. Yang

The Internet in Indonesia's New Democracy
David T. Hill and Krishna Sen

Chinese Cyberspaces
Technological changes and political effects
Edited by Jens Damm and Simona Thomas

Critical Asian Scholarship is a series intended to showcase the most important individual contributions to scholarship in Asian Studies. Each of the volumes presents a leading Asian scholar addressing themes that are central to his or her most significant and lasting contribution to Asian Studies. The series is committed to the rich variety of research and writing on Asia, and is not restricted to any particular discipline, theoretical approach or geographical expertise.

Pan-Asianism in Modern Japanese History

Colonialism, regionalism and borders

Edited by
Sven Saaler and J. Victor Koschmann

LONDON AND NEW YORK

First published 2007
by Routledge
2 Park Square, Milton Park, Abingdon, Oxon OX14 4RN

Simultaneously published in the USA and Canada
by Routledge
270 Madison Ave, New York, NY 10016

Routledge is an imprint of the Taylor & Francis Group, an informa business

Typeset in Garamond Pro by
Book Now Ltd
Printed and bound in Great Britain by
Antony Rowe Ltd, Chippenham, Wiltshire

British Library Cataloguing in Publication Data
A catalogue record for this book is available from the British Library

Library of Congress Cataloging in Publication Data
Pan-Asianism in modern Japanese history: colonialism, regionalism and
borders/edited by Sven Saaler and J. Victor Koschmann.
        p. cm.–(Asia's transformations)
Includes bibliographical references and index.
1. East Asia–Relations–Japan. 2. Japan–Relations–East Asia. 3. Japan–Foreign
relations–1868– 4. Regionalism–East Asia. I. Saaler, Sven, 1968–
II. Koschmann, J. Victor.

DS518.45.P36 2007
327.5205–dc22   2006023280

ISBN 10: 0–415–37215–1 (hbk)
ISBN 10: 0–415–37216–X (pbk)
ISBN 10: 0–203–96546–9 (ebk)

ISBN 13: 978–0–415–37215–2 (hbk)
ISBN 13: 978–0–415–37216–9 (pbk)
ISBN 13: 978–0–203–96546–7 (ebk)

Contents

Contributors

Roger H. Brown is Associate Professor of History in the Faculty of Liberal Arts at Saitama University. He researches Japanese political and intellectual history from the 1920s through the 1940s, and is currently writing a book on the nationalist thought and political activities of Yasuoka Masahiro.

Kristine Dennehy is Assistant Professor in the Department of History at California State University, Fullerton. Her dissertation dealt with "Memories of Colonial Korea in Postwar Japan" and her current research interests include repatriation from colonial Korea and projects which serve to integrate modern East Asian history into the world history curriculum at the secondary school level.

Kevin M. Doak holds the Nippon Foundation Endowed Chair and is chairman of the Department of East Asian Languages and Cultures at Georgetown University. He has written widely on issues related to ethnicity, nationalism and regionalism in East Asia. His most recent book, *A History of Nationalism in Japan: Placing the People*, is forthcoming from Brill Academic Publishers.

Hatsuse Ryūhei is Professor of International Relations at the Faculty for the Study of Contemporary Society at Kyōto Women's University. He was formerly president of the Japan Peace Studies Association and Professor of International Relations at Kōbe University. His publications include *Dentōteki uyoku Uchida Ryōhei no kenkyū* (A Study of the Traditional Right-winger Uchida Ryōhei) and many articles on human security and contemporary problems of international relations.

Katō Yōko is Associate Professor at the Department of Japanese History, Faculty of Letters of the University of Tokyo. She has written books on the middle-ranking army officers of the 1930s and their visions of how to reform the Meiji state, and on the Japanese conscription system between 1868 and 1945. Her latest book is *Sensō no Ronri* (The Origins and Logic of Japanese Wars).

John Namjun Kim is Assistant Professor of Comparative Literature, German and Japanese at the University of California, Riverside. He received his PhD in German Studies at Cornell University and has published on the intersection of German idealism and the Kyōto school of thought. He is currently completing a book on violence and modern subjectivity since Kant and Kleist, and is co-editing a volume on the work of Naoki Sakai.

J. Victor Koschmann is Professor and Chair of the Department of History at Cornell University. He has researched and published on the Tokugawa and pre-World War II as well as postwar periods of Japanese history. His current interests include the discourses on East Asian community and economic ethics during the 1930s and the period of total war.

Kuroki Morifumi is Professor Emeritus at Fukuoka International University. He researches early Pan-Asianism, particularly the history of the pan-Asian organizations Kōa-kai and Ajia Kyōkai and the Pan-Asianism of Ueki Emori. He is the co-editor of a collection of primary sources relating to the history of the Kōa-kai and the Ajia Kyōkai.

Li Narangoa is Reader at the Australian National University, College of Asia and the Pacific. She has published on Japan's policies towards Mongolia during the early twentieth century and on the formation of national identities in Asia. Her current interests are borders, empires and nationalism in Northeast Asia. She co-edited *Imperial Japan and National Identities in Asia, 1895–1945* (RoutledgeCurzon, 2003) and *Mongols from Country to City: Floating Boundaries, Pastoralism and City Life in the Mongol Lands* (NIAS Press, 2006).

Miwa Kimitada, born and raised in Japan, had just turned 16 years old when Japan was defeated in the war then known as the "Greater East Asian War." He earned his Master's and PhD degrees at Georgetown and Princeton Universities, respectively. After teaching international history at Sophia University in Tōkyō for 43 years, he retired in 2000. He has published numerous books and articles on questions relating to nationalism and Pan-Asianism in modern Japan.

Oguma Eiji is Associate Professor of Sociology and History at Keiō University. He is the author of *Tan'itsu minzoku shinwa no kigen* (The Myth of the Homogeneous Nation), *'Nihonjin' no kyōkai* (The Boundaries of 'the Japanese'), *'Minshu' to 'aikoku'* ('Democracy' and 'Patriotism') and many articles relating to questions of nationalism in modern Japan.

Sven Saaler is Associate Professor at the Graduate School of Arts and Sciences, University of Tokyo. He was formerly head of the Humanities Section at the German Institute for Japanese Studies (DIJ) in Tokyo. His research focuses on the history of Pan-Asianism and recent debates about the Yasukuni Shrine and Japanese history textbooks. He has recently published *Politics, Memory and Public Opinion* (Iudicium, 2005).

Michael A. Schneider is Associate Professor of History and Co-Director of the Center for Global Studies, Knox College, Illinois, USA. He is the author of a forthcoming book on the Japanese colonial empire. He is currently engaged in various projects on consumerism, gender, and foreign policy in twentieth-century Japan.

Dick Stegewerns is Associate Professor of Modern Japanese History and Comparative Culture at Ōsaka Sangyō University. His main fields of research are the intellectual and political history of modern Japan, the history of international relations in modern East Asia, and the history of Japanese cinema. He is the author of numerous articles on these subjects and editor of *Nationalism and Internationalism in Imperial Japan: Autonomy, Asian Brotherhood, or World Citizenship?* (RoutledgeCurzon, 2003). He has just completed the book *Adjusting to the New World: Japanese Opinion Leaders of the Taishō Generation and the Outside World, 1918–1932.*

Christopher W. A. Szpilman is Professor of Modern Japanese History and International Relations at Kyūshū Sangyō University. He is the author of numerous articles on Japanese conservatism and Pan-Asianism in the early twentieth century and co-editor of a collection of writings by Mitsukawa Kametarō.

Preface

As recent research increasingly emphasizes, the idea of the nation-state, a completely natural phenomenon for most contemporaries, is a rather recent creation with a history of not more than one or two centuries. The idea of *overcoming* the nation-state and national boundaries established by nation-states, marked by boundary stones in earlier ages and by electric barbwire in recent years, is almost as old as the idea of the nation-state itself. Pan-movements expressed the attempt to overcome or relativize the idea of the nation and create some sort of regional identity or polity. At times, pan-movements and pan-ideologies were no more than extensions of nationalism, but in general, above all, they emphasized the limitations of the national idea and put forward a transnational combination of thought and identity that went beyond national boundaries. Some pan-movements also served as vehicles for expansionism, colonialism, and the legitimization of colonial rule and (transnational) empire-building. This volume addresses questions relating to the history and ideology of Pan-Asianism in Japan from the late nineteenth century to the present, and aims to illuminate the broad variety of transnational approaches that have been put forward with the ultimate aim of defining and constructing an East Asian region – still an ongoing task.

The contributions collected in this volume are based on presentations given at a conference organized in Tōkyō by the German Institute for Japanese Studies (DIJ) in the fall of 2002.[1] The editors, also speaking for the contributors to this volume, would like to express their gratitude to the DIJ and the Japan Foundation for funding this conference, without which this volume would never have materialized. The editors also appreciate the generous support of the DIJ for translations of the Japanese papers. We would like to thank Roger Brown and Alistair Swale for translating the Japanese papers and, above all, the contributors for their patience and cooperation in responding to our questions and suggestions, but also for raising questions and commenting on other papers. We also thank the reviewers for their opinions, Paul Sorrell and Stefan Säbel for editorial assistance, Mark Selden for helping to make a book out of a collection of articles, and everybody at Routledge for their help in bringing the production of this volume to fruition.

We have rendered East Asian names in the original order, surname first, and have Romanized East Asian languages according to the Hepburn system for Japanese, the Revised Romanization of Korean from 2000 for Korean and Pinyin for Chinese. In the case of personal and place names in Chinese and Korean with established renderings in Western languages, such as Chiang Kai-shek or Shantung, we have decided to use these renderings. Pinyin in these cases is provided in brackets on the first mention (Jiang Jieshi, Shandong).

Keenly aware that a volume on a transnational ideology should not be limited to analyzing the manifestations of this ideology in only one nation-state, we hope that this volume will stimulate further research on regionalism in East Asia.

1   Pan-Asianism in modern Japanese history

Overcoming the nation, creating a region, forging an empire

Sven Saaler[1]

Pan-Asianism between nationalism and regionalism

In studies of international relations in East Asia, the phenomenon of regionalism – i.e. regional cooperation and integration based on a shared perception of the region's present, past, and future – is receiving growing attention. Regional approaches in East Asia are still heavily burdened by the legacies of the past, as shown by the recent discussions about the Yasukuni Shrine issue and the territorial disputes between Japan and her neighbors. Another important and controversial aspect of these legacies is Pan-Asianism, an ideology that served not only as a basis for early efforts at regional integration in East Asia, but also as a cloak for expansionism and as a tool for legitimizing Japanese hegemony and colonial rule. The history of Pan-Asianism is therefore highly ambiguous, as previous research[2] has demonstrated, and it is this ambiguity that still continues to pose a major obstacle for regional integration in contemporary East Asia.[3] This volume aims at exploring the ideology and the movement of Pan-Asianism as a precursor of contemporary Asian regionalism, thereby bringing historical perspective to bear on recent approaches to regional cooperation and integration.

Regionalism, as Peter Katzenstein has argued, "offers a stepping-stone for international cooperation between unsatisfactory national approaches on the one hand and unworkable universal schemes on the other."[4] Europe is widely seen as a pioneer in regional integration and in the quest to overcome the nation-state; while in Asia, regional approaches, although *en vogue* in journalism and academia, have yet to produce comparable institutional manifestations in international relations.[5] However, recent initiatives such as ASEAN+3[6] and Free Trade Agreements between Asian countries illustrate the growing importance of regional cooperation and integration.[7] In this context, references to historical precedent, i.e. nineteenth-century and prewar Pan-Asianism, are conspicuously avoided, made a taboo, or even taken as a "negative model."[8] This approach stands in contrast to the ubiquity of historical pan-Asian discourse in prewar Japan and Asia, as the contributions in this volume demonstrate.

The concept of a "pan"-movement originated within the framework of European history and international relations and thus, at first sight, may seem an inappropriate tool for analyzing Asian history. However, since the end of the nineteenth century, terms such as "Asian solidarity" (*Ajia rentai*), "Raising Asia" (*kō-A*), "Asianism" (*Ajia-shigi* or *Ajia-shugi*), "Pan-Asianism" (*Han-Ajia-shugi* or *Zen-Ajia-shugi*) and "Asian Monroe-ism" (*Ajia Monrō-shugi*) have had a wide circulation in discussions of foreign policy-making as well as in the discourses leading to the construction of modern identities in East Asia. Pan-Asianism developed in the discursive space between national identities and possibilities for transnational cooperation. It appeared in a wide variety of forms, as the variety of terms in use demonstrates, and it was also used in different ways. In all its historical manifestations, Pan-Asianism emphasized the need for Asian unity, mostly *vis-à-vis* the encroachment of Western colonialism and imperialism, but also emphasizing indigenous traditions, as will be shown below. Over time, the content of pan-Asian thought, including even the definition of "Asia," evolved as much as the consequences of its utilization in foreign policy. While Pan-Asianism was originally directed against Western influence and colonialism, it also functioned as a tool for legitimizing Japan's claim for hegemony in East Asia and Japanese colonial rule, i.e. as a way for Japan to deal with the emerging nationalisms of other Asian nations.[9]

Indeed, as a result of its prewar history, the idea of Pan-Asianism, and therefore Asian regionalism, has been much discredited. However, pan-Asian rhetoric continued to be employed in the postwar period, most notably in the quest to define so-called "Asian values" in response to the supposed universality of Western thought. Given the persistence of pan-Asian thought, and notwithstanding its problematic historical background, the phenomenon of Pan-Asianism obviously possesses a strong transnational character which appeals to intellectuals as well as politicians throughout Asia, notably at a time when economic bonds among Asian nations have reached high levels. When employed in efforts to establish a collective regional identity, pan-Asian thought has the capacity to cut across nation-state boundaries[10] and appeal to certain cohesive factors, such as culture and religion, language and script, shared historical experience, geography, and race. By addressing these aspects of Pan-Asianism in Japan[11] from the late nineteenth century until the postwar period, this volume aims at making both an empirical and a theoretical contribution to the study of Pan-Asianism and the historical background of regionalism as a factor in international relations.

The roots of Pan-Asianism

Pan-Asian ideology was an omnipresent force in modern Japan's foreign policy as well as in the process of the creation of a "Japanese" identity. In the Meiji era (1868–1912), it evolved into an ideology that was the antithesis of the government's "realist" foreign policy, which aimed at joining the club of "great powers" (*rekkyō*). Early pan-Asianist writings, in a rather "romantic" and "idealistic" manner, emphasized Japanese commonalities with Asia and aimed at uniting Asian peoples and countries against Western encroachment. In the process of the construction of a modern regional identity, Asianism was part of the criticism of modernization, against which pan-Asian thinkers advocated a "return to Asia" (*Ajia kaiki*) – a return to Asian culture and values.[12] Identification with Asia was not always an affirmative experience, as the quest for "casting off Asia" in Fukuzawa Yukichi's (1835–1901) famous "Datsu-A-ron" suggests; but Asia, as the contribution by Oguma Eiji in this volume points out, always functioned as a mirror for Japanese efforts at defining Japanese identity. Asia was "the spatial and temporal object through which Japanese defined themselves," as Stefan Tanaka has put it.[13] The resulting discussion about whether modern Japan was a part of the West, or rather of Asia, was central to modern Japanese discourse on national identity.[14] During this discourse, "Japan vacillated between insisting on being not Asian at all, and declaring itself the epitome of Asianness."[15] With the passage of time, the growing power of the Japanese nation-state and growing Japanese self-confidence, emerging as a consequence of growing power, eventually militated against a return to Asia, but led instead to ever-strengthening Japanese claims of *superiority* over Asia and *leadership* in Asia culminating in the "new order" of the 1930s and the "Greater East Asian Co-Prosperity Sphere" of the early 1940s.

The early roots of Pan-Asianism go back to the mid-nineteenth century, when China and Japan were forced to "open up" their long-isolated countries to foreign pressure and enter the system of international relations, dominated by the European imperialist powers. During that process, both China and Japan struggled to redefine their place in the new international order. Historically, a system of inter-state relations and tributary trade centered on China, also called the Sinocentric world system,[16] had been the framework holding East Asia together as a region. Japan had long been part of this system through relations conducted with China over the Ryūkyū Kingdom, controlled by the Japanese Satsuma domain, and through relations with Korea over Tsushima, as well as through its own tributary relations with China prior to the Tokugawa era.[17] At the same time, Japanese scholars had long challenged the "central" role of the "Middle Kingdom," China, in this system. Scholars of the *kokugaku* school such as Hirata Atsutane (1776–1843) had claimed that *Japan* was the "Middle Kingdom," since the unbroken imperial line of Japan (*bansei ikkei*) demonstrated that the island empire was the "Land of the Gods," not China, where dynastic changes and "Tartar rule" were frequent.[18] In this theory of "Japan as the Middle Kingdom" (*Nihon chūka-ron*) lay the seeds of the Japanese claim of superiority over China and the Japanese claim to leadership in Asia (*Nihon meishu-ron*).[19]

Notwithstanding the collapse of the Sinocentric world order in the second half of the nineteenth century, Japan could not immediately replace the old order with a pan-Asian "new order" under Japanese leadership. After the "opening" of the country in 1854 and the Meiji Restoration of 1868, Japan, above all, devoted her energy to securing national independence in view of the threat to it posed by Western imperialism. We can identify two approaches to dealing with the Western threat: aligning with other Asian nations to present a unified front, or joining the Western system of international relations and strengthening Japan economically and militarily in order to enable it to survive on its own. The Meiji government, faced with overwhelming Western military strength – which had been demonstrated on occasions such as the bombardment of the town of Kagoshima in 1863 or the fighting in the Shimonoseki Straits in 1864 – chose to adjust to the Western "Law of Nations" and secure national independence through modernization and the creation of a strong economy and a strong military (*fukoku kyōhei*). Only a few voices rejected this approach. Katsu Kaishū (1823–99), a Bakufu official who also worked for the Meiji government, advocated a Japanese–Chinese alliance (*Nisshin teikei*) as early as in the 1860s, an option taken up again by politician Sugita Teiichi (1851–1929), author of *Kōa-saku* (A Policy for Raising Asia), in the early Meiji era.[20] Authors like Fukuzawa Yukichi, too, before embracing a policy of "casting off Asia" argued for Japan becoming the leader (*meishu*) of a united Asia.[21]

During the Meiji era, a number of political associations were formed that fervently advocated the ideal of "solidarity with Asia" (*Ajia rentai*) or the notion of "raising Asia" (*kō-A*) or "developing Asia" (*shin-A*). These organized pan-Asianists criticized the government's foreign policy of cooperating with the Western powers. In order to promote a pan-Asian foreign policy, independent of the government, they maintained close contacts with opposition groups in Korea and China. The most influential of these early pan-Asian organizations were the Kōa-kai (Society for Raising Asia, founded in 1880), its successor organization Ajia Kyōkai (Asia Association) and the Tōa Dōbun-kai (East Asian Common Culture Association, founded in 1898).[22] While these organizations were above all an instrument of the opposition to criticize the foreign policy of the government, some also received government funds to pursue their ideals. Societies such as the Gen'yōsha (Black Ocean Society, founded 1881) or the Kokuryūkai (Amur Society or Black Dragon Society, founded 1901) worked in close cooperation with the government.[23] The Kokuryūkai under the leadership of Uchida Ryōhei (1874–1937) developed into *the* pan-Asian organization *par excellence*, lobbying intensively for a regionalist approach in foreign policy.[24] But also the above-mentioned Tōa Dōbun-kai, headed by court noble (*kuge*) Prince Konoe Atsumaro (1863–1904), cooperated closely with the government, for example in 1900 when it founded the Institute of East Asian Common Culture (Tōa Dōbun Shoin) in Nanjing with government funding;[25] throughout the following decades it produced China specialists who were frequently hired into government service. The first director of the Tōa Dōbun Shoin, Nezu Hajime (1860–1927), a former army officer, had founded another institute for the promotion of closer Sino-Japanese relations as early as 1890, the Research Institute for

Sino-Japanese Trade (Nisshin Bōeki Kenkyūjo), together with Arao Sei (also Kiyoshi, 1859–96), another retired army officer.[26]

However, the early pan-Asian movement could not yet gain influence on foreign policy-making, because of the government's realist course and its efforts at establishing a positive image of Japan in the West. Since the end of the nineteenth century, in Europe fears of a "Yellow Peril," the notion of a unified "yellow race" threatening European supremacy and European colonial control of parts of Asia, had gained prominence.[27] The Japanese government made continuous efforts to avoid adding fuel to Yellow Peril fears. Therefore, it refrained from using pan-Asian rhetoric and, at times, suppressed the pan-Asian movement and jailed authors of pan-Asian writings. For example, Tarui Tōkichi (1850–1922), who in the 1880s had written an "Argument for a Union of the Great East" (*Daitō Gappō-ron*) in which he rejected the Western Law of Nations and argued for a union of Japan and Korea, was arrested for participating in the Oriental Socialist Party and his manuscript was lost. However, after his release he rewrote the tract and it was published in 1893, becoming of major importance in pan-Asian circles.[28]

While Tarui was subject to government suppression, other writers who are nowadays considered representative of pan-Asian thought, such as Okakura Tenshin (Kakuzō), did not even make the effort to address their fellow countrymen. Okakura (1862–1913), who in 1903 coined the famous phrase "Asia is one,"[29] did not write for a Japanese audience,[30] but rather for an Indian one. Moreover, he could not have possibly promoted Asian unity against the West in Japan, since the government had just signed an alliance with Great Britain – the colonial master of India and other parts of Asia. Okakura's works, authored originally in English, were translated into Japanese only during the 1930s and his influence on earlier pan-Asian discourse must be considered marginal.[31] The efforts of the government to prevent "Yellow Peril" fears were not limited to the national scene. Japan also developed an active "PR campaign" abroad. In 1904, for example, when Japan set out to wage war on Czarist Russia, the Japanese government dispatched diplomats to Europe and the United States to head off the resurgence of "Yellow Peril" propaganda and influence public opinion in Japan's favor.[32] Suematsu Kenchō (1855–1920), a diplomat who was dispatched to Europe, emphasized in a speech given to the Central Asian Society in London that nothing resembling a pan-Asianist ambition to unite Asia against the West existed in Japan:

> Of late, there has been much talk about the Yellow Peril, or the possibility of a Pan-Asiatic combination; this appears to me ... nothing more than a senseless and mischievous agitation. ... Can anyone imagine that Japan would like to organize a Pan-Asiatic agitation of her own seeking, in which she must take so many different peoples of Asia into her confidence and company – *people with whom she has no joint interests or any community of thought and feeling?*[33]

Notwithstanding Suematsu's assertions, with the beginnings of Japanese colonial expansion – the annexation of Taiwan, Karafuto, and Korea – pan-Asian rhetoric became a part of the policy to integrate the Empire, as Oguma Eiji's studies have shown.[34] Still mostly unrelated to official government policies, we can also cite activities by pan-Asian agitators to strengthen contacts with their counterparts in Asian countries after 1905, above all with revolutionary circles aiming at the overthrow of the *ancien régimes* in Korea and China. For example, Chinese reformers Kang Youwei (K'ang Yu-wei) and Liang Qichao (Liang Ch'i-ch'ao) were received by Japanese pan-Asianists in 1898 when they were forced to flee Beijing; revolutionary leader Sun Yat-sen (Zhongshan, Jp. Son Bun, 1866–1925) and also Korean dissidents such as Kim Ok-kyun (1851–94) were frequently-seen guests in pan-Asian circles in Japan during the Meiji period. Since the 1910s, leaders of the Indian independence movement and anti-colonial leaders from the Arab world also visited Japan more frequently,[35] indicating an enlargement of the geographical limits of the "Asia" envisaged by Pan-Asianism. However, the support of Indian and Arab revolutionaries was in conflict with the government's realist approach to foreign policy, the core of which was the Anglo-Japanese Alliance of 1902. Great Britain, who saw her rule over India threatened by Japanese support of Indian revolutionaries, frequently demanded that the Japanese government expel Indian revolutionaries, and until the 1920s Japan felt obliged to do so.[36]

As a result of spreading pan-Asian sentiment, a concrete proposal for an East Asian Federation (*Tōa renpō*) – probably for the first time since Tarui – was made in a series of articles in the journal *Nihonjin* (The Japanese) in 1907. The author, Tanaka Morihei (1884–1928), was a rather obscure occult leader, and therefore this particular publication failed to have much influence, but his proposition gives evidence of an increasing significance of pan-Asian discourse in society and a new connection of pan-Asian thought with religious forces.[37] Pan-Asianism also could slowly make inroads into the world of politics, clearly as a result of an increasing Japanese self-confidence after the victory in the Russo-Japanese War of 1904–5. While early Meiji Japan had been a weak state on the brink of colonization, at the beginning of the Taishō period (1912–26) Japan had become a regional power and a recognized member of the so-called "great powers" (*rekkyō*) or "first-rate powers" (*ittōkoku*). Until World War I, politicians who borrowed pan-Asian rhetoric were still the exception,[38] and the government continued to be hesitant in giving pan-Asian activists its backing.[39] It was only after World War I that Asianism penetrated deeply into government circles and official diplomacy, by then having become a realistic option for Japanese foreign policy-making. In an article written for the Kokuryūkai magazine *Ajia Jiron* (Asian Review) in 1921, scholar and journalist Nagase Hōsuke (1865–1926)[40] expressed his hopes that Pan-Asianism had finally reached the stage of implementation:

> The fate of Asia has to be decided by Asians – this phrase has been heard among officials in our country for quite a while. However, it is a sad fact

that, until just prior to the Great War, this kind of statement was not very welcome and it remained in the realm of idealism (*risōron*). But fortunately, today the opportunity for the realization [of this notion] has come. I have recently met with representatives from the Bashkirs and the Confucian Tartars for intimate talks, and they, too, stated that they believe that the organization of an Asian League (*Ajia renmei*) should not be difficult. We have to leave the phase of discussion behind us and move swiftly to the stage of realization.[41]

Pan-Asianism, as Nagase's remarks show, had developed from a vague romantic and idealistic feeling of solidarity into an ideology that could be applied in the sphere of *Realpolitik*. It was in this context that the contents and meaning of Pan-Asianism were defined explicitly for the first time and, as a matter of fact, the term "Asianism" came into wide use for the first time in the years 1916–17. While in the Meiji period pan-Asianist discourse had been expressed in vague slogans such as "raising Asia" (*kō-A*) or "Asian solidarity" (*Ajia rentai*), the terms "Asianism" and "Greater Asianism" gained prominence only after the appearance in 1916 of a work by a young Lower House member, Kodera Kenkichi (1877–1949), *Treatise on Greater Asianism* (*Dai Ajiashugi-ron*) – the first publication with the term Asianism in its title.[42] Not even the well-known pan-Asian associations of the Meiji and Taishō periods, such as the Kokuryūkai, had used the term before. In the years after Kodera's publication, "Asianism" and similar terms became popular catchphrases in journals and academic writings.[43]

Pan-Asian rhetoric now also took new forms,[44] such as the "Asian Monroe Doctrine" advocated by Tokutomi Sohō (1863–1957) in the years around World War I, stressing that the fate of Asia must be decided by Asians.[45] Inspired by the new "League of Nations" other writers, such as Sugita Teiichi, demanded that Japan should advocate the foundation of an "Asian League" (*Ajia renmei*) in order to keep the West out of Asia after the end of hostilities in Europe. Similar to Nagase, for Sugita, an Asian League by now had to include:

> not only the Buddhist countries that have already achieved some kind of spiritual (*seishinteki*) bond. We rather have to strengthen this bond and use it to bring together the peoples of India and Persia with the Muslims of Turkey, Afghanistan and Baluchistan and firmly secure it so that no other power can succeed in suppressing the members of this League.[46]

The prominence of Asianism in broad sectors of society and politics had come about as a consequence of the growing consciousness of Japanese national strength and the rise of Japan as a leading regional power. At the same time, the definition of "Asia" within Asianism was enlarged to include India and Western Asia, as also could be seen in the activities of Ōkawa Shūmei (1886–1957), who in 1917 founded the Zen-Ajia-kai (All-Asian Association).[47]

Since the spread of pan-Asian thought in Japan was, above all, a consequence of growing Japanese national strength, it was increasingly seen with suspicion in other Asian countries. As early as in 1919, Chinese scholar Li Dazhao (Li Ta-chao, 1888–1927), one of the leaders of the 4 May Movement of 1919, argued for a union of weak Asian nations in a "New Asianism" in order to oppose Japan's "Greater Asianism."[48] In 1924, in a famous speech in Kōbe, Chinese revolutionary leader Sun Yat-sen warned the Japanese that Japan had to choose between becoming "a willing handmaiden of Western imperialism or … the great bastion of East Asia's Kingly Way."[49] The popular newspaper *Nihon* (Japan) had already given a response to Sun's warning. While the newspaper had harshly criticized imperialism as such and Japanese participation in imperialist policies in 1899, in 1903 it had reversed its stance, stating that "the meaning of 'imperialism' [for Japan] will be decided according to whether we will take the side of the victims (*giseisha*) or the side of the imperialists."[50] As a consequence of such changing attitudes, Pan-Asianism soon would evolve into rhetoric legitimizing Japanese colonial rule over Asia, and due to this contradictory use of pan-Asian ideals, "Japan grew more and more distant from old Asia."[51]

In light of these developments and of increasing Sino-Japanese frictions, some Japanese advocates of Asian regionalism in the 1910s and 1920s started pointing out that Asian regionalism "was of no practical value if China were not participating."[52] But only few Japanese pan-Asianists could see that Pan-Asianism had started to take a different direction, turning into a tool for legitimizing Japanese hegemony in East Asia. One rare example is Miyazaki Torazō (better known as Tōten, 1871–1922), who had supported Sun Yat-sen's revolutionary movement and has been considered a representative of early, "romanticist" Pan-Asianism.[53] At the end of World War I, Miyazaki criticized the ethnocentric dimension of contemporary Pan-Asianism, claiming that China had to play the central role in the creation of a new Asia and, in quite a realistic manner, rejected that a Japanese leadership was an option. For Miyazaki, "Japan did not have the power to influence [the development] of the five continents;" it was only China that had the civilizational prestige, sufficient resources and manpower as well as the territory to play the central role in a future "Asian League." Miyazaki considered Japan completely unsuitable for leadership in Asia, because his home country had already turned from a weak, oppressed country into an oppressor herself. The "Asian League" that Miyazaki envisaged as a product of an Asian revolution, however, had to be a League of weak and oppressed states, and therefore Japanese leadership, for Miyazaki, was out of the question, particularly so long as Japan did not give up its own colonies and grant Korea and Taiwan independence.[54]

As a consequence of the continuing disagreement about the meaning of Asianism within Asia, the so-called "Pan-Asian Conferences" (literally Conference of Asian Peoples, *Ajia minzoku kaigi*) held in 1926 in Nagasaki, in 1927 in Shanghai and in 1934 in Dairen (Dalian) ended without any tangible results. While the Japanese planners had aimed at keeping their government out of the conferences by organizing them as non-government events, away from the political center, in Nagasaki,[55] the delegates from other Asian nations detected a strong Japanese desire to legitimize Japanese leadership, or even hegemony, through the promotion of Pan-Asianism *per se* instead of promoting Asian unity *vis-à-vis* the West. In Japan, the press was divided, most emphasizing the failures of the conferences, while some commentators described the pan-Asian overtures offered at Nagasaki as "fantasies" and "idealism."[56] Even though the final declaration at the Nagasaki conference included the goal of creating an All-Asian League (*Zen-Ajia renmei*), it seems clear that Pan-Asianism had finally mutated into an "extended nationalism,"[57] above all serving the Japanese claim for leadership in Asia. Further conferences were planned for the following years, but apparently never materialized. Inter-Asian dialogue about the meaning of Pan-Asianism therefore virtually ended in the late 1920s.

The contents of pan-Asian thought

At the same time that the pan-Asian movement was becoming more influential in political circles, its ideology became more concrete and better defined. During most of the Meiji period, as Takeuchi Yoshimi has pointed out, Asianism was a loose set of ideas rather than a coherent ideology.[58] Takeuchi had in mind the activities of pan-Asian activists who, without adhering to a clearly defined ideology but rather out of vague and romantic feelings of "Asian-ness," supported independence and revolutionary movements in various Asian countries. Particularly well-known are the efforts of the early Kokuryūkai members in assisting the early uprisings of Sun Yat-sen and the anti-American uprising of Emilio Aguinaldo (1869–1964) in the Philippines, the struggle of Miyazaki Tōten for the cause of Sun Yat-sen,[59] the efforts of Ōi Kentarō (1843–1922) to assist Korean reformers and the assistance given by Sōma Aizō (1870–1945) to Indian revolutionary Rash Behari Bose (1886–1945).[60] Since many of these activists were connected to the early Movement for Freedom and People's Rights (*jiyū minken undō*), the export of the revolution to Asia – a contribution to the overthrow of the *ancient régimes* in Korea, China, etc. – was a central part of the motives of these activists.[61]

While Meiji-era Asianism was a vague sentiment rather than a consistent ideology, we observe important changes during the Taishō period. As Louis Snyder in his standard work on the "pan"-movements has pointed out, these movements in general "may be described as politico-cultural movements promoting the solidarity of peoples united by common or kindred languages, group identifications, traditions, or some other characteristic such as geographical proximity."[62] Pan-Asianism in the late Meiji and the Taishō eras, likewise developed from a vague feeling of Asianness into a clear concept of regional integration, for which regional solidarity and identity, however defined, were deemed necessary bases. The first commentator to clearly define the "base of Asianism" (*Ajiashugi no kiso*) was the above-mentioned Kodera

Kenkichi in his 1916 "Treatise on Greater Asianism."[63] In general, pan-Asian writings in Japan referred to the following commonalities when proclaiming an "Asian identity":

- The cultural unity (*dōbun*) of the peoples and nations of East Asia, based upon the common use of Chinese characters (*kanji*).
- The "racial" kinship of East Asian peoples and ethnicities (*dōshu*), which, in the Western categorization of "races," all belonged to the so-called "yellow race" (*ōshoku jinshu*).
- The geographical proximity and historical legacy of the Sinocentric order mentioned above, representing a traditional framework for inter-state relations in East Asia, but also close economic relations.
- The feeling of a "common" destiny (*unmei kyōdōtai*) in the struggle of Asian and/or colored peoples against Western imperialism and, at times, against Westernization and/or modernization. While the first three notions limited the geographical definition of "Asia" mostly to East Asia, it was as a consequence of this fourth concept that in the years after the Russo-Japanese War of 1904–5 other parts of "Asia," i.e. Western Asia, South Asia and the Arab world, came to play a role in Pan-Asianism.

The first two categories constituted the central elements of pan-Asian thought, and they were fused in the slogan "same culture/script, same race" (*dōbun dōshu*) which is commonly found in pan-Asian writings in East Asia from the beginning of the movement.[64] The Tōa Dōbun-kai – the East Asian Common Culture Assocation – incorporated part of this slogan in its name, and the head of the association, Konoe Atsumaro, was an early protagonist of "racial unity" and the "alliance of the yellow races" (*ōshoku jinshu dōmei-ron*).[65] In Japan's foreign policy, the push for the inclusion of a racial non-discrimination clause in the Charter of the League of Nations during the negotiations at the Paris Peace Conference in 1919 was one expression of this racially tinged Pan-Asianism – although this claim was never intended to include discrimination against, for example, Koreans *within* the Japanese Empire.[66]

Another factor that was frequently emphasized by pan-Asian writers was Confucianism, a religion and a social code that had originated in China but had become one of the most important pillars of the Meiji era Emperor-system (as well as the preceding Tokugawa Shogunate). While Confucianism as a common legacy of Japan and China (and Korea) was frequently emphasized in pan-Asian writings, and Japan's continuity with an "Asian past" was acknowledged, some intellectuals, as Stefan Tanaka has demonstrated, also aimed at separating Confucianism from China. They continued to respect the Orient (*tōyō*) in its antiquity, but separated it from contemporary China (*Shina*) – seen as "a disorderly place."[67]

A more important facet of Pan-Asianism than the construction of a systematic Asian identity to legitimize pan-Asian activities and policies, however, was the opportunism inherent in pan-Asian ideology. Pan-Asianism, above all, was an activist ideology, and the rationale underlying the ideology was adjusted over time in quite opportunistic ways. While Itagaki Taisuke (1837–1919), leader of the early Movement for Freedom and Civil Rights, central figure in the short-living Taiwan Assimilation Society (Taiwan Dōka-kai), and an influential politician throughout his life, had emphasized in 1887 that "the differences in terms of manners and customs (*fūzoku shūkan*) between our country and the Asian countries are large," by 1913 he was dwelling on the common interests of Asian countries in fighting Western imperialism for the sake of freedom and independence in the future and pointing to their "common destiny":

> The antagonism between the Orient and the West is linked with the question of the survival of the Asian race (*Ajia jinshu*). This is not a problem of India, of China (*Shina*), of Persia, or of Japan. Rather, all Asian countries today are sitting in the same boat.[68]

In 1914, the year in which he helped founding the Taiwan Assimilation Society, his earlier concerns about the differences between Asian nations seemed to have almost completely vanished:

> In view of the pressure from the European powers, not only are the interests and the general [political] situation of Japan and China the same. Both countries are in a position to easily reach a mutual understanding between their two peoples (*kokumin*) due to the fact that they belong to the same race and share the same culture (*dōbun dōshu no kuni*), due to their sharing the same family system and the same social system (*shakai soshiki*), due to their similarities in everyday lifestyle,... in a word, due to their having *basically no differences in terms of manners and customs* (*fūzoku shūkan*).[69]

It is clear from such statements that attitudes towards the necessity for regional cooperation – for which a base in common racial, cultural, and linguistic features was deemed essential – changed and were adjusted in a flexible manner over time, according to the changing international environment and Japan's situation within the international arena.

Equality and hegemony

The key problem with analyzing the historical phenomenon of Pan-Asianism – which has made previous research such a balancing act – is the fact that many of its protagonists came from Japan, and that Japanese pan-Asianists, in a period of growing *Japanese* national strength, tended to claim Japanese leadership in a pan-Asian regional order that was intimately associated with Japanese colonialism. As a consequence, ideals such as Asian solidarity and equality, as favored by early pan-Asianists,[70] were pushed into the background and the feeling of a "common destiny" mutated into a sense of a *Japanese* "mission"[71] with a strong religious notion: Japan as the "Land of the Gods" had the "holy mission" to liberate Asia as a first step to unite mankind. However, even claims for Japanese leadership have to be seen in the context of anti-colonialism directed against Western influence in Asia.[72] To be sure, Japanese leadership and a Japanese role model at times also were acknowledged in parts of Asia, particularly after Japan's victory over Russia in 1904–5.[73] But such appraisals of a Japanese model disappeared soon, particularly after pan-Asian rhetoric was drawn upon to legitimize Japanese colonial rule.

After a phase in Japanese foreign policy in the second half of the 1920s that has been characterized as "cooperative" or "internationalist" and in which pan-Asian writings temporarily lost some influence,[74] the escalation of Japanese (military) expansion on the Asian continent once again brought pan-Asian rhetoric to the fore in the early 1930s. In 1933, a number of influential politicians and military officers founded the Greater Asian Association (Dai Ajia Kyōkai), one of the first pan-Asian associations that included a large number of figures close to government and that worked to help implement the government's utilization of pan-Asian concepts.[75] Although it has been stated that Pan-Asianism never became government policy in prewar Japan,[76] the government employed pan-Asian rhetoric during the foundation of Manchukuo in 1932,[77] when leaving the League of Nations in 1933, and when declaring a "New Order" for East Asia in November 1938 and the "Greater East Asia Co-Prosperity Sphere" (*Daitō-A Kyōeiken*) in 1940.[78] With the establishment of the Agency for the Development of Asia (Kōa-in) in 1938 and the Greater East Asia Ministry (Daitō-A-shō) in 1942,[79] government agencies were created with a mission to implement pan-Asian themes and the "New Order" in East Asia.[80] Influential leftist and even Marxist scholars, such as Miki Kiyoshi (1897–1945), Tanabe Hajime (1885–1962) or journalist Ozaki Hotsumi (1901–44), and political scientists such as Takahashi Kamekichi (1891–1977) and Rōyama Masamichi (1895–1980),[81] all of whom argued for the creation of an "East Asian Community" (*Tōa kyōdōtai*), were now co-opted into government efforts to strengthen the ideological foundations of a "New Order" in East Asia. However, an influential current among intellectuals also continued to produce "collective forms of identity that were not immediately reducible to the state," above all ethnic-romanticist nationalism – a variant of nationalism "that would survive the collapse of the wartime state to remain a problem today."[82]

In many of the schemes for a "New Order" or a "Co-Prosperity Sphere," we find echoes of the historical Sinocentric system of international relations, but now with Japan at the centre, finally replacing the "Middle Kingdom" China. In many wartime documents concerning the "Greater East Asia Co-Prosperity Sphere," there is an explicit regional order with Japan (with Korea and Taiwan as parts of the Japanese Empire) at the centre, surrounded by four zones: a zone of "independent" states or, rather, "puppet states"[83] (Nanjing-China, Manchukuo, and Thailand); a zone of semi-independent protectorates

(Burma, the Philippines, and Java); a zone of regions directly administered by Japan (*chokkatsuryō*), containing "key areas for the defence of Greater Asia";[84] and a zone of colonies that would remain under the rule of European powers.[85] Whereas the "pan"-ideology served as the foundation for the necessity of a regional union, the "tradition" of a centralist-hierarchical order of states, now with Japan at its center, was instrumentalized to legitimize a Japanese leadership based on "traditional" East Asian thought.

The climax of hegemonic Pan-Asianism in Japanese foreign policy was seen in November 1943, when the representatives of six Asian governments – Japan, Manchukuo, China, Burma, Thailand, and the Philippines – met in Tōkyō at the Greater East Asian Conference (Daitō-A kaigi) or "Assembly of Greater East Asiatic Nations" and discussed the future of Asia.[86] After a lengthy address by Japan's Prime Minister, Tōjō Hideki, and speeches by the representatives of the other participating nations as well as the Indian observer, Chandra Bose, the summit issued a Joint Declaration, the *Daitō-A sengen*. It stated the aim of fostering "common prosperity" through "mutual aid and assistance." Asian countries should form alliances in order to be permanently liberated from "intervention, (foreign) rule and occupation." The declaration was directed against Western influence in Asia and can be seen as a counter-declaration to the Atlantic Charter, signed on 14 August 1941 by US President Franklin D. Roosevelt and British Prime Minister Winston Churchill. The Tōkyō Declaration accused the United States and the British of "seeking their own prosperity" only and oppressing "other nations and peoples. Especially in East Asia, they indulged in insatiable aggression and exploitation, and sought to satisfy their inordinate ambitions of enslaving the entire region. . . . Herein lies the cause of the recent war." The declaration claimed that the major goal of Japan's ongoing war in East Asia was the successful liberation of the region "from the yoke of British-American domination, and . . . constructing a Greater East Asia in accordance with the . . . principles" of mutual cooperation.

The text of the Tōkyō declaration remained ambivalent due to its hybrid character – it was the result of intensive discussions within Japan, particularly between the military and the Foreign Ministry. In practice, the declaration had to be further adjusted to the realities of ongoing warfare and therefore degenerated into mere propaganda,[87] notwithstanding the impression of one Manchurian representative that:

> the faces of each and every one was yellow, the hair black and differing not in the least from us. Indeed, we could not but feel anew that Asia was one family, as in a cordial and friendly atmosphere we chatted and laughed through the medium of interpreters.[88]

As a tool of the military, the Tōkyō Declaration eventually served to mobilize support from the "Asian family" and gain access to natural resources.[89] Pan-Asianism as expressed at the Tōkyō Conference was above all part of the military-inspired drive for economic autarky in order to carry on warfare against the world's superpowers, Great Britain and the United States.[90] The liberation of Asia was never an *original* war objective for the military, as statements made prior to the outbreak of war attest,[91] and consequently Japan, with "cynical carelessness ... took up and cast off its allies" in some parts of Asia, ignored large parts of the Asia it claimed to unite or liberate and, instead of promoting the overcoming of national boundaries, at will redrew boundaries according to the necessities of warfare.[92] As Hatano Sumio in his brilliant work on Japan's Asian policy during the Asia-Pacific War has pointed out, the declaration of independence for Burma and the Philippines in 1943 was above all an attempt to prepare "Japan's case" for the postwar era – at a time when defeat was already certain. While the military aimed at mobilizing support for the ongoing war effort, Japan's diplomats around Shigemitsu Mamoru prepared "historical justification" (*rekishi benmei*) for the "coming war trials," thereby contributing to the emergence of an interpretation of the war as a "war of Asian liberation."[93]

The social base of prewar Pan-Asianism

Louis Snyder in his work on "pan"-movements claims that Pan-Asianism – different, for example, from Pan-Germanism – "never managed to win a mass base" and "never became an organized movement."[94] That Pan-Asianism by the 1930s had become a powerful, although diverse, movement, and a strong political force, should be obvious from what has been said above. But did Pan-Asianism have a mass base, did it attract popular support? To be sure, the numerous pan-Asian organizations, although giving proof of a continuing current of Pan-Asianism in politics and thought, were not mass organizations. The Kokuryūkai, one of the most well-known pan-Asian organizations, had 57 members at the time of its foundation and no more than 1,000 at the height of its popularity in the years around World War I. Most organizations mentioned in this chapter never had more than a few hundred active members.[95] Only some pan-Asian associations founded in the 1930s succeeded in attracting a larger following. For example, the Tōa Renmei Kyōkai (East Asian League Association), founded by major general Ishiwara Kanji (1889–1949) in 1939, by 1943 had about 15,000 members.[96] During wartime, pan-Asian agitators at times could mobilize mass support for political rallies. The Tōkyō Conference of November 1943 was accompanied by a "People's Mass Meeting for the Solidarity of Greater East Asia" in Hibiya Park, which was attended by over 120,000 people (although some of the demonstrators surely might have been "guided" to the rally by the authorities).[97]

What is most important, however, is not the membership of the pan-Asian societies itself, but the extent to which these societies and their members could exert influence on political decisions. From what has been said above, it seems clear that the pan-Asian movement was influential and well-connected. Although at the beginning of the Meiji period Pan-Asianism was associated with the political opposition, by World War I it had entered the world of politics and by the end of the 1930s, albeit in mutated form, it had become an integral part of Japanese foreign policy – notwithstanding later assertions to the contrary by the first Minister for Greater East Asia. In an analysis of the unofficial history of the pan-Asian movement published in 1936 by the Kokuryūkai,[98] Chinese scholar Zhao Jun has shown that many influential figures at some point joined the ranks of the pan-Asian societies.[99] Of the figures acknowledged by the Kokuryūkai as "pan-Asianists," 36 percent were, not surprisingly, above all members of pan-Asian associations – what Marius B. Jansen has called "professional patriots" – and did not have permanent jobs.[100] However, 17 percent were members of the Imperial Diet or official office-holders; 15 percent were civilians working for the military and another 15 percent were military officers on active duty; 9 percent were newspaper journalists or publishers and 7 percent were businessmen.

Apart from these political and social connections, the continuity of Pan-Asianism in intellectual discourse and popular opinion also shows the importance of the ideology it represented. Pan-Asianism was not a short-lived phenomenon. Throughout the period analyzed here, many of the major Japanese journals and newspapers – above all the *Chōya Shinbun* (Capital and Country Newspaper), the *Kokumin Shinbun* (People's Newspaper), *Nihon oyobi Nihonjin* (Japan and the Japanese), *Taiyō* (The Sun), *Ajia Jiron* (Asian Review) and *Tōhō Jiron* (Eastern Review) and others – continuously published articles by pan-Asian writers and contributed to the diffusion of pan-Asian ideas. Through these journals, pan-Asian writers addressed an important and influential part of the elite and succeeded in establishing Pan-Asianism in the consciousness of key figures in politics and society. Pan-Asian writers also seemed confident about their achievements. In 1933, Tachibana Shiraki (1881–1945), editor-in-chief of the magazine *Manshū Hyōron* (Manchurian Review), in an article entitled "New Theory of the pan-Asian Movement" announced "a new era of popularity for Pan-Asianism."[101] Indeed, many Japanese soldiers who had fought in Southeast Asia and were indoctrinated by pan-Asian propaganda confirmed after the war that they believed that they were fighting for a pan-Asian cause, i.e. for the liberation of Asian peoples.[102]

In intellectual circles, pan-Asian themes were discussed right up until the last days of the war, particularly in the context of efforts to "overcome modernity." As late as 1945, scholars such as Hirano Yoshitarō (1897–1980), strongly influenced by Marxist ideas, claimed an "East Asian universalism" which, in his opinion, had developed in the East Asian village (*furusato*), where the high moral virtues associated with community (*seimeiteki kyōdōtai*), familism (*kazokushugi*), and the agrarian commune (*nōson kyōdōtai*) had been growing for "many thousand years."[103] While during the 1920s the "harmonization of Eastern and Western civilization" (*Tōzai bunmei chōwa*) had been promoted as the way for a self-confident Japan to cope with the West,[104] in the 1940s the attempt to "overcome modernity" gained momentum. The writings of Hirano and other scholars prepared the ground for a further transformation of the ideology of Pan-Asianism – now into a social ideology with a strong anti-modernist bias. As such, it survived into the postwar era, in the writings of scholars such as Takeuchi Yoshimi (1910–77), and reappeared in the 1990s debate about "Asian values."

Pan-Asianism and regionalism in postwar politics and discourse

After the war, Pan-Asianism, given its history as an ideology legitimizing Japanese colonial rule, was discredited and became a taboo for a certain period. However, from time to time it resurfaced in Japanese political discourse and sometimes led to friction between Japan and her neighbors. In recent years, the divisive legacy of Pan-Asianism has become a major obstacle to strengthening regional cooperation and integration in East Asia. Particularly damaging have been recurring remarks by Japanese politicians aiming at legitimizing or glorifying prewar Japanese colonial rule as a means of liberating Asia from European colonial rule or euphemizing Japanese colonialism as "benevolent."[105]

However, there have also been constructive discussions about regionalism. In the 1950s and 1960s, a leftist, anti-imperialist Pan-Asianism, with roots in prewar Japan, above all in the communist-influenced Research Bureau of the South Manchurian Railway Company,[106] resurfaced,[107] but failed to gain much ground in Japanese politics and was rather marginalized in political discourse. The last contemporary relic of this Asianism on the *left* of the political spectrum today is the harsh criticism by the Japan Communist Party (JCP) and the Socialist Party (SP) of Prime Minister Koizumi Jun'ichirō's neglect of Asia, or "the region," in foreign policy. The failure, or rather non-existence, of Koizumi's "Asia policy" (*Ajia gaikō*), as alleged by the JCP and the SP, in addition to some mainstream newspaper commentators, has led to the isolation of Japan in Asia[108] and has made Japan into a tool of US ambitions to strengthen its position as "the only superpower."

However, voices emphasizing the importance of regional integration, or at least cooperation, are not entirely absent in Japan. In recent years, voices within academia have emerged that advocate the idea of a "common Asian house" (*Ajia kyōdō no ie*) or an "East Asian Community" (*Higashi Ajia kyōdōtai*).[109] Developments towards economic cooperation in East Asia can be observed in the growth of nonstate networks.[110] Even though the influence of these advocates of an "East Asian Community" on actual policy-making remains limited, some politicians, such as Foreign Minister Asō Tarō in a speech in December 2005, have taken up the vocabulary of the new regionalism to promote friendly relations with Asian nations.[111] Riding on the wave of discussions of "Asian values" in Southeast Asia, anti-Western circles in Japan have joined the promotion of an Asian "identity". One example is the right-wing populist Mayor of Tōkyō, Ishihara Shintarō, well-known co-author of "The Japan That Can Say 'No'," who in 1994 also co-authored "The Asia That Can Say 'No'," together with Malaysian Prime Minister Mahatir bin Mohammad.[112]

The most influential voices advocating stronger cooperation within Asia or Asian solidarity are to be found in the media and in government-linked, but largely independent, research organizations. These advocates of a "New Asianism" or "neo-Asianism"[113] emphasize the necessity for Japan to not rely solely on "the West" – i.e. the United States – in foreign policy, and justify the need for Japanese rapprochement with Asia through the sharing of a common culture and geographical proximity – i.e. the "natural" character of a Japanese alignment with Asia. Representatives of this "New Asianism" include scholars like Matsumoto Ken'ichi, journalists such as Funabashi Yōichi, and former diplomat and present president of the Japan Foundation, Ogura Kazuo. Funabashi has taken up the above-mentioned notion of a "common Asian house" and promotes it in the media. Matsumoto, who actively promotes the legacy of Takeuchi Yoshimi, is commenting on Japan's relations to Asia in the media but is also active on government advisory boards, in both instances stressing the need for rapprochement with China.[114] During the 1990s, the heyday of the "Asian values" debate, Ogura criticized Orientalist views of Asia in the West and proposed a superior Asian civilization based on "Asian values." However, at the beginning of the twenty-first century, it seems as if the discussion of "Asian values" has come to an end, and Ogura and Matsumoto now concentrate on promoting the understanding of China in Japan.[115]

This kind of work seems highly necessary, as opinion polls show that popular attitudes to China among the Japanese have reached a historical low. In a regular opinion poll on foreign policy attitudes conducted by the Japanese Cabinet Office since the 1970s, positive attitudes to China at one time stood at over 80 percent. After the Tiananmen incident in 1989, public opinion in Japan was divided, but over 50 percent of respondents to the poll still "felt a closeness" to China (*shinkinkan o kanjiru*). Japanese–Chinese frictions over the visits of Prime Minister Koizumi to the Yasukuni Shrine since 2001, and resulting anti-Japanese riots in China and the shrill responses in the Japanese media to these events, have shattered public opinion on China. In 2004 and 2005, the number of respondents who do "not feel close to China" (i.e. dislike China) rose sharply, while the number who still "feel close to China" reached historical lows – 38 percent in 2004 and 32 percent in 2005.[116]

The background to these changes has to be seen not only in a growing Japanese nationalism, but also in the resurgence of a nostalgic Pan-Asianism in Japan, which retrospectively aims at rehabilitating *prewar* Pan-Asianism. This kind of backward-looking Pan-Asianism is also at the core of the Yasukuni Shrine issue, since the museum at the shrine, the *Yūshūkan*, presents the war as a just cause, one fought for the liberation of Asian peoples.[117] Although this view may not be widely held in Japan today,[118] the existence of even more disturbing memorials than the Yasukuni Shrine, such as the "Raising Asia Kannon" (*Kō-A kannon*[119]) in Atami or the "Great Monument to the Holy War in Greater East Asia" (*Daitō-A seisen taihi*[120]) in Kanazawa, underline the potentially inflammatory character of a retrospective Pan-Asianism.

The often-cited "history problem" Japan struggles with, and particularly current interpretations of the history of Pan-Asianism, therefore still constitute a major obstacle to the development of fruitful forms of Asian regionalism in the future. Addressing these issues need not be viewed as Japan bending to Chinese or Korean demands, but rather should be considered the key task for the future of regionalism in East Asia and for Japan's role in the regional integration of this dynamic region, a process that will continue to gain momentum in the future, with or without Japan playing a creative role.

Part I

Creating a regional identity

Ideal and reality

2 Pan-Asianism in modern Japan

Nationalism, regionalism and universalism

Miwa Kimitada

The definition and origins of Pan-Asianism in Japan[1]

The primary concept of Pan-Asianism that underlies this volume may be stated as follows: an ideology or facet of thought representing an extension of Japanese nationalism overseas, based on the Japanese belief that the Japanese share common physical traits with their continental neighbors, Koreans and Chinese, or that they belong to an East Asian world system with historical roots. The most obvious common denominator of this historical world system was the use of Chinese ideographs, through which various ideas were interchanged among the peoples of this region. These were not necessarily exclusively Chinese in origin, like Confucianism. In fact, not only Buddhism, which originated in India, but also Western concepts, after being transferred into Japanese from Western languages in modern times, were disseminated from Japan to intellectuals in this East Asian world. As a result, by the mid-twentieth century, the written *Chinese* language had become as much Japanese, especially in the field of modern scientific literature, as the Japanese had been Chinese.

A second type of Pan-Asianism premised a regional identity as Asians upon the distinction between Asia and the "West." This kind of regional identity arose as a reaction to fear in the West of a "Yellow Peril," and was closely linked to the idea of a "White Peril" – the threat to Asian independence posed by the European powers of the West – which seemed to Asian contemporaries to be much more real than the vision of a "Yellow Peril."

In other words, there were two types of Pan-Asianism in modern Japan, based on the preponderant self-identity of its exponents. When exposed to the militarily superior and aggressive expansionist threat from the West, some Japanese, motivated by their communal identity as Asiatics, believed they should work together for the common goal of regional security, while others were more inclined to believe in their national uniqueness and capability of establishing Japan's own national security on their own. The former sentiments became Pan-Asianism based on an Asian identity, while the latter in effect constituted a form of self-appointed *leadership* of the Japanese to save the rest of East Asia as well as themselves – a viewpoint which was only enhanced by the messianic complex of the Japanese.

The guiding norm of this nationalist Pan-Asianism was the concept of *kokutai* (national polity or the embodiment of national particulars), which was based on the mythological origins of the imperial house and the idea of the "family state" (*kazoku kokka*), incorporating the Japanese people, which derived from the imperial family. Although the ideology of *kokutai* was only reasserted officially after the publication of *Kokutai no hongi* (Cardinal principles of the national polity) in 1937, another notion, which later came to be coupled with *kokutai*, had already been established in 1919 – the slogan of *hakkō ichiu* ("the eight corners of the world under the one heaven of benevolent imperial rule"). This was part and parcel of the concept of Japanese uniqueness based on *kokutai*. Both notions were founded on the ancient literature of *Kojiki* and *Nihonshoki*. The two together made up Japan's messianic complex that would dominate Japanese attitudes to other nations in war and peace.

Already in 1823, *kokugaku* scholar Satō Nobuhiro (1769–1850) had constructed a scenario for the conquest of Korea from the north. As the Japanese military marched to the northern border of Korea, he planned to win the hearts of local tribes in Eastern Siberia through generous gifts of rice. His plan was designed as the strategic and tactical application of the notion of imperial benevolence outlined in Satō's *Udai kondō tairon* (Grand theory of uniting all things under the heavens) and *Udai kondō hisaku* (Secret strategy of uniting all things together under the heavens).

Maruyama Masao (1914–96) has interpreted this seemingly aggressive scenario of bringing a territory on the Asian continent under Japanese control as a fear-oriented daydream at a time when Japan, enjoying both external and internal peace maintained by its centuries-old national policy of seclusion and exclusion, was endangered by Western warships coming ever closer to its territory. In this connection, the images of China held by the Japanese intellectuals of Satō's generation and during the Tokugawa period (1603–1867) are telling. For instance, even a man of such academic stature as Ogyū Sorai (1666–1728) maintained that the title of "Great (*dai*) Empire" was more appropriately applied to Japan, as in "Dai Nihon," than to the Ming Empire of China (1368–1644), as in "Tai Ming."[2]

For some of these scholars, China was the land of Confucius that commanded their respect, and they wholeheartedly accepted its civilization as superior to Japan's. But there were others who viewed the China of the Qing dynasty (Ch'ing, 1644–1911) as a dangerous giant that expanded into neighboring countries through military force. Both images resulted from imported Chinese books such as *Sheng-wu-chi* (Imperial Military Exploits), authored by Wei Yuan in 1842 and imported into Japan as early as 1844. Among the first in Japan to read this book dealing with Qing China's military exploits were Yoshida Shōin (1830–59) and Sakuma Shōzan (1811–64).[3]

Pan-Asianism in Meiji Japan: leaving or leading Asia?

In the wake of the "opening" of Japan in 1853–54, there were two types of responses among the Japanese as to how to react to the Western powers. One was to observe the existing laws among nations in the belief that it would be a surer way to guarantee national security. The other was to denounce international law as merely the means by which the powerful Western nations could justify their aggression against weaker nations of Africa and Asia.

The former opinion was held by men like Nishi Amane (1829–97), augmented by their traditional trust in the Confucian precepts that had kept peace and order in the historical East Asian world. They optimistically accepted the international legal system, in part because the laws among nations were presented to them via the familiar ideographs and idioms of Confucian texts. In contrast, Saigō Takamori (1827–77) held the opposing position. Yoshida Shōin expressed a mixture of the two attitudes when he remarked that whatever the Japanese had lost to the Western nations as a result of the agreements imposed upon them, they could regain by in turn imposing international legal norms on Korea and China.[4] In fact, the Western legalistic approach helped Japan in both nation-building and empire-building as proven, for example, in the conduct of warfare in the Sino-Japanese War (1894–95) and the Russo-Japanese War (1904–5).

We hardly can overemphasize that *fear* was the motivation for the Japanese entry into a world system dominated by the West. Japan's fear was amplified by the repeated humiliation of China at the hands of the Western powers. Indeed, even as those powers propagated hysteria regarding a "yellow peril," after Japan's defeat of Russia in the war of 1904–5, they in turn were vividly perceived as a "white peril" by people in Asia. This feeling of a European threat was one basis for regional identity, further strengthened by the prior existence of a historical East Asian world system, and also by racial affinity and shared cultural heritage. An early product of this shared sense of fear and commonality was the first Sino-Japanese Treaty of Amity of 1871. This was the first treaty ever signed between East Asian states as "equal partners," but it was also the last – since the next, concluded between Japan and Korea in 1876, was already an unequal treaty, with Japan now adopting the style of gunboat diplomacy exercised by the Western powers and best exemplified by American commodore Matthew C. Perry a little over two decades before. Through it, Japan secured extraterritoriality in Korea.

Here, it seems appropriate to cite a young Korean scholar-diplomat, Huang Zun-xian, who, in 1880 while serving in Tōkyō, wrote an essay on the defense of Korea. He argued emphatically that the greatest menace posed to his country was *Russian* expansionism from the north. In order to cope with this threat, he strongly recommended his country's cooperation with Japan and the United States. The essay was given Huang's superior, who was visiting Tōkyō, and he in turn presented it to the Korean king. This young Korean diplomat in Tōkyō had been in touch with leading Japanese statesmen such as

Yamagata Aritomo (1838–1922) and Inoue Kaoru (1836–1915). While they shared a mutual concern regarding the Russian menace, Huang's sense of urgency was far more intense. On the other hand, China, which still considered itself the suzerain of Korea, was seriously suspicious of Japan's ambitions there.[5]

The first test of the idea of a common enemy and a cooperative defense among East Asian countries came in 1884, during the military clashes between the Chinese and the French over the Chinese vassal state of Vietnam. China's Southern Fleet was soundly defeated during the fighting, and the French occupied not only most of Vietnam, but also Formosa. This exploded the myth that China and Japan could hold a common defensive line at the Formosan Straits against maritime powers such as France that were expanding northwards and threatening the capitals of Tōkyō and Beijing.

For Japanese such as Fukuzawa Yukichi (1835–1901), it followed that as long as China remained ineffective in securing control of the strategically vital Formosan Straits, sooner or later the Japanese must capture Formosa. This was part of the background for Fukuzawa's essay *Datsu-A-ron* ("Casting off Asia") that was published in March 1885; the other part was the failure of a coup d'état in Seoul in December 1884, which led to the suppression of the pro-Japanese modernization faction. The essay called for Japan to behave henceforth like a Western nation toward Korea and China. Fukuzawa argued:

> We have waited long enough for them to become modern nations together with us in the hope of raising East Asia to a compatible level of civilization with Western nations. But should we associate with them as cordially as we used to, the Western powers would take us for these neighbors of ours whom they consider hopelessly tradition-bound and backward.[6]

Around the same time, parliamentarian Shimada Saburō (1852–1923) proposed that, in order to resolve the impasse between Japan and China over Korea, war should be waged to demonstrate which of the two countries was the stronger, thereby finally settling the dispute over who should be the leader (*meishu*) of the region. This, in my opinion, constitutes another thread in Japanese intellectual history that would eventually surface in the 1930s in the policy pronouncement of the "New Order in East Asia" (*Tō-A shin chitsujo*). It was a modern version of the traditional ideology of the Chinese Empire, restructuring the region as hierarchically as before, but this time with Japan at its apex. The principle of order would be the "imperial benevolence" of the Japanese emperor, now replacing the benevolent emperor of the Middle Kingdom.

Pan-Asianism and colonialism

How did the ideas of "leaving" and "leading" (Asia) develop in the decade following the First Sino-Japanese War of 1894–95? One characteristic of the war was that the Japanese government made it a point to strictly observe (Western) international law in order to impress the Western powers and win acceptance as a full member of the community of nations. The peace treaty of Shimonoseki, signed after the end of hostilities, awarded Japan a huge chunk of continental Chinese territory as the spoils of victory, as well as Formosa and the Pescadore Islands. Even after the Tripartite Intervention, which forced Japan to retrocede the Liaotung (Liaodong) peninsula, Formosa and some nearby islands were confirmed as Japanese territory. Its victory in the war against Russia in 1904–5 completed Japan's hegemony on the Korean peninsula, for which moral support was lent not only by the United States, but by England, which renewed the Anglo-Japanese alliance. During this period, Japan had continuously "Westernized" itself in terms of international law, and a completion of the project of "casting off Asia" (*datsu-A*) would come with the annexation of Korea to Japan in 1910. Japan at last had become not only a unified nation-state, but also an empire and a colonial power.

In an essay published in 1963, Takeuchi Yoshimi contrasted Fukuzawa's *Datsu-A-ron* as evil and imperialist against Tarui Tōkichi's *Daitō gappō-ron* (Argument for a Union of the Great East) of 1885, which Takeuchi considered a just and egalitarian approach to the question of how to deal with Korea.[7] However, I consider that the two writings cannot be so simplistically contrasted. According to Tarui (1850–1922), the Japanese imperial house could be seen as a branch of the Korean royal house. Since it is not uncommon for a main house to seek help from its branch when it is unable to stand by itself, Tarui argued, Korea should attach itself to Japan and benefit from being brought under the rule of the capable and efficient Japanese empire. I once asked Takeuchi Yoshimi whether he really intended to characterize this as "imperial benevolence," or whether he agreed that Tarui's approach was in effect as imperialist as Fukuzawa's. His response indicated that he had wanted to demonstrate that some Japanese were less self-centered and more humanitarian than Fukuzawa. "If I had found someone else who was better than Tarui, I would have used him," Takeuchi concluded, "but there was no one."

At this point, it is important to observe two things. One is the fact that the annexation of Korea was achieved by means of a Western-style treaty. On the other hand, at the time of the annexation the Meiji Emperor (reigned 1868–1912) addressed an imperial message to the emperor of Korea which included phrases reminiscent of the by then obsolete system of tributary relations in East Asia centered on Imperial China. These points help explain the ways that the Japanese reacted to the news of the Korean annexation. Nitobe Inazō (1862–1933) remains on record as having remarked that, during the summer of 1910, Japan suddenly had become just as large as France. He added that, although he did not support expansionism by force, it was the inevitable course of history for Japan to grow concentrically, eventually bringing Manchuria and the Russian Maritime Province under its territorial fold. This was the same Nitobe who had described Korea in 1906 as being on its deathbed after a long life, leaving behind a glorious history – much like the former world-wide empire of a certain country on the Iberian Peninsula. A major daily in Tōkyō, *Yorozu Chōhō*, editorialized in similar expansionist language: "Come to think of it, most of the Japanese people are Korean in origin. From now on Japanese should populate the Korean Peninsula."

It is also necessary to remember what President Theodore Roosevelt confided to Kaneko Kentarō (1853–1942) in the summer of 1905. This was shortly before the Portsmouth Peace Conference called to settle the Russo-Japanese War, when Roosevelt told the Japanese envoy that it was not yet the time to say it openly but, when the time came, Japan should declare an "Asian Monroe Doctrine." For this he promised United States support. As a staunch realist, President Roosevelt was convinced that, to keep peace in East Asia, Japan as a stabilizing regional power owed it to itself to assume the responsibility of protecting East Asia from Western colonial predators. The diplomat Ishii Kikujirō (1866–1945), the Japanese negotiator of the Ishii-Lansing agreement of 1916, acted on his knowledge of Roosevelt's encouraging words to Kaneko by confirming Japan's special interest in Chinese territory contiguous to Japan.[8] Inasmuch as Roosevelt's encouragement was an echo of the "big brother" idea behind the Monroe doctrine, the Japanese counterpart to this notion, as it would progressively take shape, was heir to the "leader of Asia" approach of the 1880s.[9]

A "new order" for East Asia: Pan-Asianism and *hakkō ichiu* after World War I

A fertile environment for political Pan-Asianism was created by the political situation during and after World War I. An early example was Prince Konoe Fumimaro's (1891–1945) essay *Bei-ei hon'i no heiwashugi o hai-su* (Opposing the Anglo-American Dominated Peace) which was published in 1918, just before Konoe went abroad to participate in the Paris Peace Conference. Except for a critical commentary that appeared in *The Millard's Review* in Shanghai, it fell on deaf ears in the West. But nearly two decades later, when crisis was intensifying on the Asian continent, "Colonel" Edward Mandell House (1858–1938), who acted as the right-hand man of US President Wilson at the Paris Conference, responded to Prince Konoe by calling for a written explanation of what he meant by a "New Order" for East Asia.

During the interwar period, the introduction of the concept of *hakkō ichiu* was the most important facet of the development of Pan-Asianism as an ideology. *Hakkō ichiu* literally means "the eight corners of the world under one roof." The collapse of several great empires in Europe, as a consequence of defeat in war or revolution, gave rise to a strong pessimism regarding the future of civilization, such as Oswald Spengler expressed in *The Decline of the West* (1918–21). Meanwhile in Korea, encouraged by the Wilsonian principle of national self-determination, the *sam-il* movement (March First Movement, 1919) emerged, demanding the restoration of Korean independence. It was in response to these developments that a professor of sociology at the Imperial

University of Tōkyō, Takebe Tongo (1871–1945) remarked that the East Asian concept and practice of *jingi* (morals) was superior to the Western concept of *seigi* (justice). He maintained that, whereas *jingi* meant humanitarian fairness based on self-giving love, *seigi* remained a merely legalistic term. This notion of *jingi*, which went hand in hand with *hakkō ichiu*, would become part and parcel of the notion of Japanese imperial, benevolent rule in Asia.

In contrast to this somewhat ethnocentric principle of good government and empire-building, an original and more ambitious manner of resolving the Korean problem was proposed in an Ōsaka newspaper in 1919. This was the proposal to create a Greater Korea as an independent state, following the model of the ancient Korean state of Goguryeo (Koguryo, Jp. Kōkuri). Territorially, this state was to comprise the Chinese territory of Manchuria, the Russian Maritime Province, and the Korean peninsula. Taken together, the topography of this enlarged state of Korea would resemble the fictitious bird of good fortune with its wings wide open, for which it was named *ōtori no kuni* (Land of the Bird of Good Fortune).

While such a notion might sound absurd today, in the political situation after World War I it was not so far-fetched. Due to a massive transfer of Japanese troops to Manchuria and the Russian Far East during the so-called Siberian Intervention (1918–22), Japan was militarily in control of all the territories concerned. However, Japanese plans in the Far East also led to estrangement from the United States, which – just as before in China – argued for an Open Door principle in Manchuria and Siberia. In effect, the United States now denounced the Japanese engagement and, even though Japan was one of the allied powers, assumed the role of watchdog to monitor Japan's aggressive behavior.

Another important development in the 1920s that fundamentally conditioned the Japanese psyche was the increasing popularity of the notion that "China is not a state but merely a civilization." Its corollary, that "being merely a civilization, it has no clearly delineated political borders," would make inroads into Japanese logic to justify expansion and territorial conquest in China.

An American political scientist, H. A. Gibbons, first made this idea public in 1918 in *The New Map of Asia*, and in Japan it was paraphrased and expanded by academics like Yano Jin'ichi (1872–1970), professor of Sinology at Kyōto Imperial University. Yano's first essay on the theme was published in the daily *Ōsaka Asahi Shinbun* in December 1921, when the Washington Conference had just opened. He maintained that for China to become a modern nation-state, it had to be divided up into four or five ethnic regions – those of the Han, the Manchu, the Mongolians, the Tibetans, and the people of Sinkiang. Another Sinologist at the same university, Naitō Konan (1866–1934), who had been writing on the Chinese people's primary concern for their family's well-being and their consequential absence of nationalistic awareness from as early as 1914, would go even further in 1938 to argue that the Chinese would not mind who ruled their country so long as they enjoyed security and prosperity. According to Naitō, they were even indifferent as to where the capital city was located or whether it was moved from one place to another, for example, from Beijing to Nanjing, or even to Guangzhou (Canton). Naitō claimed that the Chinese might very well acquiesce to their capital being relocated to Tōkyō. However, Japanese activism toward China and the possibility of a "Greater Korea" that would include parts of Siberia were straining relations between Japan and the United States, which continued to adhere to its Open Door policy in the Far East.

Even more strain was put on relations between Japan and the United States by the US anti-Japanese Immigration Act, which went into effect on 1 July 1924. A middle-aged man of the former samurai class committed ritual suicide next door to the American embassy in Tōkyō, with a letter of protest on his chest addressed to the President of the United States. This incident provided the occasion for the influential publicist, Tokutomi Sohō (1863–1957), to take a pan-Asianist stance in criticizing the American action. In his newspaper, *Kokumin no Tomo* (People's Friend), he wrote: "July 1 – this is the day when Japan's foreign policy swings away from the West to the East, disentangling itself from the United States in order to clasp hands with its Asian brothers."[10]

A full cycle had been traveled by people like Tokutomi, from fear of the "yellow peril" hostility perpetrated by the West, through cooperation with the "white" colonial powers, and finally to the assertive acceptance of the brotherhood of the "yellow" peoples of East Asia. A racial war, albeit a "cold war" for the moment, had begun; this was a propaganda war of "yellow peril" vs. "white peril," with Japan cast as the champion of the Asian peoples against the discriminatory "Whites," epitomized above all by the Americans.

Japan had made a very cautious approach to the issue of the "yellow peril" prior to World War I. So long as the Meiji oligarchs, who had seen Japan beaten by Western naval forces in the battle of Shimonoseki in 1864 and elsewhere, were in control, provocative policies such as a Sino-Japanese alliance had no chance of serious consideration by the government. It was Itō Hirobumi (1841–1909), as Resident-General of Korea in Seoul, who prevailed on the government in Tōkyō to recall from Washington Ambassador Aoki Shūzō (1844–1914) because he had argued for retaliation against US anti-Japanese immigration policies by cooperating with China. Also, in 1907, Itō ordered Gotō Shinpei (1857–1922), the newly installed president of Japan's South Manchurian Railroad Company, not to speak carelessly of a Sino-Japanese alliance for fear it would provoke unwanted "yellow-peril" hysteria in the West.[11]

Alliance with China was part of a strategic policy proposal to keep the New World of America from meddling in the affairs of the Old World. It was built on an idea borrowed from a German political scientist, Emil Schalk. To achieve this goal, Europe and the East Asian powers had to be consolidated into a single unit, and Gotō thought of the Sino-Japanese alliance only as its starting point.

But such words of caution would become rarer as the Meiji oligarchs passed away, one after another. Itō was assassinated by a Korean patriot in 1909 and Yamagata Aritomo died in 1922. Nevertheless, concern that Western racism might undermine the security of the nation was so deeply ingrained in the Japanese mind that it would surface at critical moments of decision-making in the future. At the Imperial Conference of 5 November 1941, on the eve of the "Greater East Asia War," such concerns exercised Privy Council President, Hara Yoshimichi (1867–1944). He questioned Prime Minister Tōjō Hideki (1884–1948) regarding the possibility that Hitler might make his peace with the British and Americans in spite of the Axis Alliance, leaving Japan stranded and alone in a hostile sea of racism. Tōjō answered that utmost care was being exercised to prevent the Japanese war from turning into a racial war. A German–Japanese accord signed immediately after Pearl Harbor committed the parties not to conclude a separate peace – but eventually, after six years of war, Germany was forced to surrender unconditionally in May 1945, leaving Japan alone in the war against the "white" powers.

As we have seen, Japanese Pan-Asianism relied heavily on the notions of *hakkō ichiu* ("the eight corners of the world under one roof") and *kokutai* (national polity). By 1940, both notions had become fundamental to official Japanese political parlance. The former, for example, found its way into basic policy pronouncements such as *Kihon kokusaku yōkō* (An Outline of the Fundamental National Policy), adopted by the Second Konoe Cabinet on 26 July 1940. In the same vein, *kokutai* had such pervasive symbolic importance that it alone was the focus of dispute in regard to the surrender terms spelled out in the 1945 Potsdam Declaration. Thus, the phrase "having successfully preserved *kokutai*," which opened the Imperial Rescript on Surrender (15 August 1945), was an implicit proclamation that the war had been terminated to open up the future to eternal peace. As we shall see below, moreover, certain Japanese public intellectuals continued to rely on the notion of *hakkō ichiu* for guidance in reconstructing the country and building peace in the world after the war.

Pan-Asianism as geopolitics

In the prewar period, we can identify another current of thought in pan-Asian ideology that should not be neglected, namely geopolitical notions. The policy pronouncement of the "New Order for East Asia" of 1938 was a new Japanese version of the traditional sinocentric hierarchy based on the notion of imperial benevolence. In contrast to the earlier version, the "Greater East Asia Co-Prosperity Sphere" of 1940 had to be rationalized on the basis of geopolitical notions of Western origin. It was thus conceived of as a combination of *hakkō ichiu* and the theory of an extended regional economic sphere for Japan's material self-sufficiency and military security. Geopolitical theory of Western origin was first denounced as pseudoscience in Japan, but political scientist Rōyama Masamichi (1895–1980) noticed its utility in the aftermath of the Manchurian Incident (1931), when Japan was faced with the critical problem of what to do with Manchuria.

Later, there emerged another brand of geopolitics espoused by Professor Komaki Saneshige (1898–1990) of the Imperial University of Kyōto. It was called the geopolitics of *kōdō* (the Japanese emperor's way or the imperial way). This represented a distinctly Japanese school of geopolitics, in contrast to that espoused by Western scholars like Karl Haushofer (1869–1946). The practitioners of *kōdō* geopolitics denounced the latter as *hadō* ([the way of] domination, or hegemony). As we might expect, the content of the Japanese geopolitics of *kōdō* was an amplification of the notions of *hakkō ichiu* and *kokutai*. It also reflected the intellectual current then prevalent at the University of Kyōto, known as *kindai no chōkoku* (overcoming modernity). The above-mentioned notion that "China is not a state but merely a civilization" also had originated in Kyōto in the early 1920s. Now, at the beginning of the 1940s, Komaki Saneshige, as the most prolific proponent of "Imperial Way" geopolitics, argued that Southeast Asia's international borders, which were often rivers, had not only been imposed as a result of colonial division among the Western powers but had, in effect, destroyed the agricultural communities that had once been irrigated by the waterways now dividing countries.[12]

Pan-Asianism in wartime and postwar Japan

In the weeks surrounding the outbreak of the "Greater East Asia War" on 8 December 1941, two academic organizations were inaugurated, the Nihon Chiseigaku Kyōkai (Japan Geopolitics Association) and the Nihon Takushoku Gakkai (Japan Colonization Association). Their memberships were partly overlapping and, when the latter group was founded, an old student of Nitobe's remarked that Nitobe must be rejoicing because this was something he himself might have originated.

The *kōdō* geopoliticians were not included in the Geopolitics Association. Apparently supported by the government, this association immediately started publishing a monthly journal, *Chiseigaku*, and was able to continue publishing through 1944 in spite of material difficulties that hampered other publications. Typically, the first issue for 1942 carried a front-page treatise on the geographical extent of the Greater East Asia Co-Prosperity Sphere. It argued that in ancient times, the continent of Australia had been contiguous to the Asiatic mainland and therefore logic dictated its inclusion within the scope of the Sphere.[13]

It has been more than 60 years since the total collapse of this projected regional order in both theory and reality, accompanying Japan's defeat in a war whose official objective had been to establish a Greater East Asia Co-Prosperity Sphere. In recent years, it is becoming more and more apparent that Beijing is recapturing its traditional position of supremacy in East Asia. With a centuries-old historical background of regional dominance as the "Middle Kingdom," China's return to Southeast Asia on the basis of its ancient and prestigious imperial order seems more credible as it is progressively given the status of a new and rising superpower in world politics.

At the same time, it is becoming increasingly clear that Japan will soon succumb to the Chinese imperial order thus reconstituted. The result will be a distinct regional order within the global order that is for the moment dominated by the United States. The real test is yet to come as to which arrangement will seem more just and acceptable to local people. But how did this situation come about?

At the end of the war, Japanese decision-makers insisted on preserving the national polity with the emperor at its center, and made this a condition for the acceptance of the Potsdam Proclamation. In the process, Japan neglected its responsibilities as an imperial power, which included assessing the future of Korea which was still in Japanese hands at that time. As a result, Korea was unable to move smoothly towards independence. While Japan could have prevented the eventual division of Korea, the international situation led inexorably to the Korean War and the tragedy of the Korean people that still remains so profound.

The Japanese state retained its integrity from the prewar into the postwar period, with Hirohito still as emperor. But Japan gave up the idea of constantly having to deal with the consequences of its high-flung promises to the peoples of "Greater East Asia." What happened instead was that the sense of national responsibility that must have still been alive among the Japanese people was replaced by their newly-found messianic faith in anti-nuclear pacifism. This pacifism amounted to a postwar manifestation of the national enthusiasm for wartime *hakkō ichiu*.

Partly to blame for this situation was the press code issued by the Supreme Commander for the Allied Powers (SCAP) in Japan as soon as a General Headquarters was established in Tōkyō. The code proscribed the use of wartime expressions and concepts associated with militarism and aggression, specifically naming four of these: "Greater East Asia Co-Prosperity Sphere," "Greater East Asia War," *eirei* (the spirits of soldiers who gave up their lives for the cause of the imperial state, enshrined at Yasukuni Shrine), and *hakkō ichiu*. The latter two terms had essentially provided the moral basis for the Japanese war. However, some felt that *hakkō ichiu* was still a suitable concept to maintain self-respect and moral uprightness in the postwar world, as evidenced in its use by such intellectuals as Iwanami Shigeo (1881–1946), the founding owner of Iwanami Shoten publishers. In a draft of an essay intended to be published in late 1945 on the front page of the inaugural issue of the monthly journal *Sekai* (The World), Iwanami urged the Japanese steadfastly to pursue the ideals of *hakkō ichiu*. However, as a result of the editor's precautionary self-censorship, Iwanami's essay was not printed as drafted. *Sekai's* editor might have decided to exercise caution after the term was used by others, including former army officer Ishiwara Kanji (1889–1949) in a speech entitled "Shin Nihon no kensetsu" (Construction of a New Japan) on 6 October 1945. The speech was delivered in Kyōto under the sponsorship of

Ōsaka Asahi Shinbun, but was never printed in the newspaper as intended because it was banned by the Occupation authorities.[14]

Besides men like Iwanami and Ishiwara, who found continuing validity for the construction of postwar Japan's international position in such wartime principles as *hakkō ichiu*, there was at least one opinion leader who found positive significance in Japan's defeat. This was Yasuda Yojūrō (1910–81), who had championed prewar Japan's Romantic School of literature and had helped Japanese student-soldiers to rationalize certain death on the battlefield by comparing their sacrifice to the princely deaths of medieval samurai. He believed that the emperor's decision to terminate the war presented the Japanese people with a great opportunity to return to such true national values and rebuild their nation on that footing. He identified the surrender as *ōi-naru haiboku* or "grand defeat."

Perhaps his concept could have laid a more modest, less hypocritical moral basis for the new Japan were it not for the Korean War and the Cold War, which in the meantime had made Japan indispensable to the Cold War strategy of the United States. As it turned out, however, the Japanese became the beneficiaries of peace and prosperity in the shadow of the superpowers' rivalry over nuclear armaments.[15]

Pan-Asianism between regionalism and universalism

Thus, in postwar Japan, the idea of Pan-Asianism was dead and seemed to have disappeared from the Japanese mentality. But the national energy that had gone into a total war could not simply dissipate. After all, the Pan-Asianism that the Japanese expounded and tried to make a reality was a kind of regional universalism and, once Japan had been defeated, its former advocates often turned to the universal mission of pacifism. Pan-Asianist Japanese were "reborn" as pacifists through the baptism of the atomic bombings. In their eyes, the Japanese had again become a chosen people, now pursuing the *universal* mission of *pacifism*.[16]

Typical among such advocates was Shimonaka Yasaburō (1878–1961), who began his career as a publicist and publisher in the 1920s. He embraced Pan-Asianism as a passionate activist and in 1933 organized the Dai Ajia Kyōkai (Greater Asia Association). This association attracted such elite decision-makers as Prince Konoe and the career diplomat turned politician Hirota Kōki (1878–1948), along with intellectuals such as Yano Jin'ichi and army officers such as Matsui Iwane (1878–1948) and Kagesa Sadaaki (1893–1948). In Shimonaka, the messianic complex of *hakkō ichiu* assumed new configurations: anti-nuclear pacifism emanating from the national experience of the atomic bombings, and world federalism, which also was taken up by the first postwar Cabinet and enthusiastically propagated as a matter of editorial policy by the leading newspaper, *Asahi Shinbun*.

Or take Nakajima Kenzō (1903–79), whose wartime passion for *hakkō ichiu* was transformed into a groundbreaking effort to make peace with the

Chinese on the war-torn mainland. During the war, Nakajima had written editorials for the *Jinchū Shinbun*, a newspaper published for the Japanese armed forces in occupied Singapore. His editorials were completely in line with the concept of the Greater East Asia Co-Prosperity Sphere, and he went even further than the official line required. One editorial allegedly penned by Nakajima for the 1942 national holiday issue on Hirohito's birthday urged every Japanese soldier to become an unofficial teacher of the Japanese language. "When they [Asian nationals] begin to speak even several isolated words in Japanese," he concluded, "they are already becoming the beloved infants (*sekishi*) of the emperor."

I mention Nakajima's case here as just another example of the transformation of pan-Asianist passions and the intellectual concern that had expressed itself in the arguments for "overcoming modernity" on the eve of Pearl Harbor. Defeated and disabused of their notion that such ideas would "save" Japan, these public intellectuals now went overboard to find compensatory value in, for instance, the "counter-civilization" of Mao's China, symbolized in the backyard iron-smelters promoted during the "Great Leap Forward."

Conclusion

If one defines, as I have, Japan's wartime Pan-Asianism as a combination of two principal concepts – *hakkō ichiu* and *kokutai* – and if we assume that these two elements also comprised the content of *kōdō* ideology (the imperial way), then this variety of Pan-Asianism was doomed to vanish with Japan's acceptance of the Potsdam Proclamation, for which Japan had set the precondition of preserving *kokutai* while failing to specify *hakkō ichiu*. Yet the latter ideal had been an indispensable part of the concept of the Greater East Asia Co-Prosperity Sphere and claimed, at least in theory, universal applicability as an ethically-based principle of politics.

In contrast, *kokutai* was, and remained, a concept involving particularism and ethnocentrism, applicable only to Japan and Japanese nationals (*kokumin*). Historical accidents like the exigencies of the Cold War made the all-powerful United States choose *kokutai* rather than *hakkō ichiu* as acceptably representative of prewar Japanese values and principles. The consequence, as I have pointed out above, was Japanese forgetfulness of the nation's moral responsibilities, including those that arose from their roseate promises as well as the criminal acts they perpetrated on the people of the region. On the other hand, insofar as *kokutai* was preserved, the myth of Japan's uniqueness remained little affected in the mind of its people. This mentality could not persist without affecting postwar Japanese behavior in the international arena, for better or for worse.[17]

3 The Asianism of the Kōa-kai and the Ajia Kyōkai

Reconsidering the ambiguity of Asianism

Kuroki Morifumi

Introduction

China, Korea, and Japan were confronted with modernization in East Asia by being drawn into the system of unequal treaties as the result of the forced opening of their countries after long periods of seclusion. The Treaty of Nanjing in 1841, the Treaty of Peace and Amity signed between the United States and Japan in 1854, along with the Treaty of Friendship signed between Japan and Korea in 1876, signified the beginning of that process.

This shared experience of being made subject to the coercion of Western imperialism, in combination with their geographical proximity and common membership of the "yellow" race, produced a certain sense of fraternity among the people of the three countries in question and their respective governments. It was this that provided the historical background to the emergence of a certain form of "Asianism" which at that time in Japan was rendered with the term *Kō-A-shugi* – the idea of "Raising Asia."

Asianism was a mode of conduct and thought that arose among these three main nations of East Asia to resist Western encroachment, inspire attempts to revive their fortunes and oppose the West. Unfortunately, however, relations amongst these nations were not as good as they might have been. If anything, the governments of the nations in question were in a constant state of diplomatic conflict. It was under these circumstances, with the added catalyst of Imperial Russia's encroachment on China, that Japanese Asianism was formed.

At this point it would seem pertinent to refer to Takeuchi Yoshimi's comments regarding Asianism. He remarked that Asianism was a "tendency of thinking" that aimed to somehow engage with Asia (either as aggressor or ally), and that it would probably prove difficult to subject it to historical analysis.[1] However, it goes without saying that we are presented with the fact that Asianism existed, both in terms of conduct and thought, from the end of the Edo period (1603–1867) until 1945.

Recently there has been groundbreaking research by Hazama Naoki which deals with early Asianism from the perspective of the history of Asian civilization. He divides the history of Asianism into three stages – an early, middle, and late period. The first period spans from around 1880 until the military expedition against the Boxer Rebellion in 1900; the second period extends from 1900 to the second Shantung (Shandong) expedition in 1928; and the third from 1928 to the end of the Pacific War in 1945. So far as the first period is concerned, he enumerates the various political associations that arose at the time, elucidating their various intellectual positions and clarifying the scope of their activities. In the end he arrives at the conclusion that early Asianism was a mode of thought and conduct that aimed at essentially equal relations between Japan and China.[2]

In this chapter I will deal more particularly with two of the eight organizations that were treated by Hazama; the Kōa-kai (Society for Raising Asia) and the Ajia Kyōkai (Asia Association). Given that they were the first pan-Asian organizations to be established and, to my mind, seem to encapsulate the essence of what early Asianism signified, it will be useful to clarify their thought and activities in their entirety. Moreover, I would like to highlight some of the ambiguity within the Kōa-kai's Asianism while indicating clearly the difference in character between itself and other organizations such as the Tōa Dōbun-kai (East Asian Common Culture Association).

The policy of the Meiji government toward Asia prior to the Sino-Japanese War and the formation of the Kōa-kai

In 1874 the Meiji government dispatched troops to Taiwan (*Taiwan shuppei*) with a view to securing the Ryūkyū Islands as part of Japanese territory, thus bringing itself into direct conflict with China, the "Middle Kingdom." In the following year, the Ganghwa (Kanghwa) Island Incident occurred in Korea and the year after Japan succeeded in imposing an unequal treaty on Korea that gave her privileges of extraterritoriality and exemption from customs duties on the island in question and led to the opening of Korea. Given that this was a clear violation of the traditional pecking order so far as China's notions of her spheres of influence were concerned, this only served to deepen the impasse.

In order to remedy the situation and effect some form of compromise, the Meiji Government in 1880 presented a proposal that suggested the partitioning of the Ryūkyū Islands in return for most favored nation status for Japan from China. However, China's leading statesman, Li Hung-chang (Li Hongzhang, 1823–1901) objected to the proposal and negotiations collapsed. In the meantime, Japan succeeded in opening up the Korean port of Wonsan in May of the same year and after achieving a similar concession in Busan went on to establish a diplomatic representative in Seoul – something that up until that time had been denied to Japan.[3] As is evident from the course of events that unfolded during the ensuing decade from 1880 onwards, Japan's diplomacy was preoccupied with resolving the matter of the unequal treaties with the West, yet there was at the same time considerable effort devoted to extending

Japanese territorial authority into China's traditional sphere of influence in Korea. This served only to intensify China's resolve to retaliate and thereby strained relations between the two countries.

The Kōa-kai, which was Japan's first organization dedicated to the cause of Asianism, was established in Tōkyō in February 1880 and would go on to establish branches throughout Japan and even in China and Korea. The primary figure behind its establishment was Sone Toshitora (1847–1910), a Navy Lieutenant who had served as an information-gathering attaché on China and had set up a predecessor organization named the Shin'a-kai (Association for the Advancement of Asia) in 1877. Sone had been in charge of briefing Ōkubo Toshimichi (1830–78) on Chinese affairs during negotiations for the Tientsin (Tienjing) Treaty between Japan and China in 1874 following the Japanese military expedition to Taiwan (*Taiwan shuppei*) and would therefore have most likely been directly acquainted with Ōkubo. Following the conclusion of the treaty, Ōkubo reputedly conferred with Li Hung-chang and promised to promote the establishment of language schools to nurture students who would promote deeper ties between the two countries in future. It is reasonable to conclude that Sone's establishment of the association Shin'a-kai had some connection with fulfilling the substance of what Ōkubo promised with regard to the establishment of Chinese language schools.

When the Kōa-kai was founded in 1880, its purposes were presented in the following terms: given that there were only two independent nations left in East Asia, Japan and China, and that the remaining nations of the region had succumbed to either outright invasion or subjugation by the Western powers, it was necessary for Japan to promote cooperation among the various nations of Asia, starting first and foremost with China and Korea, and thereby reverse the decline, resist the West, and advance Asian interests. In order to achieve that end it would be necessary to commence the collation of information relevant to China, Korea, and other Asian nations, and promote international exchanges on a civilian level.

The first president of the Kōa-kai was Nagaoka Moriyoshi, a Foreign Ministry official and the younger brother of the former feudal lord of Kumamoto domain. The vice-president was Watanabe Hiromoto (1847–1901), originally from Fukui (former Echizen domain) and later Foreign Ministry official. The remaining executive consisted of Sone Toshitora (former Yonezawa clan), Kaneko Yahei (an intern translator at Japan's China delegation from the former Nanbu clan), Kusama Jifuku (a popular rights proponent writing for the daily *Chōya Shinbun* hailing from Kyōto), Miyazaki Shunji (a former Bakufu official later appointed as a trainee secretary at the Amoy Consulate), along with Satō Tōru (from the former Satsuma domain). As can be seen, the executive of the Kōa-kai was made up of personnel with no clan affiliation who had varied backgrounds as either officials in the Foreign Ministry or as proponents of the popular rights movement. The Chinese Minister in Japan, He Ru-zhang, was invited to attend the founding meeting; however, he was represented instead by a deputized official. This possibly

indicated a degree of coolness towards the Kōa-kai due to the residual determination of China to express resentment over Japan's formal annexation of
the former tributary Ryūkyū Kingdom in 1879.[4] In this way the Kōa-kai was
founded with the intent of promoting cooperation between Japan and China,
but it was clear that at the point of its inception the Chinese side was not
inclined to place full trust in it.

In 1883, three years after the association's birth, the organization changed
its name to Ajia Kyōkai (Asia Association). This was mainly because Chinese
affiliates had qualms about the term "*Kō-A*" which tended to suggest that
Japan would "raise" Asia. It is also conceivable that sentiments regarding
China's great power status in Asia had some bearing on the matter as well. In
any event, regardless of the change in name, the executive and institutional
structure of the former organization was transferred unaltered into the Ajia
Kyōkai and therefore retained its essential character.

The scope of the Kōa-kai and Ajia Kyōkai's activities

In order to promote the aims of the association there were a number of practical
activities engaged in by the main chapter in Tōkyō. Primarily there was the
establishment of a Chinese language school (*Shina-go Gakkō*), which was to
provide training in Asian languages, especially colloquial Chinese and Korean,
with a view to nurturing persons who would be able to collect information on
Asia from primary resources. There were three study courses, including an
evening course, training in contemporary Chinese and Korean writing and
speaking, along with study of classical Chinese and Western mathematics.
Moreover, given that there was also a seminar based on Nakamura Masanao's
famous translation of John Stuart Mill's *On Liberty*, a work commonly
regarded as the "Bible" of the popular rights movement (*jiyū minken undō*), it
is probably fair to conclude that the atmosphere of the school was sympathetic
to that movement's outlook. This school was to produce personnel for Japan's
consulates in China. Eventually, the school became incorporated into the
Tōkyō School of Foreign Languages in 1885.

In addition to the foregoing, the association also edited and published its
own journal, *Kōa-kai Hōkoku* (Kōa-kai Report), which aimed to provide
information on Asia to members and promote communication amongst
them. The journal was published monthly and, given the prospect that there
would potentially be an extensive readership in Asian regions where Chinese
characters were in use, there was an essay column established from the four-
teenth issue onwards which contained articles presented entirely in Chinese
text (i.e. *kanbun*). The editing was presided over by the Japanese members;
however, prior to printing a copy was submitted to Chinese members to solicit
comments and corrections. As the association changed its name from Kōa-kai
to Ajia Kyōkai in 1883, the title of the Journal was also altered accordingly to
Ajia Kyōkai Hōkoku (Asia Association Report).

The association dispatched correspondents to the main cities of China and

Korea, even as far afield as Persia and Turkey. While abroad, these correspondents engaged in promotional activities for the association, signing up
members and sending regular reports on political and economic matters to
the head office which would appear in the journal. Among the members
dispatched to Asia were Matsumura Komatarō, Komamine Tadaomi, and
Yamayoshi Moriyoshi (to Beijing); Sone Toshitora and Hata Hiroshi (to
Shanghai); Eguchi Komanosuke (to Hankow); Sone Toshitora (to Hong
Kong); Igarashi Keikō and Okumura Enshin (to Wonsan); Yoshida Masaharu
and Yokoyama Magoichirō (to Persia); and Yoshida Masaharu (to the
Ottoman Empire).

General meetings were held on the first Saturday of each month followed
by a social gathering. The afternoon's proceedings would be followed by a
drinking session at which Chinese poems would be read out and discussed
with the gathering winding up usually at around 9:00 in the evening.
Moreover, in the event that there was a visiting delegation from Korea, or an
eminent guest from China, or perhaps the impending departure and return
home of one of the foreign affiliates, a special banquet would occasionally be
arranged.

One final activity of particular note is the publication of 25 issues from
1888 to 1895 of another association record, entitled *Kaiyo-roku* (Association
Announcements), which was edited by Nire Takayuki. It contained a variety
of materials which dealt with various events in Asian countries, both historical
and contemporary, as well as accounts of folk customs, anecdotes, and poetry
– all of which were rendered in Chinese. One can assume that since the *Kōa-
kai Hōkoku* was not issued during that time and that the affairs of the head
chapter were touched upon from time to time, this new publication was the de
facto association journal for that time.

The organization of the Kōa-kai

The head office of the Kōa-kai was in Tōkyō, with branches in Ōsaka, Kōbe,
Fukuoka and later also in Korea and China. At the time of the foundation of
the Kōa-kai, 77 members joined the association, 53 of them full members and
24 supporting members. Nevertheless, membership soon grew to 155, with
98 full members. Among the Japanese membership, we can identify the
following main groups: high officials from the Foreign Ministry; Japanese
diplomatic representatives in China and Korea; naval officers; educators affiliated with the Chinese language school of the Kōa-kai; members affiliated with
the newspaper *Chōya Shinbun* (Capital and Country News); China scholars
(*kangaku-sha*); those affiliated with "enlightening" organizations such as the
Keimō Gakusha or Dōjinsha; representatives of trading companies; Buddhists
from the Higashi Honganji; anti-mainstream army officers like Tani Kanjō
and Torio Koyata; along with members of the Imperial Household such as
Prince Kitashirakawa and Prince Komatsu.

Over the period starting from the foundation of the association in 1880 up until 1899, the two top executive positions of president and vice-president were filled as follows:

February 1880–April 1880	Nagaoka Moriyoshi, Watanabe Hiromoto
April 1880–May 1881	Date Munenari, Watanabe Hiromoto
May 1881–December 1881	Soejima Taneomi, Honda Chikao
December 1881–November 1882	Enomoto Takeaki, Nakamuta Kuranosuke
November 1882–January 1883	Nagaoka Moriyoshi, Watanabe Hiromoto
February 1883–January 1884	unclear
January 1884–unclear	Nagaoka Moriyoshi, Watanabe Hiromoto
May 1885–unclear	Nagaoka Moriyoshi, Watanabe Hiromoto
October 1890–unclear	Enomoto Takeaki, vice-president unclear
1895	Enomoto Takeaki, Hanabusa Yoshimoto
September 1899 onwards	Enomoto Takeaki, Hanabusa Yoshimoto

Usually upon entering the association every applicant paid a fee of two yen, regardless of whether they were founding members or affiliates. At the initial point of establishing the association, however, founding members were required to pay ten yen as opposed to the affiliate member's two. In addition, there was an additional membership fee of one yen. If we work on the assumption that monetary values in those days are roughly the equivalent of 8,000 times their original value today, this makes the cost of joining the association quite expensive. Moreover, when we compare this cost with that required to join, for example, the contemporary Liberal Party (Jiyūtō) within the popular rights movement, we find that it was only half a yen.[5] This suggests that the anticipated population base for the Kōa-kai's membership probably had almost twice the income as that of the Liberal Party membership and would be constituted of the more affluent strata of society.

The executive group in charge of coordinating the association's core activities (consisting of the president, vice-president, secretariat, and committee members) was elected by paper ballot from amongst the founding members at an annual general meeting held in April of every year. For the times, it was a relatively democratic process. All the same, the founding members had the privilege of being eligible for election to the executive with clearly delineated jurisdiction in running the affairs of the organization. The president was the association's official representative in all matters, with the vice-president standing in when, and if, incidental circumstances made it necessary. The secretariat originally consisted of five persons who were variously charged with taking care of administrative tasks such as editing the association's journal or keeping the accounts. However, in the course of the association's development there was a certain amount of fluctuation in that number (also contributed to at times by some personnel taking on dual roles). Moreover, as the number of founding members increased, the situation arose where the original executive was expanded into a committee of 12 elected officials (including the president and vice-president) which in turn operated in tandem with the secretariat to administer the organization. The supreme authority and initiative for setting the direction of the association lay with the president and the vice-president, while the secretariat remained the bearers of responsibility for administrative matters.

The political character of the Kōa-kai and the Ajia Kyōkai

In the position of president there were, on the one hand, representatives of the group of more enlightened former domain heads, such as Nagaoka Moriyoshi and Date Munenari, while on the other there were figures such as Soejima Taneomi (1832–93) and Enomoto Takeaki (1836–1908) who, though not possessing affiliations to the Meiji oligarchy, nonetheless were politicians with strong ties to Chinese and Russian affairs. Nevertheless, when it comes to ascertaining who provided the real leadership in the running of the organization it would seem, at least from a review of the documentary evidence, that it was in fact the vice-president, particularly Watanabe Hiromoto, who often held the greatest sway. One instance that possibly illustrates this best is the occasion when Watanabe in 1881 presented the association with six articles of reform that were intended to address problems of finance and organization. At the end of the document tabled to the executive there was even an unequivocal statement from Watanabe that there would be "no possibility of shifting" his position, something which indeed indicates a leading role in proceedings.[6]

The leadership group that variously occupied the offices of president and vice-president was at the time of the Restoration predominantly of a more "enlightened" outlook; however, they were all connected to the Bakufu and outside of the newly dominating Satsuma and Chōshū cliques. As a result they were inclined to a degree of criticism of the Satsuma and Chōshū dominance following the political reconfiguration. Soejima was one of the founding figures in the popular rights movement and it can be said that, in terms of having some resentment toward the politics of the oligarchy, Nagaoka Moriyoshi, Date Munenari, and Enomoto Takeaki were also inclined to have a degree of sympathy with its aims. Consequently, these figures were all part of the non-mainstream group within the politically dominant elite of the time.

Being in this situation produced a certain ambiguity for their position. It is interesting to note that Watanabe Hiromoto was apparently commissioned to write up the ordinances for suppressing the popular rights movement which suggests that the government found his expertise indispensable regardless of his being a non-Satsuma/Chōshū legal bureaucrat. Moreover, as his Tōhoku background and acquaintance with the younger Hara Takashi suggests, he had a certain affinity with the popular rights camp as well as a certain degree of status within the political establishment. However, just like Hara Takashi, he would never be able to avoid being at a certain distance from the core of political dominance that lay with the Satsuma/Chōshū (Satchō) oligarchy.

Let us turn now to the group who were charged with taking care of the association's activities – the secretariat editing the association's publications and the executive members who ran the organization's day to day affairs. At the time of founding, the secretariat consisted of Sone Toratoshi, Kaneko Yahei, Kusama Jifuku, Miyazaki Shunji, and Satō Tōru. For the *Kōa-kai Hōkoku*, the editorial duties were carried out by Kusama Jifuku, Miyazaki Shunji, Komi Genzō, Hirobe Sei, and Tei Ei-nei (1859–95). The later *Ajia Kyōkai Hōkoku* was edited by Nire Takayuki, Nakada Takayoshi, Azuma Heiji, Okamoto Kansuke, Yamayoshi Moriyoshi, and Tsuneya Morifuku.

The editorial staff had a diverse background. For example, Komi, Nire, Nakada, Yamayoshi, and Tsuneya had all been students at the Kōa-kai's Chinese language school, whereas Azuma Heiji had been a former student at Nakamura Masanao's Dōjinsha. They inherited Sone Toshitora's strong sense of the need to promote cooperation with China as well as Nakamura Masanao's idea of effecting that cooperation on an equal footing. As a result, they tended to be critical of the despising attitude displayed by the Meiji government toward China and Korea.

By contrast, Kusama Jifuku was a member of the executive of the Liberal Party who, along with Liberal Party colleague Suehiro Tetchō of the *Chōya Shinbun*, made contributions to the association's journal and enthusiastically participated in its weekly meetings. As both of these figures were prominent members in a popular rights movement political party such as the Liberal Party, they frequently made editorial contributions to the Party's publication, the *Jiyū Shinbun* (Liberty News), which were critical of the oligarchic government.

Taking both the leadership and the administrative groups into consideration as a whole, one can say that there was a certain affinity with the popular rights movement and that there was also an inclination to take up a critical position towards the government which would place them at a distance. Given the political atmosphere of the association, it is likely that the government felt inclined to keep the group at a distance as well, which probably accounts for Itō Hirobumi's refusal to join the association in 1881 when the president of the Kōa-kai, Soejima Taneomi, sent him an invitation to do so "if he had no objections."[7] It is clear that for the government, the main reason for distancing itself from Katsu Kaishū (1823–99) was the support for the Kōa-kai and the Ajia Kyōkai by the former Bakufu official.

The social base of the Kōa-kai and the Ajia Kyōkai

At this juncture there is some merit in considering just how broad a following the Asianist thought of the Kōa-kai had in society at large. Two indicators of the spread are the subscriptions for the association's journal along with the membership numbers. Within a year of the Kōa-kai's founding there were branches in Kōbe, Ōsaka, and Fukuoka, with affiliate branches being set up in the main trading cities of China and Korea. During that same period the membership rose rapidly to as many as 400 persons.[8] There were of course other members scattered in non-urban parts of the country such as Niigata included in those numbers.

An insight into the origins of that membership base is provided by an examination of the activities of Watanabe Hiromoto, the vice-president and arguably de facto leader of the Kōa-kai. In 1878, some time before the founding of the Kōa-kai, Watanabe established the Mannen-kai (Ten Thousand Years Society) as an organization to promote economic and commercial development. It was organized out of the wealthy landowners into a national organization which had as its aim the exchange of information to promote agriculture based on traditional farming methods. By 1888, the Mannen-kai had a membership of 349 persons with branches expanding from Tōkyō out to places such as Shizuoka, Morioka, Kagoshima, and Gunma.[9] Apart from this organization, he also set up in 1879 the Tōkyō Geographical Society with the aim of promoting the spread of geo-political knowledge about Japan, Asia, and the rest of the world. By 1880 it had a membership of 143 persons.[10] In this fashion Watanabe was strenuously engaging in a wide range of activities to strengthen Japan's national position and ultimately contribute towards the revision of the unequal treaties.

Generally speaking it is reasonable to assume that the ideas and opinions of the leaders of an association would be shared and supported by the members and it would seem reasonable to conclude that, if Watanabe's influence is anything to go by, that the Asianism of the Kōa-kai would have enjoyed considerable support from within the middle to upper classes of the 1880s. We should also note the influence of the pro-popular rights newspaper *Chōya Shinbun*, whose editor, Narushima Ryūhoku, and journalists (including Hirosue Tetchō, Kusama Jifuku, and Takahashi Kiichi) were all members of the Kōa-kai and promoted Kōa-kai ideas in the newspaper's pages. On that basis it would have had an influence stretching from Tōkyō to the broader newspaper-reading population throughout the country and it was certainly the case that at the time articles and lectures on Asianism were prolific.[11]

The activities of the Kōa-kai and the Ajia Kyōkai

The activities of the Kōa-kai and the Ajia Kyōkai can be divided up into five periods.

Period 1: 1880–82

This period covers the phase of extremely dynamic activity following the founding of the association. There were monthly meetings and monthly issues of the association's journal being produced regularly. It was also the time when the executive at a special session decided to admit Westerners into the association, making no distinction for eligibility based on whether they were resident in Asia or in their home countries. This suggests that the Kōa-kai was neither devoted fanatically to the cause of the "yellow" race in Asia, nor to an exclusive regionalism – it was simply concerned with the matter of releasing Asia from its condition of subservience by promoting independence.[12]

As the membership was made up of various persons who were not Japanese, including foreign diplomats and intellectuals from China and Korea, the editorials of the *Kōa-kai Hōkoku* would frequently promote cooperation amongst the Japanese Chinese and Koreans, and naturally tended to avoid issues that might offend one or the other. The main ideas and themes in the *Kōa-kai Hōkoku* were:

1   Asia's subservience in the wake of Western encroachment;
2   Asia's geographic interconnectedness (*shinshi hosha*);
3   common links amongst the peoples of Asia in terms of culture and race (*dōbun dōshu*);
4   the need for greater cooperation to resist the West, retrieve independence, and promote prosperity.

In one particularly significant article, the head of the secretariat, Kusama Jifuku, raised the question of whether Asia should seek to promote cooperation more by commercial means than by political means.[13] In response to this, Komi Genzō, then a student of the Kōa-kai's language school, submitted an article which was published in the October issue of the same year (1880). In it he advocated greater cooperation with China, suggesting that through "communication" and trade, China could be opened up on the cultural level to new developments in scholarship, law, and the mechanical arts. He was emphatically opposed to opening up China by force.[14]

In the pages of the journal there were also frank exchanges of views between Japanese and Chinese contributors. In one article Takahashi Ki'ichi went so far as to suggest that, since Japan had proceeded much further along the path of civilization and progress than China, a newspaper should be set up in either Hong Kong or Shanghai to "direct" China's "intellectual development."[15] To this a Chinese member, Wang Tao, pointed out that Japan had forced the annexation of the Ryūkyū Islands, thereby violating her traditional sphere of influence – a point that was being neglected by the Kōa-kai and inviting suspicion.[16] Another Chinese member, Wu Jian, added to these remarks by making a very pointed caution against Japan attempting to encroach on China.[17]

At this time there were in fact as many as 26 Chinese members of the Kōa-kai, including China's first official diplomatic representative, He Ru-zhang, and his successor, Li Shu-chang. Apart from such officials there were also entrepreneurs such as Wang Ti-zhai and journalists such as the aforementioned Wang Tao, who was the founder and chief editor of the Hong Kong-based newspaper *Tsun-wan yat-po* (Jp. Junkan Nippō). While the diplomatic staff such as He Ru-zhang were aware of the cultural commonalities between China and Japan and engaged with Japan's China specialists in print, they remained nonetheless unaltered in their view of China's traditional position in the regional hierarchy and considered their country as a great power. Moreover, they regarded Japan's radical program of national reconstruction based on learning from the West as an aberration, indeed something to be regarded with suspicion and contempt. And they regarded Japan's military actions in both 1874 in Taiwan and 1879 to annex the Ryūkyū Islands as an attempt to destroy the traditional hierarchy in East Asia. It was therefore deemed impertinent of this upstart country to step into the limelight and proclaim itself the focus of Asianism. Certainly the Japanese and Chinese shared a common sense of threat from the Western powers, but the Chinese also had a degree of anxiety about the Asianism espoused by the Kōa-kai – an anxiety that Wang Tao did not hesitate to voice in the editorials of his Hong Kong newspaper.[18]

In response to Wang Tao's opinion, Suehiro Tetchō made a rebuttal in the *Chōya Shinbun* condemning Wang's political conservatism.[19] He also made the arguably prescient comment that the aims of the Kōa-kai could not be accomplished overnight and that it would in fact take an extraordinary amount of patience and effort to do so. In the foregoing manner the early editorial staff of the association's journal sought to present not only the opinions of Japanese members but also represent at times the critical views of Chinese members towards Japan's foreign policy.

Period 2: 1882–84

When the Jingo military mutiny (*jingo jihen*) broke out in Korea in 1882, bringing about a fresh escalation in tension between Japan and China, the *Kōa-kai Hōkoku* attempted to depict it positively as something that in the long term would provide an important lesson in developing future cooperation, but there was no editorial that seriously addressed the causes of the conflict.

The events of August 1882 were the result of the coalescence of a political upheaval and anti-Japanese sentiment. Following the attack on the Japanese Minister's residence in Seoul, the Japanese dispatched troops to secure it. However, China also dispatched troops and there was every chance of a full-out conflagration developing in the Korean capital. Through the ensuing treaty arrangements Japan achieved a degree of resolution by obtaining the right to maintain troops at the Japanese Minister's residence in addition to reparation payments. This signified both the beginning of Japan's military infiltration of the Korean peninsula and the commencement of military conflict with China over Korea. Under the circumstances the *Kōa-kai Hōkoku* simply ran an editorial proposing the promotion of trade and commerce as the means of finding a peaceful resolution of the matter.

At the time of the incident Nire Takayuki had just completed his training at the Kōa-kai Chinese language school (*Shina-go Gakkō*) and had joined the administrative staff of the association. He had also been very critical of the move to effectively close the school by forcing its amalgamation with the Tōkyō School of Foreign Languages. His main concern was that the amalgamation would lead to the loss of a focus on Asianism and supplant it with mere language study. As we shall go on to examine further, he was developing into a particularly ardent Asianist with a strong determination to resist Western encroachment in Asia.

It goes without saying that the stand-off that ensued between Japan and China as a result of the Jingo Incident would have given Nire great cause for alarm. During 1883 he submitted in five installments to the *Kōa-kai Hōkoku* his "Outline of the Theory of Trade" by which he promoted commerce in commodities and knowledge as the means for creating greater mutual benefit and deeper trust. Indeed, he insisted that it would be precisely by the exchange of goods and knowledge that the great Asianist vision of cooperation between China, Korea, and Japan would be achieved.[20] Leading on in very much the same vein of argument, Azuma Heiji also submitted an outline of his own conception of how Asia could recover autonomy in trade matters and even discussed the potential for the eventual amalgamation of China and Japan in the future.[21] This view was arguably developed from an earlier article by Komi Genzō, which was printed in the *Chōya Shinbun* on 21 November 1879 and discussed mutual exchange in terms of "communication."[22] Other Kōa-kai members with affiliations to Ōkura Kihachirō and entrepreneurial traders from Mitsubishi also were concerned to promote commerce between Japan and her neighboring countries and made editorial contributions accordingly.[23]

Apart from expressing this joint concern to promote trade and future cooperation with China, there was also a broader concern with the relief of other peoples further afield who were similarly sharing in the sufferings associated with subjugation by the West, for example the people of Persia and Turkey. On 13 September 1882, the North African contingent of the British Army crushed the Egyptian independence movement. The following month the 32nd issue of the *Kōa-kai Hōkoku* contained an editorial entitled "The Continuing Record of Trouble," which condemned in unambiguous terms the evil of the military intervention of England and France in the internal affairs of other nations. It was a position that perhaps should not be surprising given that there were Turkish members of the association, but in any event it was depicted as a major catastrophe for the Orient as a whole.

Period 3: 1885–94

In December of 1884, an attempted coup d'etat, the Kōshin coup, was carried out in Seoul by pro-Japanese forces under Kim Ok-kyun (1851–94) against the reactionary government of the time. However, it failed after three days, despite covert support from the Japanese consulate and various freelance Japanese fighters, so-called continental adventurers, due to military invention by China. This was the first time that Japanese and Chinese forces had come into armed conflict in Korea, and within Japan calls to "punish" China, notably from within the popular rights movement, employed patriotic and anti-foreign sentiments to inflame the public into a nationwide call for war to be declared forthwith.

On 18 January 1885, a large gathering was organized at Ueno Park in Tōkyō to bring together influential persons, promote the establishment of an expeditionary force and commence hostilities. After a public meeting which attracted as many as 3,000 people – consisting of a fair proportion of the younger adherents to the popular rights movement, students, rickshaw drivers, and assorted ruffians – the participants proceeded to march through Ginza to demonstrate. Before the premises of the pro-war *Jiji Shinpō* (Daily Events News) they stopped to cheer; before the premises of Suehiro Tetchō's anti-war *Chōya Shinbun* they stopped to pelt the building with rocks and break windows before moving on.[24]

Earlier in the year, at the second meeting of the Ajia Kyōkai which was held on 30 May, Suehiro Tetchō was elected to the executive with the third highest number of votes out of the 24 committee members. Given that his anti-war stance was already well publicized, this indicates that support for his position was very strong indeed. At the same meeting the Chinese minister Xu Chang-Zu noted with concern that the majority of popular rights movement-aligned newspapers were promoting the perception of China as an enemy. He exhorted those present to "not think of ourselves as either Japanese or Chinese," but "consider ways of reviving Asia" without becoming prisoners to nationalist sentiment. Yao Wen Tong, an official at the Chinese Consulate, reiterated these sentiments and expressed his wish that the Ajia Kyōkai would go from strength to strength and thereby "fulfill the hopes of the Minister and myself."[25] So far as the Japanese government was concerned, it came to an agreement with China in the Treaty of Tientsin in April 1885 to simultaneously withdraw troops and commit to written notification prior to any future dispatch, thereby settling the matter.

The worsening of relations between Japan and China had a substantial effect on the activities of the association. Both the monthly issues of the journal and the monthly meetings became less regular, producing a trend towards a standstill. Given such a crisis in relations, Vice-President Watanabe Hiromoto called for the establishment of a policy to break the deadlock and restore peace at the association's committee meeting of June, 1885. His own suggestions for creating goodwill among Japan, China, and Korea were familiar proposals to (a) promote trade for mutual benefit, (b) advance exchanges not only on the government level but also on the broader civilian and academic level, and (c) make greater use of the Ajia Kyōkai to achieve these aims.[26] However, this argument to promote peaceful relations through trade had been wheeled out two years earlier at the time of the previous crisis by the likes of editorial staff such as Nire Takayuki and Azuma Heiji, and though it was salutary that the association's leader should voice acceptance of such a position, it was nonetheless a rather belated gesture.

In 1886 Suehiro Tetchō suggested the compilation of a "History of Asia" as a means to reinvigorate the activities of the association. The idea was to mobilize the Ajia Kyōkai organization to gather the relevant materials on the history of mutual relations in Asia and have them published, something which did in fact come into reality in a series of 14 issues of the official proceedings of the association published from 1888 to 1892. At the same time, from this period onwards any articles written in Chinese for the association's journal were all submitted to Chinese members from the diplomatic staff for proof-reading, ostensibly to gain their prior agreement and approval.[27] Nevertheless, it is also from this time that newspaper editorials in popular rights-aligned publications such as the *Jiyū Shinbun* began to show signs of transforming Asianism into an ideology justifying the encroachment of Japan on Korea.

Period 4: 1894–95 (First Sino-Japanese War)

When the new trade treaty between Britain and Japan abolishing extraterritoriality and strictures on tariffs was signed immediately before hostilities broke out with China on 16 July 1894, the Ajia Kyōkai found itself on the threshold of fulfilling the original ideal of the Kōa-kai – total autonomy from the West. However, in total contradiction of the companion ideal of achieving this on the basis of equality in Asia, it would be accompanied by the occupation of Korea and total enmity with China. It would of course be very apposite to establish what position the Ajia Kyōkai took with regard to this turn of events but, unfortunately, given the lack of association records for this time period we are unable to clarify that point with any certainty.

The membership of the Ajia Kyōkai at the May meeting just prior to the commencement of hostilities on 23 July 1894, was 250 persons – certainly much less than the 400 persons at its heyday, but nonetheless indicating a degree of continuous membership close to the figure of 270 at the association's inception. Even so, the association had undoubtedly entered a period of subdued activity compared to several years earlier. It was a sad indictment of the fact that while a certain section of the upper classes were inclined to promote peaceful relations with China, there were few, if any, who were inclined to raise their voices and address the public at large with their views. It is also testament to the manner in which Itō Hirobumi's government was prepared to harness xenophobic nationalist sentiment to pursue a war of aggression against China and accelerate Japanese society towards a continuous state of war-preparedness.

Period 5: 1896–1900

On 8 March 1896, Watanabe Hiromoto, an erstwhile leading figure of the Ajia Kyōkai, found himself delivering a congratulatory speech as the head of the local veteran's association at a gathering where he was the chief sponsor.[28] The following July he apparently confided to Ernest Satow, Britain's diplomatic representative in Japan, that deep down he had been against the war.[29] It is not altogether clear under what circumstances this statement was made but, given that it was made at a time when the euphoria of victory was still fresh in the air and any contrary utterance was impermissible, it could be taken as a frank admission of Watanabe's opposition to the war with China. Obviously there is a contradiction that emerges between the speech in March and the statement made in July, yet when we consider that he was by now the representative of his local constituency in the Imperial Diet, it is understandable that he was unable to avoid taking part in the local festivities celebrating the victory. The point remains that he was in any event opposed to the war, as were other former Kōa-kai members and supporters, such as Miyajima Sei'ichirō[30] and Katsu Kaishū. Viewed overall, the original membership of the Kōa-kai was opposed to the Sino-Japanese War, although some graduates from the association's Chinese language school eventually ended up serving in the armed forces as interpreters.

In 1898, the Western powers, perhaps reflecting an enhanced sense of China's vulnerability in the wake of the Sino-Japanese War, obtained commercial concessions in China's north-eastern territories. In the same year, as a reflection of a heightened sense of anxiety regarding these developments, there emerged a new association from amongst the ranks of Asianists: the Tōa Dōbun-kai (East Asian Common Culture Society), which was formed out of a merger of the Tōa-kai (East Asia Society) and the Dōbun-kai (Common Culture Society) under the leadership of Prince Konoe Atsumaro (1864–1904). The vice-president of this new organization at the time of its founding was none other than Nagaoka Moriyoshi, a former president of the Ajia Kyōkai, and it was two years later, in January of 1900, that the Ajia Kyōkai eventually merged with the Tōa Dōbun-kai.

The Kōa-kai and the Ajia Kyōkai had come to an end after 20 years of activity. The last remaining question is perhaps why the two groups, despite their common "Asianism," did not merge right away when the Tōa Dōbun-kai was established in 1898. The answer would seem to lie partly in the differences in the age and professional background of the two groups' membership. Another major factor was clearly the difference in their Asian outlook. The Ajia Kyōkai had always aimed to promote equal relations with China but, as is evident from the mission statement of the Tōa Dōbun-kai, the latter group conceived of itself as promoting China's "total preservation" by "assisting in China's improvement," which implied a willingness to intervene in Chinese affairs quite apart from simply promoting stronger political, economic, and cultural ties. Anxiety about this characteristic of the Tōa Dōbun-kai is probably what accounted for the delay in full amalgamation.

Promoting Asian ideals

At the time of the Kōa-kai's founding, Sone Toshitora wrote a brief introductory essay that outlined the need for creating in Asia a "way of justice" (*seidō*) which would enable Asian nations to turn their circumstances around and be a match for the Western powers' outrageous violations of Asian autonomy. This "way of justice" presented a moral basis for resisting the essentially amoral encroachment on Asia by the West. However, by the end of the Sino-Japanese War, this "way of justice" was transformed into the "Kingly way" (*ōdō*) based on the Confucian precepts of obligation and benevolence which would supplant the Western "despotic way" (or "rule of might," *hadō*).[31]

Within this transition we can glean the change in perception of his own country, which he no longer considered a minor country but rather a major power in the East Asian region.

Initially then, the Kōa-kai was promoting an alternative ideal while condemning the circumstances of Western encroachment. Apart from Sone there was also Yoshida Gisei, who taught at the Chinese language school and exhorted his students to rouse Asia out of her indifference to the advance of civilization and promote the "public good" (*kōeki*).[32] Moreover, he asserted that the difference in strength between the people of the West and the people of the East constituted an "imbalance" that violated "the will of Heaven," the rectification of which would ultimately lead to even the enlightenment of the "dark lands" of the West.[33] In this sense Yoshida conceived of both the West and Asia as being in darkness – as societies that could only be remedied through the restoration of mutual "balance."

While ideals embodied in terms such as the "way of justice," "public good," and "balance" (*heikin*) are necessarily abstract and lacking in a concrete prescriptive content, it is still noteworthy that these ideals were being presented in response to the prescription of the West which amounted to an endorsement of the strong devouring the weak. They did not adopt the imperialist or acquisitive rationale of Europe and the United States but kept their focus on the common benefit of Asia through a new ideal that embraced both the West and Asia.

The ambiguity of Kōa-kai and Ajia Kyōkai Asianism

As has been discussed in the foregoing sections, the Kōa-kai's leader, Watanabe Hiromoto, and Azuma Heiji, one the main officials in the association, both expounded on the need for cooperation on equal terms in Asia. And yet when it came to their views on Korea, their opinions nonetheless diverged. Watanabe advocated Japan's role as a leader ahead of Korea, while Azuma retained the concern to maintain equality. This in essence was the basis of a certain duality within the Kōa-kai so far as its dealings with Korea were concerned.

Watanabe's view of Korea entailed, on the one hand, a traditional contempt for the country based on a pride in the mythological invasion of the three Korean kingdoms in ancient times by the Japanese Empress Jingū and the invasions of Toyotomi Hideyoshi in the late sixteenth century. To this was added a more recently developed contempt which sprang from Japan's capacity to exact advantageous treaty provisions following the Kanghwa Island Incident in 1876 and a general perception that Japan had advanced so much further down the path of civilization and progress. This view meant that Korea was regarded as a relative weakling with little capacity for independence, so that the interest of other major powers such as China or Russia in Korea simply fueled anxiety that others would take over Korea and ultimately threaten Japan. At root this is what gave birth to the notion of assuming a leading role over Korea in the interests of Japan's national security.

Accordingly, the structure of the debate regarding cooperation amongst Japan, China, and Korea revolved around notions of maintaining a relative equality for Japan and China, while relegating Korea to an inferior position. China remained equal because, after all, it was still regarded as a "great power." But as tension mounted with China over their respective claims on Korea, the notion of equality with China also came to fall away – it became therefore simply a matter of fulfilling the aims of Japan's expansionist nationalism which sought suzerainty over Korea.

As already mentioned, Azuma did not regard Korea with contempt, but recognized both its claim to relative autonomy and its capacity to advance along the road of civilization and progress independently. As a result he also did not harbor any particular anxiety about the possibility of a third nation taking over Korea. Moreover, this meant that his conception of the best means of maintaining Japan's security lay in promoting an equal partnership with Korea, implying a "small country" nationalism. His conception of how Japan and China should relate to each other was based on a regional equality that even countenanced an alliance between the two countries.

In this fashion, the Asianism of the Kōa-kai embodied two separate notions of regionalism based on two different concepts of nationalism. Watanabe's vision was one where the regional order would be based on hierarchy – Japan and Korea would be in the same region, but Japan would be the leader in line with Watanabe's expansionist nationalism. By contrast, Azuma's vision of the regional order was one where Japan and her Asian neighbors would cooperate on equal terms based on a far less ambitious nationalism.

Extrapolating more generally on the implications of this for the history of the Kōa-kai and the Ajia Kyōkai as a whole, the difference in perceptions of Korea could be said to have engendered a rather clear distinction between the leadership – Watanabe and Nagaoka in particular – and those handling the day to day affairs of the association such as Azuma and Suehiro. Furthermore, it is clear that this divide reflected a fundamental difference in social position as well; the former representing the interests of those in power (albeit as non-Satchō elites), while the latter were representing the interests of those far from power – the likes of Christians and popular rights movement intellectuals.

From Ajia Kyōkai to Tōa Dōbun-kai

The Tōa Dōbun-kai stands as one of the most influential civilian organizations in the history of Japan's Asianism. It was the largest Asianist group from its inception in 1898 until its demise in 1945. This organization emerged in the wake of Japan's victory in an imperialist war against China as Japan went on to actively pursue a policy of encroachment on the mainland. As already noted, the documents produced at the time of the Tōa Dōbun-kai's founding indicated a willingness to meddle and interfere in China's affairs, a characteristic that the Kōa-kai and the Ajia Kyōkai did not hold in common. Consequently it becomes possible to position the activities of the Kōa-kai and Ajia Kyōkai as the "early phase" of Asianism from 1880 until 1898, this to be followed by a mid to late phase of the Asianism of the Tōa Dōbun-kai.

An incident which confirms the conclusion that these two organizations were of a different character is their respective responses to the Boxer Rebellion in 1900. In June of 1900, a meeting of the Tōa Dōbun-kai was held to discuss the appropriate response to the Rebellion. Before the main meeting there had already been six articles decided on as appropriate measures to respond to the situation.[34] They were: (i) to expound the doctrine of "complete China protectionism" to win the hearts and minds of the people of Southern China; (ii) to argue in the newspapers, etc., of Southern China in favor of receptivity towards foreign influences and avoidance of military conflict when the mood of the public became xenophobic; (iii) to offer support for the transfer of the center of political power to the South should circumstances in Beijing become politically untenable; (iv) to overcome the resistance of public officials and private citizens in China with force superior to that of the Powers; (v) to occupy Korea in the event that the Western Powers invaded China; and (vi) to take a large territory in the event that China was partitioned into spheres of influence.

When it came to deliberating on these articles in the full meeting, Watanabe Hiromoto expressed his strong opposition to the articles from (iii) onwards which clearly advocated political interference, military intervention, and the occupation of Korea. In the end these offending articles were not approved and only the "protectionist" articles were adopted.[35] In response, Konoe Atsumaro in 1900 set up a separate organization, the Kokumin Dōmei-kai (National Alliance Association), to effect the substance of articles (iii) to (vi).

Why might Watanabe have opposed the articles in question? First, he might have opposed because he opposed *any* notion of political interference, military intervention or occupation of parts of East Asia by Japan. Alternatively, there is the possibility that he merely opposed such policies out of political opportunism, i.e. in opposition to the rise of the Tōa Dōbun-kai. Given that Watanabe did not join the Kokumin Dōmei-kai at the point of its founding in 1900, it is probably safe to conclude that the former was true. Furthermore, if this conclusion is accurate, it is also likely that, regardless of his later membership in the Tōa Dōbun-kai, he continued to maintain the ideals of the Kōa-kai by opposing military intervention and promoting equal relations between Japan and China.

In sum, it can be said that the legacy of the Kōa-kai and the Ajia Kyōkai remained distinct in character from that of the Tōa Dōbun-kai and that we have to distinguish between a period of "early Asianism" that aimed at equality and cooperation with China from a period of "later Asianism" – one that was characterized by nationalist expansion at the core of "Asianist" activism.

(Translated by Alistair Swale)

4 Universal values and Pan-Asianism

The vision of Ōmotokyō

Li Narangoa[1]

Introduction

During the early twentieth century, Pan-Asianism was an important dimension of the Japanese perception of Asia and the world. Japanese Pan-Asianism was based on discourses of "same race and same culture" (*dōbun dōshu*) – an Asian brotherhood – but also on a rhetoric of pacifism, universal human love, and virtue. These values were especially dominant in the pan-Asian concepts of religious groups, ultranationalists, and military officers who had strong ties to religious sects. The pan-Asian ideal of Ōmotokyō (Great Source Sect), one of the new religious groups in early twentieth-century Japan, was most clearly based on universal pacifism, universal moral values, and virtue. Ōmotokyō's Pan-Asianism and universalist ideals impelled it to embark on an overseas mission. By considering Ōmotokyō's overseas mission, this chapter analyzes how Ōmotokyō supported its pan-Asianist stance with reference to universalist ideals, and how both those ideals and Pan-Asianism were highlighted in the organization's effort to represent Japan's national interests while simultaneously serving its own aims as a religious organization.

Ōmotokyō is an important and interesting case for three reasons. First, it was one of the oldest Japanese "New Religions" and among the most successful in terms of the number of followers which it attracted in a relatively short period of time.[2] Ōmotokyō[3] was founded in the late 1890s by Deguchi Nao (1837–1918) and Deguchi Onisaburō (1871–1948). Like many other new religious sects which emerged during the late Tokugawa and the Meiji (1868–1912) periods, Ōmotokyō was founded in response to political and economic crises in Japan; it was critical of the social and political conditions of the time. It criticized the government's Westernization policy, the new modern institutions, bureaucrats, and the established religious sects for their ignorance of the social condition of the people. It spoke for the lower social classes and for the poor farmers, and campaigned for an ideal human community, which would be based on the morality implicit in the collective consciousness of the Japanese folk. This appeal to the needs of the common people, along with the healing and the spiritual training offered by the group, attracted a great number of followers within a short period of time, particularly during and after the First World War.

Second, Ōmoto was one of the Shinto Sects that distinguished itself from State Shinto; nevertheless, it still articulated its origin upon the Shinto creation myth. Shinto was a Japanese folk religion, but at the start of the Meiji era it was declared as the state religion and was transformed into an emperor-centered state ideology. In making Shinto the state religion, however, the Meiji government faced two problems. First, this measure excluded other religions from education and moral indoctrination policies; second, Shinto beliefs traditionally included a strong element of spirit worship, which the Meiji authorities regarded as incompatible with the modern state. To solve these problems, the Meiji government abolished the institution of the state religion and presented State Shinto as a non-religious institution that would only be responsible for ceremonies in the imperial household. Shinto groups not included in this "non-religious" State Shinto were organized into *shūha* Shinto (Sect Shinto or Shinto sects). This meant that in contrast to State Shinto they remained religious institutions.[4] The policy of separating state and religion and dividing Shinto religion into a "statist" form and sectarian forms permitted Ōmoto to position itself as the "true Shinto." Ōmoto questioned the legitimacy of State Shinto, and claimed that it was a non-religious institution which did not respect the gods. The Ōmoto leader, Onisaburō, insisted that only Ōmoto's teachings expressed the true Shinto religion in its original purity.[5] This attitude contributed to Ōmoto's idea of acting as a bridge between East and West through its overseas mission, and to its ideology of unifying the world through religion, an enterprise which Ōmoto was to play a special role in. Thus, the Shinto myth which Ōmoto based its religious authenticity upon became an important element in both Ōmoto's universalism and its ethnocentric Pan-Asianism.

Third, the attitude of the sect to the state and the emperor was ambiguous, veering between protest, adaptation, and promotion: their protest evolved from a complete rejection of the socio-political system of the Meiji government to an attempt to blend the national religious myth with pragmatic political rhetoric. The original teaching (*ofudesaki*) of Deguchi Nao involved a complete rejection of the contemporary political order and of the legitimacy of the imperial system. It pronounced this system to be corrupt: it had to be destroyed and a divine realm built in its place – this would bring about a "renewal of the world" (*yonaoshi*). The new divine realm would be created by the divine power of the Ushitora no Konjin, the deity that had possessed Nao. In the long run, however, religious groups of this kind found it difficult to survive. Unlike Nao, Deguchi Onisaburō was more perceptive of the new political currents of the early twentieth century. Thus, he adapted the official state Shinto myth to Ōmotokyō's thought by linking the main Ōmoto deity, Ushitora no Konjin, with deities of the Shinto creation myths; he also fanatically propagated loyalty to the emperor to downplay Ōmoto's extreme millenarian ideal of world renewal and reconstruction and to secure its institutional existence.[6] When this attempt at the articulation of two contradicting ideas did not work, Ōmoto extended its activities beyond Japan's territorial boundaries, and it became the promoter of an ideology of territorial expansion under the banner of Asian unity and universal pacifism.

In short, Ōmoto's teachings, ideology, and activities mirrored internal Japanese social, economic, and political problems of the early twentieth century. They also reflected the ambivalent nature of Japanese pan-Asian ideology, and the fundamental contradictions between universal values, such as Ōmoto's religious pacifism, and ethnocentric pan-Asian regionalism.

Advocating universal values is the basic activity of most religious missions. Apart from the general missionary ideal of spreading universal values, Ōmotokyō had two reasons to advocate universal pacifism (or love) as part of its pan-Asian ideal. First, as a Shinto sect Ōmoto did not share common cultural roots with other Asian religions. Shinto is an indigenous Japanese religion. It was strongly promoted only from the Meiji era, whereas Buddhism had come to Japan from India via China and Korea many centuries earlier, and thus had many followers all over Asia. Ōmoto had to emphasize universal values to make Shinto more acceptable to non-Japanese Asians. Second, the mission of Ōmoto in Asia was not simply to promote Asian unity, but rather to create a basis for their missionary work all over the world. This intention was evident in their idea of "unifying the world by means of religion." Making Shinto a universal religion would place Japan at the centre of Asia and the world, because Shinto originated from Japan. Making Japan the centre of the world would also mean re-positioning Ōmoto: it would become the "great source" of universal truth. In this respect, achieving Asian unity was just a step towards a greater vision: creating a world mission.

Under the banner of universal pacifism and Asian unity

Ōmoto's first overseas missionary activities were carried out between two police raids against the sect that occurred in 1921 and 1935. In both cases, Ōmoto was suppressed by the government for *lèse-majesté*, despite its propagation of the absolute sovereign right of the emperor. The main reason behind these suppressions was the fact that Ōmoto had challenged the state: through its millenarian statements, its demands that "true" Shinto should be re-established and its organizational efficiency, which competed with the state's mobilization. The suppression of Ōmoto was also supported by various opponents of the sect: established religious organizations such as Buddhist schools, but also modern bureaucrats who rejected Ōmoto's "unscientific" healing methods and belief in spirits.[7] As a result of the first raid in 1921, many leaders, including Onisaburō, were detained, fined, or jailed. A few months later they were released, but they were kept under strict control while awaiting the court ruling. However, it took the court more than three years to arrive at final judgment. In mid 1924, Onisaburō was sentenced to five years in jail, but he and other Ōmoto leaders were released only three months later.[8]

In the situation which obtained after the 1921 suppression of Ōmoto, the obvious reason for rising interest in overseas missions was to recover from the losses caused by the first raid and the subsequent lengthy court trials. The sect was looking for a way to extend its influence to areas outside Japan, and this coincided with contemporary Japanese political and military expansion in Asia.

As a consequence of the First World War, Ōmoto leaders had started to look at Japanese social and political crises in the context of world problems. This was the beginning of the idea of a grand world family system. The resentment against the government policy of Westernization on the part of Ōmoto leaders did not arise from a narrow anti-Western view. Rather, it grew out of a strong conviction that the government should return to traditional Shinto values. Onisaburō believed that Shinto principles could be valued beyond Japan's borders. In this respect, Onisaburō shared the Japan- and Shinto-centric view of the early Shinto scholars. Japan was to become a model for the rest of the world, but the nation's standards had to be improved by a fundamental transformation before it could take its place at the centre of the world. While the pre-1921 approach had been to build a world family system from inside Japan, after the 1921 police raid against Ōmoto the method was reversed: the aim now was to improve Japan by first convincing Asia and the rest of the world to follow the Ōmoto teachings. In this context, the grand world family system represented Ōmoto's version of the universal ideals of pacifism and human love. Pacifism and love, the sect asserted, would solve the conflicts that beset Asia. Onisaburō proclaimed that all humans were brothers and sisters and that all religions came from the same origin. As Ulrich Lins in his well-researched work *Die Omoto-Bewegung* has pointed out, the followers of Ōmotokyō were now no longer nationalists; they had become pioneers of world peace who sought to bring good fortune to the entire human race.[9]

Ōmoto initiated its overseas mission with the aim of bringing East and West together and averting a war between the two civilizations. Ōmoto's world mission was inspired by two foreign organizations. The first of these was an American branch of the Bahá'i religion, which took its universal ideals from the Islamic Shi'a sect. This sect considered all peoples to be the servants of god but not the subjects of a state. Onisaburō found many parallels between Ōmoto and Bahá'i.[10] From members of the Bahá'i sect he heard that it was disseminating its world mission in Esperanto, then being promoted as a new world language. Onisaburō found this information both fascinating and useful. Esperanto had been approved by Japanese scholars such as Kuroita Katsumi, Yanagita Kunio, and Ka Seizō; in 1922 they had set up a Japanese branch of the World Esperanto Union.[11] Onisaburō became a strong supporter of Esperanto and in 1923 he started to learn the language.

The second organization that influenced Ōmoto's initiatives to embark on a world-wide mission was the World Red Swastika Society (Sekai Kōmanjikai), which was founded in 1922 by the Chinese religious group Dao Yuan with the objective of carrying out social work. The Dao Yuan had itself been founded a couple of years earlier by several well-off Chinese. Its teachings combined five major religions and philosophies: Buddhism, Confucianism, Christianity, Islam, and Daoism. The main deity, however, was the Daoist philosopher Lao Tse (Lao Zi). The members of the Red Swastika Society included well-off landowners, businessmen, military officers, and retired government officials. This organization advocated the equality of all races and religions. Ōmoto's first contact with the Chinese sect was in 1923, when members of Red Swastika Society came to Japan to bring aid to the area affected by the Kantō earthquake. The Red Swastika Society informed the Ōmoto leaders that an oracle had instructed them to work together with a religious institution in Japan for the sake of world peace. Coming to Japan they now discovered that that religious institution was Ōmotokyō. The Ōmoto leaders agreed to join forces with Red Swastika Society on the spot, and their collaboration lasted for many years. In the following year, a branch office of the Dao Yuan was set up in Kobe with the help of Ōmoto, and Ōmoto leader Deguchi Onisaburō became the Japanese representative of the office.[12]

Collaboration with this Chinese sect was the first step towards the realization of Ōmoto's universal ideals and its aim of achieving friendly relations amongst Asians. Onisaburō explained the reason for Ōmoto's collaboration as follows: "I decided to work with the Chinese Five Major Religions with the aim of collaborating with all the world religions. For Japan, for friendship between China and Japan and for world peace, I took the first step towards universal human love and virtue."[13] The Ōmoto monthly newsletter *Kami no Kuni* (The Land of the Gods) published an article in celebration of the foundation of the Kōbe Office of the Red Swastika Society. It reported that the collaboration was the "pioneering step towards the unity of humanity in the Orient" and "the basis for real Japanese–Chinese friendship and the accomplishment of the aim of making the world function as a single family."[14]

True to his words of "collaborating with all the world religions," Onisaburō also become one of the founding members of the Union of World Religions (Sekai Shūkyō Rengōkai) which was established in Beijing in May 1925. The members of this union included sects of Daoism, Christianity, Buddhism (including Chinese and Mongolian forms of Buddhism), Islam, and Shinto (Ōmoto). The general headquarters was set up in Beijing, the regional headquarters for East Asia in Ayabe, near Kyōto, at Ōmoto's headquarters. The aim of the Union was to unify the world by means of religion and to achieve global peace.[15]

Around the same time, Ōmoto also initiated missionary activities in Europe. A report on Ōmoto in the journal of the World Association of Esperanto in March 1924 had attracted great interest in the Japanese sect in Europe, and as a consequence Ōmoto established a Bureau for Overseas Mission in its headquarters in Ayabe and began a mission in Europe. To further promote its overseas missions, Ōmoto also set up an association called Jinrui Aizen-kai (Association of Humanitarian Love and Virtue) in June 1925 (or, in Esperanto, Universala Homana Associo). According to Onisaburō, *jinrui aizen* contained two major aspects: universal love between humans and a god-like absolute love and virtue. "God-like love" means a love that does not distinguish between wrong and right, enemy and friend.[16] Ōmoto set up a European headquarters in Geneva (later moved to Paris) to spread its teachings.[17] The missions in Europe and also in Latin America were meant to provide a bridge to cultural understanding between East and West with the ultimate aim of achieving world peace.

In East Asia, Ōmoto intensified its collaboration with the Red Swastika Society; with its help, Ōmoto sent missionaries to Manchuria and North China. The collaboration with the Chinese sect was seen as a pioneering act to further Asian unity by means of religion: this collaboration would be the only way to bring peace to Manchuria, East Asia, and thus eventually to the whole world. This rhetoric was very much in line with the general political discourse and public opinion in Japan. From the late 1920s Japan's influence in Manchuria increased rapidly. Japan already had extraterritorial rights on the Liaotung (Liaodong) Peninsula, but pushed for more, attempting to gain a railway monopoly over construction to gain control over transport and the economy. Anti-Japanese sentiment grew in China, and the Chinese Communists and Nationalists built a common front against the Japanese. At the same time, the Japanese public was critical of the Japanese government's "soft" China policy. Ōmoto's publications agreed with public opinion, urging that Manchuria and Mongolia should be placed under Japan's "guidance" to achieve East Asian unity. The Ōmoto leaders had close relations with high officers of the Kwantung army in Manchuria, such as Ishiwara Kanji and Itagaki Seishirō, the initiators of the Kwantung army's invasion of Manchuria and the foundation of Manchukuo. These officers used to visit the Ōmoto headquarters near Kyōto whenever they returned to Japan. Thus, Ōmoto leaders were well informed about the situation in Manchuria.[18]

Due to its close links to military officers and Japanese adventurers in Manchuria and its close collaboration with the Chinese Red Swastika Society, Ōmotokyō's mission in Manchuria and Mongolia advanced fast; the organization set up many branches throughout these territories.[19] The first missionary to Manchuria was dispatched in 1923, as soon as Ōmotokyō had established contacts with the Red Swastika Society. Thereafter, Ōmoto mission branches were set up in Fengtian (present Shenyang, in 1924), in Changchun and Harbin (1927), in Dalian (1928), in Cipingjie and Hailar (1929).[20] To promote the mission in Manchuria and to strengthen its collaboration with the Chinese Red Swastika Society, Deguchi Onisaburō and his wife Sumi, the official heir of Ōmotokyō, visited Manchuria in October 1929.[21] The number of branches in Manchuria and Mongolia reached 59 by the early 1930s. A journal with the title *Uchū* (The Universe) reported that "among the Japanese religious groups who have been carrying out missionary work in China, only Ōmoto is doing well."[22]

The mission in East Asia, which aimed to unify the region by means of religion, was carried out under the banner of "universal human love and

virtue." In February 1931, Ōmotokyō sent Fukamizu Sei as a special missionary to Manchuria and Mongolia to meet Ōmoto followers there and to
propagate the universal principles of human love and virtue.[23] In July of the
same year, the acting consul at the Japanese mission in Tieling reported to his
home office that Ōmotokyō was planning to build a new headquarters of the
Jinrui Aizen-kai in Manchuria; members had been looking for a suitable
location around Tieling.[24]

After the Japanese army's invasion of Manchuria in autumn 1931, Ōmotokyō became even more active in its missions in Manchuria and Mongolia.
More missionaries were sent to Manchuria to work with the Red Swastika
Society and to help civilians in the areas affected by the war and natural
disaster.[25] They did not criticize the Japanese army's expansion; rather they
justified it as the "will of the gods." Like other pan-Asian and nationalist
organizations such as the Amur Society (Kokuryūkai), Ōmoto presented the
Japanese army's march into Manchuria as fundamentally different from
Western expansionism, because its purpose was to abolish Western hegemony
over the world and to *liberate* Asia from Western colonialism. To prove that
the Japanese advance was not an expansionist act, Ōmoto elaborated on its
collaboration with the Red Swastika Society in Manchuria in helping civilians,
and in religious matters, and insisted on their common goal of bringing peace
to the region.[26] While Pan-Asianism became the ideological cover for Japan's
expansion in Asia, by representing the advance into Manchuria as a necessary
move to protect Asian interests, the preaching of universal pacifist love was
meant to undermine international criticism of Japanese aggression in Manchuria, and to show that such criticism represented a narrow-minded reaction
to a laudable initiative.[27]

After the foundation of Manchukuo, the Ōmoto mission was "based on the
philosophy of universal human love to provide appropriate guidance to the
backward and uncivilized local people" and to make them aware of Imperial
Manchukuo.[28] Propaganda was spread through seminars, public discussions,
and publications.[29] The Ōmoto periodicals often reported that Jinrui Aizen-
kai missionaries were active in fighting against bandits "to secure order," and,
more important, in persuading them to accept the teaching of "universal
human love and virtue," and submit themselves to the new government.
Thus, they would contribute to the harmony of the new state of Manchukuo.[30]
The missionary activities of Ōmotokyō in Manchukuo were introduced in a
series of articles in the daily *Yomiuri Shimbun* between 10 and 16 March
1933.[31] In June 1934, Deguchi Hidemaro, Onisaburō's son-in-law, vice-
president of Ōmotokyō and head of the Jinrui Aizen-kai, visited Manchukuo
with other Ōmoto followers in order to demonstrate the organization's support for the Japanese army and to inspect the branch offices of the Jinrui
Aizen-kai.[32]

Ōmotokyō propagated pacifism, universal human love and world unification through religion in other regions as well, particularly in Europe. The sect
sent missionaries to France, Germany, Austria, Spain, Italy, Hungary, Poland,

Bulgaria, but also to India and Brazil. It published information and brochures not only in Esperanto, but also in English, French, German, and Chinese.[33] In practice, however, there was a difference between Ōmoto's missions in Europe and those in Asia. In Europe, Ōmotokyō attempted to present Japan as an equal partner with the West in the effort to bring civilization to the world and to build a bridge between the West and the East. In this context, universal human love was meant to be a way to achieve peace and harmony between the West and the East. On its Asian front, however, Ōmoto empha- sized solidarity amongst Asians against Western intrusion and colonial rule. In the European mission, the Ōmoto newsletter often compared Western and Eastern cultures. Asia was presented as the cradle of world culture, which had given Buddhism, Confucianism, Islam, and even Christianity to the world. Asians could be proud of themselves because they had provided the spiritual basis for the religions and philosophies of the world. According to this view, Asians had been concentrating on the invisible spiritual and philosophical foundations of the world, while Europeans focused on material growth. As a result, most Asians had been made the slaves of the Europeans and later the Americans. "White people" mistreated Asians just because of their skin color. Asians then galvanized themselves and decided to fight White hegemony.[34] In this context, Ōmotokyō would act as a bridge between the materialist-oriented West and the spiritually-focused East. It would mediate between and help both sides.[35] Japan was presented as a paradigmatic example of a country able to balance the material and spiritual worlds. Western and Eastern culture har- moniously merged together in Japan; therefore the Japanese national mission was to work for global peace.[36]

Ōmoto's mission in Asia emphasized the pan-Asian ideal along with uni- versal values. However, after the late 1920s, universalist ideals were increasingly stressed, because the Japanese military's occupation of Manchuria challenged the foundations of pan-Asian ideology. Therefore, Ōmotokyō more eagerly promoted universal values in its Asian mission after the foundation of Man- chukuo in 1932. Universal values (love and virtue) were to refute Western and Chinese criticisms as arising from a narrow-minded view; they were designed to give locals a broader world-view and to open their minds to Japan's "guidance." As Ulrich Lins has pointed out, the idea of universalism was also intended to appeal to its followers in Japan. A Japan-centred universalism and pan-Asian ideology would mean that Ōmoto elevated "its own, Japanese, values into universal values."[37]

Mongolia as the "cradle" of East Asia

In February 1924 Deguchi Onisaburō made a "secret" journey to Mongolia while he was still under house arrest. He was forbidden to leave the Kyōto area without official permission after the suppression of Ōmoto in 1921. How- ever, with the help of certain officials, Onisaburō managed to leave the country without being caught by the authorities. His adventure in Mongolia was more than a minor episode in Ōmoto history. The journey made him a well-known public figure. This was important to Ōmoto's revival within Japan, and it advanced the sect's world mission, especially its Asian mission; thus it also furthered the dissemination of its pan-Asian ideology. Radical nationalist groups, such as Uchida Ryōhei's Amur Society, were highly inspired by Ōmoto's positive and energetic activities and Onisaburō's idea of using religion to unify Asia and the world.

Discovering Onisaburō's absence, the Kyōto Prefecture police office was highly worried. Police reports were sent to the central government in Tokyo. After a few weeks of searching, the news finally came in that Onisaburō was in Manchuria and planned to move on to Mongolia. His trip was planned and supported by Yano Yūtarō, a retired military officer, and Ozaki Tesshū, a land cultivator in Manchuria. With the help of Lu Zhankui, who was then an officer under Chang Tso-lin (Zhang Zuolin), the warlord ruler of Manchuria, Onisaburō started to organize an army. Zhang Zuolin did not officially support Lu and Onisaburō, but he agreed to supply weapons and ordered Lu to recruit soldiers. Within two months they had gathered a force of over 1,000 troops. By Zhang Zuolin's order, it was called Xibei Zizhijun (The Northwest Autonomous Army).

The troops soon began to move from Zhaonan towards the Mongolian border – without Zhang's permission. As soon as they had crossed the Manchurian border to enter the eastern part of Inner Mongolia, the banner of the force was changed to Neiwai Menggu Dulijun (Inner and Outer Mongolia Independence Army). To gain support from local Mongols, Onisaburō dressed as Dalai Lama and "nominated" one of his followers Panchen Lama. The idea of moving troops to support the independence of Mongolia now alarmed Zhang Zuolin. In early June, Onisaburō's troops were attacked by Zhang Zuolin's forces in Bayantala in the eastern part of Inner Mongolia. The army of adventurers around Onisaburō was captured and Lu Zhankui and his followers were shot. Onisaburō and his Japanese associates only narrowly escaped execution.[38]

Onisaburō later explained that his aim of traveling to Mongolia was to "participate in the holy work that would bring peace and happiness to the Asian countries and to the world" and thus eventually unify the world through religion. He argued that "Mongolia is the root (*kongenchi*) and cradle (*keirin*) of Asia" and "unifying Mongolia by means of religion was the first step towards East Asian unity and world peace."[39] Onisaburō's idea of Asia extended north to include Siberia and west to encompass Persia and Turkey. In his own words: "I wanted to cultivate Asia in the following order: first to unify Mongolia, then move to Xinjiang, Tibet, Afghanistan, Persia, Siberia and Turkey. ... "[40] He wanted to be "a pioneer," to promote the expansion of agriculture in Manchuria and Mongolia and to solve Japan's over-population problem.

Another part of the reason for Onisaburō's journey to Mongolia also was his desire to reverse the bleak situation of Ōmoto since the suppression in 1921: he rankled under the "unfair" accusation leveled against him and his followers for practicing *lèse majesté*. By going to Mongolia he thought he could accomplish two objectives: on the one hand he could do something useful that would contribute to Japanese national goals and thus demonstrate his loyalty and innocence;[41] on the other hand, he could fulfill his desire to spread Ōmoto's teachings beyond Japan's borders. The followers of Ōmoto understood Onisaburō's journey to Mongolia as a holy mission: its aim was to carry out the plans of the gods as set out in the *Reikai Monogatari* (Stories of the Spirit World), Onisaburō's most important work, according to which Onisaburō had once been active in the area of the Xingan Mountains in Mongolia. "Mongolia had an important position in the gods' plans (*keirin*) for the future."[42]

Onisaburō's utopian undertaking, his dual aim to "unify the Mongols through religion" and to "create a colony for the Japanese", failed. Onisaburō, however, achieved his goal in other respects: that is, he managed to ameliorate the crisis within Ōmoto that had been caused by government suppression and the restriction of his movements. Upon his return to Japan, he was handed a court decision sentencing him to five years jail, which had been imposed at a trial held in his absence. However, this trial was based on Ōmoto's activities before Onisaburō's journey to Mongolia and had nothing to do with Onisaburō's adventurous trip to Mongolia.

However, after his return, Onisaburō became a popular and controversial public figure. He inspired many people who had romantic ideas about Manchuria and Mongolia.[43] Media reports described him as "the man with the big dream" and "like a king in a fairy tale."[44] His undertaking became a subject for writers and theatrical performances.[45] A writer of plays, Minamida Toshirō, was inspired by Onisaburō's actions and wrote *Kyūseishu no hata no moto ni* (Under the Banner of the Redeemer).[46] He was also transformed into a popular figure to attract public attention. For example, the Esperanto Union in Japan organized a conference in October 1925 to promote Esperanto in Japan, and Deguchi Onisaburō was invited to give a lecture. The mayor of Kyoto reported to the central government that the Esperanto Union was active in propagating the Esperanto language; to attract more people they had "invited Onisaburō who receives popular attention from the public."[47] Getting attention from the public was exactly what Onisaburō wanted:

> My journey to Mongolia was like throwing a stone into the big world-lake. If I don't make splashing sounds the plan for the future is difficult. Things are happening now because many people come from Asia and Europe to visit me; that is the result of my throwing the stone by making a journey to Mongolia.[48]

Manchurian adventurers (*rōnin*), and the various groups advocating pan-Asian ideas in Japan (e.g. the Amur Society, Kokuryūkai) were particularly impressed with Onisaburō's moves. Close cooperation between Ōmoto and the Amur Society during the 1920s and 1930s was a consequence of this admiration for Onisaburō. Uchida Ryōhei (1874–1937), leader of the Kokuryūkai, later admitted that he had at first harbored prejudices against Onisaburō, like many other contemporaries influenced by official news reports after the 1921 police raid. When Uchida met Onisaburō, however, he realized that although Onisaburō might appear to be very ordinary, in terms of his thought he was incredibly creative and possessed far-sighted visions and high ideals.[49] Ōmoto supported the Kokuryūkai in their activities in Manchuria as well as in Japan and, in turn, earned a high reputation within the ranks of Amur Society pan-Asianists: a later publication issued by the Amur Society characterizes Onisaburō's Mongolian adventure as the "prelude to the foundation of Manchukuo."[50]

Uchida was inspired by Onisaburō's adventurous actions in Mongolia and his idea of unifying the world through religion; on the other hand, Onisaburō was inspired by Uchida's pan-Asian ideology. After the Japanese invasion of Manchuria in September 1931, Ōmoto and the Amur Society further intensified their cooperation. Ōmoto supported Uchida Ryōhei's lecture tour in Japan, during which Uchida focused on a solution for the "Manchuria-Mongolia Problem."[51] In Manchuria, Uchida and Tōyama Mitsuru, the leader of the Gen'yōsha, another nationalist organization, followed Ōmotokyō's lead and utilized religious organizations for their activities.[52] Uchida saw the collaboration between Ōmotokyō and the Red Swastika Society as an important step toward the realization of the pan-Asianist dream. He continued praising Deguchi Onisaburō for the advancement of the pan-Asian cause through his spiritual approach. Uchida stressed that Onisaburō's efforts had been much more effective than those of himself and his colleagues, who had been working for the cause of Pan-Asianism for several decades.[53]

Onisaburō's adventure in Mongolia played a central role in building the self-confidence of Ōmoto and advancing its mission in Asia. The sect often linked its later missionary activities with the "spectacular" undertaking in Mongolia, and commemorated Onisaburō's journey of 1924 year after year. Paintings and drawings were made to illustrate his adventure. When the sect organized an exhibition of Ōmoto's activities in 1930, Onisaburō's journey to Mongolia was represented as the very core of Ōmoto's mission in Manchuria and Mongolia.[54] In some Ōmoto branches in Manchuria, the spirits of Lu Zhankui and other Mongols and Chinese who fell in with Onisaburō's military adventure were worshipped.[55] Soon after Onisaburō's return to Japan, a rumor circulated which claimed that the Japanese adventurers in Manchuria were planning for Onisaburō's return to Mongolia as soon as he got out of jail. He never returned to Mongolia, but his interest in creating a state comprising Manchuria and Mongolia did not disappear. In 1926, he sent one of his followers, Kurihara Hakurai, to Tianjin to invite Pu Yi, the "Last Emperor" of China and later the Emperor of Manchukuo, to Kameoka near Kyōto, to talk about a possible future state in Manchuria. This projected state was to be called Mingguangguo (*Meikōkoku*, Land of the Shining Light).[56] Later, this idea was adopted, supported and eventually taken over entirely by the Kwantung army at the time of the foundation of Manchukuo.[57]

Apart from the practical purpose of creating a colony in Mongolia and Manchuria for the Japanese, Onisaburō presented his adventurous journey of 1924 in an ideological context. First the new state was to "materialize universal human love and virtue" (*jinrui aizen*) according to the will of the gods; this would help the oppressed Mongols, and settle the regional disputes between China, Russia and Japan by means of religion. The second aim was to achieve Asian unity; as "the oracle place," Mongolia was the best place to start this work. His alleged aim was "unifying Mongolia through religion and peace, to make it the basis of an East Asian alliance."[58] These missions of "peace and unification" were to be carried out by Japan and especially by means of the religions practiced in Japan, Ōmoto in particular. Onisaburō presented himself as the head of several religious groups when he traveled to Mongolia. According to his name card, he was "leader of Ōmotokyō," "President of the Chinese Five Religions and the Korean religion *Poch'ŏngyo*," and "Dalai Lama" (Reincarnation of Miroku and thus Supreme Buddhist Leader in Mongolia and Tibet).[59]

Japan as the centre; Ōmoto as the core

At the heart of the various forms of Japanese Pan-Asianism, there was a common idea: a vision of Japan as the centre of Asia and of the Japanese as the natural leaders of the Asians. In religious and moral terms, Japan was seen as a divinely-created and god-protected nation. Thus, it had the god-given duty to save Asians and eventually the whole world. This idea was based on the Shinto creation myth. The promoters of Shinto as a state religion originally sought to create an exclusive Japanese identity which rejected any foreign elements, including Buddhism. With the Japanese expansion into neighboring countries, however, traditional exclusiveness gave way to a more *inclusive* ideal, which was necessary to legitimize Japan's geopolitical interests in Asia. Shinto was not only crucial to the unification of the Japanese nation as the basis of a common identity capable of resisting Western intrusion; now it also became a means of creating a common ground for pulling together East Asia as a region. The Shinto myth provided a foundation for the claim that Japan was a divine land and for the divinely-ordained mission to "guide" Asia.

The idea that Japan should be at the centre of the world was not new. As early as in the eighteenth century, Motoori Norinaga (1730–1801) had asserted that Japan was the Land of the Gods and the origin of all countries; therefore all countries should serve Japan.[60] Ōkuni Takamasa (1792–1871), who rose to the highest position in the new State Shinto administration under the Meiji government, advocated the "one-world, one-emperor" (*bankoku sōtei*) theory. This theory was later developed to represent Japan as a holy country, "extraordinary" amongst all the countries in the world; therefore the

Japanese emperor was not only the emperor of Japan but also the general emperor (*sōtei*) of all nations.[61]

Ōmoto's leader Onisaburō shared these views. He always linked Ōmoto's pan-Asian ideals and religious universalism to Japan's "divine duty" and "mission" to bring peace to the world.[62] In Yasumaru Yoshio's words, "he [Onisaburō] linked Japanism and Shintoism with the values of universalism. He was determined to believe that Japanism and Shintoism had true universal value."[63] In March 1928, to celebrate a ceremony marking the completion of a memorial tower for the Mongol soldiers who fell during the Mongol invasions of Japan in the thirteenth century in Shikanojima in Kyūshū, Onisaburō wrote: "First to achieve Japanese–Mongol friendship and collaboration with China, then to bring peace to East Asia, and finally to spread this to the world: this is the divine destiny of our great Japanese nation."[64]

The development of Ōmoto's ethnocentrism can be divided into three stages in the context of Pan-Asianism and universalist ideas. The first stage represented Japan as the model for the great world family system which the sect propagated before the government raid in 1921. Onisaburō shared the Japan-centric views of Shinto scholars, claiming that the Japanese emperor would be ruler of the world and that therefore Ōmoto's teachings aimed to achieve a "grand family system" (world family system). He insisted that in order to build the grand world family system, which would bring peace and unity, Japan had to be a good model for the rest of the world. He was, however, very critical of the contemporary Japanese political and social system. His concept of creating a world family system was based on the idea that Japan had to reform itself before it could function as a model for rest of the world.[65] He stated that as long as there was oppression, exploitation, and injustice in Japan, it would not be qualified to rule the world. Japan had the "divine mission" to bring this grand world family system into being, and thus generate everlasting peace in the world.[66] The main focus was on internal reform, so that Japan would be fit to become the world paradigm; this focus did not have any real connection to conditions outside Japan.

The second stage was to see Japan as the representative of Asian culture and as a bridge between East and West. This idea was developed at an early stage of Ōmoto's world missionary activities, under the twin banners of Pan-Asianism and universal love and virtue. The world family system was based on the ideals of Asian unity and universal peace, and Japan was the land chosen by the Shinto gods to achieve these aims. During this period, Onisaburō's thinking was based on his understanding of the Japanese experience of learning and adapting ideas and technologies from abroad. According to him, Japan had been absorbing information and learning from outside for centuries; it was thus well informed about world culture, unlike Americans and Europeans who claimed to be the pioneers of world science but who actually were "totally blind" about Asia.[67]

The third stage, which represented Japan as the absolute centre of the world, arose from the confidence that the sect regained through their overseas missions, combined with the success of the Japanese army's advance in Manchuria. Onisaburō, who once so enthusiastically supported Esperanto as a world language to help spread his mission to the world, now saw Japanese as the world language, because it was the language spoken by the Shinto gods. He believed that the Japanese language would be used all over the world as soon as Japan was able to unify the world as a family. At first, Ōmoto had advocated the idea of universal pacifism to bring Japanese culture to the international level and to present Japan as an important contributor to world civilization. Now the argument was turned upside down: Japanese culture *was* the world culture of the future. In other words, Ōmoto's earlier view was that Japan should identify itself as part of a world culture; but now Japan was seen as the world standard – the rest of the world was expected to identify with the paradigm and follow Japan.[68] Ōmoto's ethnocentric Pan-Asianism had thus developed into a Japan-centric universalism.

The ideal of Asian unity (i.e., Ōmoto's version of Pan-Asianism) was just a first step towards achieving the goal of creating a world mission which would be based on pacifism, universal human love, and virtue. The religious dimension of pacifism as represented by universal human love, and ethnocentric Pan-Asianism as expressed in expansionism, are contradictory ideals. Pan-Asianism was a region-oriented ideology while universalism represented a world mission; thus the latter would supersede any regional or ethnic boundaries. Promoting Pan-Asianism, in terms of East versus West, implied excluding the rest of the world from the values which constituted the basis of Pan-Asianism. Universalism meant to be inclusive; however, Ōmoto's leaders did not see it that way. For them the two ideals were two sides of the same coin. Ethnocentric Pan-Asianism was the means to disseminate the universal values represented by the Japanese to the Asian region; thus it would be the first step towards achieving "world peace."

Ōmoto's missionary ambitions and ideology were at the centre of its ideal of combining ethnocentric Pan-Asianism and a Japan-centric universalism. The unification of Asia was to be carried out by Japan, guided by religions practiced in Japan, and by Ōmoto in particular. World peace could be achieved only by means of religion. Hatsuse Ryūhei has called the form of Asianism which places strong emphasis on territorial expansionist ideology "right-wing Pan-Asianism." He has categorized both Deguchi Onisaburō and Uchida Ryōhei as "traditional right-wing pan-Asianists."[69] The difference, however, was that Onisaburō was also the leader of a religious sect. As such, his aim was to spread Ōmoto's teachings or ideology, that is, to disseminate the belief that Ōmoto was the "great source" of world truth. His goal was to create a new world according to Ōmoto's vision. In this context, Ōmoto leaders were very much aware of the limitations of the pan-Asian ideology, in spatial as well as in spiritual and philosophical terms. Therefore, advocating universal pacifism was a much more attractive option for them.

As mentioned above, Onisaburō's collaboration with overseas religious sects, such as the Red Swastika Society, was undertaken in the name of Asian unity, but the ultimate aim was to achieve universal peace. He asserted that religion would be the actor in this process of achieving global peace; Ōmoto had stepped forward to play the leading role in this process. Thus, Onisaburō's collaboration with the Amur Society was also based on his concern for his own sect. Onisaburō found that the pan-Asianist ideology of the Amur Society would provide the inspiration to realize his own world mission. Moreover, the long-term experience of Amur Society members in working in Asia and Siberia was for him a valuable resource to be applied to realizing Ōmoto's mission in Asia. As Hatsuse points out, Uchida and the other Amur Society leaders sought to use Ōmoto's financial and organizational resources to bring Pan-Asianism into being, but they were utilized by Onisaburō in return.[70]

Ōmoto claimed that its missionary activities in Asia were impelled by the will of the gods. The members of the sect alleged that the values they represented therefore were universal. In other words, by bringing in the gods Ōmoto indicated that its actions went beyond merely national and regional interests to serve universal values: Ōmoto advocated the idea of equality, because from the "point of view of the gods, all human beings are brothers and sisters." In this way, Ōmoto meant to appeal directly to the people; at the same time it represented ideals which were absolute and powerful. On one hand, it sought to reach out to all Asians; on the other, it meant to point out that even emperors and politicians were subject to the same universal principles; they too should follow Ōmoto's teachings and visions.

Conclusion

In many studies on the ideological background of Japanese expansionism, Pan-Asianism is identified only as a doctrine which unites Asia and excludes the West. The case of Ōmotokyō demonstrates both that Pan-Asianism was more complex than this generalization implies, and that it was part of much more ambitious thinking about the world. For Ōmotokyō, "Asia" (however defined) represented only part of a global and universal mission. One implication of this universalist ideal was that Ōmotokyō became a persistent advocate for change within Japan itself, so that Japan could evolve into a fitting leader of and model for the world.

As a consequence, Ōmotokyō was always viewed with suspicion by state authorities. A second implication therefore was that Ōmotokyō contributed to tension within the Japanese empire, the tension between constructing the empire as an exclusively Japanese institution – by and for Japanese alone – and constructing it as an institution in which others could play an equal part. On the one hand, Ōmotokyō's doctrine was truly universal and reached far beyond the realist political aims of Japanese military planners; on the other hand, it reserved for Ōmotokyō, rather than for Japan, the role of being the "great source" of true doctrine. This ambiguity, which lay at the heart of Ōmotokyō's thinking, was also a crucial weakness in the Japanese imperial project.

5 Pan-Asianism and national reorganization

Japanese perceptions of China and the United States, 1914–19

Katō Yōko

Introduction

Japanese Asianism was described by Hiraishi Naoaki, a specialist in Japanese political thought, as "one ideological inclination appearing and disappearing in modern Japanese history," and as an idea appealing for unity with "Japan as the leader [in] resisting the pressure of the Western powers."[1] Hiraishi's definition builds on a key argument previously proposed by Takeuchi Yoshimi. For Takeuchi, Asianism was a concept of Asian solidarity (*Ajia rentairon*) put forth originally by advocates of liberty and peoples' rights. Thus, he distinguished Asianism (*Ajiashugi*) from later forms of Greater Asianism (*Dai-Ajiashugi*), as put forward from around the time of World War I by activists from associations like the Gen'yōsha (Black Ocean Society).[2]

If one takes Asianism to be an ideological inclination calling for resistance to pressure from the Western powers and for unity among Asian countries with Japan assuming the role of leader, then one should naturally see Asianism appearing in Japan when there is a rapid increase in a consciousness of foreign crisis. For the Meiji state, consciousness of foreign crisis emerged when the vital national interests of the state were thought to be menaced. What was seen to be the national interest was securing national independence and escaping the unequal treaty system.[3] Consequently, the Korean peninsula was regarded as a "line of advantage" (*riekisen*) and northeast China became the stage upon which was fought the Sino-Japanese and Russo-Japanese Wars. In 1893, prior to the Sino-Japanese War, Tarui Tōkichi (1850–1922) in his "Argument for a Union of the Great East" (*Daitō gappō-ron*) called for the unification of Japan and Korea. In 1903, prior to the Russo-Japanese War, Okakura Tenshin (1862–1913) in *Ideals of the East* claimed that "Asia is One," meaning an Asia comprised of Indian ideals, Chinese ethics, and Japanese destiny. Asianism as an ideological inclination appealing for unity under Japanese leadership had become an influential idea in Japanese society by the beginning of the twentieth century.

Furthermore, with the coming of the Shōwa era (1926–89), the vital interests that were of life and death significance to the state, and the accompanying consciousness of foreign crisis, were redirected toward resisting the

Anglo-American powers who were seeking to prevent what they saw as Japanese attempts to control China. Once again this feeling of foreign crisis gave birth to the idea of an Asia rallied beneath the leadership of Japan. For example, Ozaki Hotsumi (1901–44), in a series of papers on *The Idea of "East Asian Community" and the Objective Foundation for Its Realization* published in the late 1930s, presented a theory enabling resistance to Chinese ethnic nationalism (*minzokushugi*). Namely, he advanced the logic that unless Japan, China, and Manchuria could at once cooperate through a supra-state body to harmonize their fate and conceive a solution to Asian agricultural problems, Asia would be unable to break loose from a state of semi-colonialism.[4]

However, when considering Asianism as an ideological tendency to call for rallying under Japanese leadership in resistance to the oppression of the Western powers, there remains another constitutive element that is often neglected. In order to resist the oppression of the Western powers, in concert with the outward directed call for unity, it was necessary that there be an inward demand for national reorganization that would bring about a funda-mental restructuring of the Japanese state and institutions. Thus Asianism, in addition to being linked to arguments about Japanese regional leadership that emerged out of a sense of foreign threat, similarly attended demands for national reorganization that were likewise born of a feeling of external threat.

This fact indicates that interpretations such as those of the scholar of modern political thought Sakamoto Takao regarding the "debate over con-quering Korea" (*seikanron*)[5] or of the nation-state theorist Makihara Norio[6] concerning the Ōsaka Incident are not necessarily mistaken. Simply stated, Sakamoto argues that Saigō Takamori's (1827–77) views on conquering Korea were premised on his belief that subjugating Korea was necessary in order to recover the state's vitality, avoid blind adherence to custom, and avert collapse of the state. According to Sakamoto's interpretation, Saigō grasped that advancing overseas was part of a set with which came escaping the despotic governance of early Meiji and pursuing the necessity of domestic reform aimed at establishing constitutionalism. Makihara interprets the thinking of Ōi Kentarō (1843–1922), who played a central role in the Ōsaka Incident (1885), as follows: Although Ōi attempted to gather a volunteer force in order to support the Korean independence movement, he at the same time thought it would be unavoidable that such volunteers would also initiate a coup d'etat in Japan and realize domestic restructuring of the Japanese government. Here, too, the necessity of domestic reform and overseas advance was viewed as a set.

In modern Japan, this call for domestic reorganization originating in a sense of foreign crisis was most widely discussed during the period of the First World War. This demand for change extended comprehensively to many systemic reforms, including changing the House of Peers, the conscription system, the tax system, and recognizing labor unions and realizing a system of universal suffrage.[7] This phenomenon may be regarded as a quest for national reorganization (*kokka kaizō*). The first person to apprehend the period of the

First World War as an epoch marked by the emergence of new movements or political organizations was Maruyama Masao (1914–96), who made this case in his *Nihon fashizumu no shisō to kōdō* (The Ideology and Behavior of Japanese Fascism).[8] Concentrating on the period around 1919, when Kita Ikki (1883–1937), together with Ōkawa Shūmei (1886–1957) and Mitsukawa Kametarō (1888–1936),[9] created the Yūzonsha (Society of Those Who Yet Remain), Maruyama noted the conditions within which there was born an ideology binding together domestic reorganization and international claims. Taking up this perspective, Itō Takashi saw the special quality of this remarkable period in the appearance of political organizations comprising a reformist movement aiming to overthrow the established power structure.[10] Furthermore, Arima Manabu, from a point of view different from that of Itō, saw the political ideology that supported the organizations born during this period as National Socialism (*kokka-shakaishugi*) and explored the question of why these kinds of organizations were able to attain extensive influence in the political world of this period. As a result of analyzing the organizational conditions of the groups and their political thought, Arima sought the reason for this influence in that fact that these groups possessed both methods for coping with rural problems and prescriptions for alleviating the feeling of foreign crisis.[11]

But why did the experience of the First World War bring forth in Japan a wide-ranging movement for national reorganization? Why did the consciousness of foreign crisis increase? During the various stages of the war, what manner of incidents did this sense of foreign crisis serve to bring forth and why did these occurrences become bound up with demands for domestic reorganization?

In focusing on the rise of a new political current during the period of the First World War, Maruyama, Itō, and Arima have concerned themselves with analyzing and tracing the origins of the political groups that held power in the Shōwa period (i.e., those thought of by Maruyama as being fascists, by Itō as comprising a "renovationist faction" [*kakushin-ha*], and by Arima as being national socialists). Consequently, one can regard the immanent connectedness between the sense of foreign crisis and domestic reorganization characterizing this period as not having yet been fully elucidated. However, because the sense of crisis did accompany strong demands for Japan's domestic political reorganization, the ideas of these years need to be revisited as a problem of Asianism.

This paper will focus on Japan during the period of the First World War and the rapid emergence of the image of Japan as being under attack from the nations on either side of the Pacific, i.e., China and the United States, and consider the background and reasons for this trend. In particular, what were the accompanying images of foreign crisis that lay at the base of the many political groups that emerged during the First World War and that doggedly sought domestic reorganization?

The outbreak of the First World War and the neutrality of China and the United States

Shortly after the start of the First World War, Japan's Home Ministry directed the mayors of the nation's towns and villages to warn their constituents that although Japan was presently at war with Germany, the purpose of this conflict was "the preservation of peace in the Far East" and therefore there must be no speaking ill of the German Empire or its people. Likewise, regarding Japan's relations with neutral nations, local officials were to instruct the people not to repeat the opinions of those who were agitated, expressed "suspicious thoughts," or engaged in "mistaken speculations." What deserves attention here is the cool-headed presumption of the necessity for relations with the neutral nations of China and the United States, a perspective that is visible in the expression "our neighboring countries America and China."[12]

Under what presumed future state of affairs did the central government issue this call to be "cool-headed" regarding Japan's relations with China and the United States? To address this question, one must first note that it was not the people who were the first to be stricken by "over excitement [and] suspicious thoughts," but rather the foreign minister, Katō Takaaki (1860–1926). On 6 August 1914, Katō learned from Japan's ambassador to the United States that China, having proclaimed its neutrality in the European war, may have requested that the Americans negotiate with the belligerent countries not to turn the foreign concessions in China into war zones. Two days later Katō instructed the Japanese ambassador in China to inform the Chinese that, to begin with, from the viewpoint of Sino-Japanese diplomatic relations and geography, as well as the prevailing special Sino-Japanese relationship, this kind of request should have been submitted to Japan. Moreover, should the story of China's proposal to the United States be true, this would constitute "a serious development."[13]

The Chinese responded by explaining that, first, this particular proposal was submitted on the advice of the Chinese ambassador to the United States and, second, while it would have been appropriate to submit the proposal simultaneously to the United States and Japan, this failure was not part of an effort to shut out Japan but simply the result of a lost opportunity to negotiate with the Japanese. In further defense of the proposal, the Chinese stated that, since Japan would be unable to avoid joining the war because of the Anglo-Japanese alliance, they had hesitated to submit a request to Tōkyō.[14] Given that Japan's attitude toward the war with Germany was decided on 8 August and, on 15 August, a final ultimatum was dispatched, there were certainly grounds for the Chinese seeking help regarding "territorial security and the preservation of neutrality" from the Americans, rather than from the Japanese and the British.

On the other hand, and at roughly the same time, German officials, in order to limit the scope of the conflict and prosecute the war to their advantage, were informing their Japanese counterparts that there was no need for the two countries to wage war in the Far East. Meanwhile, in an effort to elicit the goodwill of the Chinese regarding the security of Kiao-chow (Jiaozhou) leased territory in Shantung (Shandong) province, Berlin submitted a plan to Chinese authorities calling for the return of the German leased territory. By 14 August, according to information gathered by the Japanese, concrete proposals submitted to the Chinese side were comprised of the following: (1) return of the Kiao-chow leased territory to China; (2) opening of Kiao-chow as a port of trade; (3) removal of all defensive fortifications from said leased territory; (4) disarming of all warships home-ported in said leased territory and the placing of these vessels into the custody of the Chinese government until the end of the war; (5) removal of military armaments from said leased territory with the issue of reparations to be agreed upon at a later date.[15] In the end, China declared neutrality in the war between Japan and Germany on 17 August 1914.

Considering the aforementioned developments, one can see that once England and Japan entered a state of war with Germany, the Chinese initially acted to obtain the goodwill of the United States in order to ensure their own neutrality. Although the Anglo-Japanese Alliance, which had been revised twice since being concluded in 1902, proposed to ensure "the peace of the regions of the Far East and India" and "the independence and security of China," the Chinese determined that for this war they could not rely on the framework of the alliance for their security.

So what of Japan's position *vis-à-vis* the United States? To what exactly did "suspicious thoughts [and] mistaken speculations" refer? In order to consider increasing the level of emergency military spending, the second cabinet of Ōkuma Shigenobu (1838–1922) opened an extraordinary session of the Diet (the 34th Diet). On 5 September, in a secret gathering of the full Lower House, an interpolation was held on foreign affairs issues relating to the opening of hostilities between Japan and Germany. Ogawa Heikichi (1869–1942), representing the opposition Seiyūkai, supported his inquiries as to American "interference" by introducing a special telegram from New York. According to Ogawa, the telegram reported that the US government had notified the Japanese government as follows:

> 1) the American government understands that the purpose of Japan's participation in the war is not territorial expansion in China; 2) the American government understands Japan will act within the bounds of the Anglo-Japanese alliance and with the goal of returning to China the port of Kiao-chow; 3) in the case of domestic discord in China or the occurrence of a major event in the Far East, should a case arise wherein Japan were to engage in action outside the area of the port of Kiao-chow, it will confer with the United States. Is it true that a message containing the above three points was sent?[16]

In other words, in an effort to criticize Foreign Minister Katō, Ogawa sought to learn whether the United States had constrained Japan's exercise of the sovereign right to declare war. Specifically, he inquired as to whether the Japanese government inserted "with the goal of returning to China"[17] into the final notification because without that phrase the Anglo-Americans would not have consented to Japan joining the conflict. Katō responded by clarifying matters as follows: first, regarding the final note to Germany, the Japanese government on 19 August also submitted a declaration[18] to the United States in order to communicate the note's main points. Responding on 21 August, the American side communicated the necessity of observing strict neutrality. Second, in that memorandum the United States stated its satisfaction that Japan's actions in China were in accord with the Anglo-Japanese Alliance and not calculated with the aim of territorial expansion. Finally, American officials also expressed their desire that, in the event of disorder occurring in China proper, the United States government be consulted beforehand in cases wherein the Japanese government determined a need for itself or other nations to take action. This was all, the foreign minister stated, in accord with the Takahira-Root Agreement (1908).[19]

Thus, Katō did not fundamentally rebut the information introduced by Ogawa, but treated it as being seriously mistaken and then corrected the error. The mistake lay in the three points raised by Ogawa stating that in the case of disorder in regions of China outside the area of Kiao-chow, Japan could not deal with them without the agreement of the United States. To this manner of query the foreign minister declared there had been absolutely no such demand made by the Americans. Examining the extant diplomatic documents today, one can say that Foreign Minister Katō's rebuttal was correct. In any case, Japanese dissatisfaction with a neutral America emerged from the suspicion that, in connection with Japan's final note to Germany, an American memorandum going beyond a declaration of strict neutrality had been delivered to the Japanese government. An aura of misunderstanding emerged surrounding the clause dealing with the question of how Japan and the United States would handle unrest in China proper. Specifically, there was a belief in the existence of an American demand that Japan not act in the case of problems outside Kiao-chow. Thus, the point Ogawa wanted to get at was whether or not the United States had interfered with a matter of national sovereignty such as declaring war.

On 5 December 1914, this issue was brought up again in the 35th plenary session of the Imperial Diet. The Seiyūkai's Matsuda Genji (1875–1936) queried Foreign Minister Katō along the following lines.[20] Noting it was well known that England and Japan consulted regarding Japan's declaration of war against Germany, he then asked whether it was true that the British had imposed a limit on the war zone. Katō answered that there had been absolutely no such limits requested by the British. However, a foreign dispatch dated 18 August told of a different state of affairs. Reuters reported that, according to an official announcement in the British government's *London Gazette*, the Japanese and British governments had consulted on the boundaries of the war zone and produced an agreement stating that: (1) Japanese military action would not extend beyond the China Sea into the Pacific; (2) Japanese military action would not extend beyond Asian waters of the western end of the China Sea; and (3) Japanese military action would not extend to foreign territory on the East Asian continent other than that of Germany. In other words, there could be no military action outside of Liaozhou port. That Japan had received this sort of limit was reported in the official announcement. How would Foreign Minister Katō explain this?

For the Japanese people, who with the Russo-Japanese War had come to believe the nation had achieved dual independence from Asia and from the Euro-American powers, British behavior regarding the process of declaring war was understood as interference in Japanese sovereignty. From the questioning by Ogawa and Matsuda, one can grasp the eruption of dissatisfaction by the people with the government's foreign policy in relation to what they took to be a question of national sovereignty.

Responding to the question of interference in Japanese foreign policy, Katō stated that he had received no such limitations from the British. His explanation went as follows: after the Reuters dispatch was sent he was surprised and made inquiries to the British. Japan, he continued, had of course made no such promise. Thereupon the British side explained that this was not a matter of Japan making an actual firm promise, but simply British opinion resulting from the phrase "understanding the Japanese points as appear on the right." Therefore, the foreign minister concluded, Japan had not provided a firm promise.

In order to understand Katō's actions at that time, let us turn back the clock a bit to the outset of the war and take another look at the maneuverings of Britain and Japan. Initially, because the British thought they could limit the war to the European continent and foresaw a short decisive conflict, they were not necessarily favorable toward the idea of Japan joining the fight against Germany. On 7 August, Britain requested of Tōkyō that the Japanese navy search for and deal with any disguised German cruisers operating in the China Sea. Meanwhile, the following day saw Katō present at a meeting of elder statesmen (*genrō*) and cabinet ministers a decision to not limit the purposes for joining the war, with the result that the broad war objective decided upon was to "destroy German power that threatened the interests of Japan and Britain in the Far East." Katō's enterprising spirit and quick sleight of hand placed the British in a difficult position. For starters, there was the trend toward home rule and worries about American opinion. Moreover, there was the fundamental British concern that an East Asian war might trigger disorder inside China that would then spread to all of East Asia and inflict a tremendous shock to British trade.[21] London at one point retracted its request that Japan destroy Germany's camouflaged cruisers. The Admiralty, however, viewed the power of the Japanese navy as necessary for the war effort and, on 10 August, London agreed to the view that Japan would join the war in accord with the Anglo-Japanese Alliance.[22] Nonetheless, at the same time, the British Foreign Ministry sought from Tōkyō a statement that the theatre of military operations would not extend into the western and southern China Sea or outside the German leased territory of Kiao-chow port. Nor were the scope of military operations in the Pacific to be expanded. On 13 August, the British government agreed that there would be nothing written into Japan's declaration of war against Germany regarding limiting the war zone[23] Britain thus conceded this point to Japan. The reason for this was that, on 11 August, then First Lord of the Admiralty Sir Winston Churchill, in a letter to Foreign Minister Sir Edward Grey, stated that he could not support the effort to limit the theatre of Japanese military operations and that it would be sufficient to elicit from the Japanese government some informal assurance regarding limits on the war zone.[24]

In this way, on 13 August the British agreed to Japan joining the war under the Anglo-Japanese Alliance and to the declaration of war including no reference to limitations on the war zone. However, London continued to seek a firm promise from Tōkyō assuring that the theatre of operations would in fact be limited. In the midst of all this, on 15 August Foreign Minister Katō oversaw a cabinet decision to dispatch the final notification to Germany. The contents of the ultimatum warrant closer attention. First, the purpose of going to war was said to be to "defend the general interest as expected in line with the British government's definition of the treaty of Anglo-Japanese Alliance." The final message to Germany specified the following two terms: (1) immediate withdrawal of German warships as part of demilitarizing the Japan Sea and China Sea; (2) the unconditional transfer to Japan, by 15 September, of all of the leased territory of Kiao-chow Bay for the purpose of returning this area to China.

This final note proclaiming Japan's intent to in the future return the Kiao-chow Bay leased territory to China was a clever piece of work in that the text was probably believed to have secured peace of mind outside Japan regarding Japanese actions. However, because there was no chance that Germany would acquiesce to the terms demanded, Japanese policymakers also understood the potential for it appearing as if the conditions allowing for the return to China had been rejected with the commencement of war between Germany and Japan. Indeed, following the start of the war Katō stated to the Diet that because the Kiao-chow leased territory had in fact been acquired after the outbreak of fighting with Germany, there was no need to return the territory to China. The reason given for this was that the conditions referred to a case where the Kiao-chow Bay territory was handed over to Japan prior to the start of the war. Although Katō is often thought of as an Anglophile, in the case of Japan's final prewar message he gave the British no advance warning of what was to come.

Immediately following the start of the war, in Japan this controversy was seen as marking the first misgivings *vis-à-vis* the alliance with Britain and, similarly for the first time, gave rise to a sense of threat regarding the mutual cooperation between neutral China and neutral America. What is important to emphasize here is that at the foundation of the feelings of suspicion and menace lay a strong displeasure that the right to declare war, one of the state's sovereign rights, had been infringed upon. This strong sense of fundamental foreign threat was becoming one path by which to lead the people toward demanding national reorganization.

Whither China in the prospective "postwar world"?

It is necessary to remember that, until the final stage of the First World War, it was clear to no one that Germany would rapidly collapse or that there would be a peace conference of the type held in Paris. In 1914, for a Japan that had rapidly occupied both Shantung and German possessions in the South Pacific, for all practical purposes the "postwar" arrived quickly. However, the true "postwar" would arrive five years later. In the interim what were Japanese leaders thinking? For what kind of "postwar" were they preparing? And, within their imaginings, how were China and the United States being discussed?

First, let us examine their thoughts as to the manner in which the war would end. After the frontlines solidified into stalemate in December 1914, virtually no country possessed a clear image of how the war would end or of what would comprise the agenda of any peace conference. For example, in his autobiography delegation member Matsui Keishirō (1868–1944) relates the following:

> The first meeting of the peace conference on 25 January 1919 was held in the French Foreign Ministry. The issues were: 1) responsibility of those who started the war; 2) punishment for crimes committed during the war; and 3) the labor problem. The next problem on the agenda was the issue of the League of Nations. Deferred until later were matters directly related to the settlement of the war. Raising the aforementioned three problems in the first main meeting was quite odd and received much public criticism.[25]

Rather than the question of claims against Germany, the above three issues were against all expectations given priority in discussions, the primary reasons for which lay in American and British domestic affairs. Not only Japan but other countries as well had not necessarily spent the war years preparing to deal with these three issues. For example, even in England it was anticipated that the war would end without securing a decisive victory against Germany.

In other words, Britain viewed the likelihood of a negotiated peace to be high and anticipated a German postwar economic recovery relying on large-scale exports and a policy of "dumping." For this reason, the British concluded with the major allied powers the Paris Accord of 1916, whereby the allies agreed to measures that would prevent the expected postwar dumping by Germany and preclude both Germany and Austria from receiving most-favored-nation status. The idea among the allied, or imperialist, nations was to secure through special tariffs their own economic victory.[26]

In Japan, too, the British approach carried the day, as is exemplified in genrō Yamagata Aritomo's "Case for Japanese-Russian Alliance" of 21 February 1915. Yamagata (1838–1922) argued that:

> The coalition of Russia, England and France cannot overthrow or prevent the resurgence of Germany and Austria. Nor is the opposite going to occur. The war will end in a draw or a 60 to 40 decision. In a Europe where peace has returned, planning the recovery of national strength will also naturally include military preparations. Likewise, through developing commerce and industry there will be efforts to spur competition as a means of restoring wealth. When this occurs, the stage for competition surely will be East Asia and, especially, the Chinese continent.[27]

In sum, Yamagata recognized that, in the wake of the compromise peace that would follow an inconclusive end to the war, China would inevitably become the stage for the expected return to economic warfare. At a point early in the conflict when it was unclear if the clash would last a year, there was no reason for him to expect that this struggle would become an unprecedented total war. Rather, Yamagata's fundamental presumption was that an indecisive conclusion to the conflict would be followed by economic war in China.

On 29 June 1918, the Japanese for the first time revised the "Imperial Defense Policy" of 1907. Behind this revision were Yamagata-style expectations for the "postwar." In the "Revised Opinion Paper on National Defense Policy" written in the same month, one finds the following perspective:

> Following the return of peace the position of Japan will become difficult. If the Germans win they will no doubt use Russia as a trailblazer and swoop down on the "sources of Eastern wealth" (*Tōa no fugen*). If the British win they will most likely plot the expansion of their interests from the south. As for the Americans, whichever side wins, drawing on their tremendous financial power and limitless natural resources, they can be expected to go to work managing the Pacific by crossing the Bering Strait, descending down into Primorsky Krai (Maritime Province) and monopolizing the economic interests of Siberia, thereby expanding their power onto the Chinese mainland from both the south and the north. In the final analysis, the region of postwar Asia will inevitably face either advance from the east and west by the United States and Germany or pressure from the south and north by Britain and the United States.[28]

What is noteworthy here is that the postwar was anticipated without anyone being able to foresee the decisive defeat or collapse of Germany. Consequently, when Yamagata spoke of Japan's national defense in terms of not simply securing the territory of the empire but also of going further to defend all of China,[29] just as in the case with what the British were attempting to construct through the Paris agreement, he had in mind a China that would serve as the stage for "postwar economic war." In short, it is important to note that at this stage there was as yet no idea of China as a place to plunder natural resources for national defense and in preparation for total war. China continued to be thought of as the scene for the "postwar economic war" that was expected to follow an inconclusive end to the European conflict.

However, it is insufficient to look only at the opinion of Yamagata, who was then gradually losing power. Therefore, let us examine the opinion of Tanaka Giichi (1864–1929), who was at the time establishing himself as Deputy Chief of the Army General Staff. Following his return from an inspection tour from May to June 1917, Tanaka laid out his views in a document titled "Personal Views Regarding Managing China."[30]

First, Tanaka discussed the question of who controlled the Chang Jiang sea lanes and touched on the rapid strides made by Germany. When postwar Britain and Germany returned their shipping to East Asian waters, he lamented, would not Japan's shipping industry decline precipitously? In particular, Tanaka viewed the United States as "in the future the strongest enemy that must be watched closely." Likewise, he anticipated that the pressure of great power competition expected to flow into postwar China would inevitably result in a great unsettling in the shipping industry.[31] Moreover, because one could expect that the war had left the Europeans and Americans short of iron:

> the powers will seek iron like the starving seek food and the parched seek water, and it is clear to all that they will necessarily reach a point of not discussing methods or choosing means. And the focal point of that rivalry truly exists in China and can be sought nowhere else.[32]

One can see that Tanaka's view of what to expect in postwar China was fundamentally the same as that of Yamagata.

In actuality, Germany's rapid collapse and defeat completely undercut the forecasts of a draw, and Germany's next extension of economic power in the Far East came in the late 1920s. However, what is significant is that, in line with the postwar vision held by Yamagata and Tanaka, the revision of Japan's defense policy was predicated on the prospect of a draw and on the need to take a form suitable for fighting an economic war in China. In this manner there would emerge in national defense policy simultaneous visions of China as a scene of postwar economic war and of America as the principal opponent in this economic conflict.

The question of Shantung at the Paris Peace Conference: the merging of the Chinese and American problems

In August 1921, a few months prior to the opening of the Washington Conference, Kita Ikki in the preface to his just completed *Shina kakumei gaishi* (A History of the Chinese Revolution) wrote of the failure of Japanese diplomacy at the Paris Peace Conference, commenting scathingly on how "at Versailles, China and the United States had in unison slung the mud of Japanese expulsion."[33] Kita, concerned here with the issue of Shantung, was criticizing the May Fourth Movement in China (1919) and the eruption of anti-Japanese criticism centered on Republican members of the US Senate. Significantly, he perceived a Japan under assault from America in the East and China in the West.

In June 1919, the question of Shantung was settled by the Paris Peace Conference when Japanese claims were recognized completely and implemented through Articles 156–59 of the peace treaty with Germany. These articles stipulated that all German rights and privileges in Shantung Province, including those related to Kiao-chow Bay, railways, mines and undersea cables, were forfeited to Japan. Regarding Jiangxi Railway (Qingdao-Jinan), all German rights and properties, railway stations, and factories related to the Jiangxi Railway were also placed in the custody of Japan. Looking at these conditions, it would seem that all Japanese claims were accepted completely and that there was nothing else left to be desired.

So what exactly was it that angered Kita? On this point, let us look first at the recollections of Makino Nobuaki (1861–1949), who played a central role in the Paris mission as one of the heads of the Japanese delegation. Regarding the reason for the dispute over the issue of Shantung, Makino observed as follows:[34]

> Other than the Twenty-One Demands, it was the question of Tsingtao [Qingdao] that unexpectedly became a major problem and, consequently, the issues at stake were argued about fully and repeatedly, occupying the agenda of the conference for days. Likewise, they were taken up fully outside the conference in the newspapers and this issue became the topic of the entire peace conference, with Japan's delegation serving as the target of criticism. . . .
>
> As for the origins of this problem, malcontents comprising one part of the Chinese delegation achieved predominance and excluded chief delegate Lu Zheng-xiang. Eliciting the sympathy of one part of the American delegation, they made desperate efforts in a campaign to render the treaty of the Twenty-One Demands invalid.

Judging from these recollections, Makino apparently determined that members of the Chinese delegation, meaning young American-educated diplomats such as Gu Weiju, also known collectively as representatives of "Young China," conducted an active information campaign without concern for the policies of the Beijing government. In response to this initiative, elements from within the American delegation then provided support that served to complicate the problem of Shantung.

However, is it correct to look to the composition of the Chinese delegation in order to learn what complicated the matter of Shantung?[35] Put simply, the major point of Sino-Japanese contention regarding former German interests in Shantung was, naturally, the issue of Japan returning to China the Liaozhou Bay leased territory. The Japanese emphasized that this would be returned to China after it had been handed over to Japan by Germany. The Chinese argued that because China had declared war on Germany (on 14 August 1917), any treaties between China and Germany were no longer valid and, therefore, the Liaozhou Bay leased territories and other German concessions were already defunct. Consequently, there was no reason for these concessions to be returned to China via Japan, since that country had no business involving itself in this affair.

The Japanese presented as their first piece of evidence the 25 May 1915 "Treaty concerning Shantung," signed by the Chinese government, which included an article stating that China would recognize future agreements concluded between Japan and Germany regarding Shantung. Second, they noted the February 1917 memorandum worked out between Britain, France, Russia, Italy, and Japan, which stated that in the case of a future peace conference these four countries agreed to Japan succeeding to Germany's old rights and interests in Shantung and Pacific islands south of the equator. Finally, Tōkyō referred to the 24 September 1918 "Joint Declaration Regarding the Disposition of Issues Relating to Shantung Province," which recognized Japanese control over the Shantung railway. One can say that these three agreements were the fruits of classic imperialist diplomacy.

The Chinese emphasized the following two points:[36] first, as a result of the start of war between China and Germany the treaty between the two countries was null and void and, therefore, the Chinese people desired not only the return of the Liaozhou leased territories but also of the railway and other concessions. Second, because the 1915 "treaty concerning Shantung Province" was concluded at a time when China was in dire straits, from the perspective of the Chinese, it was no more than a one-sided agreement.

In contrast, from the beginning the Japanese judged that the numerous terms found within these three agreements and official declarations, such as the annexation of the Liaozhou railway and the extension of branch lines, had been concluded with the understanding of the Chinese government. Likewise already carried out was the advance payment of 20 million yen for railway construction. Moreover, issues related to territory and the like in leased territories were not made null and void by the start of the war. As a consequence of these presumptions, Japanese officials apparently had believed that there would be no complications regarding the Shantung issue. However, that optimism would collapse on 17 April 1919 when Georges Clemenceau held discussions with Saionji Kinmochi (1849–1940), the head of the Japanese delegation, and Makino and announced that in regard to the question of Shantung, Japan was "in a difficult legal position." Clemenceau stated that he thought the legal point being developed by the Chinese, i.e., that the declaration of war meant the treaties had lapsed, would prove viable.[37]

In this set of circumstances the army and navy officers attached to the

Japanese delegation felt that rather than engaging in legal dispute over Shantung, it would be advantageous to handle the matter as a political problem. For example, army attaché Nara Takeji (1868–1962) argued that the Chinese view was not completely without reason. Since rebutting the Chinese assertion through legal argument would merely complicate matters and cause increasing trouble, clearly it was advisable to approach the matter as a political problem.[38]

Having followed this course, Japan, as specified in the final note to Germany, moved to return complete sovereignty and former German concessions to the Chinese. Despite this, Japan's assertion was not believed because Tōkyō pursued a strategy of bringing "pressure" to bear on Woodrow Wilson, Lloyd George, and Clemenceau by saying Japan would lose national credibility and that national opinion could not be controlled.

As a result, at the heads of state conference on 30 April 1919, it was decided that the Japanese position would be accepted in its entirety and incorporated into the peace treaty. However, during this process Wilson sought a statement from Japan pledging it would return the Shantung Peninsula to the complete sovereign control of China and acknowledging that what Japan would succeed to were the special economic rights formerly possessed by Germany. Japan agreed to comply with these terms.[39]

Nara and others viewed the entreaties of the Chinese delegation as having moved the American delegation to act. However, it was probably sympathy that caused Nara to view American unilateral foreign policy as being shaped in this manner. As for the Americans, the problem was rather in the actions of their country's senate.

The power of the Republican Party held sway in the US Senate and, naturally, there was much severe criticism of the Democratic President Wilson. Those attacking Wilson found a useful premise in part one of the peace treaty deliberations on the "Articles of the League of Nations," which included items limiting American sovereignty.

The Senate likewise engaged in extensive discussions that employed the "diversionary tactic" (*tekihonshugi*) of treating the Shantung issue as something of penultimate concern. One Senator remarked that "Shantung was a bribery payment made to get Japan to sign the peace treaty. As a builder of empire Japan would follow German policies. There is no way the United States can consent to this kind of treaty draft."[40] Likewise, another member stated that:

> in regard to a Japan that was attempting to snatch territory from China, bind the liberty of Shantung and enslave millions, rather than be an ally of Japan, America should instead wage war. The United States could never consent on the Shantung issue and, moreover, if war was to be inevitable, it would be better to fight now than in the future.[41]

At the peace conference in Paris held once the real postwar arrived, Japanese officials worried about how to respond after learning that the Chinese legal argument seeking direct return of the former German rights to Shantung had the support of the French and other powers. What was for Japan a distressing problem was used in the United States for the purely political purpose of attacking Wilson and, consequently, in Japan the peace conference was increasingly considered a failure.

Conclusion

Explanations of Japan's consciousness of external crisis during the years of the First World War have long taken the view that this phenomenon arose out of the Japanese people's disillusionment with their country's failure at the Paris Peace Conference to cope with the development of various nations' activist foreign policies. However, the Japanese sense of external crisis heightened by the Paris conference did not simply appear from surface anger and indignation at the foolish behavior of the Japanese delegation in failing to manage new forms of diplomacy and propaganda. Rather, Japanese dissatisfaction accumulated over the long five-year period following the beginning of the war, with such issues as national sovereignty and respect for racial dignity being regarded as matters of primary importance. As to the fundamental question of national sovereignty, considering the possibility that Japan was still under pressure from the Western powers went hand-in-hand with believing that the same nations may threaten Japan's stabilizing control over Asia.

In sum, the period of the First World War saw the following beliefs spread among the Japanese: first, perplexity at the friendly cooperation between neutral China and neutral America at the outset of the war; second, fundamental anger at efforts by their English allies and the Americans to limit Japan's theatre of operations; third, pessimistic forecasts about the unsatisfactory conditions under which the war would end; fourth, visions of malevolent Sino-American cooperation during the Paris Peace Conference; and, finally, perplexity and disappointment at the failure, because of the US Senate's view that it would constitute intervention into US sovereignty, to include in the League principles Japan's request to abolish racial discrimination, a plan viewed as extremely just and desirable. As a consequence of the above phenomena there emerged among Japanese a deeply rooted consciousness of foreign crisis that, because it did not call explicitly for Asian unity under Japanese leadership, has not been properly recognized as a form of Asianism. However, it is the author's opinion that this sense of crisis, which in turn gave birth to widespread demands for national reorganization, was indeed a variant of Asianism and, moreover, one that bore great significance for the years ahead.

(Translated by Roger Brown)

Part II

Regionalism, nationalism and ethnocentrism

6 Between Pan-Asianism and nationalism

Mitsukawa Kametarō and his campaign to reform Japan and liberate Asia

Christopher W. A. Szpilman[1]

Introduction

Pan-Asianism, as a doctrine, may be tarnished by its wartime associations with Japanese aggression, but it still has some powerful advocates. Witness Ishihara Shintarō (b.1932), now mayor of Tōkyō and then prominent LDP Diet member, who published a pan-Asianist pamphlet in 1994.[2] While proclaiming Asian brotherhood and the unity of Asian values, however, Ishihara, a prize-winning novelist turned popular politician, has repeatedly made a number of racially motivated verbal attacks on the Korean and Chinese minorities in Japan and on Koreans and Chinese in general.[3]

Ishihara's contradictory statements, embracing and rejecting Asia, reflect contradictions inherent in Pan-Asianism. For Japanese Pan-Asianism was a contradictory doctrine. It aimed to bring eternal peace to Asia, yet was discredited by its war-time association with Japanese militarism and aggression. It was anti-Western, but was partly inspired by Western writings. Though it proclaimed egalitarian Asian brotherhood, it insisted on Japanese superiority. Initially, such contradictions remained hidden from sight, but domestic and international developments brought them into the clear. Over time, they proved impossible to reconcile; Japanese nationalism prevailed and proclamations of Asian brotherhood and Asian liberation were turned into slogans to legitimize aggression in Asia. The thought and behavior of most pan-Asianists reflected these contradictions.

The pan-Asianist journalist and activist Mitsukawa Kametarō (1888–1936) was no exception in this respect. His prolific writings and his political activities reflect the shift from universalistic or regional Pan-Asianism to a nationalistic Pan-Asianism that served as window-dressing for Japan's military aggression. Though historians of Japanese Pan-Asianism have practically ignored Mitsukawa,[4] his contribution to the development of Japanese Pan-Asianism cannot and should not be overlooked. Certainly, Mitsukawa's contemporaries recognized his importance. A Kokuryūkai (Amur River Society) publication, for example, hailed him as a pioneer of Pan-Asianism.[5] He was well known as a journalist and academic, wrote popular books on Pan-Asianism, and was an influential figure in Japan's right-wing movement. It was Mitsukawa who founded the Rōsōkai (Old and Young Association) and the Yūzonsha (Society of Those Who Yet Remain), pan-Asianist organizations which historians routinely describe as the founts of Japanese fascism. He corresponded with notorious young officers, including Nishida Mitsugi (1901–37), Suganami Saburō (1904–85), Fujii Hitoshi (1904–32), and Koga Kiyoshi (1908–97), who took part in the conspiracies and assassinations of the 1930s. It was Mitsukawa who introduced Kita Ikki's (1883–1937) banned works to these military firebrands. His pan-Asian views, just as much as the views of his flamboyant comrades, Kita and Ōkawa Shūmei (1886–1957),[6] shaped the thinking of these young officers. The chances are that, without Mitsukawa, Kita would have spent the rest of his life in obscurity in China, for it was Mitsukawa who both recalled Kita from his self-imposed exile in Shanghai and introduced him to Nishida and other young and impressionable officers.

In what follows I trace Mitsukawa's contribution to the pan-Asian movement in modern Japan and explore his views on Asian unity, Japan's mission in Asia, and the threat posed by Western imperialism to Japan's and Asia's survival. All of these themes formed integral parts of his Pan-Asianism and nationalism.

Mitsukawa's life and political activities

Mitsukawa was born in 1888 in Ōsaka into an impoverished merchant family. The hardships he suffered as a boy gave Mitsukawa a social conscience and sympathy for the underdog that are less apparent in his better-known fellow pan-Asianists, Kita Ikki and Ōkawa Shūmei, both of whom grew up in relatively affluent conditions. Yet, ultimately, the poverty of his youth shaped him to a lesser extent than the humiliations he believed Japan had suffered at the hands of the Western powers. As a young boy, Mitsukawa was apparently traumatized by the 1895 Triple Intervention when France, Russia and Germany robbed Japan of the fruits of her victory over China. For Mitsukawa, the Triple Intervention was the central event of Japan's modern history, far more important than the 1889 promulgation of the Constitution, the 1902 Anglo-Japanese Alliance or even the great Japanese victory over Russia in 1904–5. He made frequent references to it in his writings. He even entitled his 1935 autobiography *After the Triple Intervention*. Ever since childhood, suspicion and fear of the West were thus an integral part of his outlook. It was this fear that turned him into a pan-Asianist and a nationalist.[7]

The Triple Intervention may not have made such a deep impression on Kita Ikki and Ōkawa Shūmei, but similarities between the young Mitsukawa and his future comrades in the Yūzonsha, all born in the 1880s, are striking. In search of some universal truth, all three flirted with Christianity as teenagers.[8] Having grown disillusioned with Christianity, they next turned to socialism and anarchism, each getting a subscription to the *Heimin Shinbun* (Commoner Newspaper).[9] All three, objecting to the anti-war stance of the socialists, drifted into their own versions of patriotic radicalism, even if Mitsukawa retained socialist sympathies for the rest of his life. All three from early on were nationalistic and anti-Western in their outlook, and it was this nationalism and anti-Westernism that shaped their pan-Asian visions.

Mitsukawa, again like Kita and Ōkawa and like many ambitious men of his generation, sought to further his education in Tōkyō. But similarities end at this point. In contrast to the relatively well-heeled Kita and Ōkawa, Mitsu-kawa incurred delays due to financial difficulties – in 1905 he was forced to drop out of school to work as a trainee for the Kyōto branch of the Bank of Japan. It was only in 1907 that Mitsukawa finally completed his secondary education and moved to Tōkyō, where he enrolled at the Faculty of Politics and Economics at Waseda University. But he did not remain a student for long.[10]

Continuing financial problems compelled him to seek a part-time job. He found a temporary position as a reporter. By 1910 he had dropped out of Waseda and become a full-time journalist with the *Kaikoku Nippō* (Maritime Nation Daily), which specialized in naval and colonial issues. The job gave him an opportunity to pursue his pan-Asian interests. As a journalist, Mitsu-kawa toured Korea – his first trip outside the Japanese Isles – and cultivated contacts with Chinese revolutionaries in exile in Japan. He also came in contact with prominent pan-Asianists, including the Genyōsha's legendary Tōyama Mitsuru (1855–1944), China hand Kawashima Naniwa (1865–1949),[11] and politicians Kōno Hironaka (1849–1923) and Inukai Tsuyoshi (1855–1932). It was Tōyama who, during the First World War, asked Mitsu-kawa to help anti-British (pro-independence) Indians on the run in Japan, and that was how he met Ōkawa Shūmei.[12]

Mitsukawa also got to know a number of senior military figures (e.g., Admirals Kami'izumi Tokuya, 1865–1946, and Satō Tetsutarō, 1866–1942; Baron Yashiro Rokurō, 1860–1930; and General Satō Kōjirō, 1862–1923), politicians (e.g., Count Gotō Shinpei, 1857–1929), and high-flying bureau-crats with strong political ambitions (e.g., Tokonami Takejirō, 1886–1935, and Nakashōji Ren, 1866–1924). In his own age group, he was particularly close to Professor Nagai Ryūtarō (1881–1944) and the *Asahi Shinbun* journalist Nakano Seigō (1886–1943), both of whom gained prominence as radical politicians in the 1920s. These disparate figures were linked by their anti-Westernism, their sympathy with pan-Asian ideals and their support for hard-line foreign policy.[13]

Given his pan-Asian views and his strong interest in current affairs, it was only natural that Mitsukawa accepted the offer of a job as chief editorial writer for the monthly *Dai-Nihon* (Greater Japan), whose first issue appeared on 1 October 1914.[14] The journal focused on "defense" and "international affairs"[15] and, as its title suggests, called for a naval build-up and aggressive foreign policy. Whether the journal received direct funding from the Imperial Navy is unclear, but a significant number of admirals (e.g., Kami'izumi, Satō, Yashiro) supported this publication.[16]

If Kita Ikki, Japan's most famous radical pan-Asianist, was an individualist who shunned membership of organizations, Mitsukawa was an organization man *par excellence*. The list of pan-Asian or right-wing organizations to which he was connected is long. As a budding journalist before the First World War, Mitsukawa joined the Ajia Gikai (Asian Conference) and the Issuikai (First Wednesday Society), organizations with pan-Asianist agendas.[17]

In November 1918, as the First World War was winding to a close, Mitsukawa founded the Rōsōkai, a study group intended to serve as "a forum to exchange ideas."[18] The eclectic Rōsōkai invited lecturers ranging from the pan-Asianist Ōkawa Shūmei and agrarianist Gondō Seikyō (1868–1937) on the right to the socialist Sakai Toshihiko (1871–1933) on the left.[19] The ages of the Rōsōkai's members were as diverse as their political views. They included retired admirals (e.g., Yashiro Rokurō) and generals (e.g., Satō Kōjirō), and even a senile veteran of the People's Rights Movement, Ōi Kentarō (1843–1922). Younger members included Shimonaka Yasaburō (1878–1961, subsequently president of the publishing house Heibonsha) and Shimanaka Yūzō (1881–1940, social and trade union activist, whose brother Yūsaku was the president of the publishing house Chūō Kōronsha). There was the philosopher Kanokogi Kazunobu (1884–1949), with his theory of world revolution, whom the British had just deported from India.[20] There was also the eccentric figure of Atsumi Masaru (1877–1928), a First Higher School graduate and Kyōto University Law Faculty drop-out, rickshaw puller, and home-grown sage, who was known as much for his lack of personal hygiene as for his philosophy based on the myth of *Momotarō* (*momotarōshugi*).[21] Under Mitsukawa's leadership the Rōsōkai accepted Takabatake Motoyuki (1886–1928), translator of Marx's *Das Kapital*, whom the liberal Reimeikai (Dawn Society) had turned down as an "extremist." The Rōsōkai – and this was perhaps its most radical aspect – included several women among its members such as Gondō Seiko, sister of the agrarianist Gondō Seikyō, and Hori Yasuko, the former wife of the anarchist Ōsugi Sakae.[22]

In August 1919 Mitsukawa and Ōkawa Shūmei, dissatisfied with the eclectic character of the Rōsōkai, founded what they hoped would be a more ideologically focused body.[23] This was the Yūzonsha, whose main policy planks were Pan-Asianism and radical domestic reform. To concentrate on the running of this new group, Mitsukawa quit his *Dai-Nihon* job.[24] The Yūzonsha had a resident ideologue in the person of Kita Ikki, whom Mitsukawa recalled from Shanghai in January 1920 to provide ideological leadership.[25] The new organization published a monthly called *Otakebi* (War Cry), bankrolled by the financier Inoue Junnosuke (1869–1932) whom Mitsukawa had got to know during his stint at the Bank of Japan.[26] Judging by the meager number of pages and its tiny circulation, Inoue could not have been too generous. Only three issues of the journal saw the light of day. The Yūzonsha's effort to form a mass movement by setting up branches at a number of universities, including the imperial universities of Tōkyō and Kyōto, was only slightly more effective.[27] Although some student activists joined, no mass movement resulted. So, in concrete terms, the Yūzonsha achieved little before it disintegrated in 1923 as the result of a personality conflict between Kita and Ōkawa.[28]

Historians have traced the origins of Japanese fascism to the pan-Asian Rōsōkai, but that is an exaggeration. It is difficult to regard the Rōsōkai, which had neither a well-defined political program nor an ideologically uniform membership, as a political organization, let alone the ultimate source of Japanese fascism – even if some participants, such as Nakano Seigō and Ōkawa, would become leaders of Japan's radical right-wing movement in the 1930s. Members had little in common apart from an interest in current affairs, dissatisfaction with the international status quo, and a marked dislike for liberalism and everything else of Anglo-Saxon provenance. Even the more focused Yūzonsha hardly qualifies as fascist. Its vague program of domestic reform and Asian liberation – not to mention the quixotic goal of replacing Japanese with Esperanto – belie its fascist reputation, even if, as in the case of the Rōsōkai, members included future leaders of Japan's right wing (some of whom became fascists).[29] It had neither a charismatic leader,[30] nor a mass membership. In fact, despite ambitious attempts at recruitment, the Yūzonsha, just like the Rōsōkai, managed to attract only a handful of members. And even though there was much talk of reform, there was virtually no action.[31]

The only perceptible action came when the Yūzonsha – paradoxically for an organization proclaiming its commitment to domestic reform – joined the Kokuryūkai, a traditional (that is, anti-reform), right-wing organization, in campaigns to prevent reforms of the Imperial Household. Thus the Yūzonsha supported the candidacy of Princess Nagako as the bride of the Crown Prince and tried to prevent the Crown Prince's projected tour of Europe in 1921.[32] Though Mitsukawa claimed that the Yūzonsha had scored a victory in this case, he exaggerated: the Yūzonsha's protests seemed to have little effect, as the Prince's tour went ahead as planned.[33]

Yet, surprisingly, these campaigns against the liberalization of the imperial institution apparently did nothing to antagonize the senior court officials who were their targets. Quite the contrary, Ōkawa and another member, Yasuoka Masahiro (1898–1983),[34] enjoyed patronage in court circles, where admirers included Makino Nobuaki (1861–1949) and Sekiya Teizaburō (1875–1950).[35] In 1924, with the support of these dignitaries, Ōkawa, Yasuoka, and Mitsukawa took over the Shakai Kyōiku Kenkyūjo (Social Education Institute) which Obi Harutoshi had founded in 1921 and which was housed within the grounds of the Imperial Palace. They renamed it the Daigakuryō (University Dormitory).[36]

Though sympathetic to Kita, in 1924 Mitsukawa followed Ōkawa into the Kōchisha, which was essentially the Yūzonsha minus Kita Ikki.[37] The Kōchisha, which proclaimed liberation of Asia as one of its goals, proved to be more long-lived than the Yūzonsha. It was still active in the early 1930s. The Kōchisha (after February 1925) published the monthly *Nihon*, but Mitsukawa ended his cooperation with it in 1926 as a result of a quarrel with Ōkawa. Perhaps he resented Ōkawa's (and Yasuoka's) elitist outlook, for, in contrast to Tōkyō Imperial University-educated Ōkawa and Yasuoka, he had no university degree. He certainly objected to Ōkawa's attempts to cultivate Makino and Sekiya and other members of Japan's political and military elite, though the immediate cause for his resignation was Ōkawa's alleged acceptance and misappropriation of funds from the Yasuda *zaibatsu*'s Yūki Toyotarō (1877–1951).[38]

It was the perceived series of humiliations Japan suffered at the hands of the Anglo-Saxons – which included the 1919 Versailles Treaty, the 1922 Washington Treaties, the 1928 Briand-Kellogg Treaty, and the 1930 London Naval Limitations Treaty – that appear to have pushed Mitsukawa further and further to the right. With each new treaty, Mitsukawa's views grew more extreme. The organizations he joined reflected this slide toward right-wing radicalism. In 1919–20, the Rōsōkai and the Yūzonsha, despite their subsequent "fascist" reputations, had relatively vague pan-Asianist and reformist agendas, but the organizations Mitsukawa joined in the 1930s had clearly-defined totalitarian programs and could fairly be described as fascist. In 1930, for example, Mitsukawa joined Shimonaka Yasaburō's Aikoku Kinrōtō (Patriotic Workers Party), which modeled itself explicitly on Hitler's Nazi Party.[39] He also joined the Shin Nihon Kokumin Dōmei (New Japan National Alliance), founded in 1932 to "mobilize the masses" while "maintaining close contacts with the middle ranks of the armed services,"[40] and the radical pan-Asianist Dai-Ajia Kyōkai (Greater Asia Society), founded in 1933, whose program included "abolition of money rule," curbs on private property, nationalization of key industries, and the liberation of the oppressed nations of the world, while creating "one cooperative system out of Japan, Manchuria and China" under the rule of the Japanese emperor.[41]

On a personal basis, Mitsukawa maintained close contacts with a wide range of like-minded right-wing radicals. In addition to his old Yūzonsha comrade Kita Ikki, whom he saw regularly, he was close to Lieutenant Fujii Hitoshi, to Aikyōjuku's (Patriotic Academy) Tachibana Kōzaburō (1893–1974), and to the Ketsumeidan's (Blood-Pledge Brotherhood) Inoue Nisshō (1886–1967), who instigated the assassinations of Dan Takuma (1858–1932) and Inoue Junnosuke (1869–1932) in 1932.[42] It was alongside these radicals that Mitsukawa campaigned against Hamaguchi Osachi's Minseitō Cabinet over the London Naval Limitations Treaty.

Involvement in right-wing politics did not affect Mitsukawa's writing activity, which proceeded without any let-up. Mitsukawa published altogether some 16 books in addition to countless articles. Many of these, such as *Ubawaretaru Ajia* (Stolen Asia, 1922) and *Tōzai jinshu tōsō shikan* (Historical View of the Struggle between the Eastern and Western Races, 1924), dealt with pan-Asian-related subjects. But he also wrote *Kokujin mondai* (The Negro Problem, 1925), one of the first Japanese works on African-Americans, and *Yudaya-ka no meimō* (Delusions about the Jewish Peril, 1929), in which he debunked various anti-Semitic conspiracy theories current in Japan. He also wrote a number of textbooks on diplomatic history. But his strong nationalism, Pan-Asianism, and antipathy to the West formed a common thread, more or less explicit, that pervaded all his works.

By the mid-1920s, his prolific writing output, no less than his extensive network of contacts, had earned Mitsukawa a reputation as an expert on international affairs. On the strength of his achievements, in 1925 he was appointed a lecturer at Takushoku (Colonial) University, whose president, Count Gotō Shinpei, was impressed with Mitsukawa's articles.[43] It was a congenial environment for Mitsukawa to work in: the university had a pan-Asianist agenda, having been founded in 1900 by Prince Katsura Tarō (1848–1913) to educate administrators for Japan's growing colonial empire; pan-Asian views were encouraged and pan-Asian instructors received with open arms. Mitsukawa's comrade, Ōkawa Shūmei, had already taught there from 1921. The new job gave Mitsukawa an opportunity to introduce his peculiar mixture of Pan-Asianism and Japanese nationalism to enthusiastic students, many of whom had already espoused pan-Asian ideas before taking up places at Takushoku University.

By the early 1930s, as Mitsukawa's rightward shift accelerated further due to the 1931 Manchurian Incident, the foundation of the puppet state of Manchukuo, and Japan's 1933 resignation from the League of Nations, Mitsukawa joined a rabidly nationalistic Shinto sect. Its religious practices involved frequent visits to the Yasukuni Shrine and a regimen of cold baths. After one such ritual ablution, Mitsukawa suffered a stroke, as a result of which he died in May 1936, aged 48.[44]

Pan-Asianism, the Asian revival, and the decline of the West

Mitsukawa's Pan-Asianism was well defined from early on. He always maintained that "Asia constitutes culturally, politically, economically, geographically and racially a single community that shares the same fate."[45] But his definition of Pan-Asianism tended to change, depending on the characteristics he wished to emphasize to his readers. He frequently (but by no means always) defined Pan-Asianism in cultural terms, opposing Asian culture to Western civilization. Pan-Asianism, he wrote in 1921, meant above all fidelity to Asian ideals: "a return to antiquity" and "a renaissance of Asian arts and letters (*bungei*)" that would allow Asia to resist the encroachments of Christian – that is, Western – civilization.[46] China, India, and other parts of Asia, he insisted, aspired to "this restorationist ideal of Asian civilization."[47] At the same time, Mitsukawa rejected the simplistic dichotomy of spiritual Asia vs. the materialistic West. Asia was indeed a spiritual civilization, which had produced Buddha, Jesus, Mahomet, and Confucius, but, he insisted, it also possessed a materialistic side which had produced the pyramids, printing, gunpowder, and navigation skills.[48] But this materialistic aspect, he regretted, had atrophied over time. Tradition and cultural values alone, Mitsukawa pointed out, were not enough to protect Japan and Asia from the West. To survive and prevail, he insisted, Japan and Asia must modernize and recover their ancient material glory.[49]

Mitsukawa's culturalist emphasis often gave way to a stress on the geopolitical and economic aspects of Pan-Asianism. This shift was closely linked to his fear of Western imperialism, which he regarded as the main obstacle to the realization of his pan-Asian ideals. The European powers, he noted in 1922, shortly after the conclusion of the Washington Conference, had conquered almost the entire Asian continent and were "plotting to subjugate Asia completely by the end of the twentieth century."[50] Asian countries, he lamented, were helpless to resist the inexorable advance of Western imperialism on their own. The former great powers, "Turkey and China, though nominally independent, are shadows of their former selves."[51] Britain had already annexed the Malay Peninsula and France Laos; both powers were now encroaching on Siam from east and west. The few independent Asian states, he warned, would lose their freedom unless Japan intervened to help them.

Nevertheless, Mitsukawa detected signs of an Asian awakening in various regions of the continent, which he attributed solely to Japan's 1905 victory over Russia. This first-ever Asian victory over a modern European power, he maintained, had dented the sense of white superiority and proved that "the yellow race (*ōshoku jinshu*) is to be feared."[52] Inspired by the Japanese triumph, Kemal Pasha had toppled the 600-year-old Turkish monarchy and forced the Western powers to revise the 1920 Sèvres Treaty. In Iraq and Syria, the nationalist Islamic movement was now opposing British and French colonialism. Afghanistan had declared war on Britain and won its independence.[53]

Inspiration, however, was not enough. Without concrete help from Japan, these stirrings of Asian nationalism were ultimately doomed to failure. Asians could not possibly win independence on their own. The rot of their spiritual decline had gone too far. Japan, he concluded as early as in 1922, was their only hope: "Only Japan could liberate Asia."[54] But it appears that by "liberation" Mitsukawa meant some form of Japanese protectorate over Asia. He specifically envisioned the formation of a "United States of Asia" under Japan's leadership. He saw no contradiction in this. In fact, he regarded such a union as necessary to guarantee Asia's authenticity and independence. But he did recognize that there were many obstacles on the road to this goal. Patience was required. "The next thirty years or so will be decisive," he wrote in 1930.[55]

Mitsukawa advocated Japan's continental mission that would bring freedom, an abstract ideal, to the oppressed nations of Asia, while bestowing upon Japan concrete benefits such as access to natural resources. Most immediately, however, Japan would benefit by exporting its excess population to Asia. Mitsukawa had for a long time been preoccupied with Japan's demographic problems. From this perspective he deplored the fact that "Japan has lacked a proper colonial or immigration policy." Overpopulated Japan had no choice, he stressed as early as 1919: it had to either "expand or perish."[56] He would reiterate this stark dichotomy whenever he could. "Japan," he insisted in 1924, "must expand overseas, no matter what." And in 1931 he repeated his arguments for mass emigration because the Japanese population, bottled up in a "small" area deprived of natural resources, was increasing at the alarming rate of 1.2 million a year.[57] To further Japan's national interests more effectively, Japanese emigrants, he insisted, must concentrate on one area. "Immediate plans must be made to develop Central and Western Asia where so far nothing has been done."[58] Colonization of this vast area by Japanese emigrants would project Japan's political power throughout Asia and establish Japan as a truly great power.

Mitsukawa gave little thought to practical difficulties. The harshness of the climate, the infertility of the land, and the unfriendly environment caused him no concerns. The Japanese, he believed, were uniquely qualified as colonists. They had "the capacity to adjust (acclimatize: *junka*)" that "the Europeans lack."[59] Unlike Europeans, moreover, the Japanese would be accepted by the local inhabitants because they were akin to them "in race, religion, life, and emotions." Indeed, they belonged to "the same race as 900 million Asians." So it was "rational" for the Japanese to help develop Asia's "abundant natural resources."[60] "As long as we, the Japanese people, are dedicated to Pan-Asianism," he insisted, "we must not forget Asian development even for one day."[61]

Such a colonial move into Asia, which Mitsukawa began vociferously to advocate in the 1930s, was made possible by what he saw as Europe's terminal illness, which he had already diagnosed several years earlier. Europe, he wrote in 1924 for example, was "facing an inevitable decline."[62] This was because "in the [Great] war, White civilization committed suicide."[63] By 1930, he had detected the death throes of the world's greatest colonial power, Great Britain, which, he noted, had "ceased to be the center of the world" as a direct consequence of the First World War.[64] "Britain's wealth" had now "migrated to New York," and the liberal Manchester School had lost its leading position in economics to the Marxists.[65] The oppressed masses in the British colonies were restive and even the native rulers, who had previously accepted British rule there, were now becoming nationalistic.[66] Under these circumstances, he had not the slightest doubt that the "British hegemony over Asia and Africa" was coming to an end. Any attempts to salvage the British Empire were ultimately doomed to failure. Britain would inexorably succumb to the same historical trends that had already made Portugal, Spain, Holland, and France irrelevant as world powers.[67]

In his diagnosis of the West's impending collapse, Mitsukawa based his thinking on pessimistic works by the German philosopher Oswald Spengler (1880–1936), the French geographer Albert Demangeon (1872–1940), and the French mystic and theosophist Paul Richard (1876–1967). The Harvard-educated Lothrop Stoddard (1883–1950), a lawyer by profession and a white supremacist by conviction, made an especially deep impression. "Recently," he wrote, "Lothrop Stoddard's *Rising Tide of Color* ... which has provided a strong proof of the rise of the non-white races ... has caused much fear among Europeans and Americans. Pan-Asianism (*Zen-Ajia-shugi*) ... casts a giant shadow over them."[68] But unlike Stoddard or Spengler, who regarded the approaching demise of European civilization with despair, Mitsukawa rejoiced at the perceived death knell of Europe, for it marked the advent of a period of greatness for Japan and freedom for the enslaved Asians.

But although he derived much comfort from the dark prophecies of these Western Cassandras, Mitsukawa was realistic enough to recognize that the great Western powers had still enough life in them to pose a threat to Japan. This volatile mixture of hopeful thinking and realism explains the almost schizoid fashion in which he swung between periods of radiant optimism, when he prophesied the West's imminent collapse, and pessimistic doom and gloom when he fretted about the great vulnerability of Japan.

The fear of America and Asian solidarity

Mitsukawa's chief source of concern was the rise of the United States, which he identified as the greatest obstacle to Japan's mission to liberate Asia. As early as 1921, in the context of the Washington Conference, Mitsukawa recognized the economic side of the American threat, which in his view was just as important as any military aspect. "America," he noted, "with its mature capitalism, has swooped down upon East Asia." American economic activity in Asia was simply another form of "aggression."[69] He reiterated the same argument ten years later. "No country in the world," he wrote in 1930, "can match the spectacular economic development of the United States in the twentieth century."[70] And although America had made no territorial claims on China, America, he believed, aimed to turn China into an economic dependency.[71] To do so, America had first to eliminate Japanese influence from continental East Asia and that was why, he explained, America threatened Japan with economic blockades and attempted to intimidate Japan by concentrating its entire fleet in the Pacific.[72]

This American "economic" attack on East Asia was, Mitsukawa believed, a natural outcome of American history, which he regarded as consisting solely of relentless territorial expansion. By the end of the 1920s, America had extended its influence over Latin America and was now, he alleged, even trying to annex Canada.[73] Though America's expansion in the Western hemisphere did not directly affect Japan, Mitsukawa brought it up to illustrate America's unquenchable territorial lust, which, he feared, would henceforth be unleashed upon East Asia.[74]

American expansionism, he warned, was no abstract danger. Through the acquisition of the Philippines in 1898–99, the United States had become Japan's southern neighbor, and it was now closing in on Japan from the east and the south. In Mitsukawa's understanding, the ulterior motive of every American action was to harm Japan's national interest. Even the apparently friendly American intercession in peace negotiations between Russia and Japan in 1905 was motivated, he maintained, by America's inherent hostility toward Japan. The United States had not, as some naively thought, wanted to help Japan. Nor had it stepped in for fear of Russian expansion. Rather, he explained, America had promoted peace at Portsmouth because it "did not want Japan to develop and expand."[75] After the peace treaty was signed, America attempted to capitalize on its intercession by "acquiring the Manchurian Railway;" and, when that attempt failed, it "tried to neutralize the railway" to prevent Japan from benefiting from her triumph. And, since the end of the First World War, in what Mitsukawa considered a sinister pattern, the United States had repeatedly bullied Japan at the Washington, Geneva, and London conferences in order to prevent her from becoming a truly great power.[76]

Although Mitsukawa feared the United States primarily because he recognized its economic and financial might, his resentment of American power was also rooted in his Pan-Asianism which, in addition to being culturalist, also had strong racialist foundations. Mitsukawa perceived world history as a series of race wars between Asians and whites.[77] And, if he advocated Asian solidarity as a key to the liberation of Asia, he also feared the revival of Western (white) racial solidarity as an obstacle to it.

The "white race" led by America, he worried, would somehow recover from its present crisis, overcome the differences that divided it, and combine to destroy Japan. The formation of a league of all "white" nations including Germany he considered unlikely, but an "Anglo-Saxon" alliance between America and Britain against Japan was a distinct possibility. Such an alliance, he believed, was indeed coming into being in 1929 on the eve of the London Naval Limitations Conference. America and Britain, he pointed out, were "forcing the entire world to adopt their so-called peace policy," which, if successful, would effectively thwart "our Empire's pan-Asian mission." The Anglo-Saxons, he feared, were now about to combine their forces to prevent Japan's "expansion into the Pacific on behalf of 800 million East Asians."[78]

Mitsukawa's grudging admiration and fear of America's economic and military power did not stop him, however, from despising the values America represented. "The Great European War," he observed, had "turned America into the World's *nouveau riche* (*narikin*)."[79] And, just as Japan's conservatives condemned the Japanese *narikin* at every opportunity, so Mitsukawa castigated American culture and society for its lack of sophistication, its crass vulgarity, its tastelessness, and its mercenary selfishness. America's new affluence, he claimed, had brought about a "frightening degeneration" of American society. The American film industry corrupted the young with its "grotesque, cruel, and depraved" movies; and the automobile industry had caused an increase in the crime rate. Beset by these problems, American society reminded Mitsukawa of "an overfed obese giant" with a heart problem. Even policies which may have been designed to stop this alleged degeneration produced deplorable results. Prohibition was a good example of such a well-intended policy. Far from strengthening the American spirit, he noted, it had caused widespread contempt for the authority of the law.[80]

While Mitsukawa rejoiced at this internal weakening of America by decadence and moral decay, he nevertheless worried that America's vices would spread to Asia. Indeed, he believed that the growing American presence in Asia – political, economic, and cultural – was already undermining the traditional fabric of Asian societies and destroying Asia's cherished moral values.

Given America's expansionist designs and morally pernicious influence on East Asia, as early as 1921 Mitsukawa concluded that war with the United States was inevitable. Though he did not explicitly compare the economic potential of the two countries, he nevertheless recognized that Japan would be at a disadvantage in such a conflict. "Tradition alone," Mitsukawa stressed, "will not protect Japan against America."[81] Neither would powerful armaments alone suffice. To prevail or at least to hold its own, he insisted, Japan must form an alliance with the rest of Asia. The American threat lent a new urgency to his advocacy of Pan-Asianism and his call for Asian solidarity. In this context, Pan-Asianism was no longer simply a matter of idealism; given the inexorability of the American threat, it constituted a *Conditio sine qua non* for Japan to prevail ultimately in its struggle against the West on behalf of Asia.

But Mitsukawa was clear-headed enough to realize the limitations of Pan-Asianism. An abstract ideal of Asian solidarity, he warned in 1926 shortly before the Shantung (Shandong) Expedition, would not be enough to protect Japan in a war against the United States.[82] Given the existing tensions between Japan and her neighbors, he noted, Japan could not count on Chinese or Korean support in its struggle against America. As soon as Japan and America came to blows, the Chinese, he feared, would betray Japan.[83] And he was sufficiently realistic in the 1920s to recognize that Japan had no chance of victory while fighting a war on two fronts against America and China.

The conclusion was inescapable. To prevail in the forthcoming struggle against America, Japan must gain Asian support. In other words, Japan must persuade China and other nations of Asia to join it as its allies. He recognized, however, that Japanese behavior was an obstacle to the achievement of this goal. Throughout the 1920s Mitsukawa continued to criticize Japanese attitudes toward China and Korea and condemned heavy-handed Japanese colonial policy in Korea.[84] Japan's behavior toward its neighbors, he pointed out, failed to live up to pan-Asian ideals.[85] The Japanese treated Chinese students in Japan with arrogance and, as a result, students returned to China from Japan with anti-Japanese views.[86] In Korea, he charged, Japan behaved hypocritically, "just like the United States, which while proclaiming freedom and equality was racially discriminating against the Japanese."[87] To change such behavior, Mitsukawa called for a "radical surgery" that would "reform the [Japanese] people's spirit."[88] Only radical domestic reforms could gain Asian support and pave the way for the unification of Asia. Only a reformed Japan, with a united Asia behind it, would be invulnerable to the Western threat; only as an autarkic state would Japan be able to launch a war to "destroy the evil American capitalist aggression."[89]

By the early 1930s, however, Mitsukawa had changed his views. His spirits had been buoyed up by reports of the Great Depression in the United States. America, whose economic might had terrified him scarcely two years before, frightened him no longer. America, he noted, might have become the most powerful capitalist empire in the world after the First World War, but it was now in "the throes of depression" and could no longer maintain its top position."[90] Indeed, he now thought it likely that "capitalist America would perish just like ancient Rome had."[91]

As his worries over the American threat receded, Mitsukawa no longer saw any need to win Chinese over to the Japanese cause. He regretted that a "misunderstanding" had arisen between China and Japan for which he blamed the Chinese, even if he conceded that Japan's policy toward China had on occasion lacked both "insight and consistency."[92] But, he claimed, conventional diplomacy could not possibly succeed in China. That was because China, far from being a single state, was splintered into warlord domains; it was rocked by civil war and plagued by banditry. Such dysfunctional anarchistic tendencies, he noted, had always been present throughout China's long history, but the situation had deteriorated beyond the point of no return due to the Nationalists' misrule.[93] Taking advantage of this dire situation, the pro-Soviet communists were gaining influence[94] while Western imperialist powers prepared to partition China among themselves. But the Nationalists under Chiang Kai-shek (Jiang Jieshi, 1887–1975), instead of accepting Japan's help, engaged in an "illegal" boycott of Japanese goods. "By refusing to cooperate with Japan," they "betrayed the ideals of Sun Yat-sen (Zhongshan, Jp. Son Bun, 1866–1925), a fervent pan-Asianist who wanted to oust the British Empire from Asia by means of Sino-Japanese cooperation."[95] Under the circumstances, he argued, "we must teach China the essential spirit of Sino-Japanese cooperation." It was no longer necessary to reform Japan. It was now Japan's task, he argued, "to reform China as quickly as possible."[96]

By this stage, Mitsukawa certainly no longer showed any qualms about the ongoing Japanese aggression in China. This transformation in attitude may have reflected a general shift in public opinion. It should not be forgotten that, following the Manchurian Incident in 1931, even the formerly liberal *Asahi Shinbun* assumed a bombastically militaristic stance. Mitsukawa's deepening involvement with a nationalistic Shinto sect, which he joined at that time, must have also played a significant role in this transformation. Whatever the cause, Mitsukawa's nationalist tone became shrill after 1931 as he discarded his earlier reservations about the injustices and abuses of Japanese colonial policy. From this uncritical position, Mitsukawa hailed the Manchurian Incident as a significant step toward the unification of Asia. By annexing Manchuria, Mitsukawa crowed, the Japanese had put an end to "the tyranny of the old Mukden military clique over thirty million people." In the new state, he hoped, echoing a propaganda cliché, the five "races" of the Manchurians, Chinese, Mongols, Japanese, and Koreans would live in perfect harmony (*gozoku kyōwa*). In short, he contended, Manchukuo was an ideal state that embodied the principle of "the kingly way (*ōdō*)."[97]

Contradicting his claim that Asia was a single entity in need of liberation, he now argued that Manchuria and Mongolia (*Man-Mō*) constituted a "special case." This area, never a part of China, was distinct geographically, culturally, and historically.[98] Indeed, he thought, it would be "unnatural to include it within China."[99] Foreign powers had previously recognized Japan's special position in the area, which "China's reckless diplomacy" and America's "infantile" interference now undermined.[100] By now Mitsukawa had abandoned his sympathy for the colonized Koreans and Chinese and resorted to a crude social Darwinian argument to justify Japan's territorial claims. "All living organisms," he noted, "grow and develop in an environment suitable to them. This is a natural law of organic evolution." So, he concluded, "in accordance with the laws of nature, the Japanese nation was entitled to colonize the neighboring areas of Manchuria and Mongolia."[101]

At the same time, he argued in a way reminiscent of Kita Ikki that Japan, unlike the rich China, Russia, Britain, and America, was a "have-not" nation with little land and no natural resources; so by annexing Manchuria, Japan was merely correcting an international injustice. "Without international equality," he insisted, "one cannot have world peace."[102] He dismissed Western criticism of Japan as hypocrisy. After all, as he pointed out, "the Europeans expelled native populations and set up a number of colonies" in the Americas, Africa, and Australia, and so had no right to criticize Japan.[103]

Such ambitious pan-Asian dreams had a tendency to turn into even more grandiose visions. On occasion, already in the 1920s Mitsukawa found Asia not big enough for Japan. "The Japanese, [who are] the sun race, must now engage in the great task" of unifying the entire world. Mitsukawa perceived various signs that augured an imminent realization of this very old mission. For a start, he noted, "the world is longing for sunlight."[104] Even the Chinese Nationalists and the Russian Communists were now, he claimed, paying homage to Japan's divine sun. The white sun appeared on a blue background in the flag of the new China and, under the new Soviet constitution, Russia's national emblem had become "a golden scythe crossed with a hammer surrounded by ears of wheat basking in sunlight."[105] These symbolic changes reflected a major geopolitical shift: the Great War had transformed a "Japan of the Far East" into a "Japan in the center of the world."[106]

This tendency to develop grandiose visions became more pronounced over time and, by 1935, Mitsukawa had lost all restraint. Gone were the criticisms of Japanese arrogance and discrimination which he had voiced in the 1920s. His Pan-Asianism had become a synonym for Japanese supremacy and limitless territorial expansion. He now invoked the indigenous prophets of Japanese nationalism, Ōkuni Takamasa (1792–1871), Satō Nobuhiro (1769–1850), and Honda Toshiaki (1744–1822), to proclaim Japan as the "Kingdom of the Middle" and "the premier state of the world." In doing so he elevated the Japanese emperor to the position of "the world's chief emperor (*sōtei*)." Japan would "save mankind" by "'emperorizing' the world (*sekai no kōka*)," that is, by "extending the great authority of the Japanese emperor throughout the entire world."[107] Mankind would be saved only if it accepted Japan's imperial system, Japan's moral values, and Japanese domination. Otherwise it would suffer the consequences of its failure to welcome the Japanese imperial liberators.

Conclusion

By 1935, a Pan-Asianism that was synonymous with unbridled Japanese chauvinism had replaced the earlier universalistic or regionalist Pan-Asianism in Mitsukawa's thinking. The notion of the emperorization of the world is so extreme that the Mitsukawa who had proclaimed pan-Asian brotherhood only a few years before is difficult to recognize. Mitsukawa, of course, was affected by the war hysteria to which Japan succumbed in the 1930s, but war hysteria alone cannot possibly account for this turn to nationalistic extremism. This metamorphosis can be grasped only if we recall the contradictions inherent in Japanese Pan-Asianism which I noted at the outset. Pan-Asianism, even in its earliest idealistic version, contained seeds of chauvinistic extremism. Japanese superiority over the rest of Asia – whether cultural, moral, or military – was always taken for granted, even when Asian brotherhood and equality were proclaimed.

Initially, these contradictions lay dormant because Pan-Asianism was less about Asian unity than about Japan's relations with the West. And initially it was the West that posed a clear and present danger both to Asia and Japan. Like most pan-Asianists, Mitsukawa feared and loathed Western imperialism and sympathized with the plight of his fellow Asians. It was, he insisted, Japan's historic role to help its fellow Asians by liberating them from Western oppression. As long as Japan's continental expansion encountered little opposition in China, pan-Asianists like Mitsukawa could maintain this universally plausible pan-Asianist position. But when the rise of Chinese nationalism, with its concomitant drive to national unification, led in the 1930s to a head-on clash with Japan, Japanese pan-Asianists, while sustaining the attack on their long-established Western enemies, began also to attack Japan's enemies in Asia, such as the Chinese Nationalists, dismissing them as cat's-paws of Western imperialism.

Mitsukawa may have wished to liberate Asia from the yoke of Western oppression, but not from oppression in general, and certainly not from Japanese oppression. Blinkered by his nationalism, he refused to recognize Japanese oppression for what it was. Contrary to what he claimed in the 1930s, Japan's continental mission was a mission of aggression, not of liberation.

The failure of Mitsukawa (and other pan-Asianists) to grasp the strength of Chinese nationalism, I think, stemmed from the essential weakness of Pan-Asianism as a doctrine. It was an abstraction derived from poring over the political map of the world in salons and libraries, not from direct experience.

As an abstraction, it was expressed in absolutes, allowed for no compromise, and could not be maintained in its idealistic form when confronted with Chinese or other Asian nationalisms.

The consequences of this pan-Asian inability to allow for compromise were disastrous. A salient example is the now notorious declaration that Japan would never negotiate with Chiang Kai-shek issued in January 1938 by the then Prime Minister, Prince Konoe Fumimaro (1891–1945), a politician with pronounced pan-Asian views. The declaration precluded any chance of reaching an understanding with the Chinese Nationalists and effectively turned the so-called "China Incident" into a full-scale war, which Japan could not win.[108]

But even in the idealistic form assumed by the ideology in the early 1920s, pan-Asianists, seemingly incapable of distinguishing between Asian brother-hood and Japan's mastery over Asia, equated the former with the latter. In 1922, for example, in a letter to Mitsukawa, a young Japanese officer, his head filled with pan-Asian ideals, wrote from Korea, where he was stationed: "wherever the Japanese go, they always build shrines even in the most remote places. Where a white *torii* stands, the territory becomes spiritually Japanese, be it China or India."[109] Contradictions between the ideal of Asian brother-hood and his own nationalism did not trouble the young lieutenant then, as they still do not seem to trouble Ishihara Shintarō now, over 80 years later. Whether this is a tribute to the resilience of pan-Asian ideals or to the persistence of Japanese nationalism, I will allow the reader to decide.

7 Forgotten leaders of the interwar debate on regional integration

Introducing Sugimori Kōjirō

Dick Stegewerns

Introduction: the region strikes back

Regionalism is a relatively new (or, alternatively, a long absent) concept in the analysis of international relations in the modern world. Whereas in the post-Cold War period it has become a pivotal term that adorns most political, economic, and cultural agendas as the *deus ex machina* that might balance the forces of globalism on the one hand and nationalism on the other, before the 1990s we find little mention of the term in this sense. Regionalism was mainly used in terms of "provincial" politics, often dealing with issues of decentralization, autonomy, or separatism and, in the few cases that it was used in the sense of the creation of some sort of transnational or supranational union, the actors were either European or South-East Asian – but definitely not Japanese.

In postwar historical writing on Japan, the absence of the concept of regionalism has been equally conspicuous. Especially in Japan itself, where the academic fields of national history (*kokushi* or *Nihonshi*) and Oriental history (*Tōyōshi*) have been and often still are almost completely partitioned off, the tendency to regard Japan as an Asian entity, and part of a region (*chiiki*) likely to include China and the divided Korean peninsula while excluding the United States, was almost non-existent. Despite the early efforts of sinologist Takeuchi Yoshimi to present China, as personified by the novelist Lu Xun, as an Asian alternative to Western modernization, and the infatuation of many Japanese intellectuals with Mao's Cultural Revolution, for historians England, Germany, and the United States acted as the most suitable models of reference. Consequently the attempt to compare the Japanese and Turkish roads towards modernization could only have sprung from a Western mind.[1]

As a result, Hamashita Takeshi's introduction of the concept of an Asian trade network (*Ajia kōekiken*) and Arano Yasunori's project to reinterpret Japanese history within the framework of Asia (*Ajia no naka no Nihon*, replacing the very popular slogan dating from Meiji days of *Sekai no naka no Nihon*) were both greeted as ground-breaking efforts in the early 1990s.[2] Nowadays every self-respecting Japanese university needs its own Asian (Pacific) Centre, and interdisciplinary research with a transnational focus has more or less become the norm for obtaining funding. But one should not forget that these are only the very recent effects of the end of the Cold War, Japan's economic downfall and China's economic upsurge, along with the Asian and world conquest by Pikachu and his (her?) descendants.

With the recent stronger focus on Asia, the analytical tool of "regionalism" (*chiikishugi*) has also re-entered the popular and academic debate in Japan since the late 1990s, where during previous decades in most cases it only surfaced in specialized discussions of prefectural agricultural policies. Regionalism's new, prominent place is probably best symbolized by the fact that it has been selected as one of the 30 key terms in Iwanami Shoten's state-of-the-art "Intellectual Frontier" series.[3] Despite the likely neutrality of the concept "regionalism," it goes without saying that Japanese calls for an East Asian version of the European Community are seriously hampered by the fact that the most obvious term for such an entity, *Higashi Ajia kyōdōtai*, will remind all with some sense of history of an earlier rather ill-advised endeavour to unite (Greater) East Asia under Japanese leadership. As a result, many commentators have now turned to the more neutral slogan of a "common house" (*kyōdō no ie*), although this metaphor also comes rather close to resonating with the war-time slogan for the unification of the world under one Japanese roof (*hakkō ichiu*).[4]

Identically, it is mostly due to the curse of Japan's uncomfortable war record that opinion-leaders and historians have also shied away from the existing and most convenient term for a regionalist agenda concerning Asia, namely Asianism (*Ajiashugi*), as a tainted "ism". It was, of course, Takeuchi Yoshimi's famous 1963 article "Nihon no Ajiashugi" which, albeit unstructured and contradictory, tried to rehabilitate the prewar Asianist discourse.[5] Despite his efforts, the remainder of the Cold War "Asianism" was either used as a tag by the many Marxist historians of modern Japanese history to indict historical personae or was simply ignored for the sake of convenience. However, in the early 1990s Asianism reappeared in academia as a respectable and essential object of study in the intellectual history of Japan and, almost simultaneously, the concept of regionalism was introduced as a framework within which to analyze modern Japanese history.[6]

The internationalist 1920s as a regionalism-free interlude?

Nevertheless, regardless of whether the drive towards regional integration is caught by the terms *chiikishugi*, *Ajiashugi*, or *rījonarizumu*, the focus of recent Japanese historical writing has been almost without exception on the period from the start of the Meiji period to the end of the First World War, and from the Manchurian Incident until the end of the Second World War (the latter period often being labeled "the Fifteen-year War"). Although many authors do not even so much as attempt to justify this hiatus, it does tend to make the interwar period (1918–31) stand out as exceptional – a period of international cooperation (*kokusai kyōchō*) with the West, symbolized by the postwar concepts of "Taishō Democracy" and "the Washington System," in which ideas of regional integration on the East Asian stage seem to be considered either absent, inopportune, or impossible.

However, although the majority of the opinion-leaders at the time were not very keen to gather under the banner of Asianism because of its rightist and ultra-nationalist connotations, there were few who did not support its central policy of kicking the whites out of Asia. Moreover, the late 1910s and the 1920s constitute a period in which ideas on the regional integration of East Asia – whether on the basis of culture, economics, or politics – flourished profusely. As I have discussed elsewhere, even Yoshino Sakuzō (1878–1933), the figurehead of Taishō Democracy, consecutively propagated a Japan-led Monroe Doctrine for East Asia and a Sino-Japanese economic alliance.[7] In this article, however, I would like to focus on a less well-remembered "Kulturkritiker" (*bunmei hihyōka*)[8] of this period: Sugimori Kōjirō (1881– 1968), a Waseda University professor in philosophy and many of the social sciences, who was also a prolific commentator on international relations and one of the most conspicuous advocates of cosmopolitanism in 1920s Japan.[9]

A case study of interwar regionalism – Sugimori Kōjirō and the creation of an autonomous Asian region

The man himself

Sugimori was born in 1881 and predestined to become a doctor, but he turned his back on the family into which he had been adopted and began studying philosophy in 1903 at Waseda, the university to which he would remain affiliated for the next four decades. Rather than the mainstream German philosophy of the day, Sugimori was attracted to the courses in American pragmatist philosophy taught by Tanaka Ōdō. Through Tanaka, the first and foremost proponent of instrumentalism in Japan, Sugimori was in his turn profoundly influenced by the teachings of "the Chicago school of pragmatism" – although he would adjust these considerably, just like his mentor had done, to the needs of his own time and place.

Sugimori graduated in 1906, but the next year he joined his alma mater once again. At first he was merely teaching German, but within a few years he had considerably expanded his teaching load by taking on classes in English, ethics, philosophy, Lipps' ethics, Nietzsche's philosophy, politics, epistemology, and theology.[10] He also contributed prominently to *Waseda Bungaku* which, under the editorship of Shimamura Hōgetsu, had developed into the stronghold of naturalist literature in the late Meiji period. From 1907 until 1912 Sugimori wrote many philosophical critiques in which he applied pragmatist theory to the fields of literature, religion, and education. These articles, which stood out not merely for his new ideas but also for his unusual literary style, brought him considerable acclaim and resulted in the publication of two short works on pragmatism.

On the basis of his writings Sugimori was seen as a new hope in the field of philosophy and was sent abroad in 1913 to further his studies, thus becoming the first (and last?) graduate from a private university to get a prestigious Monbushō scholarship in the prewar years. Not long after he reached Germany he was caught up in the Great War, which forced him to take refuge in England and stay there for the rest of the war. Although Sugimori had been trained in the German language from an early age, he did not despair and managed to write – albeit in somewhat pompous and archaic English – his first major work, *The Principles of the Moral Empire*, which was published by the University of London Press in 1917. In March 1919, Sugimori brought an end to his stay in England, which had overrun its initial schedule by four years, and no longer in fear of German submarine attacks embarked for Japan.

As was usual for those returning from study abroad in those days, Sugimori was welcomed home at his university with a promotion, in his case to the position of Professor of Philosophy. However, apart from this academic recognition, he also found his services in strong demand by the major magazines of the day. Although he had hardly published a word in his native country during the time he was abroad, Sugimori had nonetheless gained himself a reputation through the good reviews his book had received in the major London newspapers and in the leading philosophical journal *Mind* (reviewed by F. C. S. Schiller). A philosopher praised in the West had to be introduced to Japan as well, especially if the man was Japanese and, soon after his return, long articles in his hand adorned the pages of the prestigious journals *Chūō Kōron*, *Kaizō*, and *Taiyō*. Through his many articles for these and other magazines and newspapers, along with his regular appearances in round-table discussions such as those organized and published by the *Tōyō Keizai Shinpō* of his friend Ishibashi Tanzan, Sugimori's voice was hard to ignore. Considering the consistent demand from publishers for his work throughout the 1920s, his must have been a popular voice.[11]

Notwithstanding the fact that contemporary commentators invariably noted Sugimori's obscure literary style, adorned with many self-coined words, they also had to admit that this did not seem to detract at all from his popularity and that his many books and articles were widely read. Sugimori himself, to whom any form of modesty was completely unknown, was also keenly aware of his status as a name that sold and is said to have haughtily refused to write for any journal that would not print his contribution as a leading article.[12]

Finally, Sugimori also wielded political influence through Nakano Seigō, the eloquent and very popular "populist nationalist" politician, whom he is said to have served as chief adviser on ideological matters.[13] However, in contrast to his lifelong friend Nakano and to many other opinion-leaders of his day, Sugimori did not participate in the widespread political activism of the 1920s. Instead, he stuck to academia and built himself a prominent and solid position at Waseda University, where he functioned as an academic jack-of-all-trades, teaching philosophy, ethics, epistemology, theology, sociology, political science, and state theory for the various faculties of politics and economy, law, commerce, and letters.[14]

The particularist concept of the large autonomous region

What we now commonly label as the First World War was not seen as a global crisis by most contemporary Japanese spectators. Although their own country was fighting on the side of the Allied Powers, to them it was a European War (*Ōshū sensō*). Sugimori, who was in Europe for the duration of war, was no exception to the rule and all but ignored the Japanese role in the war. Moreover, although Sugimori had been forced to leave Germany at the outbreak of hostilities and was based in London most of the time, there is hardly a trace of partiality to be found in his writings and he failed to make any moral distinction between the two groups of nations at war.[15] Instead he took nationalism to task as the main culprit for the war. While Sugimori was not opposed to nationalism in general, he was dissatisfied with the quality of the nationalism of his day.[16] He maintained that national policy, and political, moral, and national education in most countries, were circumscribed by a Hegelian veneration of the state. This had resulted in a nationalism which was founded neither on individualism nor on internationalism and which in turn had given rise to an absurd system of national states, each of which assumed moral as well as legal preeminence.[17] In such a situation of "international anarchy," Sugimori noted, unswerving belief in the balance of power system would inevitably culminate in another world war. Accordingly, he loudly propagated cosmopolitanism (*sekaishugi*) as the basic component of world political reform and envisioned the ideal of a single world society, which he often called "the world village (*chijō ichison*)." He was convinced that, with sufficient progress in "the modern trends of individual autonomy and cooperation," the state organism would gradually grow into a world organism. To this end he advocated a new state philosophy, "a nationalism based on universal moral values," in order to foster "an international nation" (*kokusaimin*).[18]

Despite such convictions, Sugimori showed little interest in the internationalist endeavour to establish a League of Nations. For him, the most pressing issue facing Japan as a result of the reshuffling of the international order in the wake of the war was of a less idealistic nature. The United States was increasingly expanding its influence in the Pacific region and was clearly reaching out towards China – the central stage for Japanese economic and military expansionist ambitions since "the settlement of the Korean issue" in 1905. Moreover, China was hardly autonomous, even to the extent that there were continuous calls for the international management of the country, and it completely lacked the power to withstand outside pressures.[19]

However, from the point of view of Sugimori (and the majority of Japanese commentators), it was not so much China itself but rather Japan that would be most affected by this situation. He emphasized that "it is an economic fact that Japan is, and in the future always will be, dependent on Chinese raw materials" and that "a Japan estranged and isolated from China is powerless."[20] Accordingly he considered Chinese "autonomy" essential for Japan's survival and stressed that the United States should stay out of China. By contrast (and contrary to the notion of Chinese autonomy), Japan had to increase both its involvement and presence on the Chinese mainland.[21]

It is clear that this blunt line of argument contained little that would convince those outside Japan's borders. Of course, Sugimori was aware of this problem and admonished the government that "our particularistic national objectives should stand firmly on international universalist goals."[22] The need to keep the United States out of China, and Japan in China, had to be positioned within an acceptable universalist framework. The solution Sugimori came up with was the concept of a "regional bloc," a grouping of states situated at an intermediate stage within the world-wide trend towards increasing international cooperation.

Although Sugimori had touched on the subject immediately after the First World War,[23] it was the invitation to the Washington Conference that provided the impetus to elaborate on it and bring it to fruition. Regrettably, he explained, the unification of the world into one society – "the world village" – was at present still unfeasible, but this did not mean that mankind's development was doomed to be halted within the confinements of the nation-state. Due to the progress made in the fields of communication, transport, and international relations, mankind could proceed and thus – since in Sugimori's vocabulary a possibility automatically implied an obligation – mankind had to proceed to a higher level of cooperation, namely "the large autonomous region" (*dai-jichiku*) which he characterized as a pragmatic compromise between the still strong forces of nationalism and the long-term goal of cosmopolitanism.

Sugimori regarded mankind as the essence, and the state as nothing but an instrument – an historical phase which, in the case of Japan, had come into effect with the abolition of feudal domains and the establishment of the centrally ruled prefectures (*haihan chiken*) in 1871. Now, in the late summer of 1921, the time had come for the next logical step, the abolition of the nation-state: "The present age demands that we create the three large autonomous entities of Greater America, Greater Europe and Greater Asia." This division, Sugimori explained, was based on rational considerations of race, geography, and history (and thus not on such criteria as civilization, culture, or morality, by which he considered "the yellow race" far inferior to the white).[24] Greater America would consist of the United States, Canada, and the Central and South American countries. Greater Europe was to encompass not only the various European countries, but also included the whole African continent – although Sugimori frequently forgot to mention this "appendix" altogether. Greater Asia would comprise Japan, China, Siberia, and "some South Asian regions."[25]

According to Sugimori, to date most progress in the field of regional unification had been made on the American continent. He maintained that the United States and the various Latin American republics shared a grand political ideal and had already succeeded in creating an organizational and operational framework by means of the Pan-American Union and the Pan-American Conferences. In contrast, the pan-European movement was still immature, since the various nations could not overcome even their minor differences. Nevertheless, Sugimori perceived a glimpse of an endeavour towards a united Europe in the form of the Genoa Conference in the spring of 1922, despite the fact that the conference turned out to be a complete failure.[26] Yet the most problematic region was Asia where, in line with its status of most inferior region, a pan-Asian movement was still "all but non-existent, mainly because of Sino-Japanese friction." He exhorted his own country to give everything for the good of the regionalist cause. He even urged it to turn itself around, away from the United States and towards the Chinese continent, so that the coast of the Sea of Japan would become "the front of Japan" (*omote Nihon*), in the hope that the Japanese could form "an international autonomous region" with China by 1950.[27]

It should come as no surprise that Sugimori's admonitions to establish a form of regional cooperation were invariably aimed at his own country. A social Darwinist in heart and soul, he always thought in terms of hierarchy and therefore it was natural to him that the projected "large autonomous region" would be led by one superior, ruling nation, which would shoulder the heavy responsibility of making the whole scheme a reality. Identical to later concepts devised or adopted by Japan – such as "*gozoku kyōwa*" (Harmony between the five ethnic groups), "*Tō-A kyōdōtai*" (the East Asian Community) and "*Dai Tō-A kyōeiken*" (the Greater East Asian Co-Prosperity Sphere) – harmony within the "large autonomous region" did not imply equality amongst the various Asian nations to be included.[28]

In the case of Greater America it was obvious that the United States had already assumed the role of leader and unifier of the region. Many contemporary political commentators protested vehemently against the "large political and economic autonomous entity" that country was developing on the American continent under the Monroe Doctrine, on the grounds that it went against the universalist trend of the day. On the contrary, Sugimori considered "*monrō-shugi*" (Monroe-ism) a reflection of that same universalist trend. Greater America, he explained, was a sphere of substantial common interests created by the culturally superior nation of the region, the United States, and he urged Europe and Asia to take the healthy ambition of the leader of the Americas as an example.[29] Whereas Sugimori was not sure who to assign with the honourable task of the unification of Europe, designating successively Germany, England, and the Soviet Union seemingly on a whim,[30] this problem did not arise in the case of Asia. Sugimori's "Greater Asia" was not much more than a euphemism for a working alliance between the Japanese empire and China. As the natural leader of the region and its only independent power, there could not be any doubt that it was Japan that had to take the heavy responsibility of unifying Asia. "Japan is the only Asian nation with the power of autonomy. China is half-dependent in outlook, thanks to the good services of Japan, yet dependent in substance and will fall under white hegemony once Japan falls away."[31]

In fact, he explained, Japan had already enjoyed the opportunity to take this role ever since its victory in the Russo-Japanese War. Yet, whereas it should have cooperated with the neighbouring Korean, Chinese, and Siberian nations and formed a large-scale political and economic autonomous entity, after 1905 Japan had instead become overly imperialistic and expansionistic. On the basis of the principle of "culturalism" (*bunkashugi*), Sugimori pointed out that the *fait accompli* created by Japan's imperialism did not have sufficient moral value to create the nucleus of a new Asiatic society. It was in the fields of culture and morality that Japan had proven to be lacking and where it still had to exert itself in order to attain the credentials – in the sense of cultural and moral superiority – to realize friendly cooperation with its neighbours and with the other regions.[32] In this context, he added elaborately, the Japanese should try to use their militaristic gains from the past to a good end, as a basis upon which to build the new large autonomous region of Greater Asia. Therefore he did not acknowledge any need to give up Japanese rights and interests in South Manchuria and Inner Mongolia before the powers assembled at the Washington Conference. On the contrary, such an act could only be counter-productive when judged by the criterion of the universal trend towards internationalism, and he demanded that the other powers recognize this as well.[33]

Asian autonomy as the key to transcending civilizational inferiority

Sugimori's conception of a world divided into three large autonomous regions, determined by the factors of geography, race, and history, thus functioned as an argument to keep the United States out of China, to establish Japanese leadership over the country instead, and to retain Japan's possessions, rights, and interests in Manchuria. Like many contemporaries, he used "race" as one of the pretexts for disqualifying the United States and for qualifying Japan as the dominant power in East Asia – but, unlike the Asianists, his particularist argument was not based on a concept of Asian superiority or unity. The "inferiority of the yellow race" was too obvious to Sugimori to enable him to take up the line of argument of the superiority of Oriental civilization, culture, and morality, which otherwise would have neatly suited his social Darwinist theories on human competition and progress.

First of all, Sugimori completely rejected the notion of a separate Eastern civilization. The idea of separate Eastern and Western civilizations (*Tōzai bunmeiron*) he thought complete nonsense; there was but one universal civilization. Accordingly, the difference between Eastern and Western civilization was not one of kind but of degree – to be more specific, it was nothing other than the contrast between the superior (*yūnō*) Western man and the inferior (*retsunō*) Eastern man.[34] Sugimori went even further by claiming that the cultures of the yellow and the black races were not worth the name of culture because they were cultures of "non-beings." These peoples existed only in a biological sense; from the point of view of culturalism they were non-existent. He maintained that Eastern civilization or culture, as reflected in Buddhism, Confucianism, Shintoism, Hinduism, and Islam, lacked any scientific basis and thus had not led to freedom but to paralysis. As a result, the Asian nations were now no longer in command of even the most basic condition to achieve "progress through creation"; they had lost their autonomy and their right to live had been annexed within the right to live of the white nations.[35] Sugimori accordingly considered the European invasion of Asia not evil, but inevitable in the light of Asia's shameless moral deficit, and approved of Western hegemony over Asia as legitimate.[36]

Although he sporadically referred to the fact that white oppression of the non-white was no longer morally acceptable in the postwar era, his main argument took a different course. He began by expressing his gratitude towards the superior white race for its cultural achievements and its involvement in Asia, but continued to say that in the light of global problems such as overpopulation and the fear of the decay of human culture, the non-white nations also had to rise (again) to become "noble human beings" (*takaki jinrui*).[37] Now, in Sugimori's pyramid of moral behaviour, to achieve such progress meant that first and foremost attention had to be directed to the basic condition of national autonomy:

> Nations that do not have political autonomy ultimately lose the power to contribute to world culture. ... Political independence is a precondition of the universal human goal of stopping the growth of world population.[38]

However – and here we come to the crux of Sugimori's argument – he emphasized that real autonomy could only be realized by means of self-help. The subsequent moral stages of responsibility and creativity – the latter being the supreme level on which a nation for the first time could actively contribute to human culture – could only be attained successfully if one could rest on a stable, self-realized, indigenous basis of autonomy. He thus did not regard Asia as the "white man's burden." On the contrary, "the Asian people themselves have a responsibility towards the whites to increase their power of autonomy."[39] The liberation of the Asian nations, Sugimori concluded, would be beneficial to the whites so there was no ground for them to object; and for the desired autonomy to be genuine they were not to interfere, not even in a positive sense. Their role was to create the framework for Asian autonomy to come into being – that is, to acquiesce in a temporary pause in the international struggle for survival on the Asian front. Some form of protectionism had to be applied to the yellow and black races so they could cultivate their power of autonomy to the level necessary for them to compete with the white man and contribute to the progress of human culture.[40]

Self-help, the keyword in contemporary development aid policies, was thus used by Sugimori in the 1920s to keep the United States out of Asia. Yet the same criterion did not apply to Japan. Although Sugimori was adamant that the Asian race had to practice self-help, using such slogans as "self-help for the non-whites" (*hakujin igai no jinrui no jijo*) and "Asian autonomy" (*Ajia jichi*), he never asserted that each Asian country had to take care of itself. In other words, Japan as a non-white Asian nation was fully entitled to help its ailing neighbours. Moreover, since the country was the only non-white nation to realize its international autonomy and responsibility, it was even morally obliged to do so: "Japan stands between the developed and the underdeveloped [nations] and must be determined to advance on both sides."[41]

Whereas further expansion of Western influence in Asia was rejected on the grounds that it ran contrary to the principle of self-help, "the expansion of Japan's influence amongst the yellow and the black peoples is synonymous with the creation of international autonomy and responsibility amongst them."[42]

The universalist criterion of utilizationism

However, at the beginning of 1927 it looked as if the Chinese Nationalist forces were going to unify the whole of China and were seriously going to take upon themselves the task of restoring national sovereignty and, while they were at it, of nationalizing foreign property – two objectives which clearly threatened Japan's position in Manchuria. Thus for the first time since the Sino-Japanese War of 1894–95, China looked likely to be the main, or at least the direct, enemy of the Japanese empire.

In response, Sugimori adjusted his particularist argument of regional self-help, which was predominantly aimed at keeping foreign intruders out of East Asia and was not geared towards the new situation. Facing an intra-regional opponent, he now needed a universalist argument, which he found in the concept of "utilizationism" (*shiyōshugi*), in order to establish a distinct hierarchy among the countries within the region and to adjust their internal borders. This new self-crafted "ism", which never gained a wider currency than Sugimori's own use of it, approximated the Marxist dictum that only those who were directly involved in the production process were allowed to own the means of production. In the case of national society, it implied support for workers and tenant farmers against capitalists and absentee landlords – but when applied to international society it added up to anything but support for "the international propertyless class," as the coloured nations were often characterized.[43]

Sugimori believed that imperialism and capitalism should be criticized to the extent that they are merely aimed at possession – in other words, to the extent that they are anti-social. Yet the denunciation as exploitation and aggression of the entrepreneurial expansion of foreign countries into the territory of "ethnic nations" that cannot develop their land by themselves and sometimes cannot even settle it was nothing but irresponsible sentimentalism.[44]

In Sugimori's court of utilizationist morality and functionalist socialism traditional imperialist claims to territory were judged critically, but still extremely considerately, when compared to territorial claims based on collective heredity and self-determination by "*sangyōryoku naki minzoku*" (ethnic nations without industrial power). "The possession of territory without utilizing it is no longer in line with the machine age," was the cool verdict of Judge Sugimori in 1927. It was unethical to uphold political borders dating from before the industrial revolution. Industrial and political power were the new ethical preconditions for the possession of territory. It thus seemed unjust if a high development of industrial power was nipped in the bud due to a lack of natural resources. It was equally unjust to leave great reserves of natural resources unexploited. What was more, it would be a moral sin for Japan to be satisfied with its present territory. Therefore, it should no longer shun the term "territorial ambition" (*ryōdo-yoku*) and would be fully justified in expanding into China.[45]

In short, while Sugimori was willing to acknowledge the rights of developed "have" countries like the current great power, America, and the former great power, Great Britain, he was also very sympathetic towards the ambitions of the other "have-not" countries, Germany and Italy. But unlike Yoshino Sakuzō and other representatives of the Taishō generation of opinion-leaders, he could not regard the theoretically sovereign state of China as a country with equal rights. This was also his main argument in the face of Western protest against Japan's intervention in Manchuria in 1931. The United States and the various member states of the League of Nations, he explained, were making the fundamental mistake of treating Japan and China as equals; they had misunderstood the difference in position between a nation that gives protection and one that receives it.[46]

Another concept Sugimori adopted at this time was the idea of an East Asian Monroe Doctrine. *Monrō-shugi* was probably the most suitable "ism" he could find to combine a justification for Japan's arbitrary intervention with an air of universal compatibility. It is true that Sugimori had never been opposed to the American-instigated Monroe Doctrine. However, whereas he had formerly characterized "Monroe-ism" as a rational elaboration of his own peaceful idea of the formation of large autonomous regions, it now assumed a different function. It became the basis upon which to justify the use of force against neighboring countries under the pretext of "preserving law and order within one's own backyard." Considering that the concept of a Monroe Doctrine for East Asia first became popular during the First World War, it is not strange to see Sugimori advocating a re-evaluation of the Twenty-One Demands of January 1915, which the members of the Taishō generation now considered the point at which Japan had decisively gone astray.[47]

Whereas, even in his earlier cosmopolitanist phase, Sugimori had frequently shown his strong social Darwinist inclinations by sketching a scenario of superior nations assimilating inferior nations, this process of increasing international integration was still circumscribed by the fact that it was based on spontaneous subjugation due to the cultural and moral power of the superior nation. It was nothing more and nothing less than a noble "war of thought" (*shisōsen*).[48] Yet now, in contradiction to his own numerous remarks stressing gradual reform and questioning the utilizationist qualifications of his own country, his ideas of a moral imperialism based on regional cooperation yielded to the contaminated concept of imperialism by sheer force. In his enthusiasm for Japan's brave new "positive policy" on the Asian continent, Sugimori came up with increasingly inventive justifications for it. The following is a striking example from the end of 1932:

> There is no people with a stronger personal will to survive than the Chinese. ... Therefore the existence of the Chinese without a state and a national territory of their own is thoroughly conceivable. One can imagine the Chinese becoming a second sort of Jews. ... As individuals they will do anything just to survive. ... The future of the ethnic nation-state is not eternal. ... It will gradually and progressively dissolve. The advent of the world state, the human state, the supra-ethnic national state, the supra-racial state, the *Civitas Maxima*, is both a materialistic inevitability as well as a spiritual necessity. With the advent of such an era, the day of the Chinese will also have arrived – because in a sense it will mean that the Chinese, who have lost their national territory, will enjoy the honour of being the forerunners of this world state.[49]

In his defence of the Manchurian Incident, the universalist trend of utilizationist cosmopolitanism reached its absurd climax when the whole of the Chinese nation was to be lifted from the ground while the Japanese nation became increasingly tied to the Manchurian soil. In hindsight one may conclude that through his mixture of utilizationism and regionalism, Sugimori had merely ended up concocting a variant of the well-known civilization–race (*bunmei-jinshu*) mixture, in which the universalist element was used *vis-à-vis* China in order to put Japan in a superior position and the particularist element was used *vis-à-vis* the West to give Japan special prerogatives in East Asia.[50] His mentor Tanaka Ōdō by this time had come to stress the "irreparable cultural loss to the entire world that accompanied the political subjugation of any nation" and pointed out that "Universal trends have to be filtered through the particular history and culture of each people. The development of every nation, no matter how belated and confused, must be autonomous and voluntary."[51] However, in Sugimori's coercive cosmopolitanist (not to be confused with internationalist) trend of utilizationism there was no mercy or respite whatsoever for underdeveloped (ethnic) nations that had not yet caught up with the modern industrial age.

Continuity and discontinuity in the debate on regional integration of the 1920s and 1930s

Most overviews of Japanese regionalist ideas abruptly interrupt their story at the end of World War I, only to pick it up once again at the beginning of the 1930s by highlighting the figure of Rōyama Masamichi (1895–1980), a Tokyo University professor who in all probability holds the honor of introducing the term "regionalism" (in the transnational sense) to the Japanese language.[52] Quite out of line with his mentor Yoshino Sakuzō, Rōyama had worked his way up to the position of foremost ideologue of the East Asian Community (*Tō-A kyōdōtai*), the embodiment of "the New Order in East Asia" (*Tō-A shin-chitsujo*) proclaimed by the Konoe Fumimaro Cabinet in November 1938. It is undeniable that Rōyama's political influence was far greater than that of Sugimori, who had to work through the very prominent but only moderately successful politician Nakano Seigō. However, it is evident that Rōyama was not very innovative and owed much to senior members of the Early Shōwa generation such as Sugimori.

One cannot help noticing the basic similarities of their regionalist schemes. They both ignored or downplayed the Chinese (ethnic) national right of self-determination, rejected the corresponding Chinese nationalist demands, and in the end saw no other solution but to completely deny the Chinese a national state of their own. In doing so they stressed the priority of the regional common good, which in sharp contrast to China did not demand substantial sacrifices from Japan.[53] Although Sugimori preferred the criteria of production and utilization, and Rōyama consumption and (national) livelihood, this was hardly more than a different choice of wording dictated by the dominant political discourses of their day, Marxism and cooperativism respectively. While both Sugimori and Rōyama were very much in tune with the trends of their time and considered themselves harbingers of modernity, this can hardly rescue them from the accusation that their "modern" ideas of regional integration boiled down to "developmental dictatorship."[54] While there would have been no harm in calling for regional awareness and encouraging potential partners to join an "Asian autonomous region" (Sugimori) or an "East-Asian community with a common destiny" (Rōyama's *unmei kyōdōtai*), forcing such concepts down the other's throat was a completely different matter. The lack of intellectual courage to consider things from the Chinese point of view and to seriously confront the incontestable fact that Japan and China had become enemies at war in the late summer of 1931 (or, for those who do not subscribe to the concept of a Fifteen-year War, in the early summer of 1937) resulted in the creation of frail constructions of coerced community, which were not only bound to implode at the earliest opportunity but also to form an obstacle ("the curse of the *kyōdōtai*") to all Japanese postwar attempts to become part of and play a leading political role in Asia up until today.

During the 1920s there was also a different, more enlightened variety of East Asian regional integration, in the sense that it had more of an eye for the reality of Chinese nationalism and accordingly stressed that the interests of China, as an autonomous nation in its own right and not as part of a larger region, had to be taken into full consideration. This line of thought was best represented by the idea of a Sino-Japanese economic alliance (*Nisshi keizai dōmei*), as endorsed by such exponents of preceding generations as Takahashi Korekiyo, Horie Kiichi, and Yoshino Sakuzō. Theirs was a discourse of give-and-take, which had direct implications for Japan's imperialist position on the Asian continent, and thus inevitably had to make way for the increasingly expansionist discourse in the wake of the Manchurian Incident.[55] Whereas many members of the Taishō generation were blacklisted or forced to implement self-censure, especially in matters concerning international relations in East Asia, representatives of the Early Shōwa generation now took over central stage. Sugimori, for his part, ended up as president of the Nihon Hyōronka Kyōkai (Japan Commentators Association).[56]

Conclusion

There was no lack of debate on the political, economic, and even military and cultural integration of East Asia in the so-called "internationalist" interlude of 1918–31, and it was this continuity that ensured that the regionalist and Asianist concepts of the 1930s did not come "out of the blue" but were to a large extent part of the intellectual baggage of the preceding decade. Having said this, it is only to be deplored that, from the rich legacy of ideas on regional integration of the 1920s, the type of regionalism given a further lease of life was predominantly the variety that was blind to the self-deceit involved in advocating integration without giving up Japan's imperialist rights and interests.

Although the prewar "Great Empire of Japan" (*Dai-Nippon Teikoku*) and the present day Japan of course are different entities, there seems to be a considerable amount of continuity in the way the Japanese look upon themselves and the rest of the world. For instance, judging by the fact that my local convenience store was recently festooned with slogans proclaiming "Asia one family" on the basis that the chain to which it belongs had opened its 10,000th branch store in "Asia," we may be forced to conclude that attempts to link the country to a greater (East) Asian region are often still based on extremely shallow and self-centered arguments.[57] Japan would do well to reflect on the history of its relations with its Asian neighbors and seriously confront the fact of the rapid rise of China's economic and political power in the region. Otherwise it might very well find itself looking from the outside in at new attempts at creating East Asian communities in the political, economic, security, and other spheres in the near future.

8   Were women pan-Asianists the worst?

Internationalism and Pan-Asianism in the careers of Inoue Hideko and Inoue Masaji

Michael A. Schneider[1]

Introduction

Inoue Hideko and Inoue Masaji each produced a travel narrative of their 1921–22 round-the-world voyage. Hideko began her account with a letter, an invitation from American women to participate in peace activism at the Washington Naval Conference. Masaji, her husband, began his narrative with a preamble on the decline of the West. Exposed to the popularity of Oswald Spengler's pessimism, Masaji saw postwar diplomacy on the verge of a global race conflict. Introducing their 1937 travel narratives, Hideko marveled at the massive redwood forests of California's Yosemite Park, while Masaji told a whale story. Three days out of Japan, their ship, the *Heian* (tranquility) *Maru*, slammed into an unfortunate whale. As the ship spun back to inspect the bloodstained sea, white seagulls tore flesh from the carcass.[2] The contrasts here are telling. Hideko stressed the inclusive, social dimension of diplomacy; Masaji emphasized the submerged race thinking that threatens to destroy it. Hideko celebrated the international scene in its pacific glory; Masaji lamented its intrinsic violence.

The contrasting tenor of these travel narratives reminds us that travel, like most human undertakings, is a gendering activity. Travelers see the world through a lens of gender. International travel and the international political system underwriting it are likewise gender systems, mechanisms for defining masculine and feminine social roles quite apart from the biological traits necessary, or in the case of modern travel, unnecessary to undertake them.[3] Pan-Asianism, an ideology intimately tied to travel and politics, must also be seen as a gender system. This essay explores Pan-Asianism as a gender system, a system of social roles, and a discourse about those roles that both builds on available notions of masculine and feminine traits while at the same time defining and refining those roles. Rather than consider an array of male and female pan-Asianists, I offer the study of two linked individuals: Inoue Hideko (1875–1963) and her husband Inoue Masaji (1876–1947), both internationalists and pan-Asianists.[4] They were not unique in abandoning their interwar internationalism to support Japan's wartime expansionism, but their careers as travelers allow us to consider the special allure of Pan-Asianism for internationalists. Their contrasting gender logics in foreign policy allowed these individuals to traverse between their commitments to internationalism and Pan-Asianism differently. Although the hypermasculinist politics of fascist expansionism are widely understood, the complimentary appeal of masculine and feminine interpretations of Pan-Asianism is critical to understanding the appeal of Pan-Asianism. In the end, we might decide that the different gender roles in international politics serve as a more consistent truth than the sharp distinction between internationalism and Pan-Asianism that is used to interpret the lives of Japan's women in wartime.

Blaming the messenger

A gender perspective helps us shed new light on the central tension, one might say paradox, in pan-Asianist thought. Pan-Asianists issued universalistic appeals to Asians to unite behind culturally non-specific goals such as peace and prosperity, all along asserting that a unique, non-Western ethos bound Asians together. In the case of Japan's wartime Pan-Asianism, the universal and transnational claims of pan-Asianist ideologues grated against the particular necessity of Japanese military and economic leadership.[5] What is instructive about the case of Inoue Hideko and Masaji is not so much their garden-variety Pan-Asianism and their rationalizations of Japan's leadership, but instead the intensity of their earlier universalism, their internationalism and cosmopolitanism of earlier decades. In this ideological realm, we see the gender-specific choices confronting women and men in international politics. Hideko and Masaji embodied their appeals to internationalism and universalism differently and thus turned to Pan-Asianism differently in terms of that embodiment. A woman entering a discussion on foreign policy issues in pre-war Japan invariably brought her body with her. In other words, her contribution to foreign policy debate had to identify a female issue from which to formulate a feminine foreign policy. Men, of course, brought their bodies too, but foreign policy discussions are constructed overwhelmingly in a way to render male bodies invisible. Examination of the masculine imagery in fascist discourse is one way to counter this apparent difference.[6] This paper will focus more on the appeal of pan-Asianist discourse for women. Specifically I want to understand how the conflation of female sex with feminine foreign policy aided women's commitments to wartime Pan-Asianism.

The fact that women had to argue differently in foreign policy discourse has led historians to assess their ideological commitments differently and shape moral judgments on political outcomes. I would not support a generalization that the Pan-Asianism of women was somehow more objectionable, more contemptible, more earnest, fiery, or fanatical than that offered by men. There is, nevertheless, the accumulation of post-hoc judgments, paraphrased in this essay's title, which draw attention to the problematic relationship of women to foreign policy. Echoing the vituperative debates over the history of women under National Socialism, a dominant theme in Japanese historiography has been to look with thinly veiled horror on the poor performance of Japan's leading women during war.[7] As Ueno Chizuko summarizes this historiographic trend:

> On the question of the wartime responsibility of prewar women intellectuals, a re-reading of texts has been undertaken, reflecting the paradigm shift in women's history from a view of "victims' history" to "victimizers' history." This has been undertaken with a fundamental thoroughness to come clean on the "pasts" of all the key women intellectuals of the prewar feminist movement.[8]

The resulting scholarship shows that women's support for Pan-Asianism was paradoxical.[9] Prominent political feminists like Ichikawa Fusae were open participants in wartime mobilization of women for fear that they would otherwise lose earlier political gains.[10] In the interest of promoting women's health, prominent medical doctors like Yoshioka Yayoi were enthusiastic about patriarchal eugenic theories that complimented Pan-Asianism.[11] Christian women like Tsune Gauntlett were stunningly compliant, justifying Pan-Asianism through their charitable women's work in war-torn China.[12] Through her wartime study of Japanese matriarchy, anarchist poet and feminist historian Takamure Itsue justified expansionism as a vehicle for women's liberation.[13] At the intersection of these individual cases is the painful realization that women leaders found themselves promoting territorial expansionism in the interests of greater women's participation in public life. To do so, however, they carried the banner of masculine, cultural nationalist discourses that systematically limited further women's participation in foreign policy and moreover limited control over their own lives and bodies.

Compounding this cruel irony, these women leaders have borne the accusation, similar to that leveled against many leading women in fascist states, that their endorsement of expansionist ideologies was critical to the appeal of expansionism. In this view, without leading women to turn the broad mass of the people from peace to ardent war mongering, expansionist ideologies had less chance of success. Hideko was purged from her position as president of Japan Women's College by the American occupation in 1946. Students, fearful of her continued influence on campus, petitioned SCAP to expand the purge to include her allies in the school administration. "Mrs. Inouye and Mrs. Ōhashi [Hiroko, her successor] devoted themselves heart and soul to whipping the whole hesitating women folk of Japan into war that they never courted," one petition argued. Continuing with the theme that women's foreign policy should be pacifist, they derided her as "not a true educator but a petticoat politician, a Tōjō in woman's garb."[14] In recent histories, Hideko has suffered from an uncharitable neglect; one of the most highly placed women in prewar Japan has gone almost completely unstudied. As historians struggled with their suspicions of leading feminist women, liberal and moderate women have been summarily ignored for their complicity. This double burden – women as clear victims of expansionism, but fundamentally responsible for the appeal of its enabling pan-ethnic ideologies – is a troubling historiographic conclusion. We must resist the charge leveled by *Chicago Tribune* Berlin correspondent Sigrid Lillian Schultz, herself a rare female foreign policy reporter, who declared in 1940, "Women Nazis are the worst."[15] Pan-Asianist women such as Hideko help us understand their betrayal of earlier international commitments as instead the product of the complex position of women in foreign policy discourse.

Genders of internationalism

Hideko's apostasy and turn to fascism is made troubling by the staunchness of her internationalism. She was Japan's leading female internationalist of the 1920s. She consistently promoted the cause of world peace within Japan and at international conferences. Educated in the United States as a specialist in home economics, she advocated cosmopolitan, modern consumer lifestyles for all Japanese. She rose to the position of president at Japan Women's College (1931–46) and as professor and president promoted international education for women. She served as head of Japan's Women's Peace League and in that group's name, attended the Women's World Conference on Arms Limitation running alongside the Washington Conference of 1921–22. And she was the leader of the Japanese delegation to the most important women's conference of the 1920s, the pan-Pacific Women's Conference of 1928. With the onset of the "China Incident" (*Shina jihen*) in 1937, she nevertheless began spouting every rank pan-Asianist slogan. Touring by car and bus across Germany in 1937, she celebrated the positive results of the *Kraft durch Freude* (Strength through Joy) program in providing consumer opportunities in travel and the arts. She moreover attested to the pervasive happiness of daily life in the German countryside as a success of Nazi leadership.[16] After her return, she served the Greater East Asian Ministry (*Daitō-A-shō*) in bringing pan-Asianist educational reforms to occupied China. She was decorated by the Emperor and served in many public positions as a leading woman of wartime Japan. She was one of the few women purged during the US occupation.

Subsequent critics of Hideko pointed to her husband as the vehicle for her rise to prominence in Japan. Much of the evidence suggests a different picture: two careers sustained by a mutual affection for foreign travel, which raised both to prominence based on the international expertise they acquired. Roughly the same age, they led full but largely independent careers. Masaji was briefly a Diet member (1924–29) but worked more prominently as an advocate of Japanese overseas emigration. He was one of the more well-traveled prewar Japanese, circling the globe seven times, a feat that would have been impossible had he not married into the affluent Inoue family. Masaji, originally Adachi Masaji, washed out of a naval school and joined the Inoue family at 18.[17] Through some linguistic competence and a willingness to travel, he acquired a number of appointments as an interpreter, journalist, and lecturer.

These skills eventually landed him a job in Shanghai with the early pan-Asian society, Tōa Dōbun-kai (East Asian Common Culture Association), in 1899. That organization supported his studies in economics and colonial policy in Vienna and Berlin. With these credentials and commitment to "developing Asia" (*kō-A*), he received many government appointments as an analyst of Japan's empire beginning in 1904 and published on both travel and the colonial world.[18]

One might have expected that a longer career in colonial administration would have been in his future, but Masaji was drawn to frolicking in the Asian playground. More practically, he worked toward the goal of making more Japanese competent cosmopolitans, especially when it served the goal of addressing Japan's alleged overpopulation problem. During his second world tour in 1910–11, he later recalled, "I changed from Toyotomi Hideyoshi to [Kiyokawa] Hachirō, from Hachirō to Cecil Rhodes."[19] Masaji meant that his career up to that point had shown the limits of his two earlier modes of pan-Asian activism. On the one hand, he gave up on the notion of pan-Asian unity as a military achievement, the Hideyoshi mode.[20] He similarly rejected the life of a political *rōnin* and a faith in anti-Westernism a la Hachirō. In the end, he settled in as an economic expansionist. He promoted Pan-Asianism as a civilian enterprise with a vision encompassing not only China and Japan's colonies but also the wide reaches of Asia outside of Japanese political control.[21] To compliment his expansive, Rhodes-like vision, Masaji turned a successful profit through investments in a Malay rubber plantation.

By the 1920s, Masaji advocated a pragmatic internationalism, reformulating his Pan-Asianism as an extension of the new world order after Wilson. I say "pragmatic" to highlight that his internationalism amalgamated an idealistic vision of Asian development with practical rationalizations of Japan's foreign policy needs. He saw post-World War I global society on the verge of a revolutionary transformation that would impose the economic axiom of "the greatest good for the greatest number." If this change led to a global race conflict and the retreat of whites from Asia, it would be a result of the Japanese having been truly "disciplined in an internationalist spirit" (*kokusaiteki seishin no kunren*). The spokespeople for this new era of global peace and racial equality could be Japan if it were "populated by many Confuciuses and many Abraham Lincolns."[22] He thus conceded the fact that the post-World War I era was a triumph for universalistic values.

Masaji consciously crafted his pan-Asianist agenda to be polymorphous and adaptable. When elected to the Diet in 1924, he declared no affiliation with any political party. In the mood of government criticism of militarist administration in the colonies, he was vaguely anti-colonial. He concluded by the 1920s that Japan's colonial development programs, which developed Korean rice for Japanese consumers, were doing nothing more than "foisting [Japan's] troubles off on the Koreans." Instead he encouraged the Japanese to embrace emigration outside their empire. Not only would emigration alleviate domestic population pressures but it would also contribute to the cultural internationalist goals of increasing the geographic reach of individual cultures while promoting a global synthesis of human culture. He called this "internationalization of the nation" (*kokumin no kokusaika*) a "spiritual movement" and "sacred program" to "achieve the internationalism that is increasingly advocated nowadays."[23] Leaving the Diet in 1929, he rose to the head of the semi-official Overseas Promotion Corporation (Kaigai kōgyō kabushiki kaisha), the umbrella organization for overseas emigration support. He served on many League of Nations advisory committees and represented Japan at many international conferences on population.

Masaji's pragmatic assessment of Japan's need for a vigorous internationalism in the 1920s matched well the masculine worldview of an international traveler and global thinker. His cosmopolitan rhetoric coexisted with a pan-ethnic worldview, which filtered into his many travel accounts. Full of manly tales of adventure trekking across central Asia, they carried that racial template that not only were all Asians brothers, but that among other things, Asians were also brothers with Magyars in Hungary, whom he viewed favorably.[24] Masaji was troubled by his view that Japan lacked inspirational leadership, truly manly men, so he wrote books and essays celebrating the great men of history – Cecil Rhodes, Hara Takashi, and Mussolini, the last as early as 1928.[25] By the late 1920s, Masaji imbibed the changing mood of international politics from the weakness of Wilsonianism to the bare-knuckled and brawny leadership of Mussolini. He rewrote his paean to Lincoln and cosmopolitan values by noting the need for physical changes in the scrawny Japanese, inferior even to Koreans in their capabilities for hard labor.[26]

The contrast I would like to draw is Hideko's inability to choose Masaji's path. Where Masaji built his internationalism on typical masculine imagery of political realism, Hideko built her internationalism on the presumption that a woman's claim to speak on foreign policy had to reflect some natural endowment. In other words, international politics needed an infusion of feminine considerations. It is not surprising then that her claim to speak authoritatively about international politics grew from the position of a home economist. She tied the cosmopolitanism of the new Japanese home to a larger project of global peace bound to a nurturing ideology.

> This is the reason that European and American women talk of the ideals of universal womanhood and universal motherhood, that women should increasingly harness the natural endowments which have been given them, develop areas of activity different from men, and seek to contribute to the development of culture and the promotion of human happiness. Now women are in touch with the large home of the nation-state, city, town, and village, seeking to reform and advance their health, habits and morals, improve the conditions of factories, control the physical well being of men and women workers, and take a direct interest in social policy of schooling and children's health. Bearing this responsibility to

guide and protect, they are expanding the scope of women's natural endowment, which is really the extension of so-called home life.[27]

This quote states repeatedly that the cosmopolitanism that justifies women's participation in international relations will be found in the material and physical changes it brings in the human body.

Given wartime pan-Asianists' definitions of Asian-ness by reference to the virtues of women as the bearers of the race, one could reasonably be tempted to see Hideko's appeal to motherhood and biology as an antecedent of her subsequent Pan-Asianism. Within the discourse on population, the Japanese accepted as an article of faith that Japan was an overcrowded island that needed to send a significant portion of its population elsewhere. The predatory world of nineteenth-century imperialism had convinced most political leaders that, on social Darwinist principles, Japan had to remain an expanding society. Home economics sustained such reasoning under a eugenic internationalism. Naruse Jinzō, founder of Japan Women's College, had influenced Hideko's views on eugenics. He had promoted women's education in large measure because of his eugenic ambition to reform society through pro-natalist policies. Japanese eugenicists never tired of observing that the Japanese were the shortest people among the world's powers and that the only positive trend was that educated classes were at least taller. The various eugenics societies that rose and fell during the 1910s to 1930s shared a complex agenda to remedy this failing. On the one hand, they wanted to promote "ethnic advancement" through rationally managed marriage and reproduction. And yet, they advocated overseas emigration to alleviate population pressures, even though they knew the poorest and probably least educated and least fit to emigrate were the ones they wanted to see leave. At the same time, in league with emerging industrial food processing companies, these societies promoted consumption of beef, milk, and sugar to make people healthier and grow taller.[28]

I do not want to suggest that the eugenic thought infecting home economics at this time was a kind of genetic flaw that subsequently allowed internationalists to embrace the racist assumptions of Pan-Asianism. Instead I want to argue that the dominant realist paradigm in foreign affairs demanded that women provide practical and concrete benefits to their internationalism, that it be obvious in their bodies and explicit in their rhetoric. Eugenic beliefs served as the minimum requirements for participation in foreign policy discourse. In Hideko's case, we see a common conflation of sex and gender. On the one hand, she appealed to the hard biological concerns of ethnic modernization on a global standard. On the other, she sought to justify women's participation in international affairs through ascribed features of femininity, available to all. To address these concerns, home economists like Hideko imagined the mundane home as an ever-expanding social institution that was equally justified by the new internationalism and, in turn, reached out to embrace that internationalism. The successful, middle class magazine *Shufu no tomo* (The Housewife's Companion) published essays with an explicit understanding of the international context for a reformed home life. Staff writer Kobashi Miyoko argued that the "womb" in which the new domestic culture had gestated had also produced a new unified field of cultural activity. Diplomacy, social reform, and consumerism constituted a single field of feminine political activity. "The renovation of state and society begins with people. At the same time, the renovation of humanity must be firmly rooted in home, state, and society, and thus must cooperate with the world. Today's women must want to be educated to be able to grasp with the same sensitivity as they would their own affairs, the affairs of society, state and by extension the world."[29]

Inoue Hideko echoed these sentiments in her travel account of post-war Europe and the Washington Conference. Her message was that the education of women, their calls for political rights, and the desire to emerge from centuries of oppression necessarily called on them to see their responsibilities as playing out in an arena as broad as the whole system of international peacemaking and arms control. She calculated women's contribution to world peace as a question of military expenditure. "With 40% of Japan's budget devoted to armaments, it is difficult to achieve true cultured lifestyle (*bunkateki seikatsu*)." As she stated at the disarmament conference, "every woman in Japan cannot but wish ardently for disarmament."[30] She nevertheless reflected the aversion to birth control found across the political spectrum, even among reformers like her husband who were deathly afraid of the problem of overpopulation. She noted with shock the discussion on birth control in Washington in 1921. "To tell Japanese to limit their population is no different than telling people with insufficient food to kill themselves."[31]

Masaji and Hideko adopted different forms of internationalism, reflecting two gendered conceptions of international relations. Masaji's amalgamated or opportunistic internationalism drew on masculine imagery of a solitary and rugged cosmopolitan adventurer, who could presume to cobble together contrasting internationalist projects to address national aims in a realistic way. He never felt the need to justify his internationalism in any explicit way as being connected to the fact of his male sex. Hideko's internationalism was in many ways truer to the influential Wilsonian form of the day. She stressed the sweeping impact of modernity in transforming the home, national consciousness, and the international arena of great power rivalries. Thus she questioned underlying masculine conceptions of military aggrandizement in foreign affairs and promoted a cosmopolitan, consumer peace state. She justified these views ultimately as an extension of her "natural endowment." We know, of course, that Wilsonianism was highly vulnerable to attacks from the ideological right, especially after 1929, and the 1930s militarism took intense interest in female sexuality and women's bodies.[32]

Different Pan-Asianisms

Masaji and Hideko predictably followed different paths to Pan-Asianism. Each accommodated their internationalist stance differently to the new politics of the 1930s and, in the end, rationalized their Pan-Asianism on different assumptions about gender. A simple generalization would recognize Hideko's belated turn to Pan-Asianism and its holistic, rather than piecemeal, transformation. Hideko rationalized her pan-Asianist stance as an obvious departure from her earlier views, but a departure consistent with the new realities of the late 1930s. Masaji, by contrast, asserted the basic continuity of his views over his career. Far from an aberration or ideological gymnastics of urgent times, his pan-Asianist vision, he argued, finally realized its potential for an all-encompassing vision of Asian economic development. What is most obvious is that the same gender devices that each used to justify their earlier internationalism were enrolled in the service of Pan-Asianism. Masaji amalgamated an independent vision of Asianism's success while Hideko clung to a feminine and bodily appeal to Pan-Asianism.

Continental expansion during the 1930s provided, in Masaji's mind, new practical opportunities for achieving Asian unity. He reoriented his push for Japanese emigration immediately after the Manchurian Incident to include that new possession.[33] Although he had warned the Japanese consistently about the meager expectation one could have for Japan's territorial empire and advocated expansion into South America throughout the 1920s, he turned to the Asian continent as a bold new opportunity, underwritten by the dream of Asian unity. His earlier advocacy of emigration to the south Pacific increasingly aligned itself with the neo-mercantilist strategies for a "Southward Advance" into that area. The depiction of his personal entrepreneurship in Southeast Asia was celebrated under the rubric of promoting the nation's interests. In fact, militarism, which never appealed to him much because of his respect for Japan's civilian leadership, flourished in 1938 through the poetry of fascism.

> Returning east from their long journey
> Despite the rain, passing time and again through the Roman citadel
> The Black Shirt army feels its spirits raised
> The voice of Mussolini thundering everywhere.[34]

To describe the new Japanese occupations of East Asia, he conjured up the image of a large torso of Asian development nurtured for decades in China, with one arm stretched over Manchuria and the other over Southeast Asia.[35]

The many new books Masaji produced in this period of semi-retirement displayed emblematically the gender inflection of wartime Pan-Asianism. He pulled all the different strands of his earlier career in the international sphere into a conglomeration of masculine ascriptions of this work. Quoting an old diary, this 1944 passage folded his entrepreneurial years into the scheme of the "Greater East Asian Co-Prosperity Sphere" (*Daitō-A kyōei-ken*).

> As evidence of the fervent dedication to my work, a faith flaming with singular resolve, during those years in the south, I wrote in my diary, "It is satisfying to unite devotion and work in this world. My aim, needless to say, is to benefit my country and to benefit the world. To devote half a life [to developing Southeast Asia] is my sincerest hope, my essential nature. And though taking on this task may be judged a return to a world before Jimmu,[36] it is no idle boasting but a result of firm conviction. The vestiges of Hideyoshi's distant era, although they reside deep in us, no longer express themselves. To stand on the ground, waste neither brush nor paper, working silently until the work is done – this is the life I've led and this is how my labors began."[37]

He marveled at his personal devotion to his cause. He displayed autonomy and resourcefulness stripped of the restrictions of culture, silently and self-lessly working, fed only by conviction. Recounting bouts with malaria, he transmuted the personal sacrifice of his health and energies into a will to sacrifice for the nation. These sacrifices, however, were not petty gains, since Japan's national interests were coterminous with the goals of global development, a transcendent idealism.

This quote is also interesting in its attempt to recover Masaji's entrepreneurial spirit as a national and Asian achievement. Whereas his 1920s encouragements to pursue such spirit invariably emphasized the international benefits of strong personal character, his Southeast Asia experiences were now rededicated to the military or bureaucratic career he had, in fact, not pursued. The same pattern appeared in reflections on his years promoting overseas emigration. In 1937, he visited the Vancouver grave of the internationalist Nitobe Inazō (1862–1933) to celebrate his vision of cultural cosmopolitanism.

> To put it plainly, Japan and the US have the Pacific lying between them but have no substantial causes for friction between them. Even in the case of the Anti-Japanese Exclusion Law, which blunted the late Doctor Nitobe's will to come to the U.S. despite hoping to be "A Bridge Across the Pacific," it is still possible to see paths leading to a suitable accommodation consistent with his vision.[38]

As war between the United States and Japan raged against any hope of accommodation, he rationalized his earlier advocacy of emigration to South America, that is, outside Asia, as consistent with wartime pan-Asianist dogma.

> In this war, with the exception of Argentina, central and south America has fallen under the power of the United States. The efforts of our 200,000-odd comrades have been cut short. Have these seeds simply

withered and died? No, our goal must be to develop Asia and push ahead with the establishment of a new world order. I believe that, in the ideal expression of *hakkō ichiu*, those people and their efforts must certainly be resurrected.[39]

His writings over the period demonstrate that Masaji believed he had followed a seamless transformation from internationalism into the Pan-Asianism that, in his view, he had been promoting all along.

It was by contrast more difficult for Hideko to maintain a similar cultural cosmopolitanism in the face of the increasingly strident calls for a new Asian order. The Japanese home also had to serve as proving ground for a new Asian self. Hideko also occupied ever-higher positions of influence. She had become the first woman president of Japan Women's College in 1931. She served on the organizing committee for the 1933 International Women's and Children Exposition along with strident cultural nationalists like Ōshima Masanori and Southern Manchurian Railway vice-president and future cabinet minister Hatta Yoshiaki. In the late 1920s she had been appointed as the only woman to the Confectionery Research Society established by Meiji Confectionery Corporation. She served on its governing body until the society was disbanded under the pressure of wartime controls on consumption. She traveled to occupied China as an advisor on women's education and she was to represent Japan at a 1941 women's conference in Germany, a conference canceled due to Soviet entry into the war.

Her work with the Confectionery Research Society points out the unstable ground for Hideko's earlier cosmopolitanism. By the mid-1930s, the society's annual conferences had soaked up the cultural nationalist arguments that Asian values must be clear, not only in hearts and minds, but also in and on bodies themselves. In his opening remarks for the 1935 meeting, Director Sōma Hanji argued that:

> Western confections were brought in as a new Anglo-European form that has no longstanding basis in Japan. Nowadays we dispense with imitation and cultivate Japanese particularity. ... Thus, in our food culture, unless something clearly surpasses our native culture, the people of our nation will not be satisfied with it.

Presentations explored confections based in rice and the "preferred tastes of the Yamato race." Many speakers expressed the urgency that food science must "keep up with the trends of the times and enhance the beautiful custom of our brilliant national polity." Even in the face of this intense nationalist commentary, Inoue Hideko stated the obvious. This society's interests were in the universal human love of sweet things. "To extract confections from our home life would indeed make for a dark and dismal society." Unlike many other presentations, records for the conference indicate no applause following her speech.[40]

Hideko and Masaji's 1937 trip to the United States and Europe impressed her with the need to update her cosmopolitanism to match the trends of the times. Speaking on the new responsibilities of women in foreign relations, she commented dryly on American hypocrisy. Observing the vastness and under-development of the Texas Panhandle, she wondered: "The gates are shut and the entry of foreigners is strictly refused. Is this really not blasphemy before God?"[41] She abandoned the claims of universal motherhood and international activism and adopted instead the acceptable language of the stabilizing presence of woman on the home front. "To tie China and Japan together through the power of education and ensure that the honored casualties of war have not died in vain, that is the [role of] true home-front woman."[42]

Hideko later argued that she never succumbed to the irrational and anti-modernist excesses of some pan-Asianist rhetoric. There were many instances on which she clung to her universalist positions on the home and education. At the 1938 meeting of the Confectionery Research Society, she persisted in her view that the international arena showed clearly enough that development of sweets was an artifact of modern cultural development. Tokyo was in the last analysis an urban environment in which Western foods and desserts had flourished, even more so than Japanese foods. The impending wartime controls on consumption, she argued, would have to contend with these facts.[43] In lectures on education, she insisted that special roles for women, even their subservience to men in an Asian context, did not relieve the state of its obligation to educate women for the tasks the new Asian order demanded of them. Thus she consistently pointed to an international context to lambaste the state for failure to modernize women's education. "Everywhere the world is on the move ... and yet women's education in Japan is the most retarded in the world."[44] Or as she complained under wartime budget constraints in 1942: "The facilities of the state dedicated to a so-called more comprehensive or liberal education have been abandoned. It is not only the state that has neglected women's education, but also, because the state has neglected it, the whole nation places no emphasis on it either."[45]

Hideko thus retained an element of her earlier internationalism: the changing international context, war, influenced the nature of women's participation in affairs of the state, but it did not alter the fact of that participation. The continuing advancement of women and women's issues demanded increasing responsibility to participate in society – the opening of doors, the expansion of opportunities – in the service of national mobilization and, by extension, Japan's responsibility to guarantee the peace of East Asia.[46] Her calls were cloaked, however, in the cultural politics of Asianism. As she stated in 1938: "The epoch-defining task of struggling with East Asia's 500 million to create a new culture that has yet to appear in world history ... has been placed in the home."[47] Under such logic she advocated Japanese women's involvement in the war effort in neighborhood associations much as did more ardent feminists.[48]

What made her Pan-Asianism seem somehow "worse" then was her argument that the participation of women in the new Asian order grew from intrinsic qualities of female sex. In wartime conditions, she admitted time and again, distinctions of gender and differentiation of public life based on sex became stricter. This was the cost of hitching women's lives to a global context.

> The extraordinary string of national events – the Manchurian Incident, withdrawal from the League of Nations, the China Incident, the Great East Asian War – have led to a wholesale return to the imperial way in national thought and life, while also compelling deep reflection on women's essential mission. The desperate phase of the Great East Asian War, in particular, demands a transformation in women's views of the state, lifestyles, and accordingly, education.[49]

Postwar critics of Hideko, especially students and alumna of Japan Women's College, regarded her as the most insidious militarist threat, imagining her as a bad seed, a feudal remnant, a "petticoat politician," buried in the venerable halls of learning.[50] Such views reflect Hideko's own arguments that participation of the pan-Asian order must be achieved within women's bodies. As she commented in 1944:

> Particularly today, when the fortunes of the nation hang in the balance, it is imperative to realize the gravity of the situation through our bodies. Therefore in actions that weary our bones and draw out our sweat, that is, through the labor of the flesh, we must internalize [the war's] significance.[51]

Her critics correctly argued that she called on women to acquire a deep-seated commitment to Japan's Asian mission. But her critics went on to argue that women's militarism posed a greater threat to postwar democracy: male militarists were easily identified and purged. In the first post-defeat issue of the Japan Women's College newspaper, Hideko called on Japan's women to recognize the inherently different roles women would play in the new postwar culture state. They should not mistakenly ignore the genetic and natural differences which present women with unique issues in the public sphere. Once again Hideko called on women to view the international sphere through their bodies.[52]

Inoue Hideko was purged in May of 1946, officially for her appointment as vice president of the Japan Youth Association (Dai Nippon Seishōnen-dan) in 1941 and its affiliation with the Imperial Rule Assistance Association (Taisei Yokusan-kai) in 1942. These purges became the subject of criticism for oversimplifying the question of wartime responsibility. They certainly established mechanical definitions of victim and victimizer. Hideko defended herself to SCAP on these grounds. She asserted that she had resisted her initial appointment and opposed the affiliation with the IRAA. "I have devoted my life to the cause of female education and from the outset such social aspects as politics have failed to interest me."[53] Some Japan Women's College students feared that a six-month delay granted her purge and the naming of her ally as successor would mean the school would "remain a hotbed of feudalistic thoughts all the same, in opposition to social democratization."[54] Major R.W. Arrowood of the SCAP Civil Information and Education Section assured two graduates that "no exception would be made in the case of ultra-nationalistic or militaristic educational officials" and Hideko's purge would proceed in November 1946. Arrowood felt compelled to remind the women that their political activism on issues of international significance, though, had its limits. "Care was taken," he reported, "to explain to the Japan Women's College graduates the difference between the [r]ight kind of student democracy and an unbalanced emotional attitude arising out of an extremely distorted misconception of democracy."[55]

Conclusion

I would like to suggest that the perception that women's support for Pan-Asianism was more culpable or more tragic is as much a product of our assumptions about international relations as it is about the depths of women's commitments to Pan-Asianism. Women commenting and participating in international relations were vulnerable on two counts. First, they were driven to justify their entry into foreign policy debates on overt associations with their own bodies. This is not to say that men were not speaking about their bodies. Masaji wrote endlessly about trekking, adventures in exotic locales, and the youthful vigor demanded and yet reinvigorated by his international activities. If, in retrospect, we see a decades-long dissertation on the aging male body, he was never asked to admit to such an interpretation at the time. Few women, by contrast, attempted to argue on the basis of abstract principles of international relations, abstractions that women might have the right to celebrate or dispute. Their issues had to be women's issues. By extension, then, their participation in international relations was almost exclusively in the realm of cultural politics. Hideko's commentary on foreign policy consistently appeared hand in hand with her topics and experiences as a home economist. Her husband Masaji's participation, by contrast, required no overt claims on the intrinsic qualities of his body.

The wartime pan-Asianist vision of Japanese leadership used inflexible gender-specific roles for women as bearers of national values to bolster the mission of Asian unity. In the 1930s, women who advanced their careers did so by endorsing sharply distinguished roles for women, consistent with the views of cultural nationalist ideologues. For Hideko, whose interest was in expanding women's participation in the area of international relations, this meant promoting Japanese women and the Japanese home as exemplars for Asia. Women like Hideko thus found themselves in an unusual position. Having endorsed internationalism throughout the 1920s and 1930s to argue that women deserved a greater role in Japan's foreign relations, she turned to Pan-Asianism in the 1930s to sustain the idea of women's competence in international affairs. To see Inoue Hideko as simply a fellow traveler of male pan-Asianist ideologues is to overlook the complimentary relationship of two attitudes toward gender and foreign policy. Male theorists of Pan-Asianism struggled minimally to square their support for a new expansionist ideology with their earlier sympathy for international cooperation. Adapting to new circumstances is what any reasonable foreign political realist would do. The case of Inoue Hideko suggests that women could deploy no such claim on the universal theories of international relations. Instead they struggled with the paradox at the center of Pan-Asianism: defending Japan's particular aggression in Asia as consistent with a universal striving of all women.

Part III
Creating a regional hegemony

Japan's quest for a "new order"

9 Visions of a virtuous manifest destiny

Yasuoka Masahiro and Japan's Kingly Way

Roger H. Brown

Introduction

In 1924, Chinese revolutionary Sun Yat-sen (1866–1925) closed his address before an audience in the port city of Kōbe by challenging Japanese to determine whether their country would become "a cat's-paw of the West's Despotic Way (*seihō hadō*) or a bastion of the East's Kingly Way (*tōhō ōdō*)."[1] Sun's death the following year spared him the irony of seeing his reliance on Confucian terminology to express pan-Asian idealism turned against him in Japan's ultimate answer to his query, which was, in the apt phrasing of Marius Jansen, "to justify a rule of Might with Oriental maxims of Right."[2] Indeed, given the often glaring gap between the principles of virtuous rule and the brutalities of militarist despotism that marked Japan's "Holy War" (*seisen*) to establish a New Order in East Asia, it comes as no surprise that historians have tended to conceive of Japan's wartime Pan-Asianism as merely "false ideology" (*giji-shisō*) in the service of nationalist aggression.[3]

This inclination is nowhere more evident than in considerations of the "Kingly Way." Appearing in *The Mencius*, the term *ōdō* (Chinese: *wangdao*) has long been used to designate virtuous governance based in benevolence, an approach contrasted with *hadō* (Chinese: *badao*), or rule through despotic force. Scholars looking at Japan's invocation of this Confucian dualism during the 1930s tend to describe cursorily the term's classical origins, highlight its divorce from political reality, and tether its invocation specifically to the rationalization of Japan's puppet state in Manchuria.[4] Confucian ideals of virtuous governance thus become little more than the opportunistic idiom of Japanese aggression, figuratively pulled off the shelf in rapid response to the creation of Manchukuo (1932). Accordingly, Japanese ideologues are described as gathering hurriedly to help "design the doctrine of the kingly way ... as the philosophical underpinning of the new state."[5]

By taking a less dismissive look at one version of the Kingly Way ideal, this paper seeks a more expansive understanding of the beliefs informing Japan's pursuit of a pan-Asian "manifest destiny." While questioning neither the role of nationalist hubris nor the rationalization of aggression apparent in Japan's invocation of Confucian ideals, the following examination is premised on the idea that ideological articulations of this kind do not represent "false ideology," but rather draw on an "interrelated set of convictions or assumptions that reduce the complexities of a particular slice of reality to easily comprehensible terms and suggests appropriate ways of dealing with that reality."[6] Likewise, the presumption here is that ideologues and policymakers alike rely on fundamental notions about "human nature, the constituents of power, and national mission" that in turn reflect beliefs derived from particular historical experiences, cultural contexts, and social status.[7] Consequently, when Japanese ideologues sought to influence, justify, and find meaning in their country's actions, they produced evidence that historians can utilize to understand more fully these ideas and their role in Japan's drive for a New Order in East Asia. Finally, rather than present the Kingly Way ideal as yet another case of Asians futilely invoking traditional thought while trapped within the hegemonic embrace of a ubiquitous "modernity" pioneered by Europeans – and thus join the chorus of radical discontinuity informing much recent historiography – the following interpretation treats the contingent restructuring of traditional modes of knowledge as constituting an integral part of modern experience.[8]

Among the aforementioned ideologues was the Confucian scholar and nationalist Yasuoka Masahiro (1898–1983). A 1922 graduate of Tokyo Imperial University, Yasuoka enjoyed a long career as a private scholar-advisor to court officials, reformist bureaucrats, business leaders, and military officers. Initially connecting with key individuals later associated with the radical right wing, such as Kita Ikki (1883–1937) and Ōkawa Shūmei (1886–1957), Yasuoka forged his most sustained and important contacts with conservatives and moderate reformists, individuals whom he cast as the "men of character" (*jinkakusha*) – or, in the Confucian idiom, "superior gentlemen" (*kunshi*) – needed to "shepherd the people" (*bokumin*) toward a restoration of proper governance in line with Japan's national essence. Although he served as a leading ideologue to bureaucratic reformers of the early 1930s, by the end of the decade Yasuoka opposed the more radical political reform championed by advocates of the Imperial Rule Assistance Association (Taisei Yokusan-kai). Likewise, when confronted with Japan's military defeat, he sought to facilitate preservation of the *kokutai* ("national polity") by revising the emperor's Imperial Rescript on Surrender of 15 August 1945 to cast the monarch's decision as an act of benevolent intervention. Beginning in the late 1940s, Yasuoka rebounded from purge by American occupation authorities to become a spiritual mentor to postwar prime ministers and businessmen, ultimately bequeathing a symbol of his conservative concern for political stability to later generations through his choice of the reign name Heisei ("Realized Peace"). Nonetheless, despite Yasuoka's presence next to those in power during both the prewar and postwar eras, historians have devoted remarkably little attention to trying to understand his thought and activities.[9]

Educated both in the Confucian classics and within the Neo-Kantian environs of the Taishō era (1912–26) higher schools, Yasuoka developed a nationalist message incorporating the Confucian's focus on moral self-cultivation with the Neo-Kantian's interest in cultural authenticity. Combining Confucianism's axiomatic concern for proper governance with a nativist faith in the centrality of Japan's imperial house, he invoked the Kingly Way for the first time while participating in the ideological and political activities of the post-World War I nationalist movement. Yasuoka thus appropriated Confucian idioms to articulate his vision of virtuous rule *within* Japan, as well as without, and first did so nearly a decade prior to the creation of Manchukuo. As Japan's efforts to establish regional hegemony led first to war with China and then with the Western powers, Yasuoka continued to employ his discourse on Japan's Kingly Way, his knowledge of China's dynastic history, and his message of Japanese moral self-cultivation in order to articulate a singular "manifest destiny" for Japan to realize on the world stage. In doing so, he revealed an intriguing mix of nationalist self-righteousness and moralistic self-censure. The latter impulse, however, did not lead Yasuoka to fundamentally reconsider his faith in the virtue of Japan's self-ordained duty to lead Asia, stubbornness exemplified well in his relatively mainstream views on how to negotiate an end to the war with China, and emblematic in general of ideologies of national mission.

The Kingly Way as Imperial Way

The Manchurian Incident of September 1931, occurring against a backdrop of economic depression and political uncertainty, convinced many Japanese that they had entered a "period of crisis" (*hijōji*) requiring a new departure in both domestic politics and foreign relations. Domestically, this approach manifested itself in a shift in political power from party politicians to civilian and military technocrats. In the realm of foreign affairs, the creation of Manchukuo in early 1932 and Japan's subsequent withdrawal from the League of Nations energized those dissatisfied with the Washington order's approach to international relations in East Asia. Along with desiring a new foreign policy, these individuals sought a "renovation" (*kakushin*) of the ideological premises that would support such a departure.

It was in seeking to explain this new approach that terms such as *ōdō* and *ōdō rakudo* ("a peaceful land governed by the Kingly Way") became ubiquitous in the discourse on Manchuria. The Shibun-kai (Confucianist Society), for example, quickly put out a special edition touting the Kingly Way as the appropriate political ideal for the newly created state of Manchukuo.[10] Nonetheless, the utilization of this particular Confucian ideal was not without precedent. Indeed, one finds the Kingly Way invoked within pan-Asian discourse as early as the Meiji period (1868–1912). For example, Lieutenant General Ishiwara Kanji (1889–1949), a leading conspirator in the Manchurian Incident and well-known advocate of the Kingly Way, was first exposed to the concept much earlier in his career through contacts with a disgruntled former China hand and diplomat named Nanbu Jirō (1835–1912).[11] In 1883, influenced by late Tokugawa arguments for Asian cooperation against Western imperialism, Nanbu had conspired to overthrow the Qing government, thereby facilitating a moral revival in China and a Sino-Japanese "union of culture and progress" that would lead to "the renovation and independence of all Asia."[12] While Nanbu's activities ended his career in the Foreign Ministry, during World War I the cabinet of Terauchi Masatake (1852–1919) gave Kingly Way rhetoric an official trial run of sorts when government negotiator Nishihara Kamezō (1873–1953) employed the idiom in an effort to smooth the way for Japan's financial expansion into China.[13] Following the war, the Kingly Way was even offered as an Asian-style idealism appropriate for the international order being restructured in Versailles.[14] Employing the vocabulary of Confucian idealism to give substance to pan-Asian visions of revival and to serve national interests thus was an approach that well predated the creation of Manchukuo.

This fact is further exemplified in the thinking of Yasuoka, who by the early 1920s not only was applying the Kingly Way to his vision of Asian liberation, but also making Confucian ideals of benevolent rule central to his discourse on domestic political reform, the nature of Japan's national polity, and the ultimate realization of Japan's world destiny.[15] The restored Kingly Way envisioned by Yasuoka rested on a Confucian view of personal moral cultivation as indivisibly linked to the realization of proper governance. Incorporating Neo-Kantian concerns with personal cultivation and the creation of human value in the realm of culture, his perspective easily extended to encompass a pan-Asian project directed toward a renaissance of "Oriental civilization" (*Tōyō bunmei*) based in knowing oneself as an "Oriental." In the preface to his 1921 survey of famous Chinese philosophers, for example, Yasuoka criticized the Japanese and Chinese for neglecting the common cultural legacy that held the key to realizing both their personal identity and the liberation of Asia from the control of Western powers.[16] The following year, striking a more optimistic note, he lectured on how embracing the limitless vitality of personal character cultivated in accord with Asia's ethnic spirit promised consequences of international significance. The Great War, Yasuoka asserted, demonstrated that the civilization of Europe consisted of "countries in their twilight (*tasogare no kuni*)" and, consequently, heralded an auspicious opportunity for Asians to restore their civilization to its rightful position in the world.[17]

An avid student of the neo-Confucian philosopher Wang Yangming (1472–1528), Yasuoka saw self-cultivation as providing the intuitive insight for political action. Prefacing an essay titled "On the Kingly Way," he wrote that "in original Oriental learning the point is that knowledge is demonstrated through action and action deepens knowledge; as our personal activism is immeasurably deepened, so too is this extended from the individual to the state and beyond."[18] While modern learning may have departed from this truth, he argued, his goal would be "to bring forth learning originating in personal character."[19] Yasuoka's reading of Wang Yangming played a key role in shaping his understanding of human cultivation as the foundation for personal activism, and resulted in his devoting an entire book to the Ming philosopher and gaining some recognition as an expert on Wang's style of neo-Confucianism.[20] Commenting on his attraction to Wang's thought, Yasuoka contrasted its "true human learning" with the rationalized, mechanistic outlook and "cold learning" of the modern world, perceiving in Wang's ideas "learning that pulsates with complete character" and that conveyed to the human spirit a "grand vitality."[21] In publishing his study, Yasuoka professed hope that Wang's "philosophy of personal character," imbued with the means for "grasping and establishing a self-aware existence," would serve to spur a revival of the "Oriental spirit."[22]

For Yasuoka, establishing a properly self-aware existence required embracing cultural identity and the state in the pursuit of realizing a "boundless idealism" that would counteract the destructive effects of modern materialism. Following this axiom would produce creative individuals cultivated in their natural, true culture (*shin no bunka*), which for the Japanese meant embracing and living according to the Way of the Gods. The properly governed state, in turn, would reflect this cultural legacy and be animated by the vital ethnic energy of its populace. Moreover, Yasuoka wrote, "just as people are divided between superior gentlemen (*kunshi*) and men of small caliber (*shōjin*), countries can be distinguished as cultured and uncultured (*ka'i no ben*)."[23] He identified an uncultured country as one that wantonly pursued materialism and the accumulation of coercive power, thereby becoming just another aggressive state within the brutish arena of international affairs. Yasuoka argued that such an approach, being based solely on materialism and economic self-interest, could never provide the powers of discernment needed for realizing pure idealism and creating a cultured nation. In contrast, a cultured nation was one that mastered the Way, exhibited true culture, and extended a humanistic spirit throughout international society.[24]

Having linked his definition of the Kingly Way to the cultivation of ethnic identity and the creation of an idealistic state, Yasuoka then discussed military preparedness, political life, and education with an eye toward "putting the ideals of the state into practice."[25] While nominally critical of great power competition rooted in self-interest, Yasuoka in no way rejected the possession and use of military force. A country cultivated in the Way, he argued, would necessarily employ military force in the same righteous manner as would an exemplar of *bushidō* – "The Way of the Warrior." Rather than erecting a bastion of militarism (*gunkokushugi*), a powerful yet cultured people would instead create a state exhibiting respect for the virtues of the military arts (*shōbu-teki kokka*). Yasuoka believed that Japan was such a country, and that so long as the Japanese adhered to the Way, they would employ violence only in pursuit of virtuous goals. In this sense, he continued, the principled benevolence of the Kingly Way could also encompass and direct a righteous yet composed anger at injustice and despotism. Even a cultured and just country, therefore, had to ready itself for those occasions when force was required. In this sense, Japan should be as the true samurai, meaning one who did not seek violence yet nonetheless prepared body and soul for that eventuality.[26]

The political ideal of the Kingly Way, however, does not center on the use of force, but rather stresses the persuasive influence of the virtuous ruler and his ministers upon the people. Valuing modern political science over true political philosophy, Yasuoka argued, those of the contemporary world had little awareness of the need for experiencing Heaven's "absolute luminous virtue" (*zettai-teki naru meitoku*) as the basis for governing one's desires and moral consciousness. Proper governance would guide each individual back to this principle and thereby foster a harmonious and unified political consciousness, one that elicited reverence (*kei*) from each individual.[27] Yasuoka identified the individual who embodied "absolute luminous virtue," together with political sovereignty, as being the ruler (*Tenshi*, or "Son of Heaven") who unified the essence of the state with the individual and Heaven. In Japan's case, this profound virtue (*gentoku*) resided in the sacred and inviolable emperor (*Tennō*). However, rather than use this premise to call for direct rule by the emperor, as was common for some members of the right wing, Yasuoka argued that the political realization of imperial virtue depended on those officials who actually governed. In order to advise the ruler and guide the people properly, these ministers and bureaucrats needed to be "men of talent" (*jinzai*) who also understood and embraced their moral responsibilities as the emperor's officials. While identifying this approach to governance as a conviction that united the Orient, Yasuoka nevertheless saw an analog in the words of Italian republican revolutionary Giuseppe Mazzini (1805–72) who, he wrote, explained democracy as "the progress of all, through all, under the leading of the best and wisest."[28] Although Yasuoka rejected popular democracy as inappropriate to Japan's *kokutai*, he perceived in these words recognition of the rightful role to be played by men of character who would stand above and guide the masses. Such a moral elite, he believed, was necessary to the smooth functioning of any properly governed society.

One of the primary tasks Yasuoka assigned to this upright officialdom was the prevention of revolution (*kakumei*) through continual renewal or restoration (*ishin*) of the Way. If the country diverged from recognition of the ruler's virtue – an inherent part of its cultural essence – then revolution became possible and the dynasty was thereby threatened. In the philosophical home of the Kingly Way, China, "revolution meant dynastic change" (*kakumei wa sunawachi ekisei de atta*).[29] In Europe and the United States, monarchy and republicanism had given rise to a chaotic society wherein people and ruler stood at odds. In contrast, Yasuoka wrote:

> there is only one country where revolution never results in dynastic change, only one country where revolution resides in imperial virtue and where perpetual vitality is renewed, and that is our Japan.[30]

Nor, he believed, were the Japanese estranged yet from their sovereign. However, like many nationalists and conservatives, Yasuoka perceived the years following World War I as a time of peril:

In the fifty-eight years since the Restoration, now is definitely the time for deep political reflection. If we wish to avoid the sight of revolution before our very eyes, then we had better become strong advocates of the Kingly Way immediately![31]

A central goal of proper governance was thus to prevent revolution through the fostering of perpetual renewal that reaffirmed the centrality of the imperial house and the indispensable role of those officials who advised the ruler, administered the state, and shepherded the people.

While military preparedness and correct top-down governance in line with Japan's national essence provided the normative state structure after which to aspire, Yasuoka emphasized that the key to renewing the Kingly Way lay in proper education, meaning learning that concentrated on cultivating a correct self-awareness of this ethnic essence. Referring again to Mazzini, Yasuoka noted approvingly the Italian nationalist's identification of education as the life of the state, adding that this was a truth long recognized in East Asia, where traditionally "nothing was viewed as more important to the Kingly Way than education." After all, Yasuoka was fond of noting, one need only refer to the first line of *The Mean*, which reads, "What Heaven has endowed is called the nature. Following the nature is called the Way. Cultivating the Way is called education."[32]

Elaborating on this connection between personal cultivation and the state, Yasuoka argued that because those involved in education were responsible for fostering the moral character of their charges, "even more so than politicians and soldiers they must be superior patriots deeply cultivated in the Way."[33] Moreover, their goal should lie not in mere instruction, but rather in cultivating in the hearts-and-minds of youth an idealistic spirit. Consequently, a reformed education system would train teachers capable of mentoring idealism and moral character. Yasuoka believed this was necessary because, in contrast to earlier generations of youth who possessed creative power, purity, and reflexive insight into truth, students graduating from the contemporary education system "lacked ideals and moral cultivation (*murisō-mushūyō*)," and the potential consequences of this were serious:

People educated in this fashion naturally only perceive what is shallow and cannot discern the Way. They cannot understand the Way and therefore cannot follow nature, do not know Heaven. Thus individuals lack in morality and religion, while for the state military preparedness, governance, and education collapse, the Kingly Way is lost, and loyalty to the emperor declines. ... One who steps forward today and devotes himself to the Way can truly save Japan and redeem the world. What I wish for is a return to the Way and the instilling of the Three Mainstays and Five Constant Virtues (*kōjō*)! Experience the Japanese spirit and assist in the Kingly Way of restoration (*ishin no ōdō o yokusan seyo*)![34]

The origins of Yasuoka's discourse on the Kingly Way thus lay in the domestic political and ideological conditions of Taishō Japan, a period he perceived as characterized by both a decline in moral character and a heightened threat of political revolution. As the 1920s progressed, Yasuoka developed these ideas further in league with patrons and political allies at court and within the bureaucracy, emerging as a leading ideologue intent on defending the emperor-centered state and the prerogatives of non-party officials in an age of mass politics.

Accordingly, Yasuoka was well prepared to contribute to the rapid expansion of Kingly Way discourse that characterized the years following the Manchurian Incident. Indeed, the sudden convergence between foreign policy crisis and domestic political competition was clearly evident in his Kokui-kai (National Mainstay Society). Growing out of Yasuoka's efforts to spread moral reform and cultivation (*kyōka-shūyō*) through his private academy, the Kinkei Gakuin (Golden Pheasant Academy), the Kokui-kai served as a leading forum for attacking the supposed ineptitude of party-led governments and helped to staff the first "national unity cabinets" of the early 1930s.[35] However, while known primarily for its role in these domestic political struggles, the society concurrently championed a pan-Asian approach to foreign relations, with members welcoming the creation of Manchukuo as a first step toward re-ordering Japan's ties with Asia and the Western powers. Combating communism and weakening Western influence, they asserted, would allow for the establishing of an "international Shōwa," meaning in essence an East Asia governed in line with Confucian principles and Japanese ambitions.[36] Trustee Konoe Fumimaro (1891–1945), for example, used the society's newsletter to repeat his critique of the Washington order as merely a vehicle for perpetuating Anglo-American hegemony and to offer the Kingly Way as an alternative principle upon which to base Japan's foreign relations.[37] Indeed, the main thrust of the society's foreign policy writing highlighted the need for Japanese moral and cultural leadership in fostering a new order. Since it was believed that the best policies would flow from a fuller understanding of the thought, character, and emotions of Manchurians, a central component of this vision of a morally re-centered foreign policy was the need for facilitating greater cultural exchange between the Japanese and other Asians. With this in mind, society trustee Okabe Nagakage (1884–1970), later Education Minister in the cabinet of General Tōjō Hideki, championed the Nichi-Man Bunka Kyōkai (Japan–Manchuria Cultural Cooperation Society), which was established by the Foreign Ministry in October 1933.[38]

A notable trait of ideologies of national mission, however, seems to be the manner in which national self-interest and faith in the ultimately beneficial character of the actions of one's own country can render both ideologue and policymaker alike incapable of the compromise necessary for such mutual cooperation. In Yasuoka and his patrons one can already see the blinkered approach to other Asians that would mark Japan's foreign policy in the decade ahead. The way in which belief in their country's "destiny" to lead East Asia functioned among the "best and wisest" of the Kokui-kai is exemplified well in the perspective of its founder. In an article entitled "Considering Manchuria," for example, Yasuoka criticized the arrogance of many Japanese toward the inhabitants of Manchuria, pointing out the natural hostility such behavior engendered.[39] In a separate piece, he also chided Japanese for defending their country's actions in terms of crass self-interest and special rights, rather than emphasizing how Japan was laying her national destiny on the line in a moral and righteous cause.[40] However, this apparent sensitivity to the sensibilities of other Asians and willingness to hold Japanese to an idealized moral standard existed in constant tension with, and generally was countervailed by, a firm faith in the justice and necessity of the Japanese destiny to be first among Asians. Rather than call this providence into question, Yasuoka would argue repeatedly in the years ahead that the key to overcoming intra-Asian frictions lay in reforming Japanese moral character and thereby exhibiting the principled behavior that would persuade other Asians to cooperate in the creation of a Greater East Asia.

In the wake of the Manchurian Incident, Yasuoka contributed further to this vision of benevolent leadership with a compilation of writings entitled *Oriental Political Philosophy: Studies in the Kingly Way*.[41] Bridging domestic and foreign affairs, he argued that the fundamental issue facing Japan at this pivotal moment was inculcating leaders with "belief in the Orient's political ethics of ruler and minister, and in the sublime and grand principles of the Kingly Way."[42] The details of policymaking and administration were, he proposed, secondary matters, particularly when one considered Japan's regional obligations and "the prospects for a Manchurian state established on the model of Kingly Way governance."[43] What mattered was bringing about peace and stability by cultivating the people and raising them to a more noble personal existence. Whether in Manchuria or in Japan, Yasuoka argued, politics was about cultivating and teaching the people for, as pointed out by Chinese historian Sima Guang (1019–86), "moral guidance is the urgent affair of the state (*kyōka wa kokka no kyūmu nari*)."[44]

Reliance on the texts of Chinese philosophical tradition did not prevent Yasuoka from making Japan the preeminent standard bearer of virtuous governance. Reiterating a point made a decade earlier in "On the Kingly Way," he argued that, while a product of Chinese political thought, that land's fractious and revolution-prone national polity had prevented the actual realization of these sublime ideals. Therefore, what China had experienced in practice was rule by despots (*hasha*), rather than benevolent kings (*ōsha*). Nonetheless, this political philosophy retained its universal relevance, and the most fertile soil for realizing this ideal had proven to be that of Japan, where a pure polity centered on the unbroken rule of the imperial dynasty brought forth the true Kingly Way, which Yasuoka identified with the Imperial Way (*kōdō*).[45]

This reliance on Chinese thought to define Japan's Kingly Way implicates a larger debate among ideologues of the period. During the course of the 1930s, the exact nature of the relationship between the ideas of the Kingly Way and the Imperial Way became a point of controversy among nationalist ideologues. As ruminations on the qualities of Japan's national polity intensified, some theorists sought to affirm the inviolable purity of the Imperial Way by rejecting any association with the presumably alien Kingly Way, whereas others denied any need to draw such a stark philosophical line between China and Japan. Satomi Kishio (1897–1974), for example, a close advisor to Ishiwara Kanji, shared Yasuoka's view that Japan's Imperial Way was a superior version of the Kingly Way theorized in Chinese Confucianism.[46] Likewise, Satomi's position received approving notice from Nakayama Hitoshi, an associate of Yasuoka and a professor at Manchuria Foundation University (*Manshū Kenkoku Daigaku*).[47]

Other nationalists, however, recoiled at the idea of the Imperial Way being anything other than *sui generis* and heaped scorn on those who dared to place Japan's *kokutai* in comparative context. A prime example of this perspective was provided by Professor Minoda Muneki (1894–1946), perhaps best known for his attacks on constitutional scholar Minobe Tatsukichi (1873–1948), Sinologist Tsuda Sōkichi (1873–1961), and colonial theorist Yanaihara Tadao (1893–1961). Minoda, however, was by no means averse to targeting other rightists and he criticized Yasuoka for, among other sins, utilizing foreign thought and focusing on the role of the emperor's officials, rather than of the emperor himself. For his part, Yasuoka took pains to distinguish his brand of Japanism from that of other theorists, whom he portrayed as simple-minded and anti-foreign chauvinists.[48]

While a firm believer in the sanctity and uniqueness of the imperial institution, Yasuoka's thought was too heavily indebted to Chinese political philosophy and its Japanese variants to embrace the idea of an Imperial Way entirely divorced from foreign insights. Rather, the attributes of the Kingly Way as articulated in Confucian thought became representative of East Asian political philosophy in general. Similarly, in a manner reminiscent of the way in which the Confucian and samurai theorist Yamaga Sokō (1622–85) identified Japan, rather than China, as the Central Efflorescence (*chūka*), Yasuoka affirmed the superiority of the Japanese polity through its supposed ability to exemplify the virtues of the Kingly Way in a manner superior to that of China itself. As Yasuoka explained in a 1933 speech at the Japan Youth Hall:

> it is in Japan that the Kingly Way is being most nearly carried out; the most unalloyed example of the Kingly Way is the Imperial Way.[49]

Japan's Imperial Way thus became "the highest example of Oriental philosophy," rather than the incomparable expression of Japanese uniqueness. Moreover, he proclaimed, being blessed with the truest version of the Kingly Way obligated Japan with a national mission to employ this virtuous vision in order to reform the contemporary world's materialistic civilization.[50]

Specifically, fulfilling this obligation meant extending righteous governance to the rest of Asia. Writing on "The Kingly Way Principles of Governing Manchuria," Yasuoka rationalized the creation of Manchukuo by arguing that the Japanese, in seeking to realize their particular national mission, were simply engaging in what all countries do – projecting their values and nationalism to be the basis for international order. After all, he protested, did not Europeans and Americans portray their morality as representing humanity and their nationalism as constituting internationalism? Did not the Russians seek to use communism to remold the world in their image? Why, he asked, should Japanese be any different?[51]

In fact, Yasuoka continued, they were not, for the Japanese indeed possessed their particular "divine" guiding moral force. Moreover, they were linked to the region of their ambitions by historical bonds of race and civilization:

> The Japanese people radiate this vitality and they burn with this principle. Is it not natural and inevitable that geographically, historically, [and] racially, they would seek to extend that virtuous influence to the East Asian region with which they have the deepest ties?[52]

What is more, he determined, while the Japanese may share the ideal of national mission with others, they were in fact in a position to engage in a mission that would transcend simple aggressive expansion. Again echoing his 1924 essay on the Kingly Way, he asserted that while military expansion by an uncultured people would end in simple "violent aggression," the principles of Heaven and "true ethnic-national development" (*shin no minzoku-teki hatten*) sometimes necessitated action to "spread virtue" and to realize "true culture."[53] So long as they avoided the trap of relying upon force alone and recognized that ultimate success hinged upon the implementation of rule that transformed and pacified the people, Yasuoka concluded, the Japanese were in a position to create a virtuous new order in East Asia. The key, he cautioned, was that "the military force of the emperor's soldiers must not be of the Despotic Way – it must be of the Kingly Way."[54]

Thus, the same principles of rule that applied to domestic restoration were applicable to expansion on the continent, during which Japan's "patriotic and benevolent gentlemen" (*shishi-jinjin*) would offer moral guidance, encourage an air of principle, clarify rewards and punishments, warn against the spread of shallow culture, and cultivate purity and simplicity among the masses. In either location, the tenets of principled governance centered on guidance of the people in accordance with the Way, instruction of the people through virtue, and provision for the welfare of the people through the meritorious deeds of men of talent. Together these three tenets comprised benevolent rule and stood in contrast to rule through force, a fourth approach and one guaranteed to bring forth discord.[55] In essence, Yasuoka applied his ideal of domestic governance by a moral elite who "shepherd the people" to Japan's relations with the rest of Asia. In the foreign arena, however, all Japanese were to assume the burden of "shepherding" their Asian brethren toward the ethnic self-awareness and political restoration needed to put an end to Western domination, realize an Asian renaissance, and restore proper equilibrium between East and West.

"Dismounting to rule" and Japanese self-cultivation

When fighting broke out between Japanese and Chinese forces in July 1937, Yasuoka responded by approving of Japan's actions while calling for correct "kingly" behavior on the field of battle until order could be restored.[56] Providing a quick and apologetic historical retrospective, he assigned responsibility for the first Sino-Japanese War of 1894–95 to the Qing court for seeking to prevent Japan from turning Korea into a modern and independent nation, and determined the subsequent annexation of Korea by Japan to have been an unavoidable step taken for the greater good of East Asia. Seeing a similar dynamic at work in Manchuria, he portrayed the Japanese as rescuing the Manchurians from the depredations of a failed Chinese republican revolution. Japan's ultimate goal in North China, he concluded, should be similarly "kingly" and directed toward enforcing order and establishing stability, with force to be employed solely "for the purpose of waiting for and establishing ties with a new ruler."[57] While seeking Chinese acquiescence to a Japanese-led new order, Yasuoka relied on Confucian ideals of virtuous governance as the preferred method for restoring peace and stability, a position he supported with his reading of China's dynastic histories. The war thus served to heighten his belief in the need for the Japanese to become moral exemplars capable of persuading other Asians of the righteousness of Japan's wartime mission.

During the earliest stages of the fighting, Yasuoka called for the re-establishment of peaceful relations with China, benevolent rule in Manchuria, the eradication of communist machinations, and greater cultural exchange between the Japanese and Chinese.[58] As the fighting intensified, however, he identified the Guomingdang (GMD) of Chiang Kai-shek (Jiang Jieshi, 1887–1975) as Westernized, oppressive, and estranged from the Chinese masses. Ironically, the GMD thus came to share something with its enemy, the Chinese Communist Party (CCP), which the stridently anti-communist Yasuoka cast as the product of an alien and artificial modernism. However, in a fashion unthinkable regarding the CCP, he held out some hope for the GMD, or at least for GMD-associated elites, postulating that "the thorough shock" of the current conflict and concurrent spread of disorder might combine to bring forth "true Chinese men of character" who would see the wisdom of cooperating with their Japanese counterparts.[59] As with his earlier writing on Manchuria, Yasuoka claimed that so long as Japan's actions flowed from its ethnic vitality the result would not be aggression but the extension of imperial virtue, the fostering of Asian cultural renewal, and the blunting of the communist "red peril." Thus, while condemning the fighting as bad for East Asia, he affirmed Japan's "righteous cause" (*taigi*) and essentially placed the burden for making peace on the Chinese.[60]

Meanwhile, Japan's leaders split between those who saw an opportunity for settling the "China problem" through military victory and those who, for various reasons, favored a rapid peace settlement. Yasuoka lent his voice to the latter group, criticizing those Japanese who argued that the current conflict would be resolved with the occupation of Shanghai or Nanjing. What was necessary for achieving Japan's objectives, he countered, was to spread "the light of the Kingly Way" to the Chinese masses, a task that required more than merely toppling China's warlords.[61] To underscore the futility of relying on military force alone, Yasuoka pointed out that while the Chinese may have failed to realize the Kingly Way, they nonetheless possessed a fearsomely vital ethnic spirit best exemplified by the endurance of Chinese culture. Although it was true that China had been conquered repeatedly, in the end the conquerors either left or adopted Chinese ways. While averring that the Chinese would be foolish to continue the war in the expectation that the Japanese, too, could be defeated or Sinicized, he also cautioned that the Japanese would be equally foolish to think that force alone could resolve the current crisis.[62]

Yasuoka employed Chinese dynastic history to bolster his case further and to provide edifying models for Japanese political leaders. In October 1937, for instance, he offered the approach of Kangxi (1654–1722), the second Manchu ruler of the Qing Dynasty, as an example of how to pacify China.[63] While the Han Chinese viewed the Manchu as foreign usurpers, Kangxi was able to assuage Chinese officialdom by utilizing Confucian ideals of proper governance and by putting the literati to work bolstering the study of the classics. Here, Yasuoka wrote, was a "reference source for Japan's China policy," which should also focus on ideas and culture in order to formulate an effective "thought policy" (*shisō taisaku*).[64] Moreover, he concluded, successfully applying the lessons of China's past would permit Japan to complete the revolution botched by the republican and nationalist governments.[65] In this way, the Japanese would guide the Chinese to the realization of a new China based in the principles of the Kingly Way but realized within Japan's New Order for East Asia. Likewise, in a speech given the following year before the Japanese Foreign Policy Association, Yasuoka again discussed the need to revisit the great ministers of Chinese dynastic history and, echoing the point made by a Confucian advisor to the founder of the Former Han Dynasty (202–8 BCE), admonished his audience that "while it is necessary to take the realm from horseback, the realm cannot be ruled from horseback."[66]

The war in China and his vision of virtuous governance also spurred Yasuoka to even greater concern with driving home the point that successfully "dismounting to rule" required that the Japanese embrace their own ethnically self-aware style of moral self-cultivation. In order to create a New Order in East Asia, he argued, properly cultivated Japanese of character and ability needed to appear and persuade the Chinese of the justness of such an endeavor. In an article from December 1937, for example, Yasuoka called for men of talent and character to step forward and assist in implementing proper governance, asserting that their success or failure in accomplishing this goal would decide Japan's fate for a century to come. Therefore, he continued:

> [w]hat Japan needs at this time – more than material and more than wealth – is people; promising men of talent (*jinzai*). In due course, the China Incident will likely become the East Asia Incident. The need for men of talent is limitless: those gifted with speech, those who can write, experts in industry and business, insightful men of morality, learning, and ability suitable for shepherding the people (*bokumin ni teki-suru gakutoku-saishiki aru mono*), educators, men of religion, artists, doctors … the list is endless. In any case, from masters of every conceivable field to men of superior moral character (*taijin-kunshi*), we require an endless number of great men.[67]

Not only did this brief essay encapsulate concisely a central point of continuity within Yasuoka's prescription for realizing both domestic restoration and international destiny in accord with the Kingly Way, it previewed well his primary concern when discussing what war demanded of his fellow Japanese.

Eight months later Yasuoka expounded in greater detail on the imperative of restoring Japanese self-cultivation in the service of the New Order. Speaking before a "moral cultivation group" (*shūyōkai*) on "The Future of Self-Cultivation as Revealed by the China Incident," he reiterated that no problem facing Japan was more important than the issue of self-cultivation (*kyōyō mondai*).[68] Since the Meiji period, Yasuoka wrote, the Japanese had been educated increasingly in the ways of Western civilization. Yet it was cultivation in East Asian learning, he argued, that would decide Japan's fate in the wake of the Manchurian and China Incidents. The status quo "mechanistic cultivation" and its socialist, capitalist, and liberal democratic variants, Yasuoka asserted, had produced contemporary Japanese who were utilitarian and calculating, and who lacked the spirit of self-sacrifice for the state that had characterized their ancestors.[69] Therefore, he concluded, "as Japanese venture forth to confront the current crisis" and to implement proper governance on the continent, it was imperative there be implemented at home "a grand renovation in the self-cultivation of the Japanese."[70]

Yasuoka's concern with the consequences of failing to revitalize Japan's ethnic spirit and to imbue the Japanese with the proper style of self-cultivation was not limited to Japan's relations with China but, once war spread to the Pacific, carried over to the larger goal of realizing the Greater East Asia Co-Prosperity Sphere. Speaking before the Japan Industrial Club in the summer of 1942, Yasuoka pondered the prospects of the Japanese successfully emerging as the leaders of Greater East Asia.[71] Fate, he determined, had made it Japan's destiny to govern "one billion" Asians and, consequently, the Japanese were faced with one of two possibilities. Either they would harmoniously integrate these different ethnic peoples (*iminzoku*) under Japanese leadership or they would find themselves faced with growing resentment and ill will. In China and Manchuria, he lamented, there were signs that it was the latter pheno-menon that was occurring. Indeed, as a consequence of boorish Japanese behavior, there was palpable hostility toward the Japanese and virtually no mixing of populations: Chinese were with Chinese, Koreans were with Koreans, and Japanese were with Japanese. To underscore his point, Yasuoka recounted several examples before cautioning his audience that Japanese should imbibe a serious lesson from such tales.[72] Rather than conveying a need to rethink the "righteousness" of Japan's pan-Asian mission, however, for Yasuoka the warning to be heeded centered yet again on how poor moral character and uncouth behavior threatened to undermine Greater East Asia. Consequently, he reiterated that successful realization of their national destiny required that the Japanese possess the "self-cultivation and magnanimity of a superior people."[73] So long as they lacked these qualities, Yasuoka warned, Japanese would be unable to harmonize with and thereby successfully lead other peoples. "Through education," he concluded, "Japanese must limit-lessly cultivate grand virtue. This issue will decide Japan's fate. If this is not done, I see Japan's expansion as Japan's peril."[74]

Meanwhile, Yasuoka's Kingly Way idealism carried over into his involve-ment in the behind-the-scenes efforts of certain Japanese and Chinese to negotiate an end to the fighting in China. Despite the January 1938 statement by Prime Minister Konoe Fumimaro that Japan would have nothing more to do with Chiang Kai-shek's GMD, within months members of the Japanese government were meeting secretly with Chiang's representatives in an effort to arrange a truce. However, these discussions and Yasuoka's role in them are emblematic of the inability of Japanese officials to compromise either their objectives or sense of mission in order to pursue meaningful negotiations with their Chinese counterparts. Indeed, the evidence suggests that Japanese representatives endeavored primarily to elicit the defection of Chinese officials as a step toward creating a new Chinese government willing to cooperate with Japan's prospective New Order.[75]

The inability, or unwillingness, of even mainstream Japanese leaders to seriously compromise in pursuit of peaceful resolution to the conflict is reflected in a key letter used in the negotiations. Although long attributed to Major General Kagesa Sadaaki (1893–1948), one of the army's China hands and a key figure in the talks, the testimony of Kagesa's subordinate, Colonel Iwakuro Hideo (1897–1970), identifies the correspondence as actually having been written by Yasuoka at the request of Konoe.[76] The letter's offering of a peace mission by an obscure Song Dynasty official named Wang Lun as an example for contemporary Chinese officials to follow further bolsters the case for Yasuoka's authorship, for he repeatedly employed the example of Wang in published writings from this period. Contemporary conditions, Yasuoka asserted, required Chiang Kai-shek or Wang Ching-wei (Wang Jingwei, 1883–1944) to step forward as a great statesman, restore harmonious rule, repudiate the machinations of the Anglo-American powers, destroy the Chinese communist forces, and join hands with Japan for the benefit of

Greater East Asia.[77] The letter itself, while conceding that the Konoe cabinet's earlier refusal to recognize the legitimacy of the GMD was "unfortunate," called on the Chinese and Japanese "to embrace each other nakedly" and restore a relationship based on trust and honor. In particular, the Chinese were implored to place their faith wholeheartedly in Japan, an act that would supposedly result in the Japanese, with their *bushidō* tradition of honor, responding in a manner such that "conditions would work themselves out."[78]

Yasuoka's case for making peace thus depended largely upon Chinese recognition of Japanese sincerity and the ultimate propriety of Japan's strategic objectives. Although at the time he called for either Chiang Kai-shek or Wang Ching-wei to take the initiative, in the late 1960s, when confirming his role and intent in writing the letter, Yasuoka identified Wang as the real target of his entreaty. If so, then the ultimate goal was not to negotiate peace with Chiang but rather to entice Wang to defect and establish a new regime friendly to Japan.[79] In short, the essential qualification required of any contemporary "Wang Lun" centered on capitulation to Japan's "manifest destiny" to oversee a New Order in East Asia. Indeed, even after the war turned decidedly against Japan, Yasuoka continued clinging to the possibility of "kingly" behavior eliciting Chinese acquiescence to the Greater East Asia Co-Prosperity Sphere. In late 1944, for example, Yasuoka enclosed in a letter to former Imperial Household Vice-Minister Sekiya Teizaburō (1875–1950) a "Straightforward Plan for Dealing with the China Incident" calling for the implementation of a wide-ranging "national campaign to rescue China (*Shina kyūkoku minzoku undō*)" that would convince the Chinese of the sincerity of Japanese attempts to end American meddling and prevent the spread of Soviet-inspired communism.[80]

Although Yasuoka directed much of his attention toward China and Japan's position on the continent, he was by no means unconcerned with the potential implications of Japan's national mission within the context of the global strategic situation. For just as his discourse on the Kingly Way extended from the self to the state, the consequences of realizing benevolent rule in Asia necessarily reached beyond the region itself. Writing as war broke out in Europe, he noted that the world was split between rival ideological camps, with Germany and Italy implementing totalitarianism and authoritarianism. Meanwhile, the British, Americans, and French were championing individualism, liberalism, and democracy, while working to recruit other nations into a united front to oppose the aggression of the totalitarian powers.[81] Pondering this confrontation, Yasuoka asked rhetorically whether there was no country among the major powers that could transcend this ideological rift and rescue the pitiable small nations caught in the middle. Such an exceptional country, he judged, would require "superior leaders" buttressed by exceptional ethnic qualities. Americans, he continued, "flatter themselves" that they comprise such a nation, a form of hubris clearly visible in the speeches of President Franklin D. Roosevelt (1882–1945). However, Yasuoka noted, the United States was a member of the democratic camp of nations and, while the

Americans held decisive power over the outcome of the clash between England and Germany, the nation of Wilson and the Versailles conference could not possibly bring about world peace.

There was but one country, Yasuoka hastened to add, capable of fulfilling this role, one country that could transcend this rivalry between the great powers. Japanese, he wrote, comprised the one nation that "possessed the blessed environs and [ethnic] endowment for leading the world to true peace."[82] Consequently, it was up to the Japanese to draw on their cultural endowment, on *bushidō*, and on the Way of the Gods (*kamunagara no michi*) in order to live up to expectations by bearing this "global divine mandate (*sekai-teki shinmei*)."[83] In order to make this mandate manifest, Yasuoka urged, Japanese statesmen must purge their inferiority complex *vis-à-vis* the West and its civilization without succumbing to national chauvinism. Neither the tendency toward exaggerated self-deprecation that emerged during the years of Meiji and Taishō nor the blustery overcompensation on the rise since the Manchurian Incident, he warned, was conducive to the Japanese realizing their proper place in the world. Henceforth, he proclaimed, the Japanese must act according to their "highest humanistic ideals," which for them meant worshiping the Sun Goddess, elucidating the Kingly Way, and preaching the Imperial Way. "One can say," Yasuoka wrote, "that the world is approaching a grand turning point and, for the first time, Japan constitutes a valiant and prominent presence – are we prepared?"[84] If so, the Japanese had a contribution to make to world civilization. For in contrast to the Meiji period, Yasuoka concluded, this time it was the Western peoples (*Seiyō minzoku*) who were in a predicament and "the Japanese *minzoku* must as quickly as possible lead [them] toward correct salvation, [and] make rousing efforts to bring them into harmony with the Way."[85] In sum, for the current war to be more than a dangerous exercise in self-interested aggression – for it to be a "Holy War" – it had to be animated by the virtuous idealism of Japan's Kingly Way.[86]

Conclusion

Yasuoka's Kingly Way discourse demonstrates how the prewar ideal of virtuous rule was not necessarily simply an off-the-shelf solution to the problem of rationalizing Japan's puppet regime in Manchuria. While quite useful for validating both the creation of Manchukuo and the pursuit of larger pan-Asian ambitions, the particular version of the Kingly Way preached by Yasuoka – together with the Confucian-derived doctrines of self-cultivation and proper governance that informed his thinking – bears significant value for the understanding of modern Japan and Pan-Asianism. By limiting their attention to the convenient role played by Confucian ideals in rationalizing Manchukuo, historians have too often overlooked how these same principles informed discussion of political reform within Japan and, consequently, have been too quick to dismiss the Kingly Way ideal as merely an artifice hastily constructed for reasons of justifying foreign aggression. Yasuoka's perspective indicates some of the ideas informing this pan-Asian version of national mission are of greater substance and historical significance than such conventional wisdom suggests. For in addition to serving partisan political and national interests, ideals such as those represented with Kingly Way discourse animated and gave substance to domestic debate over the nature of the national polity and infused meaning into Japan's "divine mandate" to lead a renaissance of East Asian civilization.

As with all ideologies of national mission, the differences between the ideal and reality could be stark. Indeed, the divergence between Yasuoka's romantic vision of virtuous rule and the often despotic reality of Japan's "Greater East Asia Co-Prosperity Sphere" was frequently vast, calling to mind the warning of Sinologist Naitō Konan (1866–1934) that whenever someone attempted to implement the Kingly Way the results were the opposite.[87] Likewise, the self-assurance that accompanies the embrace of providence surely helped prevent the possibility of a more measured and truly "co-prosperous" form of Pan-Asiansm. Nonetheless, however one may judge the mix of pan-Asian idealism and self-interested aggression, Yasuoka's case suggests that understanding the path to this denouement requires a fuller comprehension of the ideology of "manifest destiny" helping to drive Japan's quest for a New Order in East Asia.

10 The temporality of empire

The imperial cosmopolitanism of
Miki Kiyoshi and Tanabe Hajime

John Namjun Kim

Introduction

The terms "imperialism" and "colonialism" are often used interchangeably
without further reflection. This is perhaps not surprising given that many
modern imperial projects entailed a colonial component and, conversely,
colonial projects an imperial one. We need to look no further than the British
Empire, the Spanish Empire, or – what is my concern here – the Japanese
Empire to see the historical coincidence of imperialism and colonialism.
However, Robert J. C. Young argues that the two are conceptually distinct
phenomena. Whereas colonialism should be considered principally as a
practice, imperialism should be considered principally as an *ideology*. "Unlike
colonialism," he claims, "imperialism is driven by ideology and a theory of
sorts, in some instances even to the extent that it can operate as much against
purely economic interests as for them."[1] Imperialism, in other words, is not
just the spatial expansion of political power. It is the expansion of an idea.
Though one should doubt if phenomena of imperialism and colonialism can
ever be exhaustively distinguished in terms of their real-world instantiations,
they should nevertheless be analytically distinguished in respect to their
ideological foundations.

If imperialism is principally an ideologically driven phenomenon, then even
those who are far removed from its "actual" practice stand in a relation of
responsibility to its effects. The maintenance of any rigorous distinction
between "practitioners" and mere "theoreticians" becomes impossible when
the question of responsibility is posed within the modern system of producing
and multiplying intellectual power through the instruments of the state. In
this sense, the figure of the philosopher in particular stands in an ethically
precarious position in respect to imperialism. While arguing for the concept
of human freedom, he might contribute to the matrix of ideas animating the
imperialist project of his state. The intellectual labor of a philosopher is as
much subject to imperial mobilization as the common citizen is subject to
military conscription. Put more polemically, the philosophers of imperial
Japan would not even need to leave the comforts of Kyōto in order to

participate in the exertion of force over subjects in regions as far flung as Manchuria or Indonesia. His acts of thinking, writing and teaching alone ensure his participation. The work of the intellectual is never too abstract or too far-removed from the life of this world as to be irrelevant to it or not to exert power over it.

Yet, a charitable reader might defend such a philosopher by asserting that his writings were merely appropriated as political propaganda by others more directly involved in creating the imperial state, or that actual policy-makers misconstrued the essence of his political philosophy. Such objections are always possible – but are also beside the point in respect to the Japanese Empire in particular. Unlike many other imperial projects, the development of this empire was driven by a total-war ideology that sought to mobilize all of the state's subjects.[2] This included philosophers.

In the following I examine the participation of two prominent figures of the so-called Kyōto School of Philosophy, Miki Kiyoshi (1897–1945) and Tanabe Hajime (1885–1962). Though significant philosophical differences lie between them, each produced a theory of subjectivity in defense of the Japanese Empire's expansion. However, contrary to what one might assume, they enact their defense of imperialism by arguing for, paradoxically, the cosmopolitan freedom that imperial subjugation would bring to East Asia. On their view, the project of Japanese imperialism spreads not only horizontally across geographical space but also vertically in historical time. In their respective theories of what one can call "imperial cosmopolitanism," the individual subject only attains subjectivity through a temporal identification with an imagined social totality that *promises* freedom. They recognized that the performative act of identifying with the social body is never spatially immediate but always temporally mediated. In as much as a subject looks to a past to find this body, it hopes for a future promising communion with that body. In this sense, the political theses of Miki and Tanabe unwittingly demonstrate the ethical ambivalence of cosmopolitanism as a real-world possibility. The promise of cosmopolitan freedom does not necessarily preclude political projects such as imperialism or colonialism. On the contrary, this promise mobilizes such political projects of domination by endowing them with a semblance of ethical legitimacy, of winning the approbation of those who will be subjugated. In view of the ethical promise that they make, freedom, and the project in which they participate, imperialism, we are faced not with questions organized by a "why" or a "what," but by a "how": How does a philosophy of cosmopolitan freedom invert into its imagined opposite, a logic of imperial subjugation? How might the formation of the modern state be predicated on the subject as a temporal being, an entity that is never simply "given" but always already thrown and projected in time? Both of these two questions ask a more basic one, namely: how is political theory temporally organized by the practice of imperialism? While the immediate "objects" of discussion in the following are two philosophers of imperial Japan and their "cosmopolitan" projects for East Asia, the scope of problems they present extends to the current concerns on the conjunction of political freedom and imperial domination.

A cosmopolitan East Asia for a new cosmopolitan world

In terms of political commitments, Miki is the more ambivalent of the two figures examined here. Born in 1897 in Hyōgo Prefecture, he first studied philosophy at Kyōto Imperial University under Nishida Kitarō (1870–1945), a neo-Kantian as well as the ostensible founder of modern Japanese philosophy. Studying later under Martin Heidegger (1889–1976) and Hans-Georg Gadamer (1900–2002) in Marburg from 1923–24, Miki developed his anthropological philosophy in an extensive study of the human form in the work of Blaise Pascal in 1925. Upon assuming a professorship in philosophy at Hōsei University in Tōkyō, he turned his attention to Marxist thought and was later briefly imprisoned for his suspected support of the Japanese Communist Party. In his work as a public intellectual, he openly condemned the National Socialists in May 1933 for their anti-Semitism and their racist views in general. In the same month, he spurned Heidegger for joining the National Socialists. However, his staunchly leftist views did not preclude him from joining the Shōwa Research Association (Shōwa Kenkyūkai), an intellectual think-tank for the then prime minister Konoe Fumimaro in 1937.[3] Thus, Miki attained a status that Heidegger sought for himself but never achieved: he became an intellectual architect for his state's political project. For him, the Empire promised not imperial domination but cosmopolitan liberation. That this promise appears absurd in respect to the historical realities of the War does not yet warrant a dismissal of his views. For it is precisely his optimistic philosophical views that demonstrate the ambivalence of modern political philosophy, namely that advancing the concept of "freedom" necessarily entails an implicit or explicit defense of subjugation.

The sense of "cosmopolitanism" relevant to Miki comes from Immanuel Kant's 1795–96 essay *Toward Perpetual Peace*, which he both appropriates and critiques throughout his writings.[4] Contrary to what one might hold, Kant's thesis on cosmopolitanism does not advocate global political unification. Rather, the central facet of Kant's theory of cosmopolitanism is the ethical relation of "hospitality."[5] In the "Third Definitive Article toward Perpetual Peace," Kant writes:

> "Cosmopolitan right shall be limited to the conditions of universal *hospitality*."
>
> Here, as in the preceding articles, the issue is not philanthropy but *right*, and *hospitality* (hospitableness) means the right of a foreigner not to be treated with hostility because of his arrival on the territory of another.[6]

On Kant's view, each subject has the right of shelter in another political community. That political community has, in turn, the obligation to treat a member of another political community as a guest. The ethical relation of hospitality is "cosmopolitan" in the sense that it establishes the basis for a system of rights and obligations between political communities throughout the globe, regardless of geographic location.[7] Simultaneously, however, Kant also condemns European colonialism for exploiting this cosmopolitan right to hospitality, praising "China and Japan" for providing the Dutch with access but not entry.[8] Possessing the right of hospitality only extends, for Kant, to the "right to visit" so that one can present oneself before one's other.[9] In this sense, the highest ethical commitment of any political community ought to be not itself, but the idea of "humanity" as a whole. The consequence of Kant's optimistic view of the ethical possibilities of political relations is a tacit affirmation of the universality of each individual subject: one is as much a member of a particular community as of a universal one, humanity as such. Cosmopolitanism – in one of two senses important for Miki – means an ethical commitment to the idea of the "human" as that which defines universality.

The second salient aspect of Kantian cosmopolitanism for Miki is its temporal structure. Though Kant does not treat the temporality of cosmopolitan ethics explicitly, he nonetheless strongly suggests that cosmopolitanism is a movement *toward* an end. Throughout *Toward Perpetual Peace*, Kant cites the "dream" of philosophers for perpetual peace,[10] uses the modal verb "ought," *sollen*, to mark our obligations for the future,[11] and, most significantly, calls the idea of perpetual peace a "goal" and a "task".[12] In this sense, cosmopolitanism exists only in the movement of a deferred end. The telos of perpetual peace is merely a regulative idea giving ethical orientation to political thought. In this respect, cosmopolitanism is both the means and movement toward the actualization of this idea in historical time. It is this dream of a future that Miki seeks in the here and now of East Asia.

Accepting its ideals but rejecting its philosophical foundations, Miki criticizes the Kantian conception of cosmopolitanism as abstract and atomistic, charging that it lacks a material and truly historical perspective on subjectivity. In an anonymously authored political treatise written under the aegis of the Shōwa Research Association, *Principles of Thought for a New Japan* (*Shin Nihon no shisō genri*), Miki invokes the second Sino-Japanese War (1937–45) as the beginning of a purportedly "new" historical paradigm for the globe.[13] He criticizes Western thought as an "abstract modern cosmopolitanism" which, he claims, functionalizes and objectifies human relations.[14] Creating a dualism between "Western" and "East Asian" cultures, he argues that the former is grounded in the principle of *Gesellschaft*, society, while the latter in that of *Gemeinschaft*, community.[15] This critique of *Gesellschaft*, is directed specifically against what he calls "liberalism, individualism, and rationalism." For him, these principles that purportedly characterize Western thought reduce humanity not only to a network of atomistic individuals, but also "erroneously" assume that the atomistic individual is the first principle of political organization. In his 1941 article "Freedom and Liberalism" (*Jiyū to jiyūshugi*), he directs his criticism of Western cosmopolitanism against the primacy it gives to the concept of the individual. Claiming that cosmopolitanism is a mere species of liberalism, he argues:

> In regard to cosmopolitanism, rather than calling cosmopolitanism a mistake, it is more accurate to say that there is an error in cosmopolitanism's abstractness. That is to say, this cosmopolitanism is not the kind that mediates nations (*minzoku*). Liberalism as individualism places individuals at the forefront in the relation between society and individuals, viewing society as the mere sum total of individuals without regard to their mutual relation.[16]

What might be taken as a sweeping charge against cosmopolitanism in general is rather a specific critique against a configuration of the cosmopolitan as an abstraction. For Miki, it is impossible to think of the individual subject outside of the complex social relations through and by which the subject is constituted. On his view, a subject is always in *excess* of what it might appear to be at any given moment. Rather than the individual, he argues for a form of political thought giving primacy to the *relation* between the individual subject and its social totality – not the totality of a particular society, but that of the globe as such.

By criticizing Western conceptions of cosmopolitanism as "abstract," Miki gestures toward the contemporaneous Japanese philosophical debate on "subjectivity." Early twentieth century philosophers such as Miki, following Nishida, made a conceptual distinction between two types of subjectivity, *shukan* and *shutai*.[17] Whereas for Kant "subject" principally means the exerciser of the "will" and the bearer of knowledge, for philosophers such as Miki its meaning is ambiguous. The subject was considered, on the one hand, as a "contemplative consciousness," or a *shukan* and, on the other, as a "practical subject," a *shutai*.[18] In other words, whereas *shukan* designates a "subject" considered as an epistemological being, *shutai* describes a "subject" as both a thinking and acting being. In Miki (as well as in Tanabe), the *shutai* has the status of a more "authentic" form of subjectivity, purportedly overcoming Western thought's emphasis on abstract knowledge over a dialectical mediation between thought and action. In his study *Philosophical Anthropology*, he describes his conception of *shutai* in terms of a transcendent and dialectical movement.[19]

> Our position in anthropology is that of active self-awareness. This is not an abstraction of the human from its body, rather it grasps the human subjectively (*shutaiteki*) and socially. However, even if taken subjectively an objective perspective must also be included as a dialectical moment. The human taken interiorly, that is taken subjectively, is an externally objective existence. By assuming the position of active self-awareness we can first grasp the human as a totality. If action were to render impossible all theories of immanence, it would be impossible to conceive of action

without admitting something transcendent. However, just as we discussed "dual transcendence," this means to acknowledge transcendence both from the exterior as well as the interior.[20]

On Miki's conception of embodied subjectivity the human exists both in itself in respect to its corporeal existence and beyond itself in respect to its external engagements with the world. Thus, "self-awareness" in Miki's sense does not connote the kind of cognitive or epistemological self-awareness found in Kant. Rather, Miki's notion of self-awareness entails human activity: self-awareness arises by making things and engaging in the world of other productive subjects.[21] By making things, I do not just relate myself to the world, I help to create it. The *shutai* is self-aware only to the extent that it *performs* this relationship toward its objects and its others. In his Marxian understanding of human agency, Miki's conception of the *shutai* is "transcendent" in a concrete rather than metaphysical sense. It participates in the constitution of the world in which it already exists by making things – works of art, commodities, dwellings – that are shared with other subjects. Insofar as its products go beyond the individual *shutai*, they not only form the basis for a community of shared cultural beliefs they also produce the basis for temporality, markers of historical time. By creating an object, one produces an instance for denoting a transformation in the matrix of objects and ideas into which one is thrown. The subject, in other words, is always implicated in the life and work of other subjects wherever and whenever this subject might exist. Nevertheless, in Miki's theory of cooperativism, an individual subject, a *shutai*, is but one instance of an imagined social totality – for Miki a putatively multi-ethnic and multi-cultural imperial state.[22]

Miki's critique of "abstract modern cosmopolitanism" thus turns on an argument for a purportedly more "authentic" form of subjectivity. Yet, his consideration of subjectivity is merely the starting point for his larger political argument in *Principles of Thought* in defense of the Japanese imperial project. He argues for a new theory of cosmopolitanism, "cooperativism" (*kyōdōshugi*), that purportedly transcends the individual interests of any particular culture through a logic of inclusion.[23] Just as an individual subject attains its authenticity through its engagement with the world, so too will the collective subject, a "nation," in Miki's argument for a cosmopolitan empire called the East Asian Cooperative Body. Directly criticizing the essentialist principles of German National Socialism, Miki offers an alternative political ideology for the Japanese Empire. His theory of cooperativism is explicitly anti-racist, standing against Japanese nationalism in particular, but nevertheless – in yet another paradox – for nationalism in general. Though he rejects Japanese exceptionalism (*Nipponshugi*), he supports nationalism as a force preserving cultural particularity. Citing the principal ideas for this community of nations, Miki writes:

> Insofar as the East Asian Cooperative Body is intended as a cooperation between nations, it must transcend the standpoint of simple nationalism.

Nevertheless, the distinctness of each nation must be recognized within this cooperative body. Therefore, second, the idea of nationalism is important insofar as it has the significance of emphasizing the distinctness of such nations. Moreover, third, the idea of nationalism contains truth in the sense that any world-historical mobilization is inaugurated by a certain nation. Even the present East Asian Cooperative Body has developed on the initiative of the Japanese nation. However, Japan itself enters into the East Asian Cooperative Body, developed under the leadership of Japan. In the sense that even Japan too must follow the principles of this cooperative body, it is obvious that its nationalism must be restricted. Japanese culture, as a potential leader of East Asia, cannot remain in a simple nationalism. It goes without saying that care must be taken against falling into an anti-foreign tendency.[24]

Though one might imagine that all forms of imperialist ideology espouse the principle of unilateral domination, the argument that Miki forwards here is one of inclusion and preservation of particularity. Transposing his theory of individual subjectivity on to the imagined collective body of a given nation, he proposes a political super-community of nations in which the freedom of the whole and that of its parts are bi-conditionally defined.[25] Thus, his proposed ideology of "cooperativism" is driven by the principle of reciprocal mediation between cultural regions. In this imperialism, cultural difference rather than domination is emphasized. He claims that cooperativism is based on the heterogeneity of cultures within the so-called East Asian Cooperative Body, specifically citing Japan, Manchuria, and China, but possibly including many other regions.[26] This heterogeneity is necessary, he argues, in order to overcome the systematic atomism of Western forms of social organization, "Gesellschaft."[27]

However, Miki's cooperativism is itself not a theory of equality among peoples. Though he stresses mutual cultural mediation between the nations making up the East Asian Cooperative Body, he also argues for the primacy of Japan within this political community. We must consider here how Miki's argument is necessarily paradoxical throughout his *Principles of Thought*. One of the two primary aims of his manifesto is to explain how the Japanese imperial project is the "liberation" of East Asia from Western colonialism and thought. The second is to show how this "liberation" is not a colonization of East Asia driven by Japanese nationalism. His strategy for fulfilling both aims is to argue for a teleological view of world history that asserts Japan as the world-historical forefront of culture by denying the "essence" of Japanese culture. On this argument, Japanese culture is occupied by a "nothingness" that has historically mediated all cultures into which it has come into contact, and thus putatively possesses the most "excellent" aspects of all. It is this culture of mediation that Miki claims will bring a new form of universality not only to East Asia but the world as whole.[28]

The starting point of Miki's argument for the world-historical role that Japan purportedly plays in the development of modern culture is his analysis of the First World War in Europe. Invoking Oswald Spengler's *Decline of the West*, he forwards the thesis that the First World War was a world-historical "auto-critique" of the West. That war, on his view, demonstrates the failures of Western forms of social organization and opens the world to the possibility of an alternative conception of world history:

> The world-historical significance of the China Incident, if viewed spatially, is that it makes the unification of the world possible by actualizing the unification of East Asia. Up to now, what has been called "world history" is in fact just European cultural history viewed from the standpoint of "Europeanism" (*yōroppashugi*). The significance of the so-called World War of 1914–18 was as an auto-critique of this Europeanism, as even Western thinkers have also noted. Awareness arose that European history was not the same as world history, that European culture was not the same as world culture. The fall of Europeanism meant the abandonment of a unified notion of world history for European thought. In the wake of the auto-critique of Europeanism, the significance of the China Incident must be to enable a true unification of the world by actualizing the unification of East Asia, and to reveal a new idea of world history.[29]

Miki's aim here is not just to critique the conflation of European history with world history but also to appropriate the latter for his proposed East Asian cosmopolis. The notion of "world history" that Miki forwards is derived from G. W. F. Hegel's conception of Spirit in the *Phenomenology of Spirit* and *Lectures on the Philosophy of History*. By Spirit, Hegel designates a suprasubject constituted by humanity as a whole, not only the collectivity of human subjects in the present but also those of the past and future. An all-encompassing being, it is a "subject" in the sense that it can assume a stance toward itself as a free and self-conscious being. However, the omnipresence of Spirit through space and time does not mean that world-historical development is evenly distributed throughout the human community. Rather, as Hegel argues – in a manner that remains rightfully controversial to this day – the historical development of Spirit occurs in historical "moments." What is important for Miki is that each stage of Spirit's development is distributed on a trajectory from the east to the west, such that as Spirit moves from East Asia, Europe, and beyond to America, it might promise its return to East Asia. The First World War was an "auto-critique" in that it was seemingly the end of Euro-American hegemony over the globe and Spirit's opening toward a new stage in world history. In as much as Miki criticizes "Western thought," his philosophy is also based on it.

Thus, Miki's treatise is a work on the principles of thought for a "new" Japan in the sense of the possibility for world-historical renewal. Japan occupies a privileged position in Miki's cooperativism because of its purported tradition of cultural inclusion. Whereas he views Western culture as reified and Chinese culture as exclusionary,[30] he argues that Japan's privileged position in the East Asian Cooperative Body is due to its ability to mediate and adopt diverse cultural practices and forms:

> what should be observed as Japanese culture's distinctiveness is its inclusiveness. From ancient times Japanese culture has developed by assimilating Chinese and Indian culture, and later Western culture. However, while adopting foreign cultures, it does not impossibly attempt to unify them into set forms. Rather, it was inclusive such that it permitted their coexistence. Belief in both Shinto and Buddhism is for Japanese people not a contradiction, rather they stand side by side. Japanese people do not feel a contradiction in viewing a Japanese painting and a Western painting in one and the same room. In this manner, the breadth and depth of the Japanese mind is located where even things that are objectively incompatible are unified subjectively. It is precisely this mind that is needed in the new Cooperative Body. Among all the nations of East Asia, the distinctiveness of each culture must be brought to life without forcing them into a single form.[31]

Miki's defense of the Japanese Empire turns on his claim that Japan will bring a culture of "inclusion" to the rest of East Asia. Beyond the problem of his monolithic characterization of the "West," "China," or "Japan," what we should note here is the promise-structure of his claim. His call to preserve and vivify the local cultures of East Asia makes a promise to the subjects of this empire. In so doing, he points to a future in which their local cultures will be endowed with the ostensibly "inclusive" character of Japanese culture. He thus offers them the possibility of attaining a cosmopolitan culture in which local and the perceived non-local coexist "without contradiction."[32] "Cooperativism," he writes, "actualizes a real cosmopolitanism" through a "mediation of nations" in which each state is opened up to all others.[33] It is in this sense that Miki also argues that the Sino-Japanese conflict is a "war of ideas"[34] and not an "imperialist invasion."[35] It was for him the promise for a new world.

That the war on the ground was indeed not a "war of ideas" but one of natural resources and that it was very much an imperialist invasion do little to dispel the force of Miki's conviction in the Japanese project for an imperial cosmopolitanism. It is precisely his conviction in this project that demonstrates how intellectual production does not stand in abstract relation to state violence. Far from being an ineffectual figure with little or no responsibility over the actions of the state, the intellectual is the locus of production for the matrix of ideas animating political projects. Miki responds to one part of the Japanese Empire's search for philosophical legitimacy by answering the question of how the social totality of the Empire not only will preserve cultural particularity but also is predicated on it. However, what he does not respond to is the subjective position that an individual forms within this promised cosmopolis. All empires operate on a certain logic of seduction such that those who are subjugated by it *desire* their subjugation. Merely preserving the particularity of the individual does not promise by itself this power of seduction. It is in this sense that Tanabe forwards his project of explaining how this desire of the individual is incited. He seeks no less than to articulate how political resistance toward one's social community is the first moment in which one identifies with that community.

Negation, mediation, and freedom in death

Miki's senior by some 12 years, Tanabe was born in Tōkyō in 1885 and wrote his dissertation on the philosophy of mathematics at Kyōto Imperial University. He studied briefly under Edmund Husserl (1859–1938) in Freiburg, where he also began his lifelong intellectual friendship with Martin Heidegger. Though he began his philosophical career steeped in phenomenology, he increasingly turned toward Hegelian dialectics by the time he assumed the chairmanship of the Department of Philosophy from his former mentor, Nishida. He developed his own philosophy of social ontology in a series of long articles written between 1935 and 1947, which are today collectively referred to as his *Logic of Species* (*Shu no ronri*).[36] At approximately the same time that Miki wrote for the Shōwa Research Association, Tanabe published a defense of his social theory in "Clarifying the meaning of the Logic of Species" (*Shu no ronri no imi o akiraka ni su*), arguing for a temporalized conception of subjectivity based on the negation of one's communal identification.[37] His theory is an attempt to justify the Japanese Empire as a multi-ethnic state and a sphere of cosmopolitan "freedom" for its subjects. However, this freedom is found only in death as the moment of absolute negativity.

Modifying Hegel's notions of the universal, particular, and singular, Tanabe's social ontology is divided into three dialectical moments: genus (*rui*), species (*shu*), and individual (*ko*). Given the historical context of growing ethnic nationalism in Japan at the time of Tanabe's writing, it is tempting to view this tripartite scheme as based on a racial biology. On the contrary, genus does not designate a collection of species, nor species a collection of individuals. His theory is explicitly anti-racist, derived not from biology but from the principles of justice (genus), totemic obligation (species) and personal resistance (individual). Each of these three designates a moment of negativity in the social world and stands in a mediating relation in respect to each other. The dialectical "logic" of the *Logic of Species* is that of the mediation and negation of social conflict arising when the individual resists the totemic dictates of the species by making an appeal to genus as a principle of universality. What does this mean?

Tanabe's social ontology is based on the movement of negation, self-alienation and reconciliation. As dialectical moments, genus, species, and individual do not designate empirical beings but forms of negation. He calls genus an "absolute negation" that both unifies and equalizes all individuals in their cultural heterogeneity:

It is a totality that internally actualizes the harmonious unity of individuals by the negative mediation of their opposition. Simultaneously, it is externally unified with other totalities, participating in the absolute totality as itself a unified individual. Such internal and external dual unity is genus. It can be thought of as itself an individual and simultaneously as the unity of individuals. The human world – in which the totality of states arises in a sublation of national class divisions, the free cooperation of individuals and, simultaneously, in international cooperation – has such a structure. In this sense, the state can be thought of as a human state and the individual as a member of the state as well as humanity. This is the concrete structure of social existence.[38]

Though Tanabe associates genus with the abstract notion of the political state as well as that of humanity, it is important to notice that genus is *not* identical to them. Rather, genus arises out of the mediation of the individual's struggle with species. In other words, genus does not refer to an object but to the individual's movement toward an ethical *idea*, such as justice. In terms of the genus–individual relation, the absolute negativity of genus is a sphere of freedom and a return from self-alienation for the individual: "Absolute negation effects a return to the self through the mediation of self-negation as a self-alienation. This is nothing but being-at-home-with-oneself, *Beisichsein*."[39] Explicitly drawing on Hegel's conception of alienation and reconciliation, Tanabe characterizes the absolute negativity of genus as that which brings the individual back to itself, or *beisich*. If a subject, for instance, rejects the social practices of her local community (species), she can call them into question (negate them) by appealing to a higher principle that would apply to that community, such as the constitutional law of her political state. Yet, even this political state might defend principles that she rejects. She could also appeal to the idea of humanity – human rights – as an ethical idea in critique of her political state. Without suggesting a hierarchy between particular political states and humanity as a whole, Tanabe argues for a conception of universality in which genus designates the final appeal that the individual can make in the struggle for freedom. It is in this sense that he calls genus "absolute negation." In calling for justice, one *negates* that for which one seeks it. This negation is "absolute" insofar as it is one's final appeal to universality.

Thus, the genus–individual relation is that of abstraction: the individual makes an appeal to an *idea* for what is just. However, Tanabe also argues that when genus mediates the individual back to itself, it also mediates it back to species. In contrast to this, Tanabe calls the individual's first relation to species "immediate." It is immediate not in the sense that its relation to the individual is that of whole and part. Instead, immediacy here refers to the individual's self-aware stance toward species. Unless I know of other cultures, ways of doing things, or other ways of believing, there is no way I can know that I exist within a particular culture. "Culture" would not even be a concept for me. My everyday practices would have a certain unreflective "obviousness," or immediacy, in respect to my being. Thus Tanabe also calls species a "sub-stratum," for it underlies our everyday practices without our reflection.[40] It is only when we reflect, or resist, species that we recognize that it in fact mediates our being.

> On the basis of its structure, it is clear that species, which was first conceived of as an immediate unity of individual subjectivity, is the absolute splitting-opposition as the negative moment of this immediate unity. I can now determine species by saying that it is nothing but unity itself that is simultaneously opposition. This applies precisely to the nation.[41]

For Tanabe, a nation is not defined in terms of ethnic homogeneity, racial consanguity, or even political unity, but by negativity. Rather than designating a group consisting of many individuals, a nation (or species) *negates* the individual in the sense that it imposes obligations to behave in a certain way, engage in social practices in a certain manner, or assume certain beliefs. As long as the individual does not resist, these obligations remain immediate to the individual. The individual remains unified with species and thus cannot even be said to be an "individual." However, even if the individual does not resist, Tanabe argues that species remains in *opposition* to this "immediate unity" insofar as it issues obligations to the individual.

To the extent that the individual follows these obligations, the individual also negates itself. It merely follows what is expected of it and, therefore, is nothing but the enactment of that expectation, pure immediacy. If I do exactly as I am expected to do without reflection in a social situation, then in one respect I am not a self. I would merely be the performance of a social expectation, a mere repetition of species. However, only if I reflect upon this expectation – either accepting or rejecting it – can I attain anything like selfhood. I will have made a "free" decision, where "free" means the capacity to negate the otherness (or opposition) of the social expectation and make it my own. I would negate my self-negation of merely following social expectations without reflection. Only then would I be "individual" in Tanabe's sense:

> Because the negation of species is the negation of self-negation, it is the for-itself actualization of an in-itself unity that includes the absolute opposition of species itself. It is the recovery of totality. The individual is the movement of the recovery of this total unity. It is the process of this return. This is why it is an active subject. In contrast to the negative aspect of the absolute negation of being-at-home-with-oneself, the affirmative aspect is nothing but the spirituality of the individual.[42]

Tanabe's notion of "individual" thus does not just refer to the mere facticity of corporeal existence but also to the movement of negation that the self-aware being enacts in its social practices. That is, the subject is an embodied being for Tanabe, but also one that is outside-of-itself, *aussersich*, as long as it does not assume a stance toward its social world.[43] It is in this sense that he argues that the subject is the "return" from being-outside-of-itself (*jikarijū, Aussersichsein*) to being-at-home-with-itself (*jikashijū, Beisichsein*).[44] Insofar as my behavior, beliefs, and practices are in large part formed through a process of acculturation over which I have little control, I am "outside-of-myself" in the sense that I am a mere reproduction of my social world. However, to the extent that I take a self-aware stance toward my behavior, beliefs and practices by accepting or modifying them, I am "at-home-with-myself" in the sense the social world into which I was thrown is *my own*. A subject in Tanabe's sense of "individual" is a self-subjection.

It would appear that the relation between species and individual is strictly oppositional, that the individual can only accept or reject the social world that it is given. On the contrary, Tanabe also argues that just as the individual transforms in this choice that it makes, so too does the species. In accepting or rejecting social practices – that is, by self-consciously continuing them or refusing to partake in them – those social practices also transform. Cultural practices, social beliefs, and historical traditions are not constants. They rely on the negative mediation of the subjects that perform them.[45] In analogy to the practice of voting in liberal-democracy, a citizen always has three choices: to affirm a policy, to reject it, or simply to abstain. The act of affirmation or rejection has a transformative effect on the life of the community. Abstention, however, has none. Whether one affirms or rejects a policy, one assumes a stance of opposition toward the given in the sense that one makes the given an *object* of one's political self-awareness. However, in abstaining, one remains a pure immediacy to the given and is thus not a "subject" in Tanabe's sense of the individual. Nevertheless, by negating species, transforming it, the individual that was once in opposition to species returns to it as an immediacy. Continuing the analogy of liberal democracy, regardless of the choice that one makes concerning the political policy in question, one stands in opposition to the life of the community and, by assuming any stance whatsoever, one asserts one's membership in that community. This is what Tanabe means by the return from self-alienation through absolute negation.

It is important to recognize that the entirety of this dialectical movement of genus–species–individual produces the conditions for the consciousness of historical time. The logic of species is not a movement "in" time. Rather, it is a movement that creates time. The action of the individual as it turns toward genus and negates species creates the historical "present." Tanabe argues that the three modes of time – past, present, and future – are the product of the dialectical activity of the individual. However, of these three, he argues that the "present" occupies a privileged position because it mediates the past and the future, insofar as it allows for the absolute mediation of the genus.[46] It "allows" for it in the sense that it makes genus into a reservoir of what the future may hold for the individual, for example, the *promise* of justice in individual's social world of species. Tanabe still goes further. Offering a *reductio* argument for his conception of time, he attempts to demonstrate that the negativity of the present, and not that of the past, constitutes social being:

By the absolute negative mediation of the present, time attains its essence in the movement of conversion. Without the instant of active pure movement, there would be no time. In particular, the pure movement of absolute negation presupposes self-negation as mediation. A simple self-sameness, which has no self-negation, would be the negation of time. The past creates the self-negative opposition of the present by opposing the future. If the spontaneous creativity of the future does not negate it, the past would be fixed, and therefore the moving instant of the present also would cease to exist. Thus, the past would lose its meaning as the past and would be nothing but the solidification of atemporal self-sameness.[47]

Tanabe argues here against a form of historical essentialism dictating that cultures are constituted by their past alone, as if cultures were merely "solidifications of atemporal self-sameness." For him, a subject's status as a being that can effect negation upon itself is the precondition for temporality. The "absolute negation" of genus (which is "pure" in Kant's universalist sense) cannot effect its own negation on species without the individual's "conversion" to it. Thus, the "movement of conversion" is an activity that belongs to the individual, who *qua* individual is always in the "present," or rather is the definer of the present. A "subject" that is "self-same" is one that has no internal difference, cannot reflect upon itself, and therefore cannot effect negation upon itself. Instead of being an individual in Tanabe's sense it would be an inert being. Such a hypothetical "subject" would be a mere stone, and for stones there is no such thing as time. However, insofar as the individual in the present can negate itself, it regards the past in opposition to the future. It is in this sense that the species is the "past" of the individual. Being an individual essentially means being the *activity* of transcending the apparent given-ness (the past) of the social world (species). In his *reductio* argument, Tanabe continues with an explication of what would be the case if there were nothing like genus, which for the individual is the future. If a subject were not able to turn to ideals, such as the principles of justice, no historical transformation would be possible or conceivable. All that would exist is the "history" of accidents. The "present also would cease to exist" in the sense that there would be no aim toward which present activity could strive to actualize. There would be no "moving instant of the present." The past would be "fixed" insofar as there would be no other temporal mode from which to regard it and reflect upon it. Thus, the "past" would not be the past in the sense of a relative relation to other historical modes. Instead, it would be but an inert being, or what Tanabe calls a "solidification of atemporal self-sameness."

Thus, the political dimensions of Tanabe's argument lie less in its tripartite scheme of genus–species–individual than in the temporality that this relation makes possible. One could translate these three dialectical moments into the politically more commonplace notions of human rights (genus), social mores (species) and lived lives (individual). If I were to live in a community that is completely dictated by given social mores without the hope of transformation, then I would live in a society devoid of any historical time, if not also a sphere devoid of subjectivity – an automated society. Only the hope for a (non-) guaranteed future can *promise* the transformation of what one is given. However, even if this future is never actualized, the mere fact that one has striven toward it for oneself or one's community means that one stakes a claim on one's membership in that community. In other words, even if one fails in the most violent way possible in one's political protest – that is, dies – one has effected a transformation of that community by asserting one's membership in it, even at the risk of death. One has effected a negation upon this community by the allowing one's ideals to effect *absolute* negation upon oneself, death. It is in this sense that the absolute negation of the future in Tanabe's logic of species is a struggle of life and death.[48]

It is this promise for a future with full membership in a transformed community that marks the imperial moment of Tanabe's logic of species. However, what we have seen up to now is a political philosophy dedicated to the project of human freedom. In resisting the socially given, demanding its transformation, one opposes the community that one rejects in order to find freedom in the one that will have been transformed. From the very outset of Tanabe's logic of species, the very possibility of one's rejection of one's community is also the condition of possibility for one's membership in it. In other words, freedom (self-negativity) both produces community and binds the self to it. Yet, the possibility of one's death alone does not constitute the "imperial" moment of Tanabe's logic of species, for one can also die in one's struggle *against* imperial domination in the (false) hope of recovering a community that is already and will always remain lost. Rather, this moment of the imperial appears where the logic of species *seduces* the subject's desire to seek her own death and to find a future freedom in a community through which she will find her "true self," though in which she will not be able to partake due to her death. This imperial moment deals less with Tanabe's controversial 1943 lecture "Death and Life" (*Shisei*), in which he exhorts students going to war to put their lives to the task of death, than with his 1939 essay "The Logic of National Existence" (*Kokkateki sonzai no ronri*) which espouses the principle that self-sacrifice for the state is a return to the self, and "hence" a return to freedom. On the relation between the individual and the totality that is the state, he writes:

> The subjectivity of the individual is also only formed in the moving mediation of both opposition and unity together within the state as a total subject. For the individual attains an affirmed existence in its self-negating self-sacrifice for the state. This sacrifice is not simply for the sake of another, since the state for which the self has been sacrificed contains the self's source of life. Rather, it is a return of the self to a true self. Self-negation turns into affirmation, and the totality opposing the self unifies

with the self. In serving the state, submitting to its commandment, the ethics of autonomous freedom does not annihilate the self, rather it makes it possible.[49]

Following Hegel, Tanabe's argument here is that individual freedom is only won within the state. However, unlike Hegel, he argues on the basis of the individual's "self-negating self-sacrifice," death. "Death" is not death for Tanabe. Rather it is the self's communion with the state which gave it life. While political philosophy since Plato has argued that one's membership (citizenship) in a state entails an obligation to defend it even at the price of death, Tanabe goes one step further. He argues for why we should *desire* our own death in our service to state. He seeks to incite this desire by making a promise: our death is not our annihilation but our freedom.

The intellectual and the state

The promise of freedom in political projects remains almost a constant in public discourse. For there is no better way of seducing someone to do as one pleases than to promise this person that they will attain freedom by following what one prescribes. In the case of Miki, the promise lies in a pan-East Asian cosmopolis in which freedom is won in not just the preservation of particularity but also its flourishing as it also mediates other cultures. For Miki, one is "cosmopolitan" only insofar as one is open to such mediation. Though Miki as a member of the Shōwa Research Association was more "directly" involved in the Japanese Empire's pursuit of an imperial cosmopolitanism, Tanabe poses the greater challenge to the question of how a philosopher might exercise a certain power over the operation of his state's political project of imperialism. Biographically, he was never a member of any state organ other than the university. Yet, it is precisely his membership in the academic world that lends him a degree of state power.

As much as one derides the university as a hot bed for ineffectual ideas – an "ivory tower" – and government as an oafishly slow-moving bureaucracy, the history of Japanese imperialism demonstrates the tight relation between the production of knowledge and the actions of the state. Empires do not develop by military means alone. Bureaucrats need to be trained. The technological means for exerting power needs to be developed. And, most important, ideas need to be produced in order to guide the actions of the state and give those actions the air of legitimacy. For both Tanabe and Miki, the idea of an imperial cosmopolitanism that will release its subjects toward a future freedom gives such legitimacy to their state's imperial project. For the state, there is no better way to legitimate its projects than by asking figures from the academic sphere to produce ideas for political policy. Few but the intellectual can turn imperial domination into a defense of human freedom or even the preservation of peace. Consider the following spirited defense of the imperial state:

In keeping with our heritage and principles, we do not use our strength to press for unilateral advantage. We seek instead to create a balance of power that favors human freedom: conditions in which all nations and all societies can choose for themselves the rewards and challenges of political and economic liberty. In a world that is safe, people will be able to make their own lives better. ... We will preserve the peace by building good relations among the great powers. We will extend the peace by encouraging free and open societies on every continent.

This passage suggesting a commitment to the ideal of cosmopolitan freedom is from neither Tanabe nor Miki. It is not even about Japan. It comes allegedly in great part from the hand of the former dean of the School of Advanced International Studies at the Johns Hopkins University, Paul D. Wolfowitz.[50] It is also the official international policy of the United States since September 2002. Though the historical concern in these pages has been narrowly focused on Miki and Tanabe, the problems addressed here are by no means restricted to the musings of two Japanese philosophers some half-century ago in their quest to rethink the world as their political state sought to remake it. Rather, the desire of philosophical and political modernity subtends these problems, a desire that expressly seeks universal human freedom *but* renders its actualization identical to death through imperial domination. Yet, the persistence of this identity across historical time and geo-political antagonisms, from mid-twentieth century Japan to early twenty-first century America, points not to the universality of imperialism – as if imperialism or "Empire" were the basic condition of the modern or the "post-modern." Instead, it points to the radical particularity with which an "ought" has been forcibly translated into an "is," such that what was to be a spread of "freedom" cannot but become a conquest of death.

11 The concept of ethnic nationality and its role in Pan-Asianism in imperial Japan

Kevin M. Doak

Introduction

Japanese Pan-Asianism during the interwar period placed tremendous weight on the concept of *minzoku* (ethnic nationality) as the sole legitimate principle of social and cultural identity. What is surprising and needs some explanation is why advocates of Pan-Asianism often relied on this concept of "*minzoku*", rather than the more direct argument that Pan-Asianism reflected a racial identity (*jinshu*) supposedly shared by those in the region. The emphasis on a common racial identity was in fact a familiar feature of late nineteenth and early twentieth century pan-Asianist discourse in general. And it should be emphasized from the outset that this move from race to ethnicity in Japanese discourse was not an absolute but a relative shift, not only because race is an element in the construction of ethnic identity, but also because the older racialist Pan-Asianism never completely disappeared. Yet we not only miss a great deal of the appeal of wartime Pan-Asianism if we simply reduce this cultural regional theory to its more biological, racialist dimensions. We would also have to sweep aside the historical reality of a rigorous insistence on the difference between race and ethnicity (or nationality) in late imperial pan-Asianist discourse. Far more than race, ethnicity was crucial to the development of wartime regionalist ideology, and the appeal of ethnicity helps to account for much of the sense of legitimacy that was associated with calls to "liberate Asia" during this era. Nor is this appeal of ethnicity dead today. It is equally important in the present, as the concept of ethnic nationality (*minzoku*) – far more than racialist beliefs – continues to underwrite much of contemporary cultural theory on the common bonds that link Japanese to other people in Asia, whether those bonds are deemed normative or actual.

In fact, scholars are often confounded by how this theory of *völkisch* nationality could reinforce regionalism, especially when they subsume the problem of *minzoku* under the category of "race." At one level, the ideological linkage between a local identity as *minzoku* and a regional identity as an East Asia Community (*Tōa kyōdōtai*) can be explained through the common grounding both shared in a theory of society as *Gemeinschaft*.[1] While this analysis helps explain the ideological functions such collectivized concepts have over individuals represented within them, it doesn't quite go far enough in explaining how this equation of national and regional identities – in principle contradictory claims – could be reconciled. In most historical instances (e.g., Nazi Germany, Milosevic's Serbia) *Gemeinschaft* and ethnic definitions ✓ of national society run directly counter to regionalism.[2]

To understand how this principle of nationality was made compatible with an ideology of regionalism, it may be helpful to begin with historical context. Like *Volk* and other ethnic approximations of nationality, the concept of *minzoku* began to appear widely in Japanese discourse around the outbreak of the First World War.[3] And like contemporary uses of the concept of ethnicity, it carried a range of ambivalent, and frequently negative, attitudes toward civic or political membership in a state, especially a multi-ethnic or "assimilationist" nation-state. It was therefore quite useful for pan-Asian imperialists, who wanted simultaneously to assert a common sense of Asian difference *from* the West, while maintaining distinctive identities *among* Asians, particularly between Japanese (whose political identity was presumed to be invested in the modern state) and the rest of the peoples of Asia (who were frequently represented as the "Völker" of the region.)[4] This cultural theory of Asian regionalism began with the assumption that everyone in the region belonged to a *Volk* (an ethnically conceived nationalized "people") and all were expected to be committed to this principle of the *Volk* as the unit of membership in the regional order, rather than to the principle of political independence for their own national state. As we will see, one of the most interesting aspects of this ethnic Pan-Asianism was the manner in which this primacy given to ethnic identity eventually gave way to a heated debate over whether ethnic identity was sharply bounded or whether it was capable of extension, ultimately to include all people in the region in one surpa-ethnic identity as a single East Asian Ethnic Nation (*Tōa minzoku*). Here, if we are not careful, it becomes easy to confuse the problem of *minzoku* with the old nineteenth-century category of "race." Pan-Asianist efforts in imperial Japan to reconcile the competing claims of nation and region, even while repudiating the "old fashioned" notion of biological race, found the concept of *minzoku* attractive as a means of revising traditional understandings of what a nation is.

As a form of regionalism, Pan-Asianism also had to confront the problem of national borders (in both the cultural and territorial senses) that were propped up by the modern desire for independent national states. One of the greatest challenges to Pan-Asianism was the emphasis on the territory of the state as a key requirement in national identity. Ernest Renan's solution – the subjective consciousness of the residents of a territory, or the "daily plebiscite" – was merely a strategy to avoid the more fundamental question: does the state's territory provide the prerequisites for nationality or is nationality, especially ethnic nationality, the condition for an independent state? If theories of ethnicity uncovered how nationality was separable from the territory of the political state, then ethnicity also enabled new ways of conceiving of regional territory. Yamauchi Masayuki captures the problem quite well:

When the distribution of a certain *minzoku* overlaps with the nation-state [*kokumin kokka*], one might conclude that territory is an index of the *minzoku*'s identity. But the causal relationship is actually just the opposite. The reason we can distinguish one specific region from another is because that territory is occupied by a specific *minzoku*. In essence, a common sense of shared territory is not a condition for being a *minzoku*, but rather when people who have become a single *minzoku* come together and reside in a place we recognize a sense of common territory.[5]

Drawing on recent developments in diasporic movements, ethnic breakups of nation-states, and especially ethnic tensions in the Middle East, Yamauchi pinpoints a weakness in traditional theories that premised nationality on the territorial state. Here, his theoretical analysis helps to clarify the problems that confronted imperial Japanese pan-Asianists as they tried to find justifications for a new regional order. Territory, it turns out, is no easier to define than nationality. Indeed, the very definition of which boundaries constitute a given region, like that of the territorial state itself, could be made dependent on the prior question of who constitutes an ethnic/national group, or a *Volk*. In short, what is the subject around which boundaries must be drawn?

One of the first attempts to answer this question in the context of Pan-Asianism after the First World War was undertaken by members of the Yūzonsha (Society of Those Left Behind). Formed in 1923 by Ōkawa Shūmei (1886–1957) and Mitsukawa Kametarō (1888–1936), the Yūzonsha was very much influenced by the shift in nationalism that followed from the First World War.[6] Ōkawa and Mitsukawa shared a sense that the new global turn toward ethnic nationality unleashed by the war was the key to understanding national identity and the problems confronting Asia as a whole. In his *Various Problems in an Asian Renaissance* (published the year before the formation of the Yūzonsha), Ōkawa outlined this new regional approach to Asia. From the very first lines of the book, he emphasized this new turn toward ethnic nationality or *Volk* [*minzoku*] to make the case for Asia as a single regional identity with one defining characteristic: the desire for liberation from the colonial yoke of the White Man. Since before the Great War, he noted, "the ethnic groups of Asia [*Ajia no minzoku*] have required first and foremost freedom."[7] Ōkawa explicitly connected his Asian revival to the anti-imperialist brand of ethnic nationalism that was capturing the hearts and minds of Serbs, Irish, Chinese, Koreans and many, many others during and after First World War.

Ōkawa and his colleagues were pivotal figures in the linking of this ethnic nationalism with new modes of conceiving of Asian regional identity. On the one hand, they were, like many of their generation, deeply impressed by the concept of race (*jinshu*). Ōkawa believed that "Asia," whatever else it was, signaled a space of common opposition to the colonial oppression by those he called "the Anglo-Saxons" or more simply "the White Man."[8] Yet, Ōkawa's sense of what held Asia together was beginning to show more complexity, developing a more historically-informed understanding in place of simplistic assertions of a common racial, or biological, identity. In the first place, Ōkawa's thinking about Asia was deeply influenced by Japan's victory in the Russo-Japanese War. This was the central defining moment for Ōkawa, who was 19 years old when the Treaty of Portsmouth was signed and when the Hibiya Riots broke out in frustration over the terms arranged by the US President Theodore Roosevelt. "Our victory," he claimed, "was the first strike against the Western ethnic nations [*minzoku*] who had not been defeated by the colored peoples for over four hundred years." Of course, nationalist pride and efforts to give "world historical significance"[9] to Japan's narrow victory over Russia were not unusual among Ōkawa's generation.

But more important for subsequent efforts to conceptualize regional unity in Asia is the way Ōkawa's discourse registers a new focus on ethnic identity within this overriding, earlier Meiji focus on race:[10]

> With this [victory over Russia], the various ethnic groups of Asia, which are members of the same race, first became clearly conscious of their identity. ... This was true not only of the ethnic groups in Asia. A spirit of opposition to the Westerners came to the fore among all ethnic groups who had been suffering the oppression of the Western European Powers.[11]

Ōkawa was resurrecting an earlier nineteenth-century conception of Asian backwardness and traditionalism (most famously associated with Fukuzawa Yukichi's 1885 short essay on "Leaving Asia" [*datsu-A-ron*]) and reframing it as a principle of revolution that would be the foundation for a new regional order. Although Ōkawa himself was deeply interested in Asian religious traditions, this new revolutionary principle was less religious in inspiration than nationalist, and it required detailed attention to the differences among ethnic and national groups within Asia.

The challenge facing the Japanese (and Ōkawa did not doubt that it was Japan's mission to save Asia from the White Man) was to find a means of creating unity from among the many different cultural and ethnic groups of Asia. In his own approach, the major units of consideration were Tibet, Siam, India, Afghanistan, Persia, Turkey, Egypt, Islamic groups under European domination, and Mesopotamia. In retrospect, it is interesting that Ōkawa largely overlooked China, although when he did refer to China, his premise of ethnic identity was front and center: consider his remark that the Chinese Revolution was being directed toward the construction of a Chinese state that would be premised on the principle of unity of the five ethnic groups.[12] The fact that many Chinese anti-Manchu revolutionaries, and even Sun Yat-sen (Zhongshan), shared this ethnic vision only lent greater legitimacy to Ōkawa's pan-Asianist appeal. Even more telling is that the Asia he sought to revive excluded Korea. Of course, in 1922 Korea was an integral part of the Japanese Empire, a historical fact that seemed to compromise his argument that ethnic

nationality, or *völkisch* approximations of society, were revolutionary principles directed exclusively against the West.

East Asia as an ethnic national order

In the context of the East Asian region, Japanese nationalists like Ōkawa were
hardly colonial subjects seeking their own liberation from the West. Nor was
Japan a divided nation seeking to become a unified political state. Nonetheless, Japanese nationalists and Pan-Asianists found in ethnic nationalism a
useful way to make sense out of what appeared to them to be Japan's internal
colonization. Internal colonization was their way of trying to represent the
Japanese as a *Volk* betrayed by its own Meiji state, a state that was merely bent
on pursuing Western models of constitutionalism at home and expansion
abroad. As the Japanese economy weakened in the late 1920s, Marxists and
others found solutions in theories of ethnic national capital (*minzoku shihon*)
and other national socialist ideas which they tried to use against the "bourgeois"
Westernized Japanese elites. *Völkisch* nationalism proved stronger than class-
consciousness for many Japanese socialists who followed Sano Manabu and
Nabeyama Sadachika in converting from Marxism to National Socialism after
1933. National Socialism was never the ideology of the Japanese government
which, in contrast to Nazi Germany, remained faithful to its imperial constitution and continued to hold public elections throughout the war. But
National Socialism was on the rise, and increasingly it directed its anger
against the Japanese state and its capitalist servants. Rather than bringing
nation and state closer together during the war, extreme nationalists and
renegade military groups created serious problems for constitutional government and for the imperial state as the problem of the nation became hotly
contested ground during the height of war. Informing politics of this era was
what Tōyama Shigeki would later refer to as "the rivalry of two forms of
nationalism."[13] At the core of the nationalist challenge to the imperial
Meiji state was the appeal of ethnic nationality, but this nationalism did
not rest easily with the multi-ethnic composition of imperial Japan. Carried to
its logical conclusion, it might not only mean independence for Korea
and Taiwan, but a radical populist government at home that would contra-
dict the principles of monarchical constitutional government established in
1889.[14]

From the middle 1930s on, theories of ethnic nationality gained tremendous sway over pan-Asian discourse in Japan. Faced with the challenge of this
revolutionary political idea, Japanese military, governmental, and quasi-
governmental agencies gradually moved towards outlining, if not always
consistently enacting, a new policy for East Asian regional order that
emphasized the priority of ethnic nationality, even while doing so often only
to coopt the idea within the political status quo.[15] In the complex give-and-
take that ensued, theories of ethnicity, which often stemmed from an interest
in domestic questions of national legitimacy, were revised and applied to a

theory of regional order that functioned to suppress national independence throughout the empire.

The most important contribution to regionalism made by this approach to ethnic national theory was the notion that there must be a hierarchical ordering of nationalities. This sense of order was given conceptual clarity in the concept of a "*minzoku chitsujo*", a hierarchy of ethnic nationalities, which was apparently coined by the ethnologist Oka Masao.[16] Oka had spent years studying ethnology in Vienna and was quite taken by the new approaches he found in Germanic *Ethnologie* that placed a priority on the *Volk* as social and cultural identity. Of course, these theories had to be fitted to Japan's regional imperialism, which was quite different from German National Socialism. But there is no question that this concept of an ethnic national hierarchy drew from Oka's interest in Germanic *Ethnologie*, as revealed in the term used to describe Japan's position in this hierarchy: the *Herrenvolk* (*shidō minzoku*; the leading ethnic nation). This notion of Japanese as the *Herrenvolk* was offered as a solution to the problem of "ethnic national harmony" (*minzoku kyōwa*) that the Concordia Society and Japanese pan-Asianists on the continent had been debating since the construction of the new state of Manchukuo in 1932.

At its most extreme, this ideological attempt to justify Japanese imperialism as the ethnic national liberation of East Asia drew from the earlier efforts of Konoe Atsumaro (1863–1904) and the Tōa Dōbun-kai (East Asian Common Culture Association) to assert that "a common script, a common race" (*dōbun dōshu*) was shared among East Asian peoples. But through the work of sociologists and ethnologists like Oka, ethnicity was articulated explicitly as a means of overcoming the older, nineteenth-century concept of biological race. A turn toward ethnicity was seen as progress over a purely biological approach to social identity.[17] Needless to say, while the pluralism implicit in the "hierarchy of ethnic nations" resonated with the belief of nationalists throughout the region in their own ethnic particularity, the idea of a hierarchy of nations in East Asia was clearly unresponsive to the demands by the more old-fashioned kind of nationalists in Korea and China for their own autonomous state. It was proving quite difficult to separate ethnic claims from territorial claims.

Just as the people in East Asia were more diverse than Japanese ideology proclaimed, Japanese nationalists also remained deeply divided among themselves, in spite of official pronouncements of national unity under the emperor. A turning point toward unity came in 1937 when Konoe Fumimaro (1891–1945), Atsumaro's son, was appointed Prime Minister. Konoe attempted to build a united front among Japanese nationalists, reaching out to anti-state activists as well as to conservative statists. After the State Mobilization Law of April 1938 consolidated national resources at home in support of the war effort, differences among Japanese nationalists, and especially anti-state nationalist activities, began to wane, while surveillance of anti-state nationalists increased under the Special Higher Police. At the same time, revolutionary nationalists were being mainstreamed, whenever possible. Two of the most notorious, Diet member Kimura Takeo and Major General (later Lieutenant General) Ishiwara Kanji, formed the East Asian League (Tōa renmei) in 1939 to institutionalize their hopes for a reshaping of East Asia along ethnic nationalist lines. As Hatano Sumio has pointed out, advocates of the League approach to Pan-Asianism saw an East Asian League as a necessary structure for resisting Western imperialism, while at the same time encouraging the expression of particular cultural identities of the ethnic national members in the League.[18] At its most theoretically liberal extreme, Kimura and Ishiwara's theory of an East Asian League (Tōa remmei-ron) allowed for the possibility that ethnic nations (*minzoku*) in the League could exercise a right to secede from the League, should their national interests so dictate. Of course, this point remained only a distant theoretical possibility. It is mainly of interest in contrasting the "idealist" (*ōdōshugi-teki*) Pan-Asianism of Kimura and Ishiwara from the more "realist" (*kōdōshugi-teki*) Pan-Asianism of Kada Tetsuji and others.

The ideology of Pan-Asianism, premised on a plurality of distinctive ethnic nations under Japanese leadership was expressed in volume two of the "Ethnic Nation Series" published in 1943 by Rokumeikan in Tokyo. Volume Two in this series was titled "The Nations of the Greater East Asia Co-Prosperity Sphere" and is most notable, not for innovative theory, but for its self-conscious goal of "not to please specialists, but to reach the one hundred million members of the Japanese nation."[19] The volume was co-written by legal scholar Maehara Mitsuo, geographer Noguchi Hoichirō and Islamic scholar Kobayashi Hajime. Maehara offered a legal argument for the necessity of autarky in his discussion of "the theory of a Greater East Asia Co-Prosperity Sphere." His lengthy contribution surveyed historical and geopolitical grounds for the Greater East Asia Co-Prosperity Sphere before returning to his own area of expertise to make the argument that existing international law, with its premise that the state (*kokka*) was the sole legitimate unit of political organization, needed to be revised to take into account the new principle of ethnic nationality.[20]

The bulk of the book was given over to Noguchi's outline of the various ethnic groups of the East Asian region and how they would fit together in the puzzle of the Co-Prosperity Sphere. Noguchi went so far as to suggest that mutual understanding would eventually lead the various ethnic groups of the region into something like a spiritual family, but the emphasis throughout was on the plurality of the members of this spiritual family, not on some brave new organic totality.[21] He described Japan's concept of a Greater East Asia Co-Prosperity Sphere as the child of two parents: its father was the English concept of a "bloc economy" and its mother was the Nazi theory of *Grossraumwirtschaft*. Japan's contribution was to draw from both theories but to re-conceive the basic unit of regional order by replacing the old emphasis on a state-centered approach to space (*Staatsraum*) with one that took seriously the claims of ethnicity.[22] Economically, Japan's regionalism was based on the theory of *Grossraumwirtschaft*, with the added virtue of affinity based on similar ethnicity.[23] Given the centrality of the problem of ethnic nationality to Noguchi's regionalism, he spent considerable time outlining the differences between ethnic nationality (*minzoku*) and race (*jinshu*), and even more on chronicling the separate circumstances of various ethnic groups throughout East Asia. In the end, his emphasis on ethnic pluralism was clear, as was his belief in Japan's mission to lead these various ethnic nations in a regional response to the West. Noguchi described Pan-Asianism as "the obligation of Japan as the leader of the Greater East Asia Co-Prosperity Sphere and its method of self defense. This must not be the method of capitalist imperialist exploitation and extortion of the various ethnic groups of Asia which Europe and America have employed in the past; rather it is a League devoted to the co-existence and co-prosperity of all the ethnic nations of the Greater East Asia."[24] And in case the pluralism and idealism were not clear enough, Noguchi implied a right of secession when he added that India would be welcome to join an East Asia League and that the Philippines and Burma had been guaranteed the honor of independence (eventually) by Tōjō Hideki, Japan's wartime prime minister.[25]

In the end, the League theorists followed the ethnologist Oka Masao, who envisioned East Asia as a hierarchical ordering of the various ethnic groups (*minzoku chitsujo*) in which each would take its own place.[26] Characteristic of their League theory of Pan-Asianism was an "instrumentalist" approach to ethnic nationality. They saw ethnic nationality as a force to be reckoned with, a potential challenge to Japanese imperialism, but they saw no reason that, in the end, ethnic nationalism in East Asia could not be molded to the agenda of Japan's war against the West.

East Asia as a single ethnic nation

In light of the relationship that the concept of ethnic nationality had with the League of Nations and Wilson's doctrine of "national self-determination" (*minzoku jiketsu shugi*), it should not be surprising that Japanese nationality theorists would appeal to a notion of a regional League while basing their concept of nationality on ethnicity. In fact, in one sense, it may be said that all the League theorists did was to transfer a Stalinist scheme for a league of ethnic nations (under the Soviet Union) to combat Western European capitalism into the notion of a league of ethnic nations (under the Japanese empire) to combat Western capitalist imperialism. What is surprising, however, is the rise of an alternative concept of Pan-Asianism, one that also drew on the appeal of ethnic nationality but which tried to reconcile the claims of ethnicity with a cultural community grounded in the notion of East Asia. Here regionalism sought to reconcile itself with nationalism through a concept of an East Asian ethnic nation that would be a singular, rather than a plural, cultural identity.

Writing in 1943, the same year as Noguchi, Professor Komatsu Kentarō of

Kansai Gakuin University presented a clear summary of the state of Japanese pan-Asianist theories of ethnicity:

> We speak of 'the formation of Greater East Asian ethnic nations' (*Dai tōa minzoku no keisei*), but there are two different ways of thinking about the meaning of the words *Dai tōa minzoku*. One way interprets the meaning to refer to making the many ethnic peoples who live in the Greater East Asian region into their own communal societies, such as the Japanese ethnic nation (*Nihon minzoku*), the Chinese ethnic nation (*Shina minzoku*), or the Thai ethnic nation (*Tai minzoku*), the Annam nation (*Annam minzoku*) or the Indonesian nation (*Indonesia minzoku*). But there is another interpretation that these words refer, not to this plurality of ethnic national communal societies, but rather to the ethnic nations of the Greater East Asia becoming one ethnic nation, that is, to the one Greater East Asian Ethnic Nation. If asked which of the two is our main concern, I would like to suggest that it is the latter interpretation, that is, the formation of a *Dai tōa minzoku* that seeks to hammer out a single Greater East Asian Ethnic Nationality and to build on that basis a single ethnic national society.[27]

Unlike other theorists of a single East Asian ethnic nationality, Komatsu actually exhausted considerable energy in trying theoretically to work out the details for this "brave new" sense of pan-Asianist ethnicity. The remainder of his essay covered all the usual criteria for nationality (or ethnicity): blood kinship, common culture and language, the difference between natural *Volk* and composite nationality, common religion, economy and politics and a common historical fate. In other words, while Komatsu noted that blood was an important factor in this East Asian ethnicity, it was not sufficient. He emphasized that the concept underlying the *Dai tōa minzoku* was not "race," but something between the German concept of *Volk* and the English idea of nation.

Komatsu's theory of a single East Asian nation was not particularly original, nor was his theory the most sophisticated version. He was simply propagating this theory in a book, *The Japanese Ethnic Nation and a New Weltanschauung*, in which government officials and State Shintoists joined with university professors to "assist through improvements in cultural work the brilliant accomplishments of our imperial Army."[28] The source for Komatsu's concept of a Greater East Asian Ethnic Nation was a body of theoretical work on ethnicity and nationality, primarily articulated by sociologists, that emphasized the contingency and plasticity of national identity. Takata Yasuma was a key figure in this sociology of nationality from the mid-1930s, although his work was part of a broader discourse that included Komatsu, Usui Jishō, Nakano Seiichi, Shimmei Masamichi, and others.[29] In broad terms, their approach to the problem of ethnic nationality may be placed within the debate between advocates of an "East Asian League" and those supporting an

"East Asian Community" (*Tōa kyōdōtai-ron*). Critics of the "East Asian League" tended to agree with Kada Tetsuji that the idea that nations have a right to join or secede from the Greater East Asian order "was a form of Western liberal tolerance, a cheap application of the ethnic national self-determinism left-over from the League of Nations, an erroneous nationality policy. The independence of backward ethnic groups in the Greater East Asian Coopera- tive Sphere," Kada concluded, "will only happen through the cooperation of powerful ethnic nations that are contiguous."[30]

No one did more than Takata to deny the right of free association of nations. As head of the quasi-governmental Ethnic Research Institute, Takata proposed a new expanded sense of *Volk* identity (*kō minzoku*) that would ethnically bind all East Asian people, even while the political state remained as a key marker of political empowerment.[31] Trained in sociology, Takata saw ethnic nationality as a functional equivalent of the Western liberal concept of society, and thus open to changes in its scope over time. For over ten years, beginning in the early 1930s, he had written extensively on the difference between *minzoku* and *jinshu*, locating his approach to the concept of *minzoku* in a broader Western literature on national identity. *Minzoku* was, he concluded, a ques- tion of cultural identity and not merely a sign of membership in a political state. He underscored the point by noting that "nationalists in Japan have, after a certain point in the Meiji period, considered Westernization the goal of state development so they tried to rid it of everything Japanese."[32] This approach was doomed to failure, Takata concluded, since it overlooked the importance of nationalism as a form of cultural identity.

After Pearl Harbor and the turn towards a war to "liberate Asia," Takata emphasized the implications for East Asia of this theory of national conscious- ness. Still emphasizing the difference between the concepts of nationality and race (*minzoku* and *jinshu*), and the difference between an ethnic form of nationality (*minzoku*) and membership in a political nation (*kokumin*), Takata applied this theory to the question of regionalism and East Asia. Drawing on the "liberal" or subjective theorists of national formation, Takata noted that:

> when external relations require ethnic groups (those with similarities in blood and culture, and thus a natural affinity for one another) to form an ethnic nation, it is completely possible that the larger group that comprises these ethnic peoples will evoke a consciousness of what we may call the 'broader ethnic group' (*kō minzoku*). ... If today we can conceive of an East Asian Ethnic Nation that unites the various East Asian ethnic nations throughout Japan, Manchukuo and China, or an East Asian Ethnic Nation that may even include the southern region, it is correctly derived from these circumstances.[33]

Takata's concept of a single East Asian Ethnic Nation was, theoretically at least, a direct refutation of the vertical approach to regional order offered by

Oka and the League theorists. He too allowed for the continued existence of smaller ethnic nations within this broader ethnic nation, but he emphasized their regional association in organic terms. There was no Western "liberal" theory of free association or right to secede from this regional identity, as members of the region were bound together in a truly national body that drew on the primacy of bio-cultural ties.

Seeking the impossible synthesis

Much of late wartime discourse on regionalism and ethnicity revolved around how to reconcile these contradictory claims: was the region to be hierarchically structured around ethnic units with the Japanese at the top? Or could one derive from the plasticity of ethnic theory a new form of ethnicity that would provide for a sense of horizontal community within East Asia? The most creative minds tried in various ways to synthesize these competing claims, to find a new communal regionalism that would, nonetheless, provide for distinct ethnic cultural identities while retaining hierarchy and Japanese control. Takata's theory of a single East Asian ethnic nation sparked enthusiasm among many theorists of ethnicity and nationality, included Komatsu and Takata's own student Nakano Seiichi.

Nakano's contribution in particular bridged the academic debate on the meaning of nationality, as he outlined how these theories might inform a new Japanese policy on nationality in the region. At the same time, his 1944 policy proposal for how to apply the ethnic nationality principle in East Asia sought to synthesize Oka's concept of East Asia as a hierarchy of ethnic nations and Takata's concept of East Asia as a single, "broader" ethnic-national community. In keeping with the dominant tendency in wartime theories on *minzoku*, Nakano began by clarifying that *minzoku genri* did not refer to race but was largely synonymous with what was known in German as the *Nationalitätsprinzip*. Drawing on Takata's theories, Nakano then argued that the proper application of this nationality principle in East Asia would avoid the pitfalls of the liberal democracies' model of nation-states and the Soviet ideology of ethnic national self-determination. Citing M. H. Boehm's *Die Nationalitätenfrage*, Nakano dismissed as "a modern western European thesis" any nationality principle that held ethnic nationality (*minzoku*) and the political state (*kokka*) to be inseparable.[34]

Nakano argued that the solution was to be found in Takata's theory of a "broad ethnic nation" that would make room for the cultural identity of East Asians. But Nakano also insisted that Takata's concept of a broader ethnic nation was the context for creating community within the hierarchy of ethnic nations in the East Asian region. He noted that:

> the basis of all East Asian ethnic nations is to be found in the position of an East Asian Ethnic Nation (Dr. Takata). Once we accept this fact, then

it is clear that the position of an East Asian ethnic nation is also the basis of the position of ethnic national complementarity [*minzoku hokan no tachiba*]. Moreover, this means that what appears as a complementary relationship among the ethnic nations is, when seen from a different angle, merely each ethnic nation making manifest its own special job. So, we can call this position of ethnic national complementarity the position of ethnic national duty. In time, as this complementarity progesses, disarray might arise in the relationship between ethnic nations and their specific duties. If we are to avoid such a development, there will need to be a hierarchy among the ethnic nations. Thus, the position of ethnic national complementarity is tightly linked to the position of an ethnic national hierarchy.[35]

Nakano believed that his concept of an "ethnic national complementarity" provided the necessary framework for a synthesis of Takata's "single East Asian Ethnic Nation" and Oka's "hierarchy of ethnic nations." As the awkward language and circular reasoning in the above quotation reveal, Nakano's "synthesis" was not a very clear or stable one. Indeed, it merely reveals the desperation behind wartime efforts to evoke an image of pan-Asian unity even as the more powerful force shaping the region was nationalism.

If Nakano's attempt at a synthesis of ethnic theories for Pan-Asianism was less than successful, the efforts by the Ministry of Welfare to outline a "global policy" based on ethnicity was even more incoherent. In 1943, around the time Nakano was working on his policy outline, the Ministry's Research Office Department of Population and Nationality completed a six-volume report, "A Study of Global Policy with the Yamato *Volk* as the Core."[36] This massive, handwritten document was prepared at the height of the war, too late to have much practical effect on the regional order, but a telling summary nonetheless of how far the intellectual discourse on ethnic nationality and *völkisch* theories had influenced sectors of the imperial Japanese bureaucracy.

As a multi-authored document, the text speaks with predictable multivocal tensions, but some key points should be noted. First, although in some places the text retains traces of the older racial interpretation of *minzoku*, overall it makes a clear distinction between the earlier nineteenth-century notion of biologically determined "race" and the new, ethnological sense of a culturally mediated concept of an ethnic national *Volk*. Early in the text, the authors make a point of noting the important distinction between *jinshu* and *minzoku*, even adding the German equivalents, *Rasse* and *Volk*, to emphasize the distinction. While summarizing Hitler's theories on "blood and soil," the anonymous authors explicitly point out that Hitler's racial theories were essentially articulations of this sense of an ethnic nation, or *Volk* (*minzoku*).[37] In short, these Welfare Ministry bureaucrats identified the core concept of their global policy with the Nazi effort to reconfigure society in *völkisch*, or ethnic national, terms, and they made explicit their understanding that this effort drew from the conceptual reforms that social, political, and anthropological discourse had been making since the First World War in moving beyond the traditional notion of a purely biologically determined "race."

But the authors of this global policy also stressed that regionalism distinguished how this problem of *Volk* identity would be implemented under Japanese imperialism from its use in Nazi Germany. They conceded that:

> Japan's approach is of course close to the German model. But at the same time, where she is different from Germany is in her intimate and inseparable relationship to Manchukuo, her relationship with the New China and the new relationships she has with the South Pacific territories: in short, her ongoing effort to develop the so-called New Order in East Asia by forming a new large, regional block.[38]

The authors went to great pains to stress that this regional order should not be mistaken as merely a rehashing of the old exploitive economic relations of imperialism. Instead, Japan's regional order was designed to address something far more troublesome than economic imbalance – although it tried to address that issue as well. The more fundamental problem was the "nationality problem" or the problem of the *Volk*. So they concluded: "the reason the nationality problem is taken so seriously, especially in Germany, is because they know that the key to victory or defeat in the Second World War ultimately hangs on a successful management of the nationality problem."[39]

It was on this issue that the policy for regionalism through *völkisch* identity floundered. The Welfare Ministry report reflected the same tensions that existed in the broader public discourse on *minzoku* where Takata's proposal to construct a new, single East Asia *Volk* was met by Kamei Kan'ichirō's argument that the solution to a Greater East Asia Co-Prosperity Sphere was to strengthen the particular ethnic identities in the region.[40] Although the report argued that one pillar of the regional policy was to encourage nationalism throughout East Asia, it never conceded an inch on the question of whether Japan should exercise leadership over the entire region.[41] But it also tried to offer a new logic of horizontal relations within this vertical order that would soften, if not completely displace, the internal hierarchy under the Yamato *Volk*. In this sense, a nationality policy for the *Völker* of Asia was the most important condition for establishing a stable, new regional order. Thus the report noted that:

> it is not necessary to point out that the political and economic structure of the East Asia Co-Prosperity Sphere as a regional economic block has as its goal the construction of a High Defense State needed to carry out the affairs. But before that plan can succeed, one has to look beyond the concept of an East Asia regional economic block, to what constitutes the base: the various *Völker* that are internally divided. We must establish a nationality policy that will bring these various *Völker* into an organic unity.[42]

In essence, these bureaucrats were still confronting the fundamental problem of Asian regionalism: the dilemma of how to hammer unity out of the plurality that has always been the reality of Asia.[43]

One searches in vain for a single, coherent policy on regional integration during the era of imperial Japan. Indeed, in 1981, the former first Minister of Greater East Asia, Aoki Kazuo, insisted that no matter how powerful pan-Asianist sentiment might have been among private intellectuals, no official policy of Pan-Asianism was ever adopted by the Japanese government.[44] As Yamamuro Shin'ichi notes, this statement is both unsurprising and beside the point. As a modern nation-state, imperial Japan was in no position to adopt a policy that might undermine the very legitimacy of the nation-state as the unit of modern political systems, nor could it completely ignore cultural arguments about Japan's historical connectedness to Asia, especially as it developed colonial relations throughout the region. Aoki's statement really discloses the uneasy relationship between ethno-cultural concepts of national identity and the kind of national identity fostered by the multi-ethnic imperial Japanese state. Intersecting both the claims of ethnicity and the scope of the Japanese empire was the problem of an "Asian" identity, a problem that grew only more intractable as the war escalated into a war against the West.

Although ethnic national discourse and ideas about ethnic identity in imperial Japan may seem marginal when viewed from a "policy studies" perspective, such issues are of central importance when one considers social ideologies and their influence throughout the region. What stands out most in these efforts to construct Asian regionalism during the wartime – and contrasts sharply with American efforts at social integration through "E pluribus unum" – is the key role ascribed to ethnic definitions of nationality. Bureaucrats in the Ministry of Welfare spoke for many, both Japanese and non-Japanese, when they approached social identity through the lens of ethnicity. "As soon as Man is born," they opined, "he already belongs to a *Volk*. In the real world, it is not possible for a Man not to belong to a *Volk*. Not only in his physical existence, but in his spiritual existence too, Man always already possesses a realistic, socialized consciousness through his 'ethnic apperception'."[45] Of course, such arguments only betrayed the "ethnic apperception" of those who made them. A more difficult question to answer – which I must leave for another time – is how widely that "ethnic apperception" was shared by Japan's colonial subjects and victims.

Part IV

Pan-Asianism adjusted

Wartime to postwar

12 Constructing destiny

Rōyama Masamichi and Asian regionalism in wartime Japan

J. Victor Koschmann

Introduction

In selecting the political scientist Rōyama Masamichi (1895–1980) for discussion, I am attempting to explore the margin, or boundary, of Pan-Asianism. That is, Rōyama's perspective on Asian unity can be located at the rationalist extreme of Pan-Asianism, some of whose proponents embraced highly intuitive, naturalistic, or culturalist visions of Asia, many of which are implicitly backward-looking. The distinction between Rōyama and the culturalist pan-Asianists can be illustrated by situating both in the framework employed by the historian Tetsuo Najita in his survey of modern Japanese intellectual history. I refer to his distinction between "restorationism," which he defines as faith in a kind of "traditional idealism" or "cultural spirit" that emphasizes human values and community, and "bureaucratism," which focuses on "effective, measurable ... performance" toward materialistic goals.[1] Culturalist Pan-Asianism – which seeks implicitly to "restore" some ontologically pure cultural unity in Asia – falls historically on the side of restorationism,[2] while Rōyama's perspective would clearly be on the bureaucratic side. Indeed, Rōyama was one of Japan's leading specialists in the field of public administration.

Despite his rationalistic frame of mind, Rōyama advocated the legitimacy and desirability of forming a Japan-dominated East Asian Community (EAC) and, eventually, a "Greater East Asian Co-Prosperity Sphere" (GEACPS), and devoted himself to achieving those objectives. With colleagues in the Shōwa Research Association, an advisory body to Prime Minister Konoe Fumimaro (1891–1945), he played a pivotal role in persuading Japanese intellectuals in universities, government ministries, journalism, and other pursuits, of the viability of Asian communal unity. In that sense, he was a kind of pan-Asianist. At the same time, I will argue that Rōyama's approach to Asian unity was scientific and rationalist, nourished by the same broad stream of social scientific development that undergirded the post-World War II resurgence of political science.

Modern political science in postwar Japan

In order to highlight significant conceptual continuities between Rōyama's wartime perspective on Asian community and the mainstream approach to political studies adopted in Japan after the Pacific War, it is useful to begin with a brief characterization of the postwar approach to politics. In his 1947 essay, "Politics as a Science in Japan," the leading postwar political scientist, Maruyama Masao (1914–96), charged that the study of politics in Japan was sterile and abstract, "for in its development it almost never had the corrective experience of shaping and being shaped by political realities."[3] The reason was that in Japan before and during World War II there had been no freedom of inquiry in the political realm. Under the system of imperial sovereignty, "any inquiry into the ultimate source of political power became taboo."[4] Since Japan's defeat, however, "political reality" was "laid completely open to scientific criticism" creating "a real base ... for the development of political science." That is, in the postwar milieu, political science could finally become "a science oriented to actualities (*Wirklichkeitswissenschaft*)."[5]

What, then, did Maruyama prescribe as the guiding principles, the criteria, for postwar political studies as a "science oriented to actualities"? In his view, the fundamental problem was that, "political investigation both regulates and is regulated by its object of study. Therefore it is the 'original sin' of political theory to be markedly subjective and to take on an ideological cast." In other words, the authentic political scientist was obliged to be existentially involved in the object of study, but also had to "aim at the highest level of objectivity ... ." The very nature of political study itself made this conflict inevitable. Maruyama sampled the views of several leading German political theorists, including Schäffle, Bluntschli, and Jellinek, and concluded:

> These approaches differ in detail, but they all agree that the distinctive characteristic of politics is a plastic futurity. This interpretation is bound up with the view that political science is not the study of pure being-as-it-is (*das Seiende*) but includes value judgements and thus is the study of being-as-it-ought-to-be (*das Sein-Sollende*) ... .

Thus, to borrow Landshut's words, it is the destiny of political science to grasp political reality "from the standpoint of its potentiality for change" (*unter dem Aspekt ihrer möglichen Veränderbarkeit*).

> Here an object does not exist in any fixed form prior to the cognitive process. ... There is a constant interchange between the subject and the object. ... In the political world the very proposal of a category or of a formulation for a problem already involves a certain evaluation of the forces at work in the sphere of actual situations.[6]

An investigation of Rōyama Masamichi's approach to political analysis shows that despite the various taboos that affected what could or could not be said about politics in the milieu he lived in, Rōyama did attend to political realities as he understood them. He also came to approach political study in a manner broadly conversant with what Maruyama prescribed, that is, as a study in which subject and object interact, a study of "being-as-it-ought-to-be."[7] In short, contrary to what we might conclude from Maruyama's blanket indictment of prewar political science as merely part and parcel of an authoritarian political system that was premised on irrationality and obscurantism, Japan's violent expansion in Asia was the product not *only* of irrational obscurantism, or even of emotional and romantic notions of Asian unity. It was also supported by the most recent social scientific approaches to politics and international relations.

Rōyama's trajectory

Rōyama's formation as a political scientist came in the 1920s, under the influence of an earlier generation of well-known scholars associated with the Taishō democratic movement. To a considerable extent, Rōyama accepted their notion of "modern political science," which included the caveat that political analysis should be "scientific." At the same time, as he wrote in 1925, Rōyama was convinced that social life could not be fully understood via the positivistic methodologies of the natural sciences. He believed that social life was concerned with the realization of value and therefore would always have a strongly teleological cast. Thus, for him, politics was ultimately a functional practice involving organized efforts toward shared goals. What he called "political society" (*seiji shakai*) amounted to "goal-oriented society" (*Genossenschaft*); in his view, human communities (*kyōdō shakai*) were constantly in the process of historicizing themselves as "goal-oriented societies."[8]

What eventually emerged from this grasp of political society, however, was not a whole-hearted commitment to "Taishō democracy" as it was developing in the 1920s but rather a conviction that democracy was being displaced by a new set of relationships among social forces, cultural ideals and the state that he later termed "constitutional dictatorship." Rōyama's turn away from Taishō democratic thought was heavily influenced by his vivid sense that a "crisis of democracy" was underway in the leading industrial countries, including Japan. He described this "crisis" in a collection of essays written in the 1920s and in 1935 published as a book, entitled *The Direction of Japanese Politics* (*Nihon seiji dōkōron*).[9] In these essays, Rōyama analyzed what he called the "second stage" in Japanese politics, an era in which, since the establishment of universal manhood suffrage in 1925, political party organization was taking the place of charismatic leadership, and political bureaucratization and professionalization were expanding rapidly.

Although Rōyama found direct evidence in his own country and others, his understanding of the crisis was filled out by European and American works on capitalism and politics. He was especially impressed with Rudolf Hilferding's model of "organized capitalism," which he saw as the basis for other transformations that comprised the crisis. Broadly conceived, organized capitalism entailed industrial rationalization, the gradual subjection of the economy to national priorities, consolidation of governmental control, planning in place of free competition, and increased use of regulatory technology. Overall, borrowing terms from the Bolshevik leader Nikolai Bukharin, Rōyama saw capitalism as moving inexorably from the "irrational" system of free enterprise to "rational" organization under the state.

As examples of rational planning and organization in the economy, Rōyama was impressed not only by the Soviet five-year plans and the rise of the Nazi Party in Germany, but the emergence out of the Labor Party in Great Britain of Oswald Moseley's "social fascism" and the American New Deal, which he interpreted as emblematic of constitutional dictatorship. He used the term, "constitutional dictatorship" (*rikkenteki dokusai*) to refer to the concentration of power entailed in governments' use of constitutional prerogatives to sidestep parliamentary institutions and administratively institute radical economic and other reforms. Historian Mitani Taichirō argues that, for Rōyama, the concept of "constitutional dictatorship" arose out of a willingness to sacrifice "parliamentarism" in order to defend "constitutionalism." Rōyama also referred to the New Deal as a "dictatorship by reason" (*riseiteki dokusai*).[10]

Rōyama began in 1933 to characterize his own standpoint toward these events as "social progressivism," which he presented as the political stance appropriate to a post-liberal and post-social democratic era. In fact, he argued that his "social progressivism" was de facto the ideology of the New Deal, although important aspects were also evident in Vladimir Lenin's administration in the USSR. He offered his clearest statement on "social progressivism" in 1939, in an essay entitled "The Formation of a National Community" (Kokumin kyōdōtai no keisei).[11]

Along with "constitutional dictatorship" and "social progressivism" he now spoke methodologically of a "contemporary political science" (*gendai seijigaku*) that was replacing the "modern political science" (*kindai seijigaku*) of the 1920s. "Contemporary political science" was focused not on the state but on something Rōyama called the "national community," which was more closely rooted than the state in the ethnic communalism of the nation (*minzoku*).[12]

Did Rōyama's turn to "contemporary political science" represent a fundamental change in the understanding of politics that he first enunciated around 1925? It appears that to some extent it did. Moreover, a major source of this change was the work of an American political scientist, W. Y. Elliot, who expounded what he called "co-organic theory." As the political historians Mitani Taichirō, Sakai Tetsuya, and others, have pointed out, Elliot's theory catalyzed a significant change in Rōyama's understanding of "function." In 1925, he had argued that political values are not end values but means values. In other words, they were functional, and political society was "functional society." Now, however, to the teleological element of functionalism he added what he called an ontological dimension. According to his new understanding, functional action was not only teleological, in the sense that it realizes or incorporates certain values and objectives, but ontological in that it manifests a set of given conditions or constraints analogous to a biological heritage. Functional means were now not only selected instrumentally to reach certain goals, but were prescribed organically – ontologically – by the very nature of the community that produced them as its "organs." Thus, political society now included not only organization directed toward end values but an inner tendency toward organic unity based on cultural values. Elliot's theory led Rōyama to understand the constitutional part of "constitutional dictatorship" in Japan in an unconventional way, as "something constructed on the intrinsic principles of the national political formation centering on Japan's 'national essence' (*kokutai*)." Thus, by the late-1930s, Rōyama was to some extent accommodating a less rational, more nativistic-sounding conceptual framework than had been the case earlier.[13] At the same time, it is especially significant that his new inclination was guided less by Japanese ultranationalists than the work of an American political scientist.

East Asian Community as Japan's Asian "destiny"

An important dimension of Rōyama's concept of "contemporary political science," and especially the role in it of "national community" in place of the state, was an orientation to regionalism that transcended the nation-state and nationalism. It was on this conceptual foundation that in the late 1930s Rōyama developed his notion of Japan's "community of destiny" (*unmei kyōdōtai*) in Asia. He noted that the American historian, Frederick Jackson Turner, had argued for the crucial importance of the "frontier" in forming the American way of life, and drew the analogy that, for Japan, the importance of East Asia as a region of destiny was similar to and, perhaps, even more compelling than of the frontier for the United States.[14] What did Rōyama mean by "destiny" here? Was he, after all, referring to the romantically culturalist belief that the Japanese were in some way "naturally" related to the Asians whom "destiny" had placed under their control? As noted above, it seems that he was not. Rōyama explicitly addressed his concept of destiny in a 1938 essay:

> The meaning of the statement that the East is a regional community of destiny is, first of all, political. It is not dependent on the constant factor that the structure of Eastern culture is regional in scope. It is, rather, created by a *sense* of destiny – destiny coming to consciousness – and, accordingly, by a political movement.[15]

By "political" Rōyama appears to mean "goal oriented." In other words, he contends that his East Asian "community of destiny" must, paradoxically, be consciously constructed as a subjective (*shutaiteki*) project. Perhaps his notion of a constructed destiny will seem less paradoxical when it is understood that Rōyama worked closely with philosopher Miki Kiyoshi (1897–1945), especially in the context of the Shōwa Research Association, and it is likely that Rōyama was influenced by Miki's philosophical language.[16] Miki's concept of destiny has to be understood historically against the background of the philosophy of technology and imagination that he was developing in the mid-1930s. In that context, historical destiny is the outcome of two inseparable aspects: purposive action and becoming, or emergence. According to Miki, "Although to act is to make something, if making did not at the same time include the meaning of becoming, history would be unthinkable. History becomes possible when construction also means emergence."[17] In other words, one might say that historical agents discover their destiny in the process of making history.

Rōyama posits several constructive principles, or what he calls "active theoretical characteristics," that could guide the Japan-led East Asian Community that, in his view, would result from Japan's "advance" into China: First, the community:

> must be a political region with a new structure (*taisei*). . . . It is a regional community and its political form must naturally be a kind of league. Second, Eastern culture is not yet a unified culture, but is rather the co-existence of heterogeneous elements. . . . Accordingly the Eastern regional community would have to respect the heterogeneity of the various national cultures . . . while moving gradually toward unity and creative development. . . .

Third, it was therefore necessary to "construct a new regional, cultural composite (*bunka tōgōtai*)" that would be connected to both "constant factors like natural, geographical conditions and variable factors such as economy, science, and technology. . . ." Fourth, the economy of the regional community must be "cooperative" rather than "imperialist," borrowing from modern imperialism some of its economic theory, techniques of management, and a willingness to cooperate with native and national capital, but always maintaining as its goal the "construction of a regional destiny." Lastly, it should not be based on autarchy or the assumptions of an economic bloc. According to Rōyama:

> [a]utarchy and bloc systems are passive, temporary regimes rather than [systems based on the] principle of world formation. . . . In the world of the future, there will be a balance among regions that subsist in organic unity between nature and culture. It will be a world of regional communities.[18]

Here again, Rōyama argues that conceptions of an East Asian Community (*Tōa kyōdōtai* – EAC) should have relatively little to do with "Asian culture" as that concept was often understood by pan-Asianists. In his view, "a regional community of destiny in East Asia could not be premised merely on the static factor of a supposedly common East Asian culture."[19] Nor could the unity of the East be a function of "belief based on intuition," for such intuitions had often been expressed without effect since antiquity, when belief in *hakkō ichiu* ("all the corners of the world under one roof") had first appeared. According to Rōyama, a similarly "intuitive" grasp of Asian unity was expressed in the Meiji period (1868–1912) by the art historian Okakura Tenshin (1863–1913) and the Chinese revolutionary Sun Yat-sen (1866–1925). While interesting, such conceptions were incapable, in themselves, of providing the basis for a dynamic East Asian Community.

The same applied, according to Rōyama, to the conceptions of Asian culture embraced by philosophers like Miki Kiyoshi when they seemed to argue that the culture of EAC must encompass both universality and particularity and therefore ultimately transcend the region of East Asia itself. Rōyama countered that, while that might be true in the long run, in the formative stages of the EAC it was most important to take account of the diverse ways of thinking of the many existing peoples and groups of East Asia. That is, "thought and cultural theory that tend toward abstraction can take on concreteness only by colliding with the particularity of people (*minzoku*) and region."[20]

In sum, for Rōyama the relevance of culture to the formation of an East Asian Community depended upon what we might call culture's concrete historicity, in terms both of activity rather than stasis and of local concreteness instead of abstraction. To be relevant, culture had to play a functional role at the conscious level in local historical movements.

Rōyama applied more or less the same criteria to race and ethnicity. When he first wrote in a theoretical vein on the EAC in 1938, some critics, such as sociologist Takata Yasuma, protested that he had too hastily written off the importance of culture and race. Therefore, when he revisited these issues in 1939, Rōyama made a special effort to credit such factors, while also trying to clarify their limitations. With regard to race, he proceeds much the same as with culture, by emphasizing the criterion of historical functionality. In Rōyama's view, critics like Takata were quite justifiably calling attention to the racial kinship between Chinese and Japanese in order to cause the Chinese to reconsider their resistance to Japanese troops. In other words, they seemed to assume that the Chinese would be more willing to accept their subordination to Japan if they could view it as legitimate tutelage within the racial family. Despite their good intentions, however, critics like Takata still had to face the fact that race was fundamentally "natural" and therefore static and meaningless in itself. Thus, he argues:

[o]f course, the mistaken Chinese nationalist (*minzokushugi*) movement might be corrected by emphasizing the sociological and/or cultural-scientific significance of the similarity by blood of the Japanese and Chinese *minzoku* and urging that it be taken into account. This is precisely Takata's point. However, an East Asian Community can be built upon the foundation of racial/ethnic community only when that foundation is infused with consciousness of [the confrontation between] White races

and Colored races at the level of the composition of the world order. So long as that is absent, the static similarity between the two peoples can never generate political movements to defend one's own racial/ethnic group. In other words, if not perceived against the backdrop of the movement of world history, the logic of Sino-Japanese racial/ethnic cooperation will fall upon deaf ears.[21]

Like cultural similarity, racial similarity would be directly relevant to Japan's efforts to bring China into an EAC only when it was linked to some form of desire in the minds of the Chinese themselves. Only as an aspect of solidarity among colored races *in opposition to* the White race could racial affinities between Chinese and Japanese be of any use in building a common community.

The "China Incident" and national subjectivity

What had finally and decisively begun to transform factors such as geographical propinquity and cultural and racial similarity into vital historical forces was a certain Zeitgeist that arose from real historical events, culminating in the so-called China Incident of 1937. According to Rōyama, only through that Incident had "the East, led by Japan, finally departed from the leadership of the European powers. In a word, it marked the East's awakening, a phenomenon whose world-historical meaning is the unity of the East." Thus Rōyama was among those who attributed to the China Incident "world-historical significance," both philosophically and politically.

Prior to Japan's decisive move into China, the world's Eurocentric structure had remained unchallenged:

> Unfortunately, when viewed in terms of the universal order centering on Europe, especially Western Europe, East Asia must be seen as particular [and thus non-universal]. This is a structural feature of the historical world, and emerges in the midst of historical processes. Considered as entities or events in the historical world, Japan and China merely appear as Oriental extensions of the international structure of modern Europe.[22]

Thus, from the perspective of Eurocentrism, Japan had been essentially on the same plane as China. However, in the modern period Japan forged ahead as a world-historical entity, striving to achieve full freedom as an autonomous national subject. This meant not only expanding her strength and international status but developing a higher level of historical self-consciousness among the Japanese themselves. Rōyama goes on:

> When viewed in a world-historical, international-structural perspective, neither Japan's spectacular development in the Meiji period nor even the strengthened national self-consciousness achieved through engaging in

war with a major Eastern European power in the Russo-Japanese War were sufficient to produce true national awareness.[23]

Indeed, only since World War I had Japanese begun to be fully conscious of their national independence and to break out of their limited international status as "Oriental watchdog in the Anglo-Japanese Alliance."

> The European war, 1914–18, and events since have demonstrated that the world includes more than Europe and the areas under its hegemony. It was in partial recognition of that reality that the League of Nations was formed. … Nevertheless, the League organization was formed on the basis of the theory of one nation one state, in the name of national self-determination and modern state sovereignty, which reached their apex in the nineteenth century. Thus, the League rejected the kind of regionalism that would have allowed the East be recognized as the East. The League organization in Geneva universalized the West and sought to incorporate the countries of the East into its universal system. … As for the East, it was expected to universalize itself through a process of Westernization focused on nationalism and the sovereign state; in the East, no regional unity would be recognized.[24]

But finally, according to Rōyama, the Japanese had begun to "be conscious of their East Asian status and to advocate solutions to the Manchurian-Mongolian and China problems from their own independent standpoint."[25] More recently, "the Manchurian Incident and the China Incident have provided the first occasions on which the Japanese people are able to grasp East Asian realities in union with Japanese ideals"; indeed – and here, of course, Rōyama and his colleagues were especially wide of the mark – the Japanese people were now able to "transcend Japanese realities and grasp the ideals of not only China but the various other nations of East Asia."

In any case, it is clear that for Rōyama, Japan's own self-formation had to parallel its emerging instrumental posture toward the external world. Without a process of radical reorganization within Japan, which among other aspects would entail a higher level of national self-consciousness on the part of the Japanese people, the regional community Japan sought would remain out of reach. A "national community" (*kokumin kyōdōtai*) had to be constructed in parallel with an EAC:

> Theory and policy for the construction of an EAC naturally call to mind discussions regarding a new order for the Japanese nation itself, and without a close connection to such discussions the discourse on EAC will be isolated and unrealistic.[26]

The "new order" (*shin taisei*) planned for Japan was variously conceived by Rōyama, Ryū Shintarō, and other Shōwa Research Association members, but in general its economic dimensions included such goals as overcoming the profit motive by means of a "new economic ethic," separating the management of business and industry from their ownership, and pursuing a centrally planned economy by organizing the various sectors of private capital and securing cooperation in what was touted as a new economic "communalism." Politically, the drive toward unity led to the voluntary dissolution of all existing political parties and, in October 1940, to the establishment of the Imperial Rule Assistance Association (Taisei Yokusan-kai) as the central political structure of the new order. In many ways, this event represented the realization in Japan of Rōyama's model of constitutional dictatorship.

Accordingly, construction of new orders both domestically and regionally comprised a great mission:

> If ... this thought structure, as the concretization of the "specific universality" and "realistic ideal" of the New Order in East Asia, could be manifested as the intellectual structure of the Japanese nation, then for the first time East Asia could be brought into full continuity with the rest of the [Western] world.[27]

Regionalism and nationalism

For Rōyama, "regionalism" was the latest stage in the evolution of the world system. East Asia was becoming a coherent region in a world that was coalescing increasingly into regional units. However, to make regionalism viable it was necessary to overcome nationalism, not just the nationalism of other East Asian areas but Japanese nationalism as well.[28]

Indeed, it was owing to nationalism that Japan's advance into China was so seriously "misunderstood" by the Chinese themselves. According to Rōyama, it was in part the fact that China developed later than Japan that was responsible for China's alliance with Western imperialism against Japan. This led to confrontation, despite the fact that, according to Rōyama, China's true interests lay rather in a common Japan–China commitment to an East Asia Community:

> [T]he unity of the East must be born of the transcendence of nationalism. Where is the motive force capable of accomplishing that transcendence? It is latent in the very expansion of Japanese nationalism toward the Asian continent. ... The principle intrinsic to Japan's advance is not imperialism but rather regionalism for the purposes of defense and development. This principle of regionalism has become manifest only recently. It is entirely natural that the immature Chinese nationalism should misunderstand and distort this as imperialism.[29]

Japanese nationalism was being transformed into a cooperative form of "regionalism" via Japan's continental expansion. Therefore, he argues, it should not be mistaken for European-style imperialism. Of course, Rōyama's discourse is stunningly blind to the savage realities of what, in respect, can only be understood as Japan's imperialist war in China.

Rōyama's articulations of regionalism often included emphasis on economic development:

> The main objective of Japan's advance onto the continent is [the formation of] a regional community of destiny. It is not continental economic management, nor is it colonial policy or a policy of commercial investment. This regional effort is constrained and controlled by the principle of cooperative economics. Moreover, it is not what is sometimes called bloc economics ... The highest objective of Japan's continental administration is contained in the plan for regional development.[30]

Sakai Tetsuya has argued that concern for Asian development and, more broadly, the "modernization" of Asia, was a constant factor in Rōyama's thought from prewar and wartime through postwar.[31] Sakai's fascinating characterization of Rōyama as an early "modernization" theorist fits well with the argument suggested here: that Rōyama's way of thinking politically – in this case focused on EAC – had much in common with that of other "modernists," including members of the younger, postwar generation like Maruyama Masao.[32]

Before considering how Rōyama responded to announcement of the next stage in Japan's regional ambitions, the "Greater East Asia Co-Prosperity Sphere," it is useful to recapitulate the methodological underpinnings of his 1938–39 conception of EAC, especially his emphasis on the need for a constructive, "subjective" (*shutaiteki*) attitude. Rōyama himself spelled it out clearly:

> If the regional community whose main characteristics I have outlined can be taken as the basic principle for the formation of a new order in East Asia, then it must appear first as a political structure. It goes without saying that the economy and culture of the existing order in East Asia will become elements of the new structure, but as I noted above they are not actively the formative elements. Ultimately, a new cooperative economy will take shape. A new culture will be created. This is essential. Nevertheless, what must precede all this and provide the motive force is politics in the broad sense. What must take precedence over all else is the will of the nations (*minzoku*) and their leaders who will actively or passively, endogenously or exogenously, become conscious of a shared regional destiny.[33]

Rōyama's functional, goal-oriented approach to politics as a "plastic futurity" also underlay his response to the extension of Japan's expansionist goals beyond East Asia proper.

Geopolitics and the "Co-Prosperity Sphere"

How would it be possible in a short period of time for Japan to establish a regional community that would extend as far as the Dutch East Indies? This issue confronted public-minded Japanese intellectuals in the summer of 1940, following Foreign Minister Matsuoka Yōsuke's announcement of the need to construct a "stable," and "self-sufficient" "Greater East Asian Co-Prosperity Sphere" that would include "not only East Asia but French Indochina, the Dutch East Indies and other areas." To Rōyama, writing in the spring of 1941, the idea of such a sphere seemed on the face of it "extremely abstract and vague."[34] When one considered the type and level of economic and other relations that currently existed among the various subregions to be encompassed, the results were not at all promising: relations between East Asia and insular Southeast Asia, especially the Dutch East Indies, continued to be "limited to minor economic interaction and a small amount of maritime transportation." In terms of the established principles of "natural, political, and economic geography," it was clearly going to be very difficult to integrate them into a functioning unit; indeed, it had to be recognized that such a Sphere would include "highly complex, conflicting geographical elements."[35]

Despite his initial doubts, however, Rōyama responded energetically. In early 1941, he sketched the outlines of a searching investigation that activated, in new theoretical language, important elements of the ideological mediations that had governed his intellectual encounter with Konoe's New Order and the EAC. First, he elaborates on the reasons for his initial skepticism regarding the Sphere. The expansive region outlined by Matsuoka included three sub-regions: (1) continental Eurasia, (2) the peninsular subregion, and (3) the insular subregion of the southwest Pacific. Drawing on the discipline of geography, Rōyama argues that the ability to knit these disparate regions into a single sphere would depend heavily upon the degree to which they had already become linked through a history of economic and other relations and were connected by viable means of transportation. In the case of the proposed Sphere, these criteria offered little reason for optimism, as it seemed obvious that "the mutual relations among these three huge regions are ... still in an underdeveloped state." Transportation was largely by sea and limited in scope and technological sophistication. According to Rōyama, "even the core area of the Sphere, which includes Japan, Manchuria and China, contains a number of obstacles to the construction of such an entity." However, the most serious and obvious obstacle to integration was the nature of the insular subregion, the South Seas, or "Nanyō." Although the island peoples of this subregion did have some historical connections with the peninsular areas of Indochina and Malaya, their relations with East Asia, including Japan, Manchuria, and China, had been extremely limited.[36] Judging from such criteria, therefore, it would be relatively difficult for Japan to rapidly bring about a wholly unprecedented degree of Japanese involvement in the area.

However, Rōyama is not content with a purely objective assessment of the potential of the Sphere. In order to go beyond the standard, empirical discipline of geography that generated his initial assessment, he introduces a new discipline that was "gradually gaining acceptance," that of geopolitics (*chiseigaku*). Following Karl Haushofer (1869–1946) and other European scholars in this new field, Rōyama defined geopolitics as a discipline that, while scientific, deals with geographical space as a historically-dynamic entity that contains important "subjective (*shukanteki*; *shutaiteki*)" elements. Such elements included "historical movements toward the formation of geographical entities such as nations (*minzoku*; *kokumin*)." Value judgments, a strong policy orientation, and the "courage" to make predictions were always implicit in the subject matter of geopolitics. Indeed, this new discipline was best viewed as a creative, projective discipline in which, according to one assessment, "objective reality does not exist." He admits that, as a result of its teleological thrust, geopolitics had drawn criticism for being "romantic" and "mystical," but insists that the objective dimension of geopolitics more than compensated for its subjective aspects. Indeed, "the duty of geopolitics is to counteract scientifically and logically any tendencies toward romanticism and mysticism." Rōyama suggests that only through the lens of such a discipline was it possible to conceive of a viable Asian community that would include Southeast as well as East Asia.[37]

Rōyama's understanding of geopolitics led him to search for "dynamic, historical movements" that were likely to affect the destiny of the Asian region. In his view, the three movements that were of decisive importance for the Sphere were, (1) the movement toward formation of nation-states (*minzoku-kokka*), (2) the imperial movement toward formation of colonies by the Western powers, and (3) movements toward national self-determination.[38] Of these, the most important to Japan were the second and third, but Rōyama adds that the movement on the part of Western countries toward formation of colonies had recently slowed, and turned from aggressiveness to defensiveness.

In sum, what tentatively emerged from Rōyama's "subjective," "predictive" exercise in geopolitical reasoning was that the Sphere could become a reality only as a fourth historical movement that would subsume Japan's own regionalism, German and Italian efforts to form a new order in Europe, and Asian movements for self-determination.[39]

Even Rōyama's "geopolitical" perspective provided little reason for optimism. He concludes:

> As we have seen, in light not only of the static foundation of the Sphere but of an equally important dynamic dimension affecting the southern area, establishment of the Co-Prosperity Sphere is definitely not the simple task hoped for by politicians and the general public but an extremely difficult project full of impediments and obstacles. The existing geopolitical conditions are not at all sufficient to bring about establishment of the Sphere.[40]

It was necessary to continue to study the region "subjectively" as well as "objectively," with attention not only to "static" factors also but to dynamic geopolitical issues related, for example, to defense, resources, and ethnic nationalism.

It seems, therefore, that for Rōyama, the Sphere could be properly conceived, not as a clearly accessible policy alternative, but only as a project that contained a substantial number of unknowns. It was a matter of will, above all. As such a project, it had to be recognized as political in essence.

Toward postwar

Along with many other social scientists, Rōyama continued throughout the Pacific War to participate in public discourse related to East Asian policy and to put his international political expertise at the service of Japan's wartime empire.[41] Clearly, therefore, that empire cannot be explained as romantic, or "restorationist"; it was not simply a matter of Pan-Asianism gone wrong. The vision of an Asian community that would represent the dialectical overcoming of Western-centered imperialism, nationalism, and liberalism was extremely attractive to modern, Western-oriented social scientists such as Rōyama. His sophisticated, constructivist methodology was markedly similar to the one that after defeat provided the foundation for the postwar political science practiced by Maruyama and many others.

It is especially interesting to note that this methodology could be used to make the case for peace as well as war. In 1949, at the height of the political crisis over the terms of a peace treaty with the Allied powers, Japanese intellectuals, including Maruyama, were in general firmly opposed to a one-sided peace treaty that would exclude the Soviet Union and other nations not aligned with the United States in the emerging Cold War. Many were also committed to an international position of unarmed neutrality for Japan. These intellectuals expressed their viewpoint most eloquently in a December 1950 statement signed by 35 members of the Peace Problems Discussion Circle (Heiwa mondai danwakai), entitled "On Peace: Our Third Statement." Maruyama Masao was a leading member of the Circle (as was Rōyama), and played a central role in drafting the statement.

The statement clearly reveals the impact of a constructive, teleological approach similar to that developed by Rōyama in the 1930s and prescribed by Maruyama in his postwar essay. The statement contends that any view of international politics "contains volitional elements," making it "impossible to achieve any objective understanding which is unrelated to a subjective position." It also pointed out that, "If we believe it possible to adjust relations without resort to arms, we will greatly increase such a likelihood."[42] The statement reflected and further sharpened a political and intellectual opposition that had emerged in Japan between "progressives," including Maruyama, who aggressively opposed a peace treaty that would bind Japan to the United States side in the Cold War, and those calling themselves "realists," who accepted global confrontation between East and West as inevitable and supported Japan's alignment with the West. In some respects, therefore, social science methodology provided one of the many forms of continuity between the regime of total war and what would come to be called "postwar democracy." The main point, of course, is not to show that postwar progressives and modernists like Maruyama Masao were still under the spell of an approach to political analysis that informed the expansionist ideology of total war, but rather to suggest that in some of its formulations the pan-Asianist ideology of Japanese dominion in Asia was more "rational" and methodologically sophisticated than is often recognized.

13 The postwar intellectuals' view of "Asia"

Oguma Eiji

In 1950, Shimizu Ikutarō, one of Japan's most popular intellectuals, commented that, "now, once again, the Japanese are Asians."[1] For intellectuals disoriented by defeat and reduced to economic impoverishment, Japan was no longer one of the Western powers but merely one of the minor countries of "Asia." From that point forward there emerged in modern Japanese history a repeated confrontation between competing inclinations to learn from the West and to reassess "Asia" and tradition. Having until now researched post-Meiji theories of Japanese ethnicity (*minzoku*) and colonial policies, here I wish to concentrate on what "Asia" meant to postwar Japan's "progressive intellectuals."

In the wake of defeat

In recently defeated Japan, the most compelling issues of the day were modernization and democratization. These, in turn, were matters indivisible from the problem of how to represent the "West" and "Asia." As one might expect, contemporary intellectuals advocated democratization and modernization modeled on "Western modernity," and were inclined to look askance toward "backward Asia." This inclination, however, was related in a number of ways to the historical context of the day.

To begin with, during the war criticism of "Western modernity" was severe. The Pacific War cast "Western imperialism" as the enemy and touted "Asian liberation." Moreover, during the 1930s it had become common currency among intellectuals to criticize a "civil society" that, following Hegelian philosophy and Marxism, they viewed as essentially synonymous with "capitalist society." For this reason, former Marxists who converted to supporting the war joined others during the conflict to criticize "Western modernity" in the name of "world historical philosophy" and to advocate the "overcoming of modernity."[2] For this reason, phenomena such as authoritarianism with the emperor at the apex and a controlled economy were praised as evidence of the "overcoming" of "modern individualism."

However, the actual conditions of the war revealed the shallowness of Japan's modernization. Nor was this simply a matter of Japan's scientific, technological, and productive capacity being inferior to that of the United States and the countries of Europe. Total war clearly exposed problems of organization and mentality, as well, beginning with intense rivalry among, and nepotism within, the Army, Navy, and civilian bureaucracy. These realities of wartime society were a far cry from the ideal types of modern rationalism that were envisioned by intellectuals. Moreover, owing to the democratization policies of American occupation forces under the command of General Douglas MacArthur, the supposedly "overcome" ideal of liberal democracy experienced a revival.

On the basis of these wartime experiences, defeat was followed by the call for a re-evaluation of "modernity." One of postwar Japan's representative intellectuals, Maruyama Masao, had in 1936, under the influence of Marxism, written an essay highlighting the limits of "modern civil society." However, in a short essay on "modern thought" published in January 1946, he asserted that, "in our country modern thought is far from being 'overcome,' for truly we have not even achieved it." Maruyama continued:

> For years, supposedly respectable scholars, men of letters, and critics, were captivated by an epochal atmosphere wherein the so-called modern spirit was most notorious, as if that word were the fundamental root of all contemporary evil, and all that remained was to "overcome" it. One can only with difficulty imagine these men's feelings of wretchedness and absurdity as in present-day Japan we are being initiated into the ABCs of modern civilization by General Douglas MacArthur. ... Under the spell of a vulgar historicism which dictates that what comes later is always more progressive than anything that had appeared earlier, our intellectuals bowed before the "world historical" significance of fascism. And now they stand perplexed before the "world historical" victory of the democratic ideal that was supposed to have been overcome.[3]

Maruyama was not the only one to note such a change. Literary critic Hirano Ken, who in 1942 had advocated "overcoming modernity," after the war participated in the founding of the journal *Kindai Bungaku* (Modern Literature) out of the "desire to make a fresh start premised on the establishment of modernity."[4]

The second contextual factor has to do with reactions against the Japan Communist Party (JCP). In conformance with Marxist theory, the party's line of criticism regarding "modernity" remained the same after defeat. Formally, the party stipulated that contemporary Japan was in the stage of absolutism centered on the emperor system. Accordingly, it adhered to a "two stage revolutionary theory," recommending that there first be a bourgeois-democratic revolution corresponding to the French Revolution, to be followed by a transition toward socialist revolution. For this reason, the party succeeded in attracting the cooperation even of liberal intellectuals who were uncomfortable with Marxism. However, the party criticized these same intellectuals for "modernism" whenever they advocated modernization and democratization in ways that conflicted with the party line.[5]

The executive committee of the JCP was comprised of people who had resisted the war and even spent more than a decade in prison without renouncing their beliefs. Liberated after Japan's defeat, they garnered wide respect. However, the party also included many intellectuals who had committed "apostasy" (*tenkō*) during the war and cooperated with the war effort through their criticism of "Western modernity;" and their postwar return to the party produced a tendency to avoid the issue of war responsibility. For that reason, when intellectuals such as Maruyama Masao and those associated with *Kindai Bungaku* engaged in a reappraisal of "Western modernity," they did so in reaction against the Communist Party.

The third factor concerns opposition between the cities and farm villages. As in many developing countries, prior to the accelerated economic growth of the 1960s, the gap between cities and the countryside was extreme, and only members of the urban middle and upper classes were able to enjoy a Western-style way of life. In this regard, it is noteworthy that most intellectuals hailed from those very classes.

However, during the period of war and recovery, the urban middle class suffered the combined impact of bombing, food shortages, and inflation, while the position of the villagers, who possessed their own food, was relatively improved. Members of the urban middle class were forced to travel to the villages and attempt to barter clothing and other belongings for food, but the farmers had little use for city dwellers and drove hard bargains. In the barracks, meanwhile, student soldiers of urban middle class origin were subjected to violence at the hands of resentful rural and lower class soldiers.

Moreover, the antipathy they felt for the wealthy Western lifestyle of the urban middle classes meant that during the war farmers and members of the lower classes were inclined to support the government's slogan of "driving out Western culture." The government, as well, criticized "soft" Western-style urban culture while praising farmers and laborers as "working warriors" who had conquered "modern individualism." Consequently, in the transition from war to defeat, the resentment harbored by members of the urban middle classes toward the wartime government and military was accompanied by an outbreak of ill will toward farming villages. In 1946, a newspaper reported that people departing from the city to the rural villages "all feel extreme bitterness toward government officials and farmers, unanimously stating that when the time of their death by starvation arrives they will expire either at the entrance to a cabinet minister's house or on the doorstep of a farmer."[6] Thus, "government officials" and "farmers" were loathed as the highest and lowest manifestations of "feudal" authoritarianism.

During the same period, economist Ōtsuka Hisao drew on the work of German sociologist Max Weber to call for the cultivation of a "modern human type" of personality, asserting that the mentality of Japan's farmers resided in a state of "Asiatic feudalism."[7] By the same token, Maruyama Masao, whose studies of Edo thought were at once a product of his academic specialty and a critique of contemporary affairs, strongly criticized the "feudal consciousness" of farmers, while advancing the idea that Tokugawa thought, having developed differently from Chinese Confucianism, had come to resemble that of the modern West.[8]

This orientation toward modernization also produced the label of "progressive faction," a generic term used to designate the various forces that criticized those thought to be responsible for the war, including the military authorities and conservative politicians, and that sought to promote democratization. This included not only communists and social democrats but, as with Maruyama and Ōtsuka, liberals who in order to promote democratization cooperated with the JCP and the Socialist Party (the latter a gathering of various non-communist left-wing organizations). The Communist Party and Socialist Party (wherein gathered numerous non-communist left-wing organizations) served as the core for this "progressive faction" (*shinpo-ha*) or "reformist force" (*kakushin seiryoku*). Meanwhile, Maruyama, who sometimes refrained from criticizing the Communist Party, was looked upon as the typical "progressive intellectual."

In general, for early postwar "progressive intellectuals" the term "Western modernity" expressed a reaction against wartime conditions. For them, emperor-centered authoritarianism and the wartime criticism of "modernity" by intellectuals, as well as the farmers who (from the intellectuals' perspective) fell in line with military authoritarianism and the assault on Western culture, were to be loathed. In contrast, what they agreed on was a "modern Western" society divorced from authoritarianism and united on the basis of equality. The more miserable the wartime experience of an intellectual and the stronger their reaction against the war and authoritarianism, the more apt they were to idealize an image of "Western modernity" and, in contrast, to lump together the negative elements of Japanese society and generalize them as "Asiatic."

The 1950s

This pejorative view of "Asia" was thoroughly transformed by the 1949 Chinese Revolution. In general, following the 1868 Meiji Restoration and especially after Japan's victory in the 1895 Sino-Japanese War, Japanese intellectuals had disdained China as a more backward country than Japan. Most Marxists were no exception. For these Japanese intellectuals it was thus a great shock that China had succeeded in realizing a socialist revolution before Japan. Moreover, the late 1940s witnessed the repeated success of Asian independence movements such as those in India and Egypt.

In 1953, historian and Communist Party member Ishimoda Shō, a longtime critic of Ōtsuka Hisao, wrote, "democracy, socialism, and communism – these words no longer belong solely to Europe. The Chinese Revolution has born witness to the arrival of an age in which the Asian masses – long thought to be governed by different principles from Europeans – are creating these systems through their own efforts."[9] About the same time, China scholar Takeuchi Yoshimi gained prominence and, in 1953, Maruyama Masao published an article criticizing his own previous views on China.[10]

This transformation in the image of "Asia" occurred in tandem with changes in the domestic and international conditions of the 1950s. One of these conditions was the intensification of the Cold War and American pressure on Japan. At the outset of the occupation, the United States sought to implement policies that would democratize and demilitarize Japan, and it was under American leadership that the principle of renouncing military armaments and war that is embodied in Article Nine of the new constitution was formulated and written. However, with the intensification of the Cold War and the onset of the Korean War, the United States turned to a policy of remilitarizing Japan as an anti-communist ally. In August 1950, under the direction of US forces, a "military police reserve" – so called in an effort to avoid contradicting the constitution's prohibition of a military – was organized. In 1954, this unit was expanded into the Self-Defense Forces.

In September 1951, during the Korean War, the San Francisco Peace Conference was held and the occupation of Japan by American forces came to an end. However, the peace treaty concluded under American leadership was spurned by the Soviet Union and countries of Eastern Europe. China and Korea were not even invited. Moreover, in accord with the accompanying US–Japan Security Treaty, the stationing of American forces in Japan continued even after the conclusion of the occupation. Furthermore, at about the same time that the peace treaty went into effect, a secret treaty provided that in times of emergency Japan's defense capabilities could be placed under the direction of the US military.

Japan's conservative political regime accepted these American demands and, through a posture of participation in the Western camp, sought to obtain security and an end to the occupation. Among conservative politicians were some who aimed for an expansion of military capabilities and a return to the old order, and others who sought security and a suitable response to American demands for an enhanced military capacity while devoting themselves to economic growth. The two groups were at odds within the conservative regime but, basically, it was the policies of the latter group that came to be reflected in practice.[11]

However, this kind of American pressure incurred a strong negative reaction from Japanese communists and those liberals inclined toward pacifism. In the midst of an expanding opposition movement directed against the San Francisco Peace Treaty and rearmament, these individuals became known for their sympathy with the anti-American and anti-Western inclinations of public opinion and for their re-evaluation of those Asian countries then winning their independence from Western control. Amongst the intellectuals of the day were also those who, quite apart from the issue of China and Asian independence movements, reacted against American pressure for rearmament by sympathizing with Europe. Conservatives were inclined to favor the English royal house on account of their interest in defending the Emperor. People avoided Germany because of its strong association with Nazism and the Axis, but some were attracted to the French anti-German resistance movement. The novelist and future Nobel laureate Ōe Kenzaburō, who became well known as a pacifist defender of Article Nine, relates that upon becoming a college student in 1953 he chose to major in French literature in reaction against the United States.[12] However, in terms of general discourse in Japan, there was an inclination to conflate the United States and Europe through the use of terms such as "the West" and "Euro-American." Reaction against the United States quickly and easily became bound up with reaction against "the West" and with a re-evaluation of "Asia."

A second development of the 1950s was a new fascination with "the people" (*minshū*) that emerged in reaction to the apparent elitism of the early postwar Enlightenment activities through which intellectuals had sought to instill democracy and modernization. Such efforts had been welcomed as a breath of fresh air in the aftermath of liberation from wartime censorship; however, by around 1948 the popularity of Enlightenment discourse had declined. Left-wing intellectuals sought an explanation for this in the paternalistic attitudes of the Enlightenment publicists, who had adopted the stance of instructor to the masses. As time went on, their activities not only failed to garner the sympathy of those masses, but elicited the self-reflection among intellectuals themselves that such activities constituted a rebirth of the very authoritarianism they were supposed to be criticizing.

Thus, from around 1950 intellectuals began to reflect on a style of Enlightenment one-sided in its dependence on Western thought and to take a new interest in mass culture. The influence of the Chinese Revolution resulted in the slogan, "Intellectuals must learn from the masses!" being spread throughout the Left. Consequently, although having until then served as an object of criticism for the Enlightenment movement, traditional Japanese culture underwent a re-evaluation and such areas as folklore studies attracted newfound attention. In the same way, culture once termed "Asian" and "feudal" also experienced a reassessment.

A third issue shaping these changes was the poverty of Japanese society at the time. Defeat in the war delivered a tremendous blow to Japan's economy. According to the United Nations' 1948 Economic Survey of East Asia, the per capita income of the Japanese people was 100 dollars, whereas for Americans the figure was 1,269 dollars. By way of comparison, in Ceylon (Sri Lanka) and the Philippines, the numbers were 91 and 88 dollars, respectively. In 1945, Japan's total urban population was calculated at 28 percent so the bulk of inhabitants still lived in rural areas centered on farm villages.

It is not surprising, therefore, that Japanese intellectuals were apt to think of Japan as a "backward Asian country." Yet, the strong inclination to perceive "Asian" conditions critically in comparison with a "Western" ideal remained strong in the immediate postwar period. After around 1950, however, amidst burgeoning anti-American sentiment and an increasing impulse to idealize "the people," skepticism toward "Western modernity" spread and the image of "Asia" improved. Of course, re-evaluation of "Asia" did not mean that modernization itself was rejected. Instead, the preference during this period was to argue for the existence in "Asia" of a type of modernization that differed from that of the West.

For example, in a 1948 essay on "Chinese Modernity and Japanese Modernity," the scholar of Chinese literature, Takeuchi Yoshimi, contrasted China's modernization against that of Japan.[13] According to Takeuchi, Japan had never since ancient times possessed its own traditional culture. Rather, the elite had always imported culture from outside (for example, from China or the West) and forced the masses to conform. Characteristic of Japan, therefore, were a repetitive process of "conversion" (*tenkō*), in which the existing culture was discarded in favor of a newly imported culture, and an authoritarian system of blind obedience to elites, who in turn blindly followed the authority of foreign cultures. The modernization of Japan since the Meiji era (1868–1912) was none other than a conversion from the stance of "expel the barbarians" (*jōi*) to "civilization and enlightenment" (*bunmei kaika*), and the political changes from prewar to wartime and from wartime to postwar – that is, from liberalism to totalitarianism and from totalitarianism to democracy – were nothing more than repeated cases of apostasy and conversion. In contrast, the strength of tradition in China, although preventing the kind of easy modernization carried out in Japan, brought forth the necessity of modernization from the level of the masses and was resulting in a successful form of modernization that made use of tradition.

Just as in the immediate postwar years when Maruyama and Ōtsuka had idealized "Western modernity," Takeuchi's assertions doubtless idealized China. However, his argument drew a sympathetic response from intellectuals confronting the success of the Chinese Revolution and the impasse of Enlightenment activism, and in 1964 *Chūō Kōron* (Central Review), a magazine popular among Japanese intellectuals, selected Takeuchi's "Chinese Modernity and Japanese Modernity" as one of the "Ten Most Influential Essays of Postwar Japan."

In line with this discourse, "Asia" also served as a standard by which to reflect on the war. In the wake of defeat, Japan's plunge into war was thought to have resulted from a failure to democratize and consolidate the individual ego (*jiga*) in the same manner as the "modern West." However, Takeuchi's essay portrayed modern Japan as having become a "slave" of modern Western civilization and, riding the coat tails of Western imperialism, having carried out aggression against "Asia." In 1951, under the influence of Takeuchi, Maruyama joined in arguing that even though Japan had modernized faster than the rest of "Asia," it had blindly imitated European imperialism and gone from being "Asia's hope to Asia's betrayer."[14]

Paralleling these activities, moreover, from around 1950 the JCP began to place major emphasis on "national (or ethnic) independence" (*minzoku dokuritsu*). Immediately after the war, the JCP had stipulated that American occupation forces were "liberating troops" and argued for the possibility of realizing a peaceful revolution while cooperating with the democratization policies of the occupation forces. However, in January 1950 the Communist Information Bureau (Cominform) published a treatise criticizing the JCP and demanding a confrontation with American occupation forces. The article was unsigned, but was written by Stalin.

The Korean War broke out in June of the same year. Having decided that Japan was now in a state of semi-colonialism under American occupation, the JCP followed the Chinese Communist Party in proclaiming the war to be a struggle for national independence (*minzoku dokuritsu tōsō*). The party then proceeded to confront occupation authorities through such issues as the anti-US base struggles and opposition to the San Francisco Peace Treaty, while also adopting a line of armed struggle against illegal militarization as a means for fomenting revolution by sowing dissention between American forces and the Japanese government.

Accordingly, intellectuals connected to the Communist Party extolled the national independence struggle in China and elsewhere and, while criticizing "Western modernity," rehabilitated the value of Japan's traditional culture. Although Takeuchi, Maruyama, and their contemporaries did not necessarily conform to the thinking of the Communist Party, the party line and their own views were consistent with one another, a development that hastened the 1950s' reassessment of Asia.

As the various processes mentioned above intertwined and reinforced one another, Japan's return to "Asia" proceeded apace. This was perfectly symbolized in Shimizu Ikutarō's proclamation in the January 1950 edition of *Chūō Kōron* that "now, once again, the Japanese are Asians." Among the factors Shimizu emphasized were that Japanese society was extremely poor in comparison with the United States and that the United States harbored deeply-rooted racial prejudice toward the Japanese. Moreover, he continued, through American pressure Japan was being forced to rearm while at the same time Japanese land was being stolen for American military bases.

However, the re-evaluation of "Asia" did not necessarily entail new concern about Japan's war responsibility toward Asian countries. From the end of the war until the 1950s, discussion of war responsibility had for the most part focused on the responsibility of politicians, bureaucrats, militarists, and the emperor for carrying out a reckless war and victimizing the Japanese people. Such inquiries were carried out solely on behalf of everyday Japanese who, together with those Japanese who were killed in battle, were defined as victims of the war. No thought was given to "Asian" victims who might have suffered at the hands of these very same Japanese.

On the occasion of the San Francisco Peace Conference in September 1951, the monthly *Sekai* (The World), which was an important organ for progressive intellectuals not affiliated with the Communist Party, published a special issue on problems related to the treaty. The 120 contributors opposed the American-led peace conference and criticized the fact that Asian countries – particularly China – were not invited. However, excepting a roundtable discussion among economists, only two writers mentioned postwar reparations to Asian countries. Moreover, even participants in the economists' roundtable argued that, given the contemporary state of its economy, Japan was incapable of paying such reparations.[15] Ultimately, as a consequence of America's international political power, those Asian countries which signed the treaty were forced to renounce the right to seek reparations.

The 1960s and beyond

With the advent of the 1960s, the domestic conditions within Japan described above changed completely. Of course, Japan's accelerated economic growth was the major factor. Having recovered to prewar levels by around 1955, Japan's economy then embarked upon the full-scale growth of the 1960s. The urban population expanded from 28 percent in 1945 to 72 percent in 1972. Meanwhile, in 1963 Japan joined the OECD and gained admission to the ranks of developed nations. Lifestyle changes were likewise dramatic. House-hold appliances such as televisions, washing machines, and refrigerators spread rapidly from the late 1950s, while changes in daily life and food culture continued apace. The homogenizing effects of mass media and mass culture, too, became increasingly obvious.

Disappearing in the course of this process was the schema, common until the late 1950s, that highlighted Japan's peculiar coexistence of a "Westernized urban middle class" with an "Asiatic peasantry." The sociologist Yamamoto Akira noted that until the 1950s, "if one went from the city to the village things were so different that one wondered if this was the same Japan. ... [I]t was not until after 1960 that the hinterlands became developed and people began thinking of cities and farm villages as part of the same country."[16]

Economic growth also changed Japan's self-image of its international stand-ing. In 1951, responding to a question regarding the superiority or inferiority of the Japanese in comparison to Westerners put to them by the Broadcast Opinion Research bureau of the Japan Broadcasting Corporation (NHK), 28 percent of respondents believed that the "Japanese are superior", while 47 percent felt the Japanese were "inferior." In contrast, by 1963 these replies had reversed, with 33 percent answering that the Japanese were "superior" and 14 percent perceiving them as "inferior." By 1968, those affirming Japanese superiority had risen to 47 percent.[17]

Accompanying the rise in Japanese self-confidence was anthropologist Umesao Tadao's publication in 1957 of "A Historical View of the Ecology of Civilization," which divided the world into "first tier" and "second tier" regions.[18] According to Umesao, the "first tier" consisted of "wet, forested regions" and corresponded to Western Europe and Japan, both of which had passed through feudalism and subsequently built modern civilizations. The "second tier" of "dry, continental regions" referred to Russia and China, which had transformed themselves from authoritarian empires into socialist states. Umesao's point was that Japan, even in regard to its indigenous culture, belonged to a different category than that of China and the other regions of Asia. Rather, Japan more closely resembled Western Europe and, for this reason, had succeeded in modernizing. These assertions by Umesao were welcomed warmly in a Japan flush with economic growth.

Among leftists, too, Japan's standing changed. In the late 1950s, the Japan Communist Party began expelling student members who were dissatisfied with the party line, and various New Left factions began to be formed. One point of contention between these new factions and the Communist Party had to do with Japan's international standing. Since 1950, the party had defined Japan as a semi-colonized "Asian" state subordinate to the United States. However, the nascent New Left maintained that Japan was already an advanced imperialist state at the same level as countries of the West and that it was advancing economically into "Asia."

Paralleling this argument was the new critique of "Western modernity." Environmental degradation had accompanied high economic growth, and by the late 1960s the result was full-blown criticism of modernization and industrial society. Meanwhile, rural and traditional culture, as well as "Asia," again underwent a re-evaluation. As noted earlier, a reassessment of rural and traditional culture had also occurred in the middle to late 1950s. However, that discourse insisted on defining Japan as an "Asian" country and was carried out by literati opposing American military pressure. Under those circumstances, affirming rural and traditional culture meant affirming the Japanese masses. Moreover, rather than disavowing modernization, this view proclaimed a unique "Asian" modernization that drew on traditional culture. However, the criticism of modernity and reassessment of "Asia" that occurred in the late 1960s identified all of Japan, including the masses, with the modern West. Therefore, all aspects of modernization became the object of criticism, while praise of rural and traditional culture turned increasingly to nostalgia for a lost rural landscape.

The same period witnessed the rise of a generation born in the postwar period. While the wartime generation were inclined to impress upon the young the severity of their wartime suffering, this postwar generation responded by emphasizing the damage their elders had inflicted on "Asia." Previous discussions of war responsibility had indicted political leaders for the harm they had done to the Japanese people, while treating the majority of the people as victims. However, with the rise of a younger generation who had not experienced the war came a tendency to treat the entire older generation, everyday citizens and political leaders alike, as victimizers of "Asia."

Accelerating that tendency was the Vietnam War. American "special procurements" of war material for that conflict accounted for 10–20 percent of total exports. Although this fell short of the 60 percent of total exports that had been accounted for by procurements during the Korean War, it nonetheless served to support Japanese economic growth.

After 1965, when there arose in Japan, as elsewhere, a student-led movement opposed to the Vietnam War, that movement tended to emphasize the suffering of other "Asians." During the Korean War, emphasis had been placed on the danger of Japan being caught up in the war and on American pressure to rearm. However, in their opposition to the Vietnam War the New Left and others stressed that Japan, standing shoulder to shoulder with Western countries as an advanced imperialist state, was assaulting "Asia."

Amidst the emphasis placed on the suffering of "Asia" by the anti-Vietnam War movement, attention also began to be paid to damage done during the Sino-Japanese and Pacific Wars. In 1967, journalist Honda Katsuichi from the daily newspaper *Asahi Shinbun* wrote *Senji no mura* (Battlefield Village), detailing the realities of the Vietnam War and in the process exposing the brutal conduct of American soldiers and the racial prejudice that underlay it. Honda also indicted the Japanese government for cooperating with the US military. Moreover, after publishing *Amerika gasshūkoku* (United States of America), in which he laid bare racial discrimination in the American South, Honda visited China in 1971 and wrote *Chūgoku no tabi* (China Travels), in which he investigated the massacres carried out by Japanese soldiers in Nanjing and elsewhere. In his preface to *China Travels*, Honda related how he was spurred on in his efforts to investigate what had happened in China by American journalists who had brought to light the Mai Lai massacre perpetrated by American soldiers in Vietnam.[19]

Although events such as the Nanjing Massacre had been exposed and garnered attention as a result of the Tokyo trials immediately after the war,[20] with the passage of time they had faded from memory. Now, however, provoked by reports of the brutal behavior of American soldiers in Vietnam and a sense of guilt for Japan's cooperation in the war, the historical precedents for victimization of "Asia" were again recalled. Also prompted by the Vietnam War were some late 1960s novels that dealt with war memories, including Ōoka Shōhei's *Leite Senki* (Leyte War Diary) and Ibuse Masuji's *Kuroi Ame* (Black Rain).

In March 1967, Japanese Christian organizations released a report exposing their complicity in the Asia-Pacific War. Philosopher Tsurumi Shunsuke, who was involved with the anti-Vietnam War movement, commented that, "if one wonders why this report appears now, twenty-two years after the end of the war, [the answer] is that the Vietnam War is demonstrating its worth as a catalyst."[21] American peace activist Howard Zinn revealed that during his visit to Tokyo in June 1966, which came at the behest of the Japanese citizens' groups in the "Peace for Vietnam! Citizens' Alliance" (Betonamu ni heiwa o! Shimin rendō, or Beheiren), he repeatedly heard the criticism that "you Americans are behaving in Asia today just as we once behaved."[22]

Accompanying news of the Vietnam War came reports from the United States of the movements seeking justice for indigenous peoples and African-Americans. In Japan, attention turned to the indigenous Ainu of the north and to resident Koreans descended from those Koreans brought to Japan under colonial rule, as well as to Okinawans integrated into the country when Japan subjugated and annexed Okinawa and the rest of the Ryūkyū Islands during the nineteenth century. These minorities were defined as an element of "Asia" who suffered aggression at the hands of the modern imperialist state of Japan. In the context of controversy over environmental destruction and discrimination against minorities, Ainu and Okinawans, as well as Native Americans, were pictured as people who coexisted with nature.

At one extreme of this discourse lay the "East Asian Anti-Japanese Armed Front" (*Higashi Ajia Hannichi Busō Sensen*). This extremist left-wing group was composed of youths who split off from the student uprisings of the late 1960s. They criticized the economic advance into "Asia" by Japanese corporations and in 1974 bombed trading companies and facilities related to the armaments industry. These radicals emphasized ancient Japan's aggression toward the Ainu, Okinawans, Koreans, and others who had lived in a "primitive communist system" in close touch with nature.[23] In a sense, the Ainu and Okinawans were being rediscovered as Japan's "internal Asia" (*uchi naru Ajia*).

Conclusion

The image of "Asia" for postwar intellectuals provides not only a mirror of Japanese national identity, but a reflection of domestic conditions. As is often pointed out, "Asia" is not a real thing. For many Japanese, "Asia" is limited to East and Southeast Asia, i.e. China and Korea, or Indonesia and Malaysia. However, for Western Europeans, "Asia" seems to refer first to the Middle East and India. Opinions differ as to whether such border areas as Greece and Russia fall within "Asia" or the "West." There are even anecdotal instances of Poles calling Russia "Asia," Germans saying Poland is "Asia," and French referring to Germany as "Asia."

Thus, "Asia" tends to represent images of the "Other" that are constructed in opposition to the "Self" in the process of national identity formation. This was the case for Japanese intellectuals, too. For them, "Asia" was the medium through which they expressed reactions and attitudes including anti-Western emotions and desires for modernization, complex feelings toward the masses and traditional culture, and conflict between generations and the issue of war responsibility. More than a true representation of the actual circumstances of Asian nations, their constructions reflected a Japanese national identity that changed amidst shifts in domestic political and economic conditions. One can, of course, say the same about "Western modernity."

This affinity for "Asia" has been apparent among both progressive and conservatives. If one were to construct a very simple sketch in order to show how "Asia" has served as an anti-Western and anti-modern symbol, it would look something like the following.

I	II
III	IV

In this diagram the perpendicular axis covers the spectrum from progressive to conservative, while the horizontal axis, running from left to right, represents a continuum from anti-Asian to pro-Asian sentiment. Therefore, Area I demarks those "anti-Asia progressives" who called for democratization in line with the criteria of the "modern West." Area II represents "pro-Asia progressives" who, while looking to the model of Asian independence movements and perhaps making an issue of Japan's war responsibility toward Asia, criticized American pressure and "Western modernity." Area III encompasses the "anti-Asia conservatives" who disdained Asia and promoted cooperation with America and Europe while working toward industrial modernization. Area IV then, is for the "pro-Asia conservatives" who, while reacting against America and "Western modernity," underscored the view of the Pacific War as being about the "liberation of Asia."

Of course, this is only a simplified diagram presenting an idealized typology. As will be evident from the historical changes outlined above, actual trends cannot be simplified in this manner. Moreover, as can be seen with Maruyama Masao, the same person sometimes takes more than one position. However, such a scheme does provide a way to display the range of variation that occurred in Japanese views of "Asia."

Similar views of "Asia" also continue to exist in contemporary Japan. In recent years, the well-known right-wing group "Society to Create New History Textbooks" (Atarashii rekishi kyōkasho o tsukuru kai) has stressed the historical view that the Pacific War was a war fought against the West to achieve Asian liberation; however, at the same time they support the US–Japan Security Treaty and are in harmonious unity with both "pro-Asia conservatives" and "anti-Asia conservatives." Likewise, Tōkyō Governor Ishihara Shintarō, known for his rightist utterances, makes discriminatory statements about Asia while co-authoring with Malaysian Prime Minister Mohammad Mahathir *The Asia that Can Say 'No'*, a book filled with anti-American opinions.[24]

The peculiar characteristics of this discourse originate primarily in relations with the West, which in turn determine views of "Asia" as the dependent variable. For example, Ishihara Shintarō is typical of conservative critics who generally are ignorant of the realities in Asian countries and who change their views of "Asia" depending upon the state of relations with the West. In other words, if relations with the West are threatening, they extol ties with "Asia," but when relations with the West settle into the background they revert to denunciations of "Asia." Needless to say, the object of the "No" in Ishihara's book is the United States.

In sum, Japanese perceptions of "Asia" mirror Japanese national identity and reflect domestic political and economic conditions. As a result, to inquire into Japan's "Asia" is also to interrogate Japan itself.

(Translated by Roger Brown)

14 Overcoming colonialism at Bandung, 1955

Kristine Dennehy

Introduction

In April of 1955, Japan participated in the Asian-African Conference in Bandung, Indonesia. The stated aims of this conference were to bring together representatives from Asia and Africa in order to "promote the ideas of sovereignty, equality, and solidarity." The year before, in 1954, the prime ministers of Burma (now Myanmar), India, Indonesia, Pakistan, and Ceylon (now Sri Lanka) had met in Colombo to discuss common issues of concern, such as the liberation movements in Indochina. At the Colombo Conference, the leaders of these nations found common ground around issues such as the demand for the respect for the sovereignty of nations and the demand for non-interference in the internal affairs of other countries.

Following the meeting in Colombo, 29 official representatives from various countries in Asia and Africa met in Bandung, Indonesia to discuss these common issues of concern. Even though the conference brought together representatives from the continents of both Asia and Africa, it was most significant for Japan in the way that it created and reinforced a common bond between Japan and the other countries of Asia. Having just regained full sovereignty a few years before with the end of the US-led Occupation, the Japanese delegates found at Bandung an opportunity to begin building new relationships with other Asian nations, many of which had been subjected to Japanese imperial rule only a decade or so earlier. In this sense, it can be said that one of the outcomes of the Bandung Conference was the creation of a new kind of Pan-Asianism in the postwar period.[1]

Among studies of Japan's postwar political and ideological trajectories, much emphasis has been placed on its close ties with the United States, within the framework of Japan's subordination to American Cold War aims after 1945. When attention is given to Japan's ties with other Asian countries, it is often in the context of Japanese attempts to move beyond its imperialist past, as people's energies became directed toward the goals of high-speed economic growth and political stability. An examination of Japan's involvement in the Bandung Conference in 1955 shows how Japanese politicians, bureaucrats, and intellectuals took advantage of this pan-Asian forum to promote a vision of Japan's future beyond the dominant force of American influence.

On the conservative end of the political spectrum, Bandung reveals the priorities of leaders like Foreign Minister Shigemitsu Mamoru (1883–1957) to re-establish links with Asia based in large part on economic investment, reminiscent of the pre-war model of Japanese tutelage.[2] For Shigemitsu, the central themes of Bandung such as "Asian liberation" and "reciprocal cooperation" resonated with the rhetoric and moral tone that he sought to propagate in the early 1940s.[3] For progressives, Bandung brought to light the domestic and international tensions that resulted from trying to position Japan within Asia in a way that was radically distinct from the hierarchical model of the late nineteenth and early twentieth centuries. Among leftist intellectuals, calls for a new kind of pan-Asian solidarity can be seen as a form of political resistance to the conservative agenda of the ruling elite in postwar Japan.

It is ironic that while many of the speeches and communiqués of the Bandung Conference stressed the oppressive nature of Asia's colonial experiences, the delegation from Japan included several members who were prominent figures in the prewar and wartime years of Japanese expansionism into Asia. Furthermore, in later years the delegates from these conservative circles would go on to serve in political and bureaucratic posts tied to a postwar agenda that clearly had its roots in the ideological constructs and nationalist sentiments of the prewar years. With the exception of socialists like Sata Tadataka and Sone Eki, most of Japan's delegation consisted of members who were affiliated with the conservative leadership that dominated postwar politics in Japan.

The lead delegate was Takasaki Tatsunosuke, Director General of the Economic Deliberation Agency.[4] He was accompanied by Tani Masayuki, adviser to the Ministry of Foreign Affairs, as well as three other officials from that ministry, Kase Toshikazu, Asakai Kōichirō, and Wajima Eiji.[5] Uehara Etsujirō represented the Democratic Party (Minshutō), while Nadao Hirokichi hailed from the Liberal Party (Jiyutō). Other high-ranking officials included Ōta Saburō and Kajiwara Shigeyoshi. Advisers from the industrial sector included Fujiyama Aiichirō, president of the Society for Economic Cooperation in Asia (Ajia Kyōkai), and Takata Gisaburō from Ishihara Sangyō. The appointment of Takasaki as the lead delegate reveals that Japan's aims at Bandung were primarily economic in nature. Representatives like Uehara and Nadao indicate the ideological dominance of what would later be called the "1955 system" with the merger of the Minshutō and Jiyutō into the Liberal Democratic Party.[6]

The mindset of bureaucrats and politicians like Nadao Hirokichi can be linked to their prewar experiences, such as Nadao's background as an official in the Home Ministry (Naimushō) and his postwar path as a member of the pro-Taiwan lobby within the LDP and as Minister of Education in the 1950s and 1960s.[7] In this capacity, he promoted policies that would re-insert a highly nationalistic tone into the educational curriculum through greater centralized control over school textbooks and appointed school board members. Known for his strong stance against the teachers' union,[8] Nadao advocated the revival of moral education through textbook lessons and pressure on classroom teachers to glorify Japan's past, rather than spend time being critical of Japan's military exploits. In this sense, Nadao was representative of the conservative establishment who thought that the American-influenced educational reforms in the early postwar years had gone too far. After the Occupation ended, they turned their attention to thwarting left-wing forces that sought to perpetuate those liberal-minded reforms. They sought to remedy what they deemed to be "excesses" by reasserting stronger controls over the national school system from their position of political dominance. This same mentality of Japanese nationalism carried over into the international political sphere, with its assumptions of pride and admiration for Japan's economic and political developments, both before and after 1945.

This contrasts greatly with the notions of Pan-Asianism that appealed to Japanese progressives in the 1950s, and beyond into the later decades of the 1960s and 1970s. For them, the appeal of Bandung was tied to the ongoing struggles for national liberation in Asia, seen most clearly in the wars for independence in Indochina. There was an explicit link between the historical perspective of these intellectuals and their contemporary political agenda. Their political activism must be placed in the broader context of the task of postwar historians like the members of the Historical Science Association (Rekishi Kagaku Kyōgikai), who insisted that a critique of Japan's imperialist past necessarily be tied to an agenda of political resistance.[9] As will be discussed further below, the Bandung Conference provided a distinctive opportunity for progressive intellectuals to align themselves with the formerly colonized peoples of Asia. In this way, Bandung embodies the ambiguity of Japan's position in the world after 1945.[10] That is to say, at the same time that Japanese intellectuals were "coming to terms" with their own country's history of imperialist aggression in Asia, they also saw themselves as uniquely suited in leading calls for an end to Western imperialist influences in areas of Asia such as Indonesia and Indochina.[11]

On the one hand, in 1955 Japan was still struggling with its imperialist past, most notably in negotiations over reparations to Southeast Asian countries like Burma, Thailand, and the Philippines.[12] In this regard, the lead delegate to Bandung, Takasaki Tatsunosuke, was involved in talks with the Philippines, while Wajima Eiji played an important role in Japan's negotiations with Indonesia around this same time.[13] Yet, on the other hand, after Japan regained its sovereignty with the end of the Occupation in 1952, it was still left with the contentious issue of a large American military presence on its soil. Progressives used this issue of Japan's subordinate position *vis-à-vis* the United States in their calls to question the status quo of Japan's place in the Cold War international order. Thus, Japan's ambiguous position was a result of two competing forces after 1945. One was the process of finding a mutually suitable way to re-establish ties with other Asian countries. The other was the struggle over redefining its relationship with powerful Western countries, particularly the United States.

The following section will provide an overview of the goals and legacy of the Bandung Conference. This will be followed by a discussion in more detail of the significance of Bandung for Japan, particularly how it became a symbolic turning point in Japan's relations with the rest of Asia, especially for progressive intellectuals in the postwar period. Marxist historians like Tōyama Shigeki looked to Bandung as an important symbol of Japanese intellectuals' support for various Asian national liberation movements (*minzoku kaihō undō*) in the post-colonial environment of the late 1950s and 1960s.[14] In particular, they stressed the pacifist, anti-imperialist features of this new kind of Pan-Asianism. Furthermore, for these progressive intellectuals, this support of the goals of Bandung became a vehicle through which they could redefine, and make more radical, the meaning and significance of the term "*minzoku*" for the Japanese people.[15] Thus, Bandung linked the Japanese people (*minzoku*) with other Asians in a way that would support liberation movements against Western imperialist powers, such as the French in Indochina in the 1950s.

The Bandung Conference

The impetus for the conference in Bandung in 1955 was a meeting of the prime ministers from five Asian countries in Colombo, the capital of Ceylon, in 1954. At this Colombo Conference, they discussed several issues of common concern.[16] First, they expressed their support for the liberation movements in Indochina against the forces of Western imperialism. In this regard, they declared that colonialism was a violation of fundamental human rights. They also expressed their support for the independence of Tunisia and Morocco and demanded a just and swift settlement of the Palestinian issue. On this issue, they expressed their sympathy for the Palestinian refugees. The participants in the Colombo conference also demanded the admission of the People's Republic of China to the United Nations, and decided that the Asian-African group at the United Nations should collaborate to promote common aims, especially *vis-à-vis* the stronger powers of Western nations who they saw as generally dominating the proceedings of the UN.[17]

One of the key points to come out of the Colombo Conference was the declaration that these countries deplored the production of atomic bombs and other weapons of mass destruction. In this way, they set the tone for a kind of pacifist agenda among themselves. They also laid the groundwork for the participating countries to keep up discussions of mutual aid and cooperation. The Prime Minister of Indonesia, Dr. Ali Sastroamijoyo, proposed the idea of an Asian-African conference that came to fruition in Bandung the following year.[18] The leaders of the delegations in Bandung decided on the following five points that set the agenda for the conference in 1955:

1   economic cooperation,
2   cultural cooperation,
3   human rights and self-determination,

4 problems of dependent peoples, and
5 world peace and cooperation.[19]

When the conference opened in Bandung, Indonesian President Sukarno made the following points in his inaugural speech. He stressed that the participants had unique duties and responsibilities to address the current problems of Asia and Africa. He emphasized that everyone there was united in working for peace and should use their national strength in peaceful ways. Sukarno also voiced a scathing critique of colonialism in the following way. He stated that, "colonialism [has not ceased], but merely changed its classic dress for a new one, in the form of economic control and the actual physical control by a small community within a nation."[20] Abdel Nasser of Egypt made comments along similar lines when he addressed the Bandung Conference as follows. He said:

> We have emerged from a long period of foreign influence, political as well as economic. At present we are faced with such problems as economic development, social and political reconstruction. It is not surprising, therefore, [that] we should feel close together, a fact that finds expression in our concepts of world peace and international justice.[21]

It is not difficult to see why Japanese progressive intellectuals would be drawn to this kind of pacifist, anti-imperialist agenda.[22] As Carol Gluck has argued, progressive intellectuals have long been "identified as the consciousness and conscience of" postwar Japan.[23] She uses the term "portmanteau progressives" to characterize this group of intellectuals as a significant force of opposition in the postwar period against the political and economic establishment of the Japanese state. In this sense, the use of the term "progressive intellectuals" here refers to a range of leftist positions which Gluck has characterized as being somewhat unified in their alignment "against the grain of the conservatives in power" after 1945. Some intellectuals who actively supported the Bandung Conference explicitly identified themselves with the aims of certain political opposition parties such as the Socialist Party or Communist Party, but this was not always the case. For Socialists, one of the attractive aspects of Bandung was the emphasis on neutrality and non-alignment amid the tensions of the Cold War.[24] For Communists, the anti-imperialist agenda and focus on national liberation movements, especially against Western powers like France and the United States, was particularly attractive.[25]

Japan at Bandung

Although Bandung became an important symbolic moment for leftists after 1955, it is important to recognize that the actual delegates from Japan to the conference were of a more conservative background. For example, as noted by Kweku Ampiah, Kase Toshikazu (1903–2004) played an important role in

Bandung. He "was third in the hierarchy of Japanese delegates to the conference. He was also Permanent Observer of Japan to the United Nations at the time."[26] In an October 1955 contribution to *Foreign Affairs*, Kase reveals his extreme disdain for his progressive counterparts in an article entitled "Japan's New Role in East Asia."[27] In particular, he minimizes anti-American sentiment in Japan and uses this international readership forum as a way to express a McCarthy-like dismissal of leftist intellectuals. He writes:

> Our policy of maintaining close cooperation with the United States is supported by an overwhelming majority of our people. Like other nations, we have a quota of people considering themselves intellectuals who make a profession of anti-Americanism; but, though very vocal, they are a small minority. Often unconsciously they are stooges for the Communists. Fortunately the broad masses of our people are more realistic, more intelligent than the 'intellectuals,' hence more aware of the perils of Communism and more firmly opposed to it.[28]

Further on, Kase is also critical of Socialists and intellectuals with regard to their opposition to Japanese rearmament in the postwar period. Kase reveals his support of the American military presence in Japan by stating "under the Security Pact, we *invited* the American forces to stay in and around Japan."[29] With reference to the end of the Occupation period and negotiations to station American forces in Japan, Kase explains that "even then the Socialists – and in general the segment of our public called 'intellectuals' – were opposed. Naturally their opposition has grown in vigor with the apparent easing of the international situation."[30] In this way, we can see the divide that characterizes the delegates in Bandung such as Kase, and those on the more progressive end of the political spectrum who aligned themselves with both the aims as well as the anti-imperialist rhetoric of the conference organizers.

From Kase's perspective, the American military was a welcome presence, and as can be seen from the quote above, the only "realistic" option of international alliance in the current Cold War climate. Kase's reference to the healthy realism of the majority of Japanese is revealing in a couple of ways. Most importantly, it provides the rationale for Japan's decision to maintain its subordinate position *vis-à-vis* the American military by identifying Communism as a recognized threat among the "broad masses" of Japanese people. It can also be linked to a particular historical perspective regarding Japanese expansionism and notions of "realism" in late nineteenth and early twentieth century international relations.[31] Just as Kase argued that fostering ties with the United States was the only realistic option for Japan in the 1950s, so too would conservative politicians and bureaucrats argue that Japan's decision to pursue greater economic, strategic, and political control in Asia around the turn of the century was the only realistic path in the face of Western imperialist expansion worldwide.

As seen in Kase's remarks above, there was a virulent anti-Communist edge to the political stance of many of the head delegates from Japan. For the most part, it can be said that their main motivation for attending the conference was to build up economic ties with other Asian countries. Ironically, this was exactly the kind of economic "second invasion" of Asia so deplored by Japanese progressives in the postwar period. Some of the delegates also represented the continuity of Japan's prewar and wartime imperialist economy in terms of the personnel in charge of Japan's economic expansionism. A striking example of this continuity is seen in the background of one of the advisers to the delegates, Fujiyama Aiichirō (1897–1985). Fujiyama was the president of Ajia Kyōkai (Society for Economic Cooperation in Asia) in 1955. He had succeeded his father, Fujiyama Raita, as president of the Dai Nippon Sugar Manufacturing Company, Ltd. The father had been a key figure in building up the sugarcane and pulp industries in Taiwan, Japan's first colonial territory. He had also been the president of Tōkyō's Chamber of Commerce and Industry.

Fujiyama Aiichirō carried on these colonial pursuits as the sugar company's president, and he had also served as the chairman of the Japan Chamber of Commerce and Industry in 1941. Because of his leading role in the economy during wartime, Fujiyama had been purged during the Occupation years, but by 1957 he had risen again to the top ranks of Japan's political elite as the Minister of Foreign Affairs under Prime Minister Kishi Nobusuke (himself an accused class "A" war criminal). Kishi (1896–1987) described his relationship with Fujiyama as "very close since the Tōjō cabinet days, and after the war I was indebted to him for allowing me to make a living by installing me as an executive of Nitto Chemicals after I got out of Sugamo [Prison]."[32] Kishi also made it clear that he turned to Fujiyama to join his cabinet in the mid-1950s based on the belief that in Japan's dealings with both the United States and Asia, "the foundation is economic relations. That is why I thought that I would have Fujiyama make full use of his talents in the economic arena, in which he had been involved until then."[33]

In the 1960s, in the era of high-speed economic growth under the leadership of LDP politicians like Ikeda Hayato (1899–1965) and policies like the income-doubling plan, Fujiyama continued to be a strong presence in directing Japan's economy. As Director-General of the Economic Planning Agency in the early 1960s, Fujiyama took issue with Ikeda's vision for economic growth, and instead stressed the importance of economic stability. In this way, he continued to influence Japan's domestic and international economic expansion and his "criticism of Ikeda's economic policies had reverberations in both political and financial circles."[34] This trajectory is a representative example of the kind of wartime continuity so strongly criticized by Japan's postwar progressive intellectuals. Yet, at the same time, this was the kind of delegate that the Japanese government had sent to take part in the Bandung Conference in 1955. Someone such as Fujiyama would have a radically different notion of Pan-Asianism, based on his own experiences as part of the *colonial elite* in Taiwan, compared to the progressives who in later years would hold up Bandung as the symbol of a pan-Asianist movement that was meant to *repudiate* Japan's own colonial and imperialist past in places like Taiwan.

The lead delegate, Takasaki Tatsunosuke, was also a "businessman-turned-politician who had once served as president of Manchurian Heavy Industries."[35] His efforts to normalize trade with mainland China in the early 1960s have been described as tinged with "continental nostalgia" because of his prewar past. However, in Bandung, he addressed the participants with a narrative of wartime Japan that raised the issue of Japan's own victimization in World War II, rather than focusing on the history of Japanese aggression. In his opening speech, he referred to the "war conflagration" (*senka*) that had spread to neighboring countries in the early twentieth century, while noting how the Japanese themselves were the only ones who had suffered the tragic damage of the atomic bombs.[36] He then went on to tie this to Japan's postwar path of rebirth as a free nation, and the Japanese people's dedication to peace and cooperation with the United Nations.

Despite the conservative establishment's unease with the radical nature of Article Nine of the postwar constitution, Takasaki highlighted Japan's commitment to contributing to world peace and made specific reference to the condition of renouncing war as a means of settling international disputes. He acknowledged the strong suspicions of Japan on the part of Southeast Asian nations because of their wartime experiences, even though this was seen as unsatisfactorily vague by delegates from countries such as Indonesia. It should also be noted that the particular reference to Southeast Asia, presumably to emphasize Japan's far-reaching expansionism after 1941, precludes a discussion of the sufferings of East Asian colonial subjects going back as far as 1895 in Taiwan.

This kind of limited focus on Japanese expansionism from 1941 reveals an important feature of historical consciousness in postwar Japan. As noted by Tanaka Hiroshi, the historical consciousness that gave shape to postwar Japanese history is one which highlights Japanese militarism only from the time of Pearl Harbor.[37] Tanaka recalls significant events that he associated with the end of the war, namely the attack on Pearl Harbor, the Battle of Midway, the bombings of Hiroshima and Nagasaki, the Emperor's surrender broadcast, and occupation by the American military. He is critical of Japan's postwar democratic education that makes no mention of the fact that Japan's surrender also meant the collapse of 51 years of rule in Taiwan, 36 years of control over Korea, and three years and several months of military administration in Southeast Asia. For most Japanese, while postwar pacifism might call for a repudiation of Japanese militarism in the 1940s, this same kind of repentant attitude was not necessarily invoked in evaluations of earlier stages of Japanese imperialist expansion.

Even though the above examples reveal a particular strand of Japanese nationalism that proved problematic at times for other Asians, this did not prevent these delegates from finding a common agenda with the other representatives. It is important to remember that the participants of the Bandung Conference were not necessarily brought together by a common political ideology. Rather, what they shared was "a common abhorrence of imperialism, whether Western or Communist."[38] One Indian observer has described the conference as a watershed moment in the following way:

> Bandung provided a practical example of co-operation on terms of equality between communist and non-communist peoples on a scale which had been unknown before. In other words, it broke through the policy of bi-polarization which was the current pattern. This turned out to be a good example of 'peaceful co-existence' among countries of diverse ideology.[39]

A more radical interpretation of its significance was expressed by Chitta Biswas, Deputy Secretary General of the Afro-Asian People's Solidarity Organization, on the thirtieth anniversary of the conference in 1985. In his words:

> it was a conference of a new type, of new emerging forces in history. It was the coming-together of peoples, who had never had the opportunity to have their independent voices in any world forum. Their voices were gagged – by their colonial masters – the British, French, Dutch, Portuguese, Spanish, Germans and others.[40]

This quote is revealing because of the way it emphasizes the history of Western, white imperialism and only vaguely alludes to the fact that one of the conference participants, Japan, had been a colonial master, complicit in gagging the voices of its subject peoples in Asia.

Japan's ambiguous position as a former imperialist power in Asia is further illustrated in David Kimche's discussion of the historical background of the Afro-Asian Movement, a movement which he says "reached its high point with the first Asian-African conference, held at Bandung in Indonesia in 1955, and remained a political force until the failure of the 'Second Bandung' meeting at Algiers in 1965."[41] Kimche traces the antecedents of this movement back to about the turn of the century and argues that events "such as the 'Boxer' rebellion in China in 1900, and, even more so, the Japanese victory over Russia in 1905 – all evidenced a new awakening among the colored peoples, the gathering of momentum of ideas and emotions which were to develop into national movements and finally into sovereign nation-states."[42] Despite the fact that Japan's defeat of Russia signaled the end of Korea's sovereignty due to Japan's dominant position on the Korean peninsula from 1905, Kimche's timeline of pan-Asianist momentum singles out Japan's military triumph in 1905 as a celebrated moment in the continuum of racially tinged activism against the imperial powers of the West.

In addition, Kimche points to Japan's role in Southeast Asia during the 1940s as a key component in the downfall of Western imperialism in areas like

Indonesia, Malaya, and Indochina.[43] Again, despite the fact that Japanese aggression in this region was similar in many ways to the imperialist advances of European countries (and Japan's motivations were similar, i.e., the need for natural resources like oil), Japan is also recognized as having played a positive role in spawning nationalist movements in opposition to the forces of Western domination. Although Kimche does not go into the details of Japanese involvement in postwar independence movements in these regions, recent research has shown that a significant number of Japanese soldiers stayed behind in these countries to fight against Western imperialism after 1945. Baba Kimihiko has summarized the findings of this research on former imperial soldiers as follows:

> Some fought alongside the Vietmin against the French. Some stayed behind in Indonesia to fight against the Netherlands in the war for Indonesian independence. Others remained in Malaysia as members of the Malaysian Communist Party and Malaysian National Liberation Army, fighting as guerrillas in the war for independence and the Malaysian civil war.[44]

In terms of Bandung's place on the historical continuum of anti-imperial and national liberation movements, most sources trace the roots of the Bandung Conference back to the Indian struggles for independence in the 1920s and 1930s. In this context, ironically, Chitta Biswas notes Jawaharlal Nehru's solidarity with other Asian nations as illustrated by his "initiative to send a Medical Mission to China as a symbol of protest against Japanese aggression."[45] So while Japan was clearly guilty of imperialist aggression in Asia before 1945, it was also uniquely positioned as a force against the renewed onslaught of Western domination, particularly in Southeast Asia against France and the Netherlands after 1945.

The legacy of Bandung

Even though memories of Japanese aggression in prewar and wartime Asia were significant factors in Japan's relations with the rest of Asia after 1945, Bandung provided a unique opportunity for Japan to align itself successfully with an anti-colonial, pacifist pan-Asian agenda. In general, there were two things that the participating nations of the Bandung Conference had in common. First, most "had an experience at one time or another of subjection to a foreign power, usually a Western power." And second, they were generally representative of "poor, underdeveloped countries with relatively low standards of living."[46] Even though Japan itself had been an imperial power during the first half of the twentieth century, by 1955 leftist proponents of Japanese participation at Bandung could point to this event as a potent marker of their solidarity with other Asian and African nations against imperialism, particularly what many Japanese leftists called the "imperialist" power of the United States since 1945.

Especially in the early years of the postwar period, Japanese intellectuals were struggling with the issue of wartime responsibility (*sensō sekinin*) and a central part of their agenda after 1945 was to question and redefine the political role of the intellectual in Japanese society. Part of this process was a reassessment of prewar notions of the Japanese people (*minzoku*) and their relations with other Asian peoples. During the prewar and wartime years, the Japanese state had effectively manipulated the construction of the Japanese *minzoku* as part of an agenda of imperialist domination, justified by a pan-Asianist ideology. In opposition to these ideological forces that had brought so much destruction and suffering to the peoples of Asia and Japan, among postwar Japanese leftists there was strong support for the rising power of the Asian nationalist and independence movements that had been gaining ground since 1945.[47] The Bandung Conference represented a new kind of solidarity among Asian nations that was forming around these issues, defined against the Cold War international order and the legacies of imperialism in Asia and Africa.

As stated above, for progressive historians in the postwar period, this new-found anti-imperialist solidarity and Pan-Asianism can be called a form of political resistance. The target of this resistance was the conservative Japanese government and their leading role in Japan's involvement (direct and indirect) in conflicts such as the Korean and Vietnam Wars, and agreements between Japan and the United States like the San Francisco peace treaty and security treaty. There were two key components in the formation of this new postwar Pan-Asianism among Japanese progressive intellectuals. One was the pacifist agenda that was central to the goals of the Bandung Conference. In particular, the leaders of the conference stressed the importance of being vigilant against "the impending danger of the spiraling arms race with atomic weapons and other weapons of mass destruction."[48] In this regard, the Japanese saw themselves as uniquely positioned to criticize the Cold War arms race, due to their experience of having fallen victim to nuclear weapons at the end of World War II in Hiroshima and Nagasaki.[49]

In recent years, a number of scholars have illuminated the importance of this notion of "victimization" (*higaisha ishiki*) that took root very strongly in postwar Japan. As John Dower has noted in his book *Embracing Defeat*, "the preoccupation with their own misery ... led most Japanese to ignore the suffering they had inflicted on others ... ."[50] In a more extensive analysis of this phenomenon, James Orr has described what he calls "the mythologies of Japanese war victimhood" among groups ranging from peace movement activists to conservative politicians.[51] In his book, *The Victim as Hero*, Orr argues that "the vision of the Japanese as innocent war victims reached its purest expression in the public dialogue over nuclear weapons." In addition, the bombings of Hiroshima and Nagasaki "provided the country with its first powerfully unifying national myth after defeat."[52]

As discussed above, Japan's lead delegate Takasaki Tatsunosuke made reference to the atomic bombings in his opening speech. For Japanese intellectuals who were critical of figures such as Takasaki and their limited historical vision, there was a tendency to stress Japan's wartime victimization from a different perspective. Because of Hiroshima and Nagasaki, they could readily make the argument that Japan was a victim of American hegemony, both historically in the final stages of World War II, as well as in the postwar period because of the way Japan was subject to the stationing of American military forces on its soil, even after the end of the Occupation.[53] Through Japan's participation in the Bandung Conference, Japanese intellectuals could now ally themselves with countries such as India, a nation that was more clearly a victim of Western imperialist aggression and exploitation. Japan could align itself with the other nations of Africa and Asia based on its common sense of victimization at the hands of the strongest power in postwar East Asia, the United States. In particular, Japanese intellectuals argued quite forcefully that Japan continued to be subject to the dangers of American nuclear capabilities. The most striking example of such danger was the so-called "Lucky Dragon Incident" of 1954, when the fallout from an American hydrogen bomb experiment in the Pacific caused radiation poisoning among the crew of a Japanese tuna boat called the Lucky Dragon.[54] In the same book by Orr mentioned above, he also describes how this incident played a crucial role in fanning popular opposition in Japan to nuclear testing.[55]

While this first pacifist component of Pan-Asianism was concerned primarily with the contemporary political situation of the Cold War world order, the other component of this new postwar Pan-Asianism was related to the historiographical agenda of progressive Japanese intellectuals. Specifically, leading Japanese historians like Tōyama Shigeki combined their scholarly critiques of Japan's imperialist past with an explicit political agenda that was extremely critical of the conservative ruling elite of Japan after 1945. By condemning their own nation's modern history as one of aggression in Asia, Marxists like Tōyama were also sending a message that the Japanese people should be on guard against repeating the mistakes of the past. As intellectuals, they felt a particular responsibility to speak up against the actions of conservative politicians who they argued were leading Japan down an eerily familiar path of remilitarization and renewed economic aggression in postwar Asia.[56]

Coming just three years after the end of the American-led Occupation of Japan, the Bandung Conference provided an opportunity for these intellectuals to express their solidarity with other countries that were also subject to the hierarchical political reality of the Cold War international order. With memories of the American occupation army's presence fresh in the minds of the Japanese, it was not difficult to argue that Japan was also subject to a kind of semi-colonial status *vis-à-vis* the United States.[57] The continued presence of American military forces in Japan, particularly on the American-controlled islands of Okinawa, was glaring evidence of this unequal relationship.[58] By identifying Japan's interests with those of the other Asian and African participants, postwar Japanese intellectuals could also celebrate their country's participation in the Bandung Conference as a turning point in making a break with its own history of imperialist domination before 1945. In addition, progressives saw this as a chance to redefine Japan's priorities in international relations, especially its close alliance with the United States. As intellectuals, they felt they had the responsibility to speak up against the actions of politicians they saw as ill advised. They defined their role in postwar society as necessarily including the role of monitor over Japan's international relations and alliances, especially where Japan's military was concerned.

In the aftermath of the Bandung Conference, this meeting was hailed as a triumph of non-alignment, a strategy that was particularly appealing to Japanese socialists. But as David Kimche has shown, in fact, the proponents of non-alignment were in the minority at the time of the conference.[59] Although one of the main organizers of the conference, Nehru of India, had envisioned the creation of a feeling of Afro-Asian solidarity around the issue of non-alignment, there was actually significant disagreement on this point at the time of the conference itself. It was not until after 1955 that prominent leaders like Abdel Nasser of Egypt moved "squarely into the camp of the militarily non-aligned."[60] Just as the complexities of these discussions over non-alignment were selectively invoked in the aftermath of the conference, so too did a somewhat mythical interpretation of events in Bandung take root among Japanese progressive intellectuals. In the wake of Bandung, Japanese intellectuals have often invoked the conference as a powerful symbolic moment in the postwar period.[61] Since 1955, it has become a marker of Japan's potential to overcome its own history of imperialist aggression. However, a closer look reveals the discrepancies between Japan's actual participation in 1955, and the way it has been remembered by Japanese progressives who have used it as a symbol in the service of a rather radical political agenda. The prewar careers of Japan's representatives, such as Nadao Hirokichi, Kase Toshikazu, and Fujiyama Aiichirō, are glossed over in a way that minimizes the influence of these postwar figures to re-establish ties in Asia.

In this sense, Bandung can be viewed as a moment in postwar Japanese history that helped to serve the interests of two very different streams of Pan-Asianism. At the conference itself in 1955, the officials from Japan represented a force of continuity from the prewar period, while in the wake of Bandung after 1955, it was picked up by the Left as a turning point with which Japanese progressives could strongly identify. It provided a way to clarify new priorities for the Japanese people that included a more explicit political struggle against the trends of postwar politics and Japan's international relations that were tied so closely to Cold War aims under the influence of American power in Asia.

15 Pan-Asianism in international relations

Prewar, postwar, and present

Hatsuse Ryūhei[1]

Introduction

Pan-Asianism has been defined as a set of ideas, feelings, or attitudes appropriated by Asians to promote solidarity and cooperation within "Asia," usually against the political, economic, and cultural influence of "the West," i.e., the Western powers that encroached upon Asia during the modern era. Pan-Asianism, or Asianism, has national, international, and transnational dimensions. Particularly in Japan, at times it has overlapped with nationalism, in the form of expansionism; at times it has been above all a reaction to Western dominance in Asia; sometimes it is little more than a vague identification with other Asian people(s) or "Asian values." While Pan-Asianism is expressed in political, economic, and cultural terms, above all it has been determined by changes in international relations.

Before World War II, Japanese Pan-Asianism was mainly political, aiming at the liberation of Asian nations from the colonial or imperial control of the West. In contrast, after 1945, economic factors became more important in the Asian world, as most of the Asian nations regained their independence and thereafter sought economic development as their primary national goal. During the Cold War, however, Asia was divided into two opposing blocs, thereby hampering economic as well as political cooperation in the region as a whole. In Japan, Pan-Asianism disappeared from the surface of political discourse after 1945, due to the prewar role of the idea as a legitimizing ideology for Japanese territorial expansion. However, in the late 1970s Japanese Non-Governmental Organizations (NGOs) began to assist community or rural development in other Asian countries. These activities can be considered a new type of transnational cooperation among Asian peoples that is in some ways reminiscent of the transnationalist thread of prewar Pan-Asianism.

The character of Pan-Asianism in each historical stage of its development has been determined by the character of international relations in Asia in the respective period. Therefore, we cannot discuss Pan-Asianism without taking into consideration changes in the structure and function of Asian international relations.

The aim of this chapter is twofold: first, to outline the changes in Pan-Asianism in the context of the foreign relations of modern Japan; and second, to locate the latest transnational forms of Japanese Pan-Asianism in the context of recent international relations. The chapter will begin with an analysis of the changes in the international system in Asia that influenced the development of Pan-Asianism, then move on to particular features of Pan-Asianism in its different historical stages, and end with examples of NGO activities, above all those of Nakamura Tetsu (1946–) and his Peshawar Association (Peshawar-kai, founded 1983) in Pakistan and Afghanistan. In this chapter I use the terms "Pan-Asianism" and "pan-Asianists" for analytical purposes, to describe the ideas, attitudes or behavior of "pan-Asianists." In other words, those "pan-Asianists," defined here so, do not necessarily claim themselves as "pan-Asianists."

Changes in international relations in Asia

The Western system of sovereign nation-states developing since the seventeenth century was quintessentially Western-centric and, within that system, legitimate actors in international relations were limited to the Western sovereign states. While the system brought development, wealth, and state-building to Western nations, it undermined non-Western nations – politically, economically, and culturally. The Western system of international relations embraced a practical code of inter-state behavior, which was, however, based on a double standard – one standard to be applied to Western nations and another to be applied to non-Western nations. While Western nations interacted as equals (at least in principle), non-Western political entities were treated in a discriminatory way, as was considered appropriate in the West.[2]

The system could function to the extent that it was underpinned by the existence of those non-Western areas that had been denied sovereignty and prosperity. The international situation changed radically in Asia after the end of World War II. Before the war, most of the Asian nations were Western or Japanese colonies. From the mid-nineteenth until the mid-twentieth century, the major political goal of Asian nations had been to regain their independence. Accordingly, the major task of pan-Asianists was to assist those nations in achieving their goal. Soon after World War II ended, one Asian nation after another became independent: the Philippines in 1946, India and Pakistan in 1947, Burma and the two Koreas in 1948, Indonesia in 1949, Laos and Cambodia in 1953, and Malaya in 1957. In 1963, Singapore further achieved independence from Malaya. In Indochina, the Vietnamese struggle for independence led to the First Indo-Chinese War beginning in November 1946 and ended by the Geneva Agreement in July 1954, which brought about the foundation of two Vietnamese states (the Vietnamese Democratic Republic in the North and the State of Vietnam/the Vietnamese Republic in the South).

Thus, many Asian nations had become independent, at least in a political sense. In April 1955, Asian leaders including Sukarno from Indonesia,

Jawaharlal Nehru from India, Chou En-lai (Zhou Enlai) from China, and U Nu from Burma gathered in Bandung, Indonesia, to convene the first Asia-African Conference.[3] Here, they declared the Ten Principles on Peace. This conference was, in a sense, a collective attempt by 29 Asian nations to declare their independence from colonial status. Accordingly, we might assume, Pan-Asianism had completed its role of assisting Asian nations to reach their independence.

However, in the 1950s and afterwards, the national goal of Asian countries shifted from political independence to economic autonomy. Even during the Cold War era, there were important internal dynamics of development at work within Asia, particularly from the mid-1970s. Economic development and growth then took off in the so-called Newly Industrializing Economies (NIES), namely South Korea, Taiwan, Hong Kong, and Singapore. Since the late 1980s, member states of the Association of Southeast Asian Nations (ASEAN) began to follow suit in terms of economic growth. A new focus for Asia was formed in Southeast Asia, crystallizing around ASEAN, which from the 1970s increasingly worked for the stabilization of inter-state relationships in the region. Pan-Asianism thus took a new form and found a new center in Southeast Asia, as opposed to the old center in East Asia, i.e., China, Japan, and Korea.

In retrospect, the first task in postcolonial Asia should have been the establishment of an international system of cooperation among the newly independent Asian countries, just as the European Community had developed in Europe from the 1950s. However, due to the unfavorable international situation, such a scenario was unlikely to be realized. The Cold War had divided Asia in two opposing blocs, and in some instances had escalated into "hot" wars, as in Korea and Vietnam. Besides, postwar Japan, although the only advanced country in the region, could never propose or promote such an internationalist scheme as a result of its prewar legacy of Japanese Pan-Asianism as an ideology for the legitimization of expansion, aggression, and colonial rule. Asian nations would have strenuously rejected any pan-Asian ideas that implied Japanese leadership or were generated in Japan and criticized such attempts as a resurgence of the prewar "Greater East Asian Co-Prosperity Sphere." This distrust of Japanese ambitions in the region is still alive today, as recent developments have shown.

After the end of the Cold War, in the 1990s Asian countries established their own inter-state system, composed of sovereign states, for the first time in history. In addition, Asian leaders began striving for dialogue with their Western counterparts on an equal basis. Two results of this development are the Asia Pacific Economic Cooperation (APEC) that was initiated in 1989 and the Asia-Europe Meeting (ASEM), starting in 1996. These new organizations were in part based on an ideology of Asian regionalism that promoted Asia's equal partnership with the American, Oceanic and European countries. In particular, Dr. Mahathir bin Mohamad, the former prime minister of Malaysia, advocated a variety of Pan-Asianism.[4]

In recent years, pan-Asianists have been increasingly seeking to counteract the United States as a hegemonic power in the region and to expel it from Asia. Many people in Asia find the level of American influence there absolutely repugnant. In addition, there still persists a level of popular skepticism about the Western model of modernization. On the one hand, these reactions have become manifest in hyper-nationalism as a counter-force against globalization in Asia, and, on the other, various attempts by Asian people at transnational cooperation among themselves.

The transformation of Pan-Asianism

As we have seen, the major political task of the modern Asian nations was to achieve political independence – a task not finished until the 1950s. In this regard, Japan was an exception. From the late nineteenth century, Japan had joined the club of the "great powers" (*rekkyō*) and, at the same time, colonized its neighbors: Taiwan, Korea, Southern Sakhalin, the Liaotung (Liaodong) peninsula (Kwantung Leased Territory), Micronesia, and, indirectly, Manchuria. This two-faced foreign policy was the mainstream of Japanese diplomacy during the modern era, based on the double standard of the behavior codes of the Western powers set within the Western state system. The ideological background for this diplomacy was embodied in the slogan "Cast off Asia, Join Europe" (*datsu-A nyū-Ō*) coined by Fukuzawa Yukichi (1834–1901), an important educator and opinion-leader in Meiji Japan, in 1884.

In contrast to the mainstream of Japanese foreign policy, Japanese pan-Asianists tried to assist other Asian nations in achieving their political independence. For example, some pan-Asianists offered financial, material, and moral support to Sun Yat-sen (Zhongshan, Jp. Son Bun, 1866–1925) and his revolutionary movement in China. They were composed of two groups: the so-called right wing of the political associations (*seiji kessha*), the Gen'yōsha (Black Ocean Society) led by Tōyama Mitsuru (1855–1944) and the Kokuryūkai (Amur Society or Black Dragon Society) led by Uchida Ryōhei (1874–1937), on the one side; and liberal democrats such as Miyazaki Tōten (1870–1922) and Kayono Chōchi (1873–1947) on the other. The former group was inclined toward what we might call "Greater Pan-Asianism," supporting the idea of Japan as a leader (*meishu*) in Asia, whereas the latter group was more egalitarian in terms of relationships among Asian nations, supporting the independence of each nation, but not necessarily claiming Japanese leadership.[5]

Uchida Ryōhei, one of the major proponents of the conservative group, attached great importance to Japan's national interest; as he once remarked, "I have been a supporter of Sun's revolution all my life. That is because his ideas and activities fit well with Japan's interests."[6] In contrast, Miyazaki Tōten emphasized the power of liberal ideas shared by his and Sun's groups, and he described himself as "in principle revolutionary and sympathetic to the revolution in China."[7] While these two politicians undoubtedly took totally different viewpoints, they shared the expectation that the Revolution would create a stable national government in China.

After the end of World War II, the international background of Pan-Asianism underwent an essential change. As most Asian nations succeeded in regaining independence after 1945, Japanese pan-Asianists lost any reason to assist Asian nations. Furthermore, in postwar Japan, the term "Asianism" was prohibited and considered a taboo in political discourse, as it could easily be confused with the discredited ideology of the "Greater East Asian Co-Prosperity Sphere." This, however, did not mean that the feelings or ideas behind Pan-Asianism had entirely vanished in the minds of the Japanese. Voices calling for solidarity among the Asian (or, at times, Asian-African) peoples, aiming at the restoration of friendly relations with mainland China, or criticizing American involvement in the Vietnam War, emphasized the possibility of dismantling the framework of the Cold War.

For the Japanese, pan-Asian emotions resurfaced in the great hopes held for the Bandung Conference (1955), which called for solidarity among Asian-African peoples. Pan-Asianism merged into the new notion of "solidarity among Asian peoples." This idea derived from a diplomatic term which the new Communist government in China had begun using in the 1950s, seeking to establish a good relationship with the Japanese "people" – as opposed to the "militarists" who had led Japan into war and devastation during the 1930s and 1940s. This slogan was also used in Japan in the 1950s and 1960s as a weapon for "progressive" intellectuals exerting pressure on the conservative government to recognize the Beijing Government instead of the Taipei Government under Chiang Kai-shek (Jiang Jieshi, 1887–1975). These intellectuals aimed at establishing a friendly relationship between Japan and China on a people-to-people basis, to the exclusion of militarist elements. However, in the 1970s, references to "the people" in slogans were in turn replaced by "citizens" in Japanese movements for peace, ecology, and human rights, which were seeking to distance themselves from class or labor struggles. A case in point was the movement for the solidarity of "citizens" in promoting peace in Vietnam and decrying United States involvement in Asian affairs in the 1970s. A very recent case involves the burgeoning discussions on global or transnational civil society. While also based on internationalism or cosmopolitanism, these trends can be understood as recent expressions of Pan-Asianism.

In postcolonial Asia's striving for economic autonomy, Japan was to provide aid in several ways. In this context, we might expect that Japanese pan-Asianists would have put forward ideas of economic cooperation with Asian nations based on mutual equality. We might also assume that, as a consequence, the policy of Official Development Assistance (ODA)[8] would be explained in terms of Pan-Asianism. To gain clarification of these points, I have investigated official statements of the postwar era, such as the policy speeches made by prime ministers at the beginning of each session of the National Diet; relevant paragraphs in *Gaikō Seisho* (The Diplomatic Bluebook) published annually by the Foreign Ministry; *Keizai Kyōryoku no Genjō to*

Mondaiten (The White Paper on Economic Cooperation and its Problems) published by the Ministry of Trade and Industry; and the *Keidanren Geppō* (The Bulletin of Keidanren) published by Keidanren (Japan Federation of Economic Organizations).

When I examined whether business groups or politicians, when explaining economic assistance to Asia, placed emphasis on the notion of cooperation and co-prosperity with Asian countries on an equal basis, I found that material reflecting a pan-Asian character, assuming equal partnership, was more or less exceptional. One of the rare cases where I found pan-Asian rhetoric was the policy speech made by Prime Minister Fukuda Takeo at the 81st session of the National Diet in spring 1977, in which he proposed to establish "a relationship of cooperation between real friends in both the intellectual and material fields," and construct "good relations with the whole region of Southeast Asia in order to share peace and prosperity with it." Another case is a sentence in *The 1969 White Paper on Economic Cooperation and its Problems*, which proposed to improve relationships with neighboring countries in Asia by "responding to their expectations, offering them friendly advice and rendering them warm assistance."[9]

While a declaration of cooperation and equality in dealing with Asian neighbors in official documents is rare, the prewar idea of "Greater Pan-Asianism" still remains strong in contemporary discourse on Japan's economic cooperation with the countries of Asia. For example, Kamei Shizuka, a Diet member of the Liberal Democratic Party (LDP), observed in 1988: "As you know, the Japanese Government has endorsed the huge sum of a six hundred billion yen loan to China, in compensation not for the damage caused by our invasion of China, but for the troubles caused by us during the war period."[10] A similar remark was made by Koyama Gorō, a leading businessman, Mitsui Bank director, and former chairman of the Association for Assistance to University Students from Asia, who observed that "ASEAN countries were able to achieve independence from long European dominance because Japan was defeated in the Greater East Asian War." And further: "We are trying to provide any type of economic assistance, apologizing for those big troubles caused by the war, for which all of us feel very sorry." While emphasizing his firm resolution to continue economic assistance, Koyama seemed unhappy about recipients who had received funding without expressing their deepest gratitude. His last words, implicitly to other Asian peoples, took the form of a querulous question: "Why and how did you achieve independence?"[11] These examples show that, regardless of the changes in the Asian international system, the ghost of *Greater Pan-Asianism*, reminiscent of prewar politics, still persists in some circles in Japan.

Japanese NGOs, however, are putting increasing emphasis on an equal relationship with Asian people(s) and nations. They have sought to draw together Asian peoples by providing refugees with emergency relief, local people with medical services, or by assisting communities in promoting social development, mainly in Southeast and South Asia. Some of their activities are predicated upon universal humanitarianism, while others are derived from pan-Asian emotions that may be called pan-Asian humanitarianism, as distinct from universal humanitarianism.

For example, Ono Satoyo, a representative of the Kampuchean Refugees Relief Program from Kyōto, remarked on the "sweet and lovely smiles" of Cambodians living in a refugee camp on the Cambodia–Thai border in the 1980s. She observed: "I think that I, as an Oriental person, have found a similarity between me and those Cambodian people who were so unwilling to complain, holding their own great grief in their hearts."[12] While Ono is not a pan-Asianist in the traditional sense – she is more concerned with upholding the universal values of human rights than opposing Western dominance – some pan-Asian elements are revealed in her emotions.

Another case of pan-Asian humanitarianism is found in the activities of Dr. Iwamura Noboru, who supplied medical assistance to rural people in mountainous Nepal in the 1960s and 1970s. He noted: "Personally and nationally, we can be redeemed by living together with Asia."[13] This was dramatically confirmed by his experience in Nepal, where he contracted dysentery and was saved by traditional medicine. A medical shaman treated him effectively. Dr. Iwamura discovered that the value of Western medicine is fairly limited in traditional society. Furthermore, when an old woman fell seriously ill, a young Nepalese man hoistered her onto his back, and walked along miles of mountain trails to Iwamura's clinic. But he would not take money for the painstaking service, embodying his words of "living together" in the behavior. Thus he learnt the wisdom of "living together" from the young man. Thus pan-Asian emotions motivated his transnational thinking and activities for the benefit of Nepalese rural people, although it had little political and economic significance at the time.

Since the 1990s, Pan-Asianism has therefore taken two forms in Japan, in tandem with the process of globalization. First, thinking and activities directed at "living in Asia" or "living together with Asian people" have become more popular with Japanese NGOs. Needless to say, not all Japanese NGOs that are active in Asia are necessarily pan-Asian in orientation. Many of them, as indicated above, rather hold values rooted in universal humanitarianism or human rights. Still, it can not be denied that transnational Pan-Asianism has been growing stronger in Japan recently, particularly in the burgeoning civil society movement. One striking example is the activities and ideas of Dr. Nakamura Tetsu and the Peshawar Association (Peshawar-kai). Nakamura and the other members of this organization, mostly from Fukuoka, have devoted their energies to medical services and rural development in Pakistan and Afghanistan since the mid-1980s, and are still active there today (see next section).

On the other hand, however, we cannot overlook the resurgence of an exclusive nationalism in Japanese society as a reaction against the processes of globalization. In part reminiscent of the prewar notion of the "Greater East Asian Co-Prosperity Sphere," this kind of nationalism aims at retrospectively justifying the invasion of Asian nations by Japan and thereby negating the Japanese postwar democracy that developed in opposition to prewar values. One obvious example of this tendency is the so-called "Liberal View of History" (*jiyūshugi shikan*) propagated by Fujioka Nobukatsu, Nishio Kanji, cartoonist Kobayashi Yoshinori, and others.[14]

Nakamura Tetsu and Peshawar-kai medical services

Dr. Nakamura Tetsu, born in Fukuoka City in 1946, is a medical doctor who graduated from the medical school of Kyūshū University in 1973.[15] In 1982, while working as a psychiatrist after graduation, he was greatly impressed with a lecture delivered by Dr. Iwamura Noboru who had been engaged in medical services in Nepal from 1962 to 1980 as a volunteer with the Japan Overseas Christian Medical Cooperative Service (JOCS). Nakamura wrote to Iwamura, stating his intention to follow in Iwamura's footsteps.[16] In April 1983, JOCS assigned him a clinical position at the Mission Hospital in Peshawar in northwest Pakistan. His position was head of the hospital's leprosy unit, a post he took up in May 1984. In September 1983, ahead of his arrival in Pakistan, Nakamura's friends established an NGO called Peshawar-kai, located in Fukuoka, to support his activities. In 2006, Nakamura and the Peshawar-kai are still involved in broadly-based cooperative projects in Pakistan and Afghanistan.

The organization's activities can be divided into three periods. In the first period (1984–90), Nakamura worked in Pakistan mainly within the framework provided by JOCS. However, after he left the Christian organization in 1990, he expanded his activities to the mountainous areas of northeast Afghanistan in order to extend medical services to the rural poor in those areas. These projects were financially supported by Peshawar-kai. During the decade from 1990 to 2000, other Japanese also became involved in medical services in Peshawar, although numbers were still very limited. The third stage began in 2000, when Nakamura and the Peshawar-kai decided to launch a number of community development projects, such as supplying drinking water, building large-scale irrigation systems, and running a pilot farm. Thus their activities were extended to cover other fields than medicine. During the last two decades, Peshawar-kai has expanded its financial commitment from annual expenses of 6,110 thousand yen in 1984 to 228,024 thousand yen in 2003 (see Table 15.1).

The first stage of Peshawar-kai's activities

At the start of their work, the major task of Dr. Nakamura and the Peshawar-kai was to treat leprosy patients. However, Nakamura had only minimal knowledge of leprosy, which is very rarely found in contemporary Japan. Therefore, between his appointment and beginning work at Peshawar, he started training in June 1983 at Oku-Kōmyō-en, a national sanatorium for

Table 15.1 Annual budget (general and special, combined)

Income (thousand yen)	1984	1985	1986	1987	1988	1989	1990	1991	1992	1993	1994	1995	1996	1997	1998	1999	2000	2001	2002	2003
1. Membership fee and donation	7,417	6,906	7,261	6,483	7,288	11,555	16,148	20,016	33,771	62,843	47,925	58,382	77,061	72,934	49,778	56,529	105,633	940,061	398,100	290,485
2. Subsidy	0	0	0	0	0	3,600	7,000	9,894	24,963	37,350	31,042	38,384	27,967	25,758	29,268	33,376	16,617	18,616	7,636	0
Foreign Office International						3,600	7,000	6,344	15,467	11,320	8,000	8,500	7,500	7,770	5,000	4,500	0	0	0	0
Volunteer Saving								3,550	9,496	19,638	21,062	28,072	18,091	15,905	22,568	27,727	16,617	18,616	7,636	0
Others										6,392	1,980	1,812	2,376	2,083	1,700	1,149	0	0	0	0
3. Business profit, garage sale, sale of books, honorarium for lecture and others	110	234	436	315	0	215	849	234	645	400	240	2,599	1,089	1,876	1,515	5,021	5,062	14,565	3,752	408
4. Saving interest	50	4	56	32	60	57	39	56	454	240	210	44	46	410	56	8	18	514	39	49
Subtotal	7,576	7,144	7,753	6,830	7,348	15,427	24,036	30,200	59,833	100,833	79,417	99,409	106,163	100,978	80,617	94,934	127,330	973,756	409,527	290,942
Forward from the previous year	2,692	4,158	2,628	1,284	1,656	1,737	921	1,714	1,023	6,960	12,271	9,188	20,619	27,891	4,155	11,845	25,434	54,405	83,536	222,684
Total	10,267	11,302	10,382	8,114	9,004	17,164	24,957	31,914	60,856	107,791	91,688	108,596	126,782	128,869	84,772	106,779	152,765	1,028,160	493,063	513,626

Expense (thousand yen)	1984	1985	1986	1987	1988	1989	1990	1991	1992	1993	1994	1995	1996	1997	1998	1999	2000	2001	2002	2003
1. Cooperation fields	4,373	7,324	7,786	4,822	5,128	13,489	19,734	26,844	49,940	72,523	77,396	82,921	93,567	111,039	*66,974	70,800	91,415	*273,584	249,071	204,820
Medical services	4,373	7,324	6,364	4,822	5,128	11,715	16,911	23,759	47,366	70,488	73,471	80,424	85,197	104,355	*66,974	63,535	51,739	81,654	91,159	82,366
Support to Nakamura's activities	4,373	5,824	4,263	3,635	3,466															
Running JAMS						11,715	16,911	23,759	47,366	67,802	65,206	56,564	59,531	39,422	25,708					
Running PLS											8,265	23,860	15,660	20,190						
Running PMS															41,265	63,535	51,739	81,654	65,566	60,103
Constructing a sandal workshop	1,500																			
Purchasing a jeep			2,101																	
Emergent cure for malaria										2,686										

Expense (thousand yen)	1984	1985	1986	1987	1988	1989	1990	1991	1992	1993	1994	1995	1996	1997	1998	1999	2000	2001	2002	2003
PMS hospital construction													10,006							
Constructing a clinic and others														44,743					25,593	22,263
Rural development and emergency relief	0	0	0	0	0	0	0	0	0	0	0	0	0	0	0	0	30,968	180,150	135,290	88,993
Digging wells																	30,968	12,616	41,655	44,405
Support for agriculture																			380	612
Irrigation canal construction																			93,255	43,976
Emergency relief FfL																		167,534		
Miscellaneous		–	1,422	1,187	1,632	1,774	2,823	3,085	2,574	2,035	3,925	2,497	8,370	6,684	6,100	7,266	8,708	9,647	22,622	33,460
Japanese local workers													5,755	3,800	3,759	3,442	5,359	7,025	17,994	20,969
Traveling and correspondence			1,197	887	1,383	1,344	1,095	2,280	1,417	1,246	2,368	1,671	1,323	1,861	1,497	2,314	2,672	486	2,161	5,844
Domestic activities			225	300	249	430	1,728	805	1,157	789	1,557	826	1,292	1,024	844	1,510	677	2,136	2,467	6,647
2. Newsletter and PR	840	697	580	826	1,082	1,436	1,905	1,931	1,810	1,905	2,408	2,172	2,380	2,311	2,452	3,237	3,743	6,667	8,811	7,377
3. Secretariat	896	652	705	810	1,087	1,319	1,604	2,116	2,146	3,293	2,697	2,884	2,944	2,709	3,502	2,720	4,175	13,238	12,497	15,827
4. Refund to subsidy																4,588		1,136		
5. Fund for Life																		650,000		
Subtotal	6,110	8,673	9,071	6,458	7,267	16,243	23,243	30,891	53,896	77,721	82,500	87,977	98,891	116,059	72,928	81,345	99,333	944,624	270,379	228,024
Forward to the next year	4,157	2,629	1,311	1,656	1,737	921	1,714	1,022	6,960	30,070	9,188	20,619	27,891	12,809	11,845	25,434	53,433	83,536	222,684	285,601
Total	10,267	11,302	10,382	8,114	9,004	17,164	24,957	31,914	60,856	107,791	91,688	108,596	126,782	128,869	84,772	106,779	152,765	1,028,160	493,063	513,626

Source: Peshawar Kaihō, nos. 6, 9, 12, 16, 20, 24, 28, 32, 36, 40, 44, 48, 52, 56, 60, 64, 68, 72, 76, 80.

Note

*Data inconsistent.

leprosy patients in Okayama, and thereafter went to the United Kingdom to study tropical diseases at the Liverpool School of Tropical Medicine from September 1983 to April 1984. In addition, after working for a year at Peshawar, he went to the Wilson Leprosy Centre in Korea to train himself in reconstructive surgery for leprosy patients for two months from June 1985.

The treatment of leprosy in Pakistan was to require various medical skills, such as reconstructive surgery, plastic surgery, neurosurgery, dermatology, and social care. However, the equipment and facilities at the leprosy unit in Peshawar were so limited that the only utensils available were a broken trolley, a gauze kettle, several broken pairs of forceps, a damaged stethoscope and some syringes. The unit had only 16 beds for admission, as opposed to 2,400 patients registered at the hospital. Nakamura's first task, in May 1984, was to remodel one room into an operating theatre. He did his best not only to rebuild the unit, but also to rehabilitate the patients.

In the 1980s, Afghanistan descended into turmoil as war was waged between the Soviet troops that had invaded the country in 1979 and the local Mujahedin fighters who fought continuous battles against the invaders. Eventually, in February 1989, the Soviets were forced to retreat from Afghanistan, and shortly afterwards civil war broke out among local warlords, leading to the seizure of power by the Taliban, who took over Kabul in September 1996. During these two decades, a series of wars produced millions of refugees who fled to Pakistan and Iran, with hundreds of thousands of people displaced within Afghanistan itself. In response to this situation, in April 1987 Nakamura and the Peshawar-kai established the Afghan Leprosy Service (hereafter ALS), which aimed to provide medical care for Afghanis in refugee camps near the border in northwest Pakistan and at the same time to seek out new leprosy sufferers in the rural areas. Nakamura and his Afghan staff would treat Afghan patients among the refugees, setting up small-scale mobile clinics in camps in the war zone. In January 1989 they reorganized and renamed the ALS into the Japan–Afghanistan Medical Service (hereafter JAMS), which aimed to provide dispensary services for general – not just leprosy – patients in rural areas of Afghanistan. With the exception of Nakamura, JAMS staff working in Afghanistan were all Afghan nationals.

However, it became clear that Nakamura's activities were overstepping the boundaries set by JOCS, which was supposed to provide manpower only for missionary hospitals in developing countries, but no financial or material assistance. Outside the hospital, in January 1987 Nakamura began to extend medical services to Afghan refugees at camps on the northwestern frontier of Pakistan, activities supported by a special fund raised for purchasing a jeep in 1986 as well as annual donations from members of Peshawar-kai and other supporters. In addition, Peshawar-kai received subsidies from the Japanese Foreign Ministry from 1989, and from the Ministry for Post and Telecommunications (derived from funds for development assistance donated by depositors of postal savings[17]) from 1991 (see Table 15.1). In June 1990, Nakamura resigned from JOCS after two terms (six years) of work, in order to plan his activities with greater independence.

The second stage of Peshawar-kai's activities

In the 1990s, Peshawar-kai extended their activities to Afghanistan itself through initiatives undertaken by JAMS. In May 1992, Afghan rural refugees started returning home on a voluntary basis in the wake of the collapse of the Communist Government in Kabul the previous month. This was done in accordance with the restoration of Jirga – traditional autonomous rule – in the villages, and in the midst of intensified internecine warfare. Already in December 1991, JAMS had opened a satellite clinic at Dara-e-Noor – a rural hamlet without any modern medical facilities in the mountainous region of north-eastern Afghanistan. This clinic was intended as a base for further work in the country. Subsequently, JAMS set up two more clinics in hamlets without doctors in the north-eastern region of Afghanistan.

In November 1993, when malignant malaria hit the Dara-e-Noor area, Peshawar-kai raised funds through a large-scale campaign in Japan to purchase anti-malarial drugs in Pakistan and send them to patients in Afghanistan. Their slogan was: "Your two hundred and twenty yen can save an Afghan life."[18] The project resulted in more than 20 million yen donated by people throughout Japan, funds which were used to save 20,000 patients in Afghanistan. Furthermore, on top of treatment services offered at the satellite clinics in Afghanistan, the Peshawar-kai launched periodic medical services to Lasht in the northernmost mountainous areas of Pakistan in April 1995, leading to the establishment of a satellite clinic in Lasht in September 1998 (open seasonally from May to November). The organization also built another clinic in a village in Kohistan in November 1999, which however was abandoned in June 2002 due to local insecurity. Up to the present, these clinics have continued to provide medical services for local people in these mountainous regions under difficult circumstances – both political and social – people who would otherwise have no access to modern medicine.[19]

In October 1994, the Peshawar-kai established the Peshawar Leprosy Service (hereafter PLS) independent of the Peshawar Mission Hospital, as its permanent staff chose to leave the hospital after a series of conflicts with the director. At the same time, it established the Peshawar-kai Rehabilitation Extension Program (hereafter PREP) that qualified for official status as a social welfare organization under the auspices of the government of the North-West Frontier Province of Pakistan. A major aim of PREP was to administer the medical activities of PLS in the country. Finally, Peshawar-kai, determined to build its own core hospital in Peshawar since 1996, opened a 70-bed hospital on a permanent basis in a suburb of Peshawar in November 1998 to enable it to fully support and control its medical activities in the region. The new hospital was to be wholly administered by Peshawar-kai Medical Services (hereafter PMS), which came into being through a merger of the former PLS and the former JAMS in December 1997. At that time the Peshawar-kai was losing control of JAMS which was under the leadership of an Afghan doctor concerned less for the rural poor and somewhat more for the better-off urban population.

The third stage of Peshawar-kai's activities

In June 2000, the number of patients suffering from dysentery underwent a sudden increase in the organization's clinics in Afghanistan. Most of the victims were children. Supposedly, this was because they had been forced to drink contaminated water during a period of water shortage in areas hit by a very severe drought. In response, in June of the same year Peshawar-kai launched a Water Supply Project as an extension of its medical work, considering the supply of clean water essential to the elimination of gastrointestinal infections such as dysentery, amoebic dysentery, and typhoid. In Nakamura's words: "First of all we should feed the local people so as to keep them alive, before worrying about their illnesses and offering treatment."[20]

The project started with the digging of wells and then expanded to the rehabilitation of abandoned karez – ancient underground canals – found in those areas. By October 2001, the Peshawar-kai had helped local people to dig more than 600 wells for drinking water by providing them with financial, technical, and administrative support (see Table 15.2). This was in contrast to the indifference shown by other international aid agencies and organizations, which chose to leave Afghanistan as a consequence of UN economic sanctions placed against the Taliban regime in January 2001.

In October 2001, the Peshawar-kai set up the Funds for Life program in Japan to deliver food to internally displaced Afghanis who had fled their homes as a result of the US bombing of Afghanistan. The group raised more than 800 million yen to distribute wheat flour (1,884 tons) and cooking oil (167 kiloliters) to starving families in Kabul, Jalalabad, and a few other towns. This program supplied food to 150,000 people until February 2002, when other international agencies and relief groups began aiding war victims. On top of the food program, Peshawar-kai opened five temporary clinics in Kabul between March 2001 and June 2002, at a time when other foreign medical facilities were not available there (see Table 15.3).

In January 2002, by utilizing the money (more than 130 million yen) left over from earlier fundraising efforts, Peshawar-kai launched the Green Ground Fund for Afghanistan, a series of programs designed to reactivate agriculture in villages torn by war and drought.

First, the Fund carried on the projects for securing water for farm irrigation which had begun a year and a half previously. In September 2004, it undertook the reconstruction of karez in the valley of Dara-e-Noor, restoring 38 waterways which had been turned into desert by the drought. It also helped the local people to dig 11 big irrigation wells in the Dara-e-Noor area. Former water sources were recovered and made available at 1,181 sites. These restoration efforts enabled almost 1,000 families to return to villages abandoned due to a shortage of water. This irrigation project for community revitalization and self-sufficiency is still in place today, and continued even during the US air attacks on Afghanistan from 2001.

Second, in March 2003, the Fund started construction of the 14-kilometer Ab-e Marwarid Canal, intended to make the best use of the abundant water

Table 15.2 Water supply project

| | Sites under construction or control | | | | | Usable water resources | | | | |
| | Dara-e-Noor | | | Other areas | All sites | | | | | |
	# well	# irrigation well	# karez	# well	#total	# total	# well	# irrigation well	# karez	# completed
July 2000	10				10					
Dec 2000	35		30	284	349	204	177		27	78
Jan 2001	42		35	278	355					
Nov 2001	59	1	38	560	658	603	573	1	30	455
Feb 2002	81	1	38	579	699	557	529	1	28	429
Dec 2002	150	5	38	704	897	848	820	5	28	760
Jun 2003	200	5	38	757	1,000	932	889	5	38	899
Dec 2003	269	11	38	776	1,094	1,030	983	9	38	1,007
Jun 2004	325	11	38	848	1,217	1,217	1,128	11	38	1,086
Sept 2004	340	11	38	889	1,278	1,278	1,181	11	38	1,146

Source: http://www1m.mesh.ne.jp/~peshawar/wp/wsp03.html (access 25 October 2004).

Table 15.3 Medical treatment

	1988	1989	1990 (no data)	1991	1992	1993	1994	1995	1996	1997	1998	1999	2000	2001	2002	2003
Number of outpatients																
JAMS Peshawar Clinic/Hospital	3,238	7,732		29,158	45,029	48,584	53,804	82,078	45,641	41,657	25,259	30,171	–	–	–	–
PLS Hospital									4,823	10,174	13,159	–	–	–	–	–
PMS Hospital												35,891	56,585	61,343	46,062	50,537
Dara-e-Noor Clinic				–	36,634	47,205	34,211	39,642	28,408	30,363	21,768	22,884	29,286	35,900	34,572	42,680
Dara-e-Paich Clinic					2,282	28,058	21,734	31,971	29,492	32,131	15,052	21,969	34,041	34,733	30,683	35,500
Wama Clinic							13,503	20,588	21,200	24,452	13,748	17,519	17,991	16,264	11,786	14,969
Lasht Clinic												1,825	3,978	4,926	3,508	4,584
Kohistan Clinic												9,165	14,266	237	1,271	–
Clinic near Peshawar				7,490	13,093	12,202	18,564	14,165	9,970	–	–					
Refugee camps and mobile clinic	5,160	4,965		5,134	4,065	8,601	2,634	7,155	3,176	2,263	1,066,650	–	7,452			
Five temporary clinics in Kabul													12,365	114,365	17,446	–
Total	8,398	12,697		41,782	101,103	144,650	144,450	195,599	142,710	141,040	1,155,636	139,424	12,365	267,768	145,328	148,270
Number of inpatients																
JAMS Peshawar Clinic/Hospital		241		398	667	735	928	1,090	965	619	337	259				
PLS Hospital									551	580	492	–	–	–	–	–
PMS Hospital												834	1,051	1,278	1,841	1,773
Total		241		398	667	735	928	1,090	1,516	1,199	829	1,093	1,051	1,278	1,841	1,773

Source: Peshawar Kaihō, nos. 20, 24, 32, 36, 40, 44, 48, 52, 56, 60, 64, 68, 72, 76, 80.

resources of the Kunar River in eastern Afghanistan. As part of the canal, a water gate, a reservoir, barrages, and a 2-kilometer waterway were completed in March 2004. As of 31 March 2003, the number of staff engaged in water supply and canal construction projects was 148 (including eight Japanese), along with 300 laborers, while by June 2003 the sites involved numbered about 1,000. Irrigation is intended to cover 1,500 hectares of agricultural fields and enable 70,000 farmers to make a living (see Table 15.2 for the water supply projects).

Third, Peshawar-kai opened a pilot farm of around 8,000 square meters in the Dara-e-Noor valley where, in cooperation with local farmers, Japanese experts have experimented with new crops and vegetables suited for arid land, and introduced livestock farming to produce more dairy products. The farm, based on organic methods, is oriented toward full self-sufficiency in agriculture for the villages involved.

The activities of Peshawar-kai today

On 2 November 2003, while flying above the construction site for the irrigation canal in Kunar province, two US helicopter gunships mistook the blasting site as a ground-based attack and hit the area with machine-gun fire. As part of the US military operation to mop up al-Qaida, this preemptive attack fortunately resulted in no injuries. However, local people's painstaking attempts to rebuild their lives had been undermined by US military operations that were ostensibly seeking to restore stability in the area. In response to this incident, Nakamura raised an outcry against the American "approach of linking rebuilding aid to military intervention," maintaining that it was far removed from "the will of the [local] people."[21]

In July 2003, Peshawar-kai, supported by 12,000 members in Japan, had one hospital, one clinic and one office in Pakistan, and three clinics, one sub-office, and three staff houses in Afghanistan. By May 2004, Japanese staff numbered 19 in Pakistan and Afghanistan, while the number of local staff stood at 250, excluding daily workers (see Table 15.4). In 2003, the total number of cases treated in the organization's medical facilities was about 160,000, with 110 medical staff employed (see Table 15.3 for the number of patients at each facility).

In the hospital, the activities of Fujita Chiyoko and other female Japanese nurses have been significant, since Afghan and Pakistani women, in keeping with Islamic tradition, never expose their skin to male strangers, even to medical doctors. They have become indispensable for caring for female patients in the Islamic world. Furthermore, in the absence of Nakamura Tetsu, Fujita has been in charge of hospital administration, also working as deputy director of the hospital. It also should be noted that the medical project includes medical education and training for local staff as well as the treatment of patients.

In August 2002, Nakamura Tetsu and the Peshawar-kai received the Okinawa Peace Prize. The award of 10 million yen was used to rebuild the

Table 15.4 Composition of staff

	20/6/02	31/3/03	1/7/04
1. Medical services			
Total number	122	115	125
Japanese	5	5	7
Pakistani projects	66		66
Afghan projects	52		52
Doctor	22	18	22
Nurse and assistant	39	21	39
Inspection	11	13	11
Sandal workshop	2	2	2
Pharmacy	2	2	
X-ray specialist		1	
Clerk		13	
Driver		13	
Porter		11	
2. Water supply and irrigation			
Total number	98	148	98
Japanese		8	
Clerk		10	
Technician and director		62	
Driver		7	
Porter		9	
Miscellaneous		44	
Worker (daily)	700	300	800
3. Agriculture			
Total number	8	5	
Japanese	6	2	

Source: Peshawar Kaihō, nos. 72, 76, 80.

Dara-e-Paich Clinic. Constructed in August 2003, the refurbished clinic was renamed the Okinawa Peace Clinic. Nakamura also received the 2003 Ramon Magsaysay Award for Peace and International Understanding from the board of trustees of the Ramon Magsaysay Award Foundation in the Philippines, which recognized "his passionate commitment to ease the pain of war, disease, and calamity among refugees and the mountain poor of the Afghanistan–Pakistan borderlands."[22]

Nakamura's Pan-Asianism

Nakamura sums up the basic principle behind his activities in the following words: "[We] go where others dare not go. [We] do what others dare not do."[23] Seriously committed to human survival, Nakamura strives to be more practical than ideological, more flexible than rigid in fundraising, more humanist than rationalist in his planning. His thinking and behavior show him to be more an Oriental type of humanist than a Western one – he is concerned with the implementation of human rights at the subsistence level endured by the Asian poor, especially of the socially and economically disadvantaged in remote towns and villages. Thus he has developed a strong sense of transnational Pan-Asianism, involving respect for individual initiatives, which needs to be distinguished from the political or economic Pan-Asianism predominant in prewar Japan. Nakamura's brand of Pan-Asianism has been made clear in his published comments:

> What has motivated us is not a trend such as international cooperation or internationalization (*kokusaika*), as is popular in a contemporary Japan, but something akin to an unrefined emotion of the heart and a sense of obligation or simple sympathy. ... What has underpinned our work is, beyond any rational reason, the sense of love and affinity, and the spirit of sincerity. From these qualities a bond has been created among us that allows us to become conscious of the thick blood shared by us all.[24]

And further:

> Once we forget about Asia and the Asian people, we shall lose our identity. This has been our consistent attitude toward our activities overseas. ... It is our people's earnest prayers for our Asian brothers and sisters, and the proactive cooperation of the local people, that has consistently given me the strength to go on.[25]

These remarks testify to the pan-Asianistic instincts that are the basis for Nakamura's activities in Pakistan and Afghanistan. However, other comments reveal an anti-Western dimension which historically has been almost inseparable from Japanese Pan-Asianism:

> [After returning to Japan in September 2001, after 9/11], of all the things I remember about Afghanistan, what impressed me most was the country people who showed me the deepest *humanity* even in the middle of an arid waterless hell. In contrast, *freedom and democracy* are continuing to massacre the people on a large scale, even while proclaiming retaliation against terrorists. Hopefully, these very retaliators, as if experiencing a nightmare, might themselves feel some regret and pain when they come across a heap of corpses of innocent civilians.[26]

And again:

> It concerns me that aid to Afghanistan is equated with the aerial bombardment of Afghanistan. The reasoning is: "As there are dangerous forces there, we must crush them." These interventionists appear to have created such a scenario and followed through on it. In such a context, the assistance offered for reconstruction is in essence not much different from

the aerial bombing that preceded it. Such intolerance and impertinence are a dangerous sign for the non-Western world.[27]

Nakamura strongly criticizes the contemporary foreign policy stance of Japan that has involved it in the Gulf War and the Afghan War on the Western side. He maintains that, by kowtowing to Western nations but paying little respect to Asia and Asian people – this decision stands in the mainstream of Japanese diplomacy since the Meiji era – Japan still wants to "cast off Asia and join the West" (*datsu-A nyū-Ō*). He comments:

> Since the start of the Gulf War, the Japanese Government has decided to firmly support the multinational Forces and has offered them massive financial support. This policy can only lead to bewilderment and enmity among local Muslim populations. In essence, it derives from the admiration for the West that Japan has adopted through its policy of "casting off Asia and joining the West" and its hankering for modernization based on the Western model. As a result, a majority of Japanese, who regard the Western world as the true international society, have revealed their insensitivity to voices from the developing countries. If we look from Peshawar, as a representative corner of the Islamic world, "the international order" which seems to be self-evident to Japanese is in fact "the Western order" that justifies local confusion and international intervention.[28]

Fukumoto Manji, an executive member of Peshawar-kai, further observes: "The reasoning behind both the aerial bombing and reconstruction is to deny and destroy the traditional rural society of Afghanistan in order to build a 'democratic state' on the Western model there."[29] Thus both the bombing of a non-Western country and the recovery assistance offered to it are based on the same idea that Western modernity is a model for all societies to follow throughout the world. A non-Western country, first, has to be bombed when it is judged to be less than democratic by Western standards, and afterwards is given assistance for recovery so as to become "democratic" in the Western sense. In both cases of destruction and reconstruction, the model proposed is not indigenous but exogenous, since it comes from the West. In such a way, the West oppresses the Orient in social and cultural terms as much as it oppresses the Orient militarily, politically, and economically.

It is this Western dominance in the social and cultural spheres that Peshawar-kai members have tried to overcome through their medical and communal activities. Nakamura criticizes the "hypocritical" attitudes of Western nations that boast of their "humanitarian aid" when they should be apologizing for their acts of destruction.[30] In contrast, he notes the role of a pacifist Japan in promoting mutual support among Asian peoples, rejecting its membership of the elite Western club, and sharing the region's joys and sorrows with its neighbors.[31]

Conclusion

I have discussed the transformation of Pan-Asianism in the context of changes in the international system in Asia. My conclusions can be summarized as follows.

First, in the modern era, when the major goal of Asian nations was political independence, pan-Asianists from Japan were engaged in assisting this political goal of other Asian countries and nations. However, by the 1930s, Japan herself had established colonial control of large parts of Asia, and Japanese Pan-Asianism increasingly was discredited as an instrument for the legitimization of Japanese colonial control. After the collapse of the Japanese Empire, during the 1950s many Asian nations gained political independence and as a result, political Pan-Asianism lost its momentum. During the 1960s and 1970s, the major goal of Asian countries was refocused on economic autonomy; however, voices from Japan, advocating assistance for this new goal, were rarely articulated in terms of Pan-Asianism. In contrast, from the 1980s on, Pan-Asianism originating in Japan came to be tied to humanitarian activities across Asian nations.

Second, contemporary Japanese Pan-Asianism is closely associated with the kind of transnationalism prevalent in Asia associated with protest against the political, economic, and cultural dominance of the West. Nakamura Tetsu's Pan-Asianism discussed in this paper is a clear example of this current in contemporary Japan. This transnational Pan-Asianism is Oriental in its worldview, although it is also positively associated with humanitarian ideals and with modern Western thinking on human rights.

In the foreseeable future, pan-Asian ideas may well pass beyond the ambit of East Asian nations to include the leaders and peoples of Southeast Asian countries. Dr. Mahathir's notions of a new Pan-Asianism, the Asia-Europe Meeting, and proposals for an Asian understanding of human rights are all manifestations of this development. Perhaps we are witnessing the development of *two* centers of Pan-Asianism, in East Asia and in Southeast Asia.

Notes

Preface

1 See: http://www.dijtokyo.org/?page=event_detail.php&p_id=210&lang=en for details.

1 Pan-Asianism in modern Japanese history: overcoming the nation, creating a region, forging an empire

1 I am grateful to Christopher W. A. Szpilman, J. Victor Koschmann, Roger H. Brown, and Mark Selden for helpful comments on earlier versions of this chapter, and all the contributors to this volume for numerous suggestions and criticisms concerning the conceptualization of the book.

2 While research in postwar Japan had long abstained from addressing Pan-Asianism, in recent years a growing number of studies have been published, the most comprehensive being Yamamuro Shin'ichi, *Shisō kadai toshite no Ajia*, Iwanami Shoten, 2001. For further Japanese and English-language studies of Japanese Pan-Asianism refer to the notes below.

3 J. Victor Koschmann, "Asianism's Ambivalent Legacy," in Peter J. Katzenstein and Takashi Shiraishi, eds, *Network Power. Japan and Asia*, Ithaca, NY: Cornell University Press, 1997, pp. 83–110; Eizawa Kōji, '*Daitō-A kyōei-ken' no shisō*, Kōdansha, 1995, particularly pp. 112–16. See also the contributions of Miwa Kimitada, Kuroki Morifumi, and Hatsuse Ryūhei in this volume.

4 Peter J. Katzenstein, "Introduction: Asian Regionalism in Comparative Perspective," in Peter J. Katzenstein and Takashi Shiraishi, eds, *Network Power. Japan and Asia*, Ithaca, NY: Cornell University Press, 1997, pp. 1–44 (quote p. 5).

5 However, recently the importance of non-state networks and the role of academia have been receiving growing attention; see for example Ming Yue, "Chinese Networks and Asian Regionalism," in Peter J. Katzenstein *et al.*, *Asian Regionalism*, Ithaca, NY: Cornell University Press, 2000, pp. 89–114; Giovanni Arrighi, Takeshi Hamashita, and Mark Selden, "Introduction," in Giovanni Arrighi, Takeshi Hamashita, and Mark Selden, eds, *The Resurgence of East Asia*, London: Routledge, 2003, pp. 1–17. See also the contribution of Hatsuse Ryūhei in this volume.

6 See the official homepage of the Japanese Ministry of Foreign Affairs, http://www.mofa.go.jp/mofaj/area/asean/asean%2b3 (last accessed on 20 April 2006).

7 See Keizai Sangyōshō (Ministry of Economy, Trade and Industry), *Tsūshō Hakusho*, Keizai Sangyōshō, 2002. (Unless otherwise noted, the place of publication for all Japanese titles quoted in this volume is Tōkyō.)

8 Prasenjit Duara, "Crossing between Old and New Nations," in *IIAS Newsletter 32*, 2003, pp. 1–3.

9 See Narangoa Li and Robert Cribb, "Japan and the Transformation of National Identities in Asia in the Imperial Era," in Narangoa Li and Robert Cribb, eds, *Imperial Japan*

and National Identities in Asia, 1895–1945, London: RoutledgeCurzon, 2003, pp. 1–22.

10 As early as in the 1920s, as Dick Stegewerns' contribution in this volume shows, Japanese writers prophesized that while the "future of the ethnic nation-state is not not eternal," it will eventually give way to a "world-state."

11 Pan-Asianism as an ideology, movement or policy is not limited to Japan, but is of course an Asian phenomenon. While pan-Asian thinkers can be found in China, Korea, Vietnam, and other Asian states as well, this volume deals exclusively with Pan-Asianism in Japan. Research on Pan-Asianism in other Asian countries is even more fragmented than research on Japanese Pan-Asianism and remains a strong desideratum for future research. Some results of recent research can be found in the various contributions in Narangoa Li and Robert Cribb, eds, *Imperial Japan and National Identities in Asia, 1895–1945*, London: RoutledgeCurzon, 2003.

12 Matsuzawa Tetsunari, *Ajiashugi to fashizumu*, Renga Shobō Shinsha, 1979, pp. 24–25.

13 Stefan Tanaka, *Japan's Orient. Rendering Pasts into History*, Berkeley, CA: University of California Press, 1993, p. 77.

14 T. J. Pempel, "Transpacific Torii: Japan and the Emerging Asian Regionalism," in Peter J. Katzenstein and Takashi Shiraishi, eds, *Network Power. Japan and Asia*, Ithaca, NY: Cornell University Press, 1997, pp. 47–82.

15 Gavan McCormack, *The Emptiness of Japanese Affluence*, Armonk, NY: M. E. Sharpe, 1996, p. 159.

16 See John F. Fairbank, ed., *The Chinese World Order*, Cambridge, MA: Harvard University Press, 1968.

17 Ronald P. Toby, *State and Diplomacy in Early Modern Japan: Asia in the Development of the Tokugawa Bakufu*, Princeton, NJ: Princeton University Press, 1984; Hamashita Takeshi, "The Intra-regional System in East Asia in Modern Times," in Peter J. Katzenstein and Takashi Shiraishi, eds, *Network Power. Japan and Asia*, Ithaca, NY: Cornell University Press, 1997, pp. 113–35.

18 Bob Tadashi Wakabayashi, *Anti-Foreignism and Western Learning in Early-Modern Japan. The New Theses of 1825*, Cambridge, MA: Harvard University Press, 1991.

19 Miwa Kimitada, "Ajiashugi no rekishi-teki kōsatsu," in Hirano Ken'ichirō, ed., *Nihon bunka no hen'yō*, Kōdansha, 1973, pp. 385–461, p. 390; Miwa Kimitada, "Japanese Policies and Concepts for a Regional Order in Asia, 1938–40," in James W. White, Michio Umegaki, and Thomas R. H. Havens, eds, *The Ambivalence of Nationalism. Modern Japan Between East and West*, Lanham, MD: University Press of America, 1990, pp. 133–54.

20 Cf. Miwa, "Ajiashugi," pp. 401–04; Hashikawa Bunsō, "Japanese Perspectives on Asia: From Dissociation to Coprosperity," in Akira Iriye, ed., *The Chinese and the Japanese. Essays in Political and Cultural Interactions*, Princeton, NJ: Princeton University Press, 1980, pp. 328–55; Kan Sō-ichi (Han Sang-Il), *Nikkan Kindaishi no kūkan. Meiji nashonarizumu no rinen to genjitsu*, Nihon Keizai Hyōronsha, 1984, p. 14; Chō Gun (Zhao Jun), *Dai-Ajiashugi to Chūgoku*, Aki Shobō, 1997, p. 28.

21 Cf. Banno Junji, "'Tōyō meishu-ron' to 'Datsu-A Nyū-Ō-ron' – Meiji chūki Ajia shinshutsu-ron niruikei," in Satō Seisaburō and R. Dingmann, eds, *Kindai Nihon no taigai taido*, Tōkyō Daigaku Shuppankai, 1974, pp. 35–64; Li Ting-Jiang, "Ajiashugi ni tsuite," in *Ajia Kenkyūjo Kiyō* 17, 1990, pp. 87–106 (section 3); Hiraishi Naoaki, "Kindai Nihon no 'Ajiashugi'," in Mizoguchi Yūzō *et al.*, eds, *Kindai-ka-zō* (Ajia kara kangaeru, vol. 5), Tōkyō Daigaku Shuppankai, 1994, pp. 265–91.

22 See the contribution of Kuroki Morifumi in this volume, on the Kōa-kai see also Vladimir Tikhonov, "Korea's First Encounters with Pan-Asianism Ideology in the Early 1880s," in *The Review of Korean Studies* 5:2, 2002, pp. 195–232.

23 Marius B. Jansen, *The Japanese and Sun Yat-Sen*, Cambridge, MA: Harvard University Press, 1954; Sven Saaler, *Pan-Asianism in Meiji and Taishō Japan – A Preliminary Framework*, Tōkyō: Deutsches Institut für Japanstudien, 2004 (Working Paper 02/4).

24 Ibid. The *Gen'yōsha*, on the other hand, even though also often described as strongly "pan-Asian," from its inception had a much stronger nationalist agenda, as we can see in the founding principles of the association.

25 Yamamoto Shigeki, *Konoe Atsumaro – sono Meiji kokka to Ajia-kan*, Minerva Shobō, 2000, pp. 116–18; Marius B. Jansen, "Konoe Atsumaro," in Akira Iriye, ed., *The Chinese and the Japanese. Essays in Political and Cultural Interactions*, Princeton, NJ: Princeton University Press, 1980, pp. 107–23; Douglas Reynolds, "Training Young China Hands: Tōa Dōbun Shoin and its Precursors, 1886–1945," in Peter Duus, Ramon H. Myers, and Mark R. Peattie, eds, *The Japanese Informal Empire in China, 1895–1937*, Princeton, NJ: Princeton University Press, 1989, pp. 210–71.

26 Kan, *Nikkan Kindaishi*, pp. 34–39; Hazama Naoki, "Renzai. Shoki Ajia-shugi ni tsuite no shiteki kōsatsu," in *Tōa* 410 (August 2001) to 417 (March 2002); Hashikawa, "Japanese Perspectives," pp. 332–33.

27 For the idea of the "Yellow Peril," see Heinz Gollwitzer, *Die Gelbe Gefahr. Geschichte eines Schlagworts*, Göttingen: Vandenhoeck & Ruprecht, 1962; and Hashikawa Bunsō, *Kōka monogatari*, Iwanami Shoten, 2000.

28 This short piece by Tarui can be found in Takeuchi Yoshimi, ed., *Ajiashugi*, Chikuma Shobō, 1963 (Gendai Nihon shisō taikei, vol. 9). See also Hashikawa, "Japanese Perspectives," pp. 334–37; Hiraishi, "Kindai Nihon no Ajiashugi," pp. 271–75; Han, *Nikkan Kindaishi*, pp. 25–34; Miwa, "Ajiashugi," pp. 412–18.

29 Kakuzo Okakura, *The Ideals of the East*, Rutland, VT and Tokyo, Tuttle, p. 1.

30 Irokawa Daikichi, "Tōyō no kokuchisha Tenshin," in Irokawa Daikichi, ed., *Okakura Tenshin-Shiga Shigetaka* (Nihon no meicho, vol. 39), Chūō Kōronsha, 1970, pp. 37–38.

31 Ōtsuka Takehiro, however, traces Okakura's influence in Ōkawa Shūmei, a pan-Asian writer who gained influence in the 1920s; cf. Ōtsuka Takehiro, *Ōkawa Shūmei*, Chūō Kōronsha (Chūkō shinsho 1276), 1995, p. 60. We find signs of Okakura's influence on Ōkawa in the latter's writings of the 1910s, such as in "Nihon bunmei no igi oyobi kachi," in *Tairiku* 3, 1913, pp. 22–32.

32 See Matsumura Masayoshi, *Pōtsumasu e no michi. Kōka-ron to Yōroppa no Suematsu Kenchō*, Hara Shobō, 1987.

33 Baron Suematsu [Kenchō], *The Risen Sun*, London: A. Constable, 1905, pp. 292–94 (emphasis added).

34 Oguma Eiji, *Nihonjin no kyōkai*, Shin'yōsha, 1998, pp. 8–9, 161–63, 198, 217, 225–30, 323–25, 334, 341–45, 645–54 and *passim*. See also Oguma's contribution in this volume.

35 See the various contributions in Selcuk Esenbel and Inaba Chiharu, eds, *The Rising Sun and the Turkish Crescent*, Istanbul: Bogazici University Press, 2003, for contacts between Japan and the Turkish and Arab worlds; see Nakajima Takeshi, *Nakamura-ya no Bōzu. Indo dokuritsu undo to kindai Nihon no Ajiashugi*, Hakusuisha, 2005 and T. R. Sareen, *Indian Revolutionary Movement Abroad (1905–21)*, New Delhi: Sterling Press, 1979, for Japanese contacts with the Indian independence movement.

36 On the circumstances that made the Japanese government change its course, see Nakajima, *Nakamura-ya no Bōzu*, pp. 120–21.

37 On the Asianism of the Ōmoto-kyō sect in the 1920s and 1930s, see the contribution of Li Narangoa in this volume; cf. also Matsuzawa, *Ajiashugi to fashizumu*, pp. 111–14.

38 Colonial administrator Gotō Shinpei was one of these exceptions. Cf. Kitaoka Shin'ichi, *Gotō Shinpei. Gaikō to vision*, Chūō Kōron-sha (Chūkō shinsho 881), 1988.

39 The government therefore had been reluctant to give support to two attempts of creating an independent Manchurian state in 1912 and 1915. However, even though these attempts failed, they did lead to the establishment of new contacts between Japanese such as Kawashima Naniwa (1865–1949) and Manchurian bands (*bazoku*) that were essential in a later period. On Kawashima cf. Chō, *Dai-Ajiashugi*, ch. 5.

40 Nagase had studied at Johns Hopkins University and Berlin University, and had worked for the imperial Army and the Taiwan Government-General before becoming professor at Waseda University. Around World War I, he wrote frequently in a number of journals and was one of the best-known commentators on foreign policy. He criticized the government's policy of cooperating with the Western powers and advocated an "autonomous" foreign policy. Nagase is the author of a six-volume biography of Napoleon Bonaparte and of numerous studies of the Balkans, the Ottoman Empire, and central Asia.

41 Nagase Hōsuke, "Nikkan heigō wa Ajia renmei no zentei," in *Ajia Jiron* 5.4, 1 April 1921, pp. 5–9, quote on p. 7.

42 Kodera Kenkichi, *Dai-Ajiashugi-ron*, Hōbunkan, 1916.

43 Sven Saaler, "The Construction of Regionalism in Modern Japan: Kodera Kenkichi and his 'Treatise on Greater Asianism' (1916)," in *Modern Asian Studies* 41:1, 2007 (forthcoming).

44 Regarding the growing diversity of Asianism around World War I, see Furuya Tetsuo, "Ajiashugi to sono shūhen," in Furuya Tetsuo, ed., *Kindai Nihon to Ajia ninshiki*, Ryokuin Shobō, 1996, pp. 47–102, especially sections 4 and 6.

45 Yonehara Ken, *Kindai Nihon no aidentitī to seiji*, Minerva Shobō, 2002; Nakamura Naomi, "Tokutomi Sohō no 'Ajiashugi'," in *Shakai Kagaku Kenkyū* 37:2, 1991, pp. 415–37. The term "Asian Monroeism," mostly attributed to Tokutomi, had been used by Gotō Shinpei since around 1910; cf. Kitaoka, *Gotō Shinpei*, p. 138.

46 Furuya, "Ajiashugi to sono shūhen," pp. 88–89; see also Matsuzawa, *Ajiashugi to fashizumu*, pp. 84–85 for further avocates of an Asian League at the end of World War I.

47 Zen-Ajia-kai was officially translated as The Asiatic Association of Japan; cf. Ōtsuka, *Ōkawa Shūmei*, p. 88. Besides Kodera, Ōkawa was one of the first writers to use the term "Pan-Asianism." Besides his use of Zen-Ajia-shugi, in an article in 1916 he also used the term Han-Ajiashugi, for example in Ōkawa Shūmei, "Kokuminteki risō juritsu no kyūmu," in *Michi* 2, 1916, pp. 34–40. On Ōkawa, see also Christopher W. A. Szpilman, "The Dream of One Asia. Ōkawa Shūmei and Japanese Pan-Asianism," in Harald Fuess, ed., *The Japanese Empire in East Asia and its Postwar Legacy*, Munich: Iudicium, 1998, pp. 49–63.

48 Chō, *Dai-Ajiashugi*, pp. 22–23.

49 Miwa, "Japanese Policies and Concepts," p. 139; see also Chō, *Dai-Ajiashugi*, ch. 6 and the contribution of Roger H. Brown in this volume.

50 Cited in Banno, "Tōyō meishu-ron," p. 60.

51 Michio Umegaki, "Epilogue: National Identity, National Past, National Isms," in James W. White, Michio Umegaki, and Thomas R. H. Havens, eds, *The Ambivalence of Nationalism. Modern Japan between East and West*, Lanham, MD: University Press of America, 1990, pp. 251–63.

52 Stegewerns, Dick, "The Japanese 'Civilization Critics' and the National Identity of their Asian Neighbours, 1918–32: The Case of Yoshino Sakuzō," in Narangoa Li and Robert Cribb, eds, *Imperial Japan and National Identities in Asia, 1895–1945*, London: RoutledgeCurzon, 2003, pp. 107–28.

53 See note 59.

54 Cf. Matsuzawa, *Ajiashugi to fashizumu*, pp. 100–1.

55 Nevertheless, a number of influential politicians, scholars, journalists, and businessmen joined the Japanese organizing body for the conference, the All Asian Association (Zen Ajia Kyōkai), which reveals a growing interest in Asianism in these circles. On the other hand, some of the Asian delegates were subject to surveillance by the Home Ministry. Cf. Nakajima, *Nakamura-ya no Bōzu*, ch. 4.2; Mizuno Naoki, "1920nendai Nihon – Chōsen – Chūgoku ni okeru Ajia ninshiki no ichidanmen. Ajia minzoku kaigi o meguru sangoku no ronchō," in Furuya Tetsuo, ed., *Kindai Nihon to Ajia ninshiki*, Ryokuin Shobō, 1996, pp. 509–48.

56 Ibid.

57 Snyder, Louis, *Macro-Nationalisms. A History of the Pan-Movements.* Westport, CT: Greenwood Press, 1984, p. 4.
58 Takeuchi, *Ajiashugi*; see also William G. Beasley, "Japan and Pan-Asianism; Problems of Definition," in Janet Hunter, ed., *Aspects of Pan-Asianism*, London: Suntory Toyota International Centre for Economics and Related Disciplines, London School of Economics and Political Science (International Studies 1987/II), p. 116.
59 See Miyazaki's autobiography, *My Thirty-three Years' Dream: The Autobiography of Miyazaki Toten*, translated by Eto Shinkichi and Marius B. Jansen, Princeton, NJ: Princeton University Press, 1982. Eto and Jansen characterize the autobiography as giving "a romantic and often melancholy account of the fate of pure motives in the impure world of Japan at the end of the nineteenth century" (p. xiii). See also Chō, *Dai-Ajiashugi*, ch. 2; Matsuzawa, *Ajiashugi to fashizumu*, ch. 3.
60 Cf. Nakajima, *Nakamura-ya no Bōzu*.
61 See particularly Matsuzawa, *Ajiashugi to fashizumu*, ch. 2 for the case of Takeda Noriyuki, one of the so-called "continental adventurers" and member of the *Kokuryūkai*.
62 Snyder, *Macro-Nationalisms*, p. 4.
63 Saaler, "The Construction of Regionalism."
64 Already one of the first pan-Asian organizations, the Kōa-kai, had emphasized that "Japan, China and Korea belonged to the same race and used the same letters." Anonymous author, Shinkoku tsūshin, in *Kōa-kai Hōkoku* 8, July 1880, p. 10. See also the contribution of Kevin M. Doak in this volume.
65 Yamamoto, *Konoe Atsumaro*, pp. 31–33, 91–94, 218–20; cf. also Jansen, "Konoe Atsumaro" and Saaler, "Pan-Asianism in Meiji and Taishō Japan," pp. 21–23.
66 Furuya, "Ajiashugi to sono shūhen," pp. 90–91.
67 Tanaka, *Japan's Orient*, pp. 108–10.
68 Itagaki Morimasa, ed., *Itagaki Taisuke Zenshū*, Hara Shobō, 1970, pp. 60 and 352.
69 Ibid., p. 388. The reader might also recall Baron Suematsu's remarks claiming the exact opposite (see above, p. 5).
70 Cf. Ōsawa Hiroaki, "Meiji zenki no Chōsen seisaku to tōgōryoku," in Nihon Seiji Gakkai, ed., *Nenpō Seijigaku 1998 – Nihon gaikō ni okeru Ajiashugi*, Iwanami Shoten, 1999, pp. 71–90; Yamada Akitsugu, "Jiyū minken-ki ni okeru kō-A-ron to datsu-A-ron," in *Chōsen-shi Kenkyūkai Ronbunshū* 6, 1969, p. 47.
71 Eizawa, *'Daitō-A kyōei-ken' no shisō*, pp. 24, 50–52, 83.
72 Cf. Hatano Sumio, *Taiheiyō sensō to Ajia gaikō*, Tōkyō Daigaku Shuppankai, 1996, p. 277 for the example of Shigemitsu Mamoru.
73 See Narangoa and Cribb, "Japan and the transformation of national identities," p. 3; Yamamoto, *Konoe Atsmaro*, 179; Jansen, *The Japanese and Sun Yat-Sen*, pp. 210–11.
74 The main rationale for pan-Asian agitation in the 1920s was opposition to Western countries' racial exclusion of Japanese (and other Asian) immigrants. See Furuya, "Ajiashugi to sono shūhen," pp. 91–97.
75 Miwa Kimitada has emphasized the function of this organization as a "brain trust" for later Prime Minister Konoe Fumimaro, similar to the better-known Shōwa Kenkyūkai. Miwa, "Japanese Policies and Concepts," p. 138.
76 Conspicuously, this statement was made by the first Minister for Greater East Asia and the chairman of the Preparatory Commission for the November 1943 Greater East Asian Conference (Daitō-A Kaigi, see below, p. 13), Aoki Kazuo, after the war. See Yamamuro, *Shisō kadai toshite no Ajia*, p. 573.
77 On the slogan of the "harmony of the five races" (*gozoku kyōwa*) in Manchukuo, see Narangoa and Cribb, "Japan and the Transformation of National Identities," p. 17; Mariko Asano Tamanoi, "Knowledge, Power, and Racial Classifications: The 'Japanese' in 'Manchuria'," in *The Journal of Asian Studies* 59:2, 2000, pp. 248–76. For official statements on the "harmony of races" see Matsukata Yoshisaburo, ed., *Manchukuo and the Assembly of Greater East Asiatic Nations*, Shinkyō: Manshū Tsūshinsha, 1943, pp. 6–7, 22–24.

78 Eizawa, *'Daitō-A kyōei-ken' no shisō*, pp. 94–95.
79 See Gaimushō, ed., *Gaimushō no hyakunen*, vol. 2, Hara Shobō, 1969; Hatano, *Taiheiyō sensō to Ajia gaikō*, ch. 3.
80 Since the Foreign Ministry's East Asia Section (Tō-A-kyoku) was absorbed into the Ministry for Greater East Asia (as was the Kō-A-in) – meaning that the Foreign Ministry was stripped of its responsibility for diplomacy towards East Asia – resistance in the Foreign Ministry to the foundation of the new ministry was naturally strong. As a consequence, Foreign Minister Tōgō Shigenori resigned in protest.
81 Regarding Miki and Tanabe, see the contribution of John Namjun Kim in this volume; regarding Rōyama, see J. Victor Koschmann's contribution. Regarding Ozaki, see Takeuchi, *Ajiashugi*, pp. 322–25; regarding Takahashi, see Sakai Tetsuya, "Tōa Shin-chitsujo no seiji keizaigaku – Takahashi Kamekichi no shoron o chūshin ni," in *Kokusai Seiji* 97, 1991.
82 Kevin M. Doak, "Ethnic Nationalism and Romanticism in Early Twentieth-Century Japan," in *The Journal of Japanese Studies* 22:1, 1996, pp. 77–103.
83 On the term "puppet state," see Narangoa and Cribb, "Japan and the Transformation of National Identities," pp. 13–16.
84 Among them were, besides the areas already under Japanese colonial rule, parts of Indonesia, Malaysia, and Vietnam – due to their abundance of natural resources – as well as parts of China.
85 See, for example, Kokusaku Kenkyūkai, *Daitō-A kyōeiken no han'i* (The Extent of the Greater East Asia Co-Prosperity Sphere); International Military Tribunal for the Far East, document no. 2229.
86 Speeches of participants and the full text of the Declaration can be found in Go [Gō] Toshi, ed., *The Assembly of Greater East-Asiatic Nations*, The Nippon Times, 1944. Cf. also Matsukata, *Manchukuo and the Assembly of Greater East Asiatic Nations* and Hatano, *Taiheiyō sensō to Ajia gaikō*, ch. 7.
87 Ibid., p. 283.
88 Matsukata, *Manchukuo and the Assembly of Greater East Asiatic Nations*, p. 102.
89 Hatano, *Taiheiyō sensō to Ajia gaikō*, p. 185.
90 On the notion of autarky in the Japanese economy and the military cf. Michael A. Barnhart, *Japan Prepares for Total War. The Search for Economic Security, 1919–1941*, Ithaca, NY: Cornell University Press, 1987 and James B. Crowley, *Japan's Quest for Autonomy*, Princeton, NJ: Princeton University Press, 1966.
91 See for example the statements by Admiral Nagano Osamu made in September 1941, cited in Miwa, "Ajiashugi," p. 461.
92 Narangoa Li and Robert Cribb, "Japanese Imperialism and the Politics of Loyalty," in Narangoa Li and Robert Cribb, eds, *Imperial Japan and National Identities in Asia, 1895–1945*, London: RoutledgeCurzon, 2003, pp. 315–18.
93 Hatano, *Taiheiyō sensō to Ajia gaikō*, p. 209.
94 Snyder, *Macro-Nationalisms*, pp. 43 and 205; see Rainer Hering, *Konstruierte Nation. Der Alldeutsche Verband 1890 bis 1939*, Hamburg: Christians, 2003 for the history of Pan-Germanism and the Pan-German League.
95 On the membership and the social base of the Kōa-kai, see the contribution of Kuroki Morifumi in this volume; concerning the social base of the religious organization Ōmotokyō, which also advocated pan-Asian views, see the contribution of Narangoa Li in this volume.
96 On Ishiwara's "Movement for an East Asian League" (Tōa renmei undō), see Kobayashi Hideo, "Tōa Renmei undō," in Peter Duus and Kobayashi Hideo, eds, *Teikoku to iu gensō. 'Daitō-A kyōeiken' no shisō to genjitsu*, Aoki Shoten, 1998, pp. 203–50.
97 See Go, *The Assembly of Greater East-Asiatic Nations*, page before the table of contents (unnumbered) for a picture of the mass rally; cf. also Matsukata, *Manchukuo and the Assembly of Greater East Asiatic Nations*, pp. 107–08.

98 Kokuryūkai, ed., *Tōa Senkaku Shishi Kiden*, Hara Shobō, 1966 (reprint).
99 Chō, *Dai-Ajiashugi*, p. 13.
100 Jansen, *The Japanese and Sun Yat-Sen*, p. 33. Uchida Ryōhei, for example, financed his political activities through donations given to him.
101 Nakajima Makoto, *Ajiashugi no kōbō*, Gendai Shokan, 2001, pp. 200–01.
102 Yoshimi Yoshiaki, *Kusa no ne no fashizumu*, Tōkyō Daigaku Shuppankai, 1987, p. 189.
103 Hirano Yoshitarō, *Dai-Ajiashugi no rekishteki kōsatsu*, Kawade Takao, 1945, p. 303.
104 Ōkuma Shigenobu, *Tōzai Bunmei no Chōwa*, Dai Nihon Bunmei Kyōkai, 1923.
105 Wakamiya Yoshibumi, *Sengo hoshu no Ajia-kan*, Asahi Shinbunsha (Asahi sensho 541), pp. 9–13.
106 Cf. Kobayashi Hideo, *Mantetsu Chōsabu*, Heibonsha, 2005, ch. 4.
107 See the contributions of Oguma Eiji and Kristine Dennehy in this volume.
108 Christian Caryl, "A Very Lonely Japan," in *Newsweek*, 31 October 2005; Funabashi Yōichi, "Koizumi gaikō, datsu-A kara nyū-A e," in *Asahi Shinbun*, 13 November 2003, p. 13; cf. also Ajia gaikō ga shinpai da, in *Asahi Shinbun*, 1 November 2005, p. 3 (editorial).
109 For example, Morishima Michio, *Collaborative Development in Northeast Asia*, London: Palgrave Macmillan, 2000; Kang Sang-jung, *Tōhoku Ajia kyōdō no ie o mezashite*, Heibonsha, 2001; Matsumoto Ken'ichi, "'Ajia komon hausu' no kanōsei," in *Ronza* 5, 2006, pp. 136–45; Wada Haruki, *Tōhoku Ajia kyōdō no ie: shin-chiikishugi sengen*, Heibonsha, 2003; Hara Yōnosuke, *Shin Tōa-ron*, NTT Shuppan, 2002.
110 See the various contributions in Peter J. Katzenstein *et al.*, *Asian Regionalism*.
111 Asō Tarō, *Asian Strategy as I See it*, Internet: http://www.mofa.go.jp/announce/fm/aso/speech0512.html (last accessed on 11 January 2006).
112 Mahathir bin Mohamad and Ishihara Shintaro, *"No" to ieru Ajia*, Kōbunsha, 1994.
113 See Peter Duus, "The 'New Asianism'," in Arne Holzhausen, ed., *Can Japan Globalize?*, Heidelberg: Physica, 2001, pp. 245–56; McCormack, *Emptiness*, pp. 166–68.
114 Matsumoto Ken'ichi, "Kinrin gaikō o tō. Atarashii Ajia kōsō o," in *Asahi Shinbun*, 26 May 2005, p. 15.
115 Ogura Kazuo, "Jōshiki ni hisomu muttsu no ayamari," in *Ronza* 3, 2005, pp. 46–51.
116 Cf. Naikakufu Daijin Kanbō Seifu Kōhō-shitsu, *Gaikō ni kan-suru yoron chōsa*, Internet: http://www8.cao.go.jp/survey/h17/h17-gaikou/index.html (last accessed on 25 April 2006).
117 Cf. Sven Saaler, *Politics, Memory and Public Opinion*, Munich: Iudicium, 2005, ch. 2.2.
118 Ibid., p. 138.
119 This temple was founded by General Matsui Iwane in 1940, upon his return from the front in China, and since 1994 has been increasingly exploited by conservative circles for a reappraisal of Matsui's role and the meaning of prewar Pan-Asianism. The "Society to Protect the Kōa Kannon" claims that since "Japan's history has been distorted in the postwar era, the protection of the Kōa Kannon is one way of correcting (*tadasu*) history." http://www.history.gr.jp/~koa_kan_non (last accessed on 20 May 2006).
120 Cf. Saaler, *Politics, Memory and Public Opinion*, pp. 110–15.

2 Pan-Asianism in modern Japan: nationalism, regionalism and universalism

1 Most of the material presented here, including my definition of Pan-Asianism, is also discussed in my earlier essay, "Ajiashugi no rekishiteki kōsatsu," in Hirano Ken'ichirō, ed., *Nihon bunka no hen'yō* (Sōgō kōza: Nihon no shakai-bunkashi, vol. 4), Kōdansha, 1973, pp. 385–462, 474–75.
2 Marius B. Jansen, *China in Tokugawa Japan*, Cambridge, MA: Harvard University Press, 1992, p. 79

3 Ibid., p. 75.

4 John Peter Stern, *The Japanese Interpretation of the "Law of Nations," 1854–1874*, Princeton, NJ: Princeton University Press, 1979, p. 81.

5 Hirano Ken'ichirō, "Interactions among Three Cultures in East Asian International Politics during the Late Nineteenth Century: Collating Five Different Texts of Huang Zun-xian's 'Chao-xian Ce-lue' (Korean Strategy)," in *Creation of New Contemporary Asian Studies*, Working Paper no. 5, Waseda University, pp. 1–3.

6 Miwa Kimitada, "Fukuzawa Yukichi's 'Departure from Asia': A Prelude to the Sino-Japanese War," in Edmund Skrzypczak, ed., *Japan's Modern Century*, Sophia University with Charles E. Tuttle, 1968, pp. 1–26.

7 Takeuchi Yoshimi, "Ajiashugi no tenbō," in Takeuch Yoshimi, ed., *Ajiashugi* (Gendai Nihon shisō taikei, vol. 9), Chikuma Shobō, 1963, pp. 36–37.

8 Hata Ikuhiko, *Taiheiyō kokusai kankeishi. Nichibei oyobi Nichiro kiki no keifu*, Fukumura Shoten, 1972, p. 28.

9 Miwa Kimitada, "'Jindōshugi' no na ni oite hanpatsu shita Nihon," in Miwa Kimitada, ed., *Nichi-Bei kiki no kigen to hainichi imin-hō*, Ronsōsha, 1997, pp. 311–14.

10 Miwa Kimitada, "Tokutomi Sohō no rekishizō to Nichi-Bei sensō no genriteki kaishi," in *Seiyō no shōgeki to Nihon* (Kōza hikaku bungaku, vol. 5), Tōkyō Daigaku Shuppankai, 1973.

11 Tsurumi Yūsuke, *Gotō Shinpei*, 4 vols, Hara Shobō, 1965.

12 Miwa Kimitada, "Japanese Policies and Concepts for a Regional Order in Asia, 1938–40," in James W. White, Michio Umegaki, and Thomas R. H. Havens, eds, *The Ambivalence of Nationalism: Modern Japan between East and West*, Washington, DC: University Press of America, 1990, pp. 133–56.

13 Miwa Kimitada, "Colonial Theories and Practices in Prewar Japan," in John F. Howes, ed., *Nitobe Inazo: Japan's Bridge across the Pacific*, Boulder, CO: Westview Press, 1995, pp. 159–75.

14 Miwa Kimitada, "Manshū jihen to 'hakkō ichiu': Ishiwara Kanji o chūshin ni," in Gunjishi Gakkai, ed., *Saikō: Manshū jihen*, Kinseisha, 2001, pp. 37–38.

15 Romano Vulpitta, *Fuhai no jōken*, Shin Chūō Kōronsha, 1995.

16 Miwa Kimitada, *Nihon: 1945nen no shiten*, Tōkyō Daigaku Shuppankai, 1986, pp. 203–33.

17 Miwa Kimitada, "'Kokutai goji' no shūsen to Nihon kokumin 'tōgō' no shōchō toshite no Tennō," in Naya Masatsugu and David Wessels, eds, *Gabanansu to Nihon: Kyōchi no mosaku*, Keisō Shobō, 1999, pp. 293–97; Miwa Kimitada, "1924 nen hainichi imin-hō no seiritsu to Beika boikotto," in Hosoya Chihiro, ed., *Taiheiyō Ajia-ken no kokusai keizai funsōshi, 1922–1945*, Tōkyō Daigaku Shuppankai, 1983.

3 The Asianism of the Kōa-kai and the Ajia Kyōkai: reconsidering the ambiguity of Asianism

1 Matsumoto Ken'ichi, *Takeuchi Yoshimi 'Nihon no Ajiashugi' seidoku*, Iwanami Shoten, 2000, p. 8.

2 Hazama Naoki, "Shoki Ajiashugi ni tsuite no shiteki kōsatsu" (1)–(8), in *Tōa*, August 2001–March 2003.

3 Shinobu Seizaburō, ed., *Nihon gaikōshi I*, Mainichi Shinbunsha, 1974, p. 120.

4 Ibid., p. 115.

5 Nagai Hideo, ed., *Shimpojiumu Nihon rekishi, vol. 6: Jiyū minken*, Gakuseisha, 1976, p. 93.

6 Watanabe Hiromoto, "Kōa-kai iji no hōan," (March 1881), *Watanabe Hiromoto shiryō* (Documents Relating to Watanabe Hiromoto, Archives of the University of Tokyo History).

7 Letter from Soejima Taneomi to Itō Hirobumi, 20 September 1881, in Itō Hirobumi kankei monjo kenkyūkai, ed., *Itō Hirobumi kankei monjo*, Hanawa Shobō, 1973–81.

8 "Meiji jūsan-nen Kōa-kai kai'in seimei-roku," in Kuroki Morifumi and Masuzawa Akio, eds, *Kōa-kai Hōkoku/Ajia Kyōkai Hōkoku*, vol. II, Fuji Shuppan, 1993, p. 280.

9 Kuroki Morifumi, "Jiyū minken undō to Mannenkai no seiritsu: hi-hanbatsu seifu kōkan Watanabe Hiromoto no shokusan kōgyō seisaku," in *Seiji Kenkyū* (Kyūshū University), 34, 1987, p. 65.

10 "Tōkyō chigaku kyōkai dai'ichi nenpō," in *Tōkyō Chigaku Kyōkai Hōkoku*, vol. I, 1880.

11 For example, in *Tōkyō Yokohama Mainichi Shinbun*, 10 and 15 January 1880.

12 *Kōa-kai Hōkoku*, 21, 28 October 1881.

13 *Kōa-kai Hōkoku*, 8, 29 July 1880.

14 Komi Genzō, "Zai-Shin Pekin (Beijing) Nakajima Takeshi kun ga Shin-Ro no sensō o ronzuru ippen o bakusu," in *Kōa-kai Hōkoku*, 11, 9 October 1880.

15 See the text of an address by Takahashi Kiichi, in *Kōa-kai Hōkoku*, 8, 29 July 1880.

16 Editorial of *Junkan Nippō* for 16 August 1880; reproduced in *Kōa-kai Hōkoku*, 12.

17 See *Kōa-kai Hōkoku*, 8. For further details refer to Hazama, "Shoki Ajiashugi ni tsuite no shiteki kōsatsu" (4), in *Tōa*, November 2001, pp. 84–85.

18 Ibid., especially the second section on the Chinese response.

19 Suehiro Tetchō, "Kōa-kai ni oite Junkan Nippō o bakusuru enzetsu," *Chōya Shinbun*, 15, 17, and 18 June 1880.

20 See Nire Takayuki, "Bōekiron ryaku," (1)–(5), in *Kōa-kai Hōkoku*, 33, November 1882 and 35, January 1883; in *Ajia Kyōkai Hōkoku*, 3, 16 April 1883; 4, 16 May 1883 and 5, 16 June 1883.

21 Azuma Heiji, "Ōrai kōtsu no ri o ronzuru," in *Ajia Kyōkai Hōkoku*, 7, 26 August 1883 and "Nisshin wa shaken o shūaku subeki o ronzuru," in *Ajia Kyōkai Hōkoku*, 8, 16 September 1883.

22 Kuroki Morifumi, "Kōa-kai no Jingo gunran e no taiō (1)," *Seiji Kenkyū* (Kyūshū University), 31, March 1984, p. 46.

23 Eminami Tetsuo, "Shina tsūshōron," in *Kōa-kai Hōkoku*, 33, November 1882.

24 Kuroki Morifumi, "Kōshin seihen to Fukuoka Nichinichi Shinbun," in Chihō-shi Kenkyū Kyōgikai, ed., *Ikoku to Kyūshū. Rekishi ni okeru kokusai kōryū to chiiki keisei*, Yūzankaku Shuppan, 1992, p. 223.

25 *Ajia Kyōkai Hōkoku*, 18, 25 September 1885.

26 "Watanabe Hiromoto-kun enzetsu," ibid.

27 Ibid.

28 See the special issue of *Fūzoku Gahō*, 111, 25 March 1896.

29 See the entry for 11 July 1896, in Satow, Ernest (Nagaoka Shōzō, trans.), *Ānesuto Sato kōshi nikki (gekan)*, Shin Jinbutsu Ōraisha, 1989, p. 163.

30 See the entry for 25 November 1896, ibid.

31 Sone Toshitora, *Ro-Shin no shōrai*, Akashi Junkichi, 1896, preface.

32 Yoshida Gisei, "Dōkai shokun ni tsugu," in *Kōa-kai Hōkoku*, 7, June 1880.

33 Yoshida Gisei, "Kōa-saku daiichi," in *Kōa-kai Hōkoku*, 11, 9 October 1880.

34 Konoe Atsumaro, *Konoe Atsumaro Nikki*, vol. III, Kajima Kenkyusho Shuppankai, 1968, pp. 186–87.

35 Kokumin Domeikai, *Kokumin Domeikai shimatsu*, Kokumin Domeikai, 1902, p. 2.

4 Universal values and Pan-Asianism: the vision of Ōmotokyō

1 I would like to thank Deguchi Sanpei for his help in collecting materials. My special thanks to the late Deguchi Yasuaki for his willingness to devote long hours to interviews and to his family for their generous help in facilitating my collection of research materials. I also thank Robert Cribb for his comments on an earlier version of this chapter and also would like to pay tribute to the intellectual work of Ulrich Lins and Yasumaru Yoshio, to whose pioneering work in the field I am greatly indebted.

2 The number of branches increased from 40 in 1917 to 148 in 1920, and the number of

followers reached 100,000 by 1920. See *Ōmoto nanajūnen-shi* [Ōmoto's 70-year History] I, Ayabe: Shūkyō-hōjin Ōmoto, 1967, pp. 467–68.

3 The name Ōmotokyō was used after 1914. Until then the religious group had used different names: when it emerged in the 1890s, it was known as Kinmeikai. When Ueda Kisaburō (later Deguchi Onisaburō) joined her in 1899, the group was called Kinmei Reigakkai.

4 Yasumaru Yoshio, *Ikki, Kankoku, Cosumorojii* [Rebellion, Prison and Cosmology], Asahi Shinbunsha, 1999, pp. 186–88.

5 Ulrich Lins, *Die Omoto-Bewegung und der radikale Nationalismus in Japan*, Munich: Oldenbourg, 1976, p. 102.

6 The Ushitora no Konjin that possessed Nao to renew the world was considered to be the Kunitakehiko no Mikoto, a god from Shinto mythology. The Sun Goddess Amaterasu sent him to earth to change the world. See Franck Frederick, *An Encounter with Ōmoto 'The Great Origin'*, New York: West Nyack, 1975, p. 53.

7 Sheldon Garon, *Molding Japanese Minds: The State in Everyday Life*, Princeton, Princeton, NJ: Princeton University Press, 1997, pp. 79–82.

8 In 1927, they were all pardoned as part of a general amnesty following the death of the Taishō emperor.

9 Lins, *Die Omoto-Bewegung*, p. 256.

10 *Ōmoto nanajūnen-shi* I, pp. 693–94.

11 Gengo kankei zakken [Language Related Issues], Historical Archive of the Japanese Foreign Ministry (Gaimushō Gaikō Shiryōkan), Gaikō Kiroku 3-10-6-4, 1920–25.

12 *Ōmoto nanajūnen-shi* I, pp. 702–03; Prasenjit Duara, *Sovereignty and Authenticity: Manchukuo and the East Asian Modern*, Lanham, MD: Rowman & Littlefield, 2003, pp. 110–12.

13 *Kami no Kuni* [The Land of the Gods], 25, February 1924, p. 24.

14 Hayashi'ide Kenjirō, "Kōmanjikyō chōsa ni kansuru ken" [Survey on the Red Swastika] (19 March 1924), Ōmotokyō to Kōmanjikai teikei no ken, Archive of the Japanese Foreign Ministry, Gaikō Kiroku 3-10-1-36-1.

15 *Ōmoto nanajūnen-shi*, pp. 768–69.

16 Deguchi Onisaburō, "Jinrui Aizen no shingi" (1926), in *Deguchi Onisaburō chosakushū*, Yomiuri Shinbunsha, 1972–73, vol. II, pp. 188–92.

17 *Ōmoto nanajūnen-shi* I, pp. 785–88.

18 *Ōmoto nanajūnen-shi* II, p. 325.

19 *Kami no Kuni*, June 1934, p. 92.

20 Ōmoto had started mission in Taiwan in the 1920s. However, in July 1920, the Governor General of Taiwan prohibited Ōmoto mission, since the missionaries were propagating the reconstruction of the world and because the followers of Ōmoto in Taiwan were sending large sums of money to the Ōmoto headquarters in Japan (*Ōmoto nanajūnen-shi* I, pp. 459–61). Ōmoto's mission in Korea started in the late 1920s and closely cooperated with the Korean Poch'ōngyo (ibid., II, p. 44).

21 *Ōmoto nanajūnen-shi* I, pp. 33–35, 42.

22 Cited in *Kami no Kuni*, 25 January 1930, p. 79.

23 "Ōmotokyō tokuha sendenshi no dōsei ni kasuru ken" [About the Activities of the Ōmoto Special Envoys], Kakkoku ni okeru shūkyō oyobi fukyō kankei zakken, vol. 1, Archive of the Japanese Foreign Ministry, Gaikō Kiroku I-2-1-0-2, 1932.

24 In November 1931, Ōmotokyō sent another group of high-ranking officials to Manchuria to finalize the plan. Ōmotokyō would provide 200,000 Yen for the construction of the building and the Red Swastika Association in Fengtian was to negotiate with the Fengtian authority about leasing land. See "Ōmotokyō Manshū sōshibu secchi keikaku ni kansuru ken" [Re: The Plan of Setting up an Ōmotokyō Headquarter in Manchuria], ibid.

25 Kakkoku ni okeru shūkyō oyobi fukyō kankei zakken, vols. 1 and 2, Archive of the Japanese Foreign Ministry, Gaikō Kiroku I-2-1-0-2.

26 Lins, *Die Omoto-Bewegung*, p. 163.
27 Ibid, p. 183.
28 "Ōmoto no kaigai sendenshi tokuha ni kansuru ken" [Re: Special Envoy as Overseas Missionary of Ōmotokyō], Kakkoku ni okeru shūkyō oyobi fukyō kankei zakken, vol. 2, Archive of the Japanese Foreign Ministry, Gaikō Kiroku I-2-1-0-2, 1933–36.
29 *Shinnyo no Hikari*, [The True Light] (weekly), 17/24 February 1934.
30 *Kami no Kuni*, March, August 1935; April 1935.
31 "Kita e obiru Ōmotokyō" 1–6, *Yomiuri Shimbun*, 10–16 March 1933 (morning edition), all on p. 8.
32 "Ōmotokyō sōtō to Deguchi Hidemaro ichigyō no kōdō ni kansuru ken" [Re: The Activities of the Vice-President of Ōmotokyō, Deguchi Hidemaro and his Followers], Kakkoku ni okeru shūkyō oyobi fukyō kankei zakken, vol. 2, Archive of the Japanese Foreign Ministry, Gaikō Kiroku I-2-1-0-2, 1933–36.
33 *Kami no Kuni*, August 1930, pp. 81–82.
34 *Oomoto Internacia* 1, no. 3, 1926: 1, cited in Lins, *Die Omoto-Bewegung*, p. 126.
35 *Oomoto Internacia* 3, no. 23, 1928: 2, cited in Lins, *Die Omoto-Bewegung*, p. 126.
36 Lins, *Die Omoto-Bewegung*, p. 127.
37 Ibid, p. 145.
38 *Ōmoto nanajūnen-shi* I, pp. 732–48.
39 Ueno Kōen, *Oni Mōko nyūki* [Oni(saburō)'s Journey to Mongolia], Santo Shinbusha, 1925 (reprint 1994), pp. 20–21.
40 *Kami no Kuni*, October 1925, p. 89.
41 *Ōmoto nanajūnen-shi* I, pp. 720–22.
42 Ibid, p. 722.
43 Ibid, p. 756.
44 "Mōko to Nihon" [Mongolia and Japan], *Hokkoku Shinbun*, 14 November 1924, reprinted in *Kami no Kuni*, 25 November 1924, pp. 66–68.
45 "Deguchi Onisaburō o shibai ni" [Deguchi Onsaburō in Play], *Yomiuri Shimbun*, 19 February 1930 (morning edition), p. 10.
46 *Kami no Kuni*, September 1934, p. 67.
47 Gengo kankei zakken, Gaikō Kiroku 3-10-6-4, 1920–25, Archive of the Japanese Foreign Ministry.
48 *Kami no kuni*, October 1925, pp. 90, 94.
49 *Kami no kuni*, August 1930.
50 Kokuryūkai, ed., *Tōa senkaku shishi kiden* [Biographies of East Asian Pioneers], Hara Shobō, 1966 (reprint), p. 39.
51 Ibid, p. 296.
52 *Ōmoto nanajūnen-shi*, II, pp. 165–73.
53 *Jinrui Aizen Shinbun*, no. 162, 23 September 1931, p. 1.
54 *Kami no Kuni*, August 1930, pp. 84–85.
55 *Shinnyo no Hikari*, 17, 25 February 1934, p. 35.
56 *Ōmoto nanajūnen-shi* II, pp. 108–09.
57 Ibid, pp. 107–12.
58 *Ōmoto nanajūnen-shi* I, p. 720.
59 Ibid.
60 Yasumaru Yōichi, "Kaisetsu" [Comments], *Deguchi Onisaburō chosakushū* II, p. 498.
61 John Breen, "Bakumatsu ishinki no Shintō shisō ni tsuite" [Shinto Thought at the End of the Tokugawa and in the Restoration Period], in *Shūkyō to kokka* (Nihon kindai shisō taikei, vol. 5, furoku), Iwanami Shoten, 1988, pp. 2–3.
62 *Ōmoto nanajūnen-shi* I, p. 366.
63 Yasumaru, "Kaisetsu," pp. 428–29.
64 *Shin'nyo no Hikari*, 12 March 1928, p. 21.
65 Lins, *Die Omoto-Bewegung*, p. 103.
66 *Deguchi Onisaburō chosakushū* II, pp. 155–73.

67 *Deguchi Onisaburō chosakushū* I, pp. 200–02.
68 Lins, *Die Omoto-Bewegung*, pp. 183–84.
69 Hatsuse Ryūhei, *Dentōteki Uyoku: Uchida Ryōhei no kenkyū* [Traditional Right-Wing: Research on Uchida Ryōhei] (Kita kyūshū daigaku hōgsei sōsho 1), Fukuoka: Kyūshū Daigaku Shuppankai, 1980, p. 373.
70 Ibid., p. 315.

5 Pan-Asianism and national reorganization: Japanese perceptions of China and the United States, 1914–19

1 Hiraishi Naoaki, "Kindai Nihon no 'Ajiashugi,'" in Mizoguchi Yūzō *et al.*, eds, *Kindaika-zō* (Ajia kara kangaeru, vol. 5), Tōkyō Daigaku Shuppankai, 1994.
2 Takeuchi Yoshimi, "Ajiashugi no tenbō," in Takeuchi Yoshimi, ed., *Ajiashugi* (Kindai Nihon shisō taikei, vol. 9), Chikuma Shobō, 1963, p. 10.
3 Oka Yoshitake, "Kokumin-teki dokuritsu to kokka risei," in *Oka Yoshitake chosakushū*, vol. 6, Iwanami Shoten, 1993.
4 The writings of Tarui Tōkichi, Okakura Tenshin, and Ozaki Hotsumi mentioned here all are included in Takeuchi, ed., *Ajiashugi*.
5 Sakamoto Takao, "Seikanron no seiji tetsugaku," in *Nenpō Seijigaku: Nihon gaikō ni okeru Ajiashugi*, Iwanami Shoten, 1998; also see Katō Yōko, *Sensō no Nihon kingendaiashi*, Kōdansha, 2002, pp. 42–49.
6 Makihara Norio, "Ōi Kentarō no shisō kōzō to Ōsaka jiken no ronri," in Ōsaka jiken kenkyūkai, ed., *Ōsaka jiken no kenkyū*, Kashiwa Shobō, 1982.
7 Regarding the types of organizations and the kind of reorganization they sought, see Itō Takashi, *Taishō-ki "kakushin"-ha no seiritsu*, Hanawa Shobō, 1978.
8 Maruyama Masao, *Gendai seiji no shisō to kōdō*, Miraisha, 1964.
9 Regarding Mitsukawa see the contribution of Christopher W. A. Szpilman in this volume (the editors).
10 Itō, *Taishō-ki "kakushin"-ha no seiritsu*.
11 Arima Manabu, "*Kaizō undō* no taigaikan," in *Kyūshū Shigaku*, 60, September 1976.
12 "Jikyoku ni kansuru naichō," "Hiji bunsho-tsuzuri shoshū" (Chiba-ken Mutsuzawa chōritsu rekishi minzoku shiryōkan shozō).
13 Gaimushō, ed., *Nihon Gaikō Bunsho, Taishō 3*, vol. 3, Gaimushō, 1966, p. 105, document no. 105.
14 Ibid., pp. 118–19, document nos. 117 and 119.
15 Ibid., p. 138, document no. 146.
16 "Ogawa Heikichi no shitsumon," *Teikoku gikai shūgiin himitsu kaigi jirokushū*, vol. 1, Kyōiku Tosho Kankōkai, 1997, p. 98.
17 Article One of the final note to Germany sought the immediate withdrawal of German warships from the seas around Japan and China, while Article Two demanded of the "German Imperial Government" the uncompensated and unconditional delivery to Japan by 15 September 1914 of "for the purpose of returning to China all of the Jiaozhou leased territory."
18 *Nihon Gaikō Bunsho, Taishō 3*, vol. 3, p. 184, document no. 205.
19 US–Japan Joint Declaration on the Pacific issued on 31 November 1908. Article Five that in the event of an incident threatening the status quo in China or the principle of the Open Door the governments of Japan and the United States agree to exchange views in order to attain a settlement.
20 *Teikoku gikai shūgiin giji sokkiroku*, 30th Diet, no. 35–36, Taishō 3 (1914), Tōkyō Daigaku Shuppankai, 1985.
21 British opinion as of 9 August, *Nihon Gaikō Bunsho: Taishō 3*, vol. 3, p. 111.
22 Ibid., p. 122.
23 Ibid., p. 135.
24 Ibid., p. 136.

25 Matsui Keishirō, *Matsui Keishirō jijoden*, Kankōsha, 1988, p. 95.
26 P. J. Cain and A. G. Hopkins, *Jentoruman shihonshugi no teikoku II*, Kibata Yōichi and Dan Yūsuke, trans., Nagoya Daigaku Shuppankai, 1997, p. 42.
27 Ōyama Azusa, ed., *Yamagata Aritomo ikensho*, Hara Shobō, 1966, p. 346.
28 Ibid., p. 375.
29 Ibid.
30 Takakura Tetsuichi, *Tanaka Giichi denki*, vol. 1, Denki Kankōkai, 1958, pp. 676–712.
31 Ibid., p. 700.
32 Ibid., p. 712.
33 Kita Ikki, *Kita Ikki chosakushū*, vol. 2, Misuzu Shobō, 1959, p. 2.
34 Makino Nobuaki, *Kaikoroku*, vol. 2, Chūkō Bunko, 1977, pp. 142–43.
35 Regarding this issue, the most precise analysis of the Chinese side is Kawashima Shin, "Dai-ichiji taisen sansen to Santō mondai kaiketsu puroguramu," in his *Chūgoku kindai gaikō no keisei*, Nagoya Daigaku Shuppankai, 2004.
36 Gaimushō, ed., *Nihon Gaikō Bunsho, Pari kōwa kaigi keika gaiyō*, Gaimushō, 1971, pp. 717–58, 892–910.
37 Ibid., p. 719.
38 "Kōwa kaigi ni kansuru Nara tokuhō, chūō/sensō shidō, gaikō bunsho/241." Archive of the National Institute for Defense Studies (Bōeichō bōei kenkyūjo senshi-bu toshokan).
39 Gaimushō, ed., *Nihon Gaikō Bunsho, Pari kōwa kaigi keika gaiyō*, p. 750.
40 "Taishō 8-nen 7-gatsu 17-nichi chaku, Beikoku chūzai bukan-hatsu gunreibu jichō-ate denpō," "11/gaichūin hō/T3-38/82, Taishō 8-nen chūzai'in jōhō, denpō ichi." Archive of the National Institute for Defense Studies (Bōeichō bōei kenkyūjo senshi-bu toshokan).
41 Ibid.

6 Between Pan-Asianism and nationalism: Mitsukawa Kametarō and his campaign to reform Japan and liberate Asia

1 I am grateful to Mrs. Hara Mari, the granddaughter of Mitsukawa Kametarō, for allowing me access to the papers in her family's possession, and to J. Victor Koschmann, Sven Saaler, Roger Brown, and an anonymous reader for their helpful comments.
2 *"No" to ieru Ajia*, Kōbunsha, 1984, co-authored with Mahathir bin Mohamad, the then prime minister of Malaysia.
3 See, for example, *Sankei Shinbun*, 8 May 2001, where he claimed that Chinese in Japan commit "crimes that are encoded in their national DNA," which he feared "may alter the character of Japanese society." See also Miyake Akimasa and Yamada Masaru, eds, *Rekishi no naka no sabetsu. 'Sangokujin' mondai to wa nani ka*, Nihon Keizai Hyōronsha, 2001.
4 As of 2001, only five articles had been published on Mitsukawa. See Christopher W. A. Szpilman, "Kaidai," *Mitsukawa Kametarō: chiiki, chikyū jijō no keimōsha*, Takushoku Daigaku Shuppankyoku, 2001 (hereafter referred to as MKC), p. 469.
5 "Mitsukawa Kametarō," in Kokuryūkai, ed., *Tōa senkaku shishi kiden*, Hara Shobō, 1966, vol. 3, p. 678.
6 See, for example, Christopher W. A. Szpilman, "The Dream of One Asia: Ōkawa Shūmei and Japanese Pan-Asianism," in Harald Fuess, ed., *The Japanese Empire in East Asia and Its Postwar Legacy*, Munich: Iudicium, 1998, pp. 49–63; Christopher W. A. Szpilman, "Kita Ikki and the Politics of Coercion," *Modern Asian Studies*, 36:2, 2002, pp. 467–90.
7 Mitsukawa Kametarō, *Sangoku kanshō igo*, Heibonsha, 1935 (hereafter referred to as *Sangoku*), pp. 20–22. *Sangoku* was reprinted by Dentō to Gendaisha in 1977 and Ronsōsha in 2004. Unless stated otherwise, the footnotes refer to the Heibonsha edition. See also *Ubawaretaru Ajia*, Kōbundō, 1921, pp. 1–2.

8 As an adolescent, Mitsukawa devoured books by Kinoshita Naoe, Ebina Danjō, Uchimura Kanzō, and other Japanese Christians. *Sangoku*, p. 72.

9 *Sangoku*, pp. 72–73.

10 "Kaidai," MKC, I, p. 443.

11 Ibid., p. 113. Mitsukawa found him a "China hand in a class of his own."

12 Mitsukawa, "Shin aikoku undō no shōshi," *Kaihō*, 5:5, May 1923, p. 85. Also *Sangoku*, pp. 132–34.

13 Ibid., p. 129.

14 Ibid., p. 127. In its design and layout, the journal consciously imitated "the quality political journal, *Taiyō.*" Its initial circulation was 12,000, but subsequently declined. Ibid., p. 119.

15 Ibid., p. 127.

16 These admirals, known for their hard-line, expansionist and anti-British views, were shunted off onto the retired list in the late 1910s.

17 See, for example, Hōryū nikki, 1 February 1911, Mitsukawa Kametarō Papers, Kensei Shiryōshitsu, National Diet Library (hereafter referred to as MKP). Mitsukawa describes the colorful atmosphere that prevailed at Ajia Gikai meetings. Members were evidently inspired to a greater extent by traditional Chinese novels such as the *Suikoden* (On the Water Marshes) than by twentieth-century political theory. *Sangoku*, pp. 96–98. The pan-Asianist Miyajima Daihachi, president of the Zenrindō, was the leader of the Issuikai. Ibid., p. 112.

18 Ibid., p. 182.

19 Ibid., p. 215.

20 Ibid., p. 196.

21 Ibid., p. 211.

22 On the participation of socialists, see ibid., p. 193; on women members, p. 198.

23 Ibid., p. 211.

24 Ibid., p. 249.

25 Mitsukawa read Kita's first work, *Kokutairon oyobi junsei shakaishugi*, as a student at the Waseda University Library where this banned book was available. It made a profound impression on him. In 1915 he read Kita's second work, *Shina kakumei gaishi*, and was equally impressed. In 1919, he and Ōkawa decided Kita would provide a blueprint for the domestic reforms that were necessary before Japan embarked on its mission of liberation. Ōkawa went to Shanghai to deliver Mitsukawa's letter inviting him to return to Japan. Kita accepted the invitation and arrived in Tōkyō at the beginning of January 1920. "Kaidai," pp. 446–47.

26 *Sangoku*, p. 249.

27 Ibid., p. 265.

28 "Kaidai," p. 447.

29 In addition to Ōkawa, Kita, and Nishida, they included Yasuoka Masahiro, Kanokogi Kazunobu, Ayakawa Takeji (1892–1966), Nakatani Takeyo (1898–1990), Shimizu Kōnosuke (1895–1981), Iwata Fumio (1891–1943), and Kasagi Yoshiaki (1892–1954).

30 Kita, by all accounts a charismatic figure, refused to lead. See, for example, Takizawa Makoto, *Kindai Nihon uha shakai shisō kenkyū*, Ronsōsha, 1980, p. 332.

31 "Kaidai," p. 447.

32 Mitsukawa's objections are set forth in "Tōgū goto'Ō no enki o kigan suru nana dai riyū" (Seven major reasons why I pray for the delay of the Crown Prince's tour of Europe). Significantly, these included the possibility of a conspiracy by pro-independence Koreans, and – an expression of pan-Asian sentiment – insistence that the Prince also visit China. He thought the tour too Eurocentric. But that was reason no. 6, almost an afterthought compared to the Korean danger at no. 2. MKP.

33 "Shin aikoku undō no shōshi," *Kaihō*, 5:5, May 1923, p. 87.

34 On Yasuoka, see Roger Brown's article in this volume (the editors).

35 Makino thought it was "rare to see such earnest young men as these two." See Itō Takashi and Hirose Norihiro, ed., *Makino Nobuaki nikki*, Chūō Kōronsha, 1990, p. 146, entry for 10 July 1924. Makino was a grandson of Ōkubo Toshimichi and thus, nominally at least, belonged to the Satsuma faction. He may have been impressed by the Yūzonsha's support for Princess Nagako, granddaughter of Prince Shimazu of Satsuma. Although rumors abounded, there seems to be no hard evidence to support this interpretation.

36 "Start my lectures at the Shakai Kyōiku Kenkyūjo." Mitsukawa Kametarō nisshi, entry for 31 January 1924, MKP. Also *Sangoku*, p. 272.

37 Although the date of the founding of the Kōchisha is not clear, Mitsukawa recorded a meeting of the Kōchikai [sic] in early 1924 and it may not have been the first. See Mitsukawa Kametarō nisshi, p. 28 January 1924. MKP.

38 On this incident, see C. W. A. Szpilman, "Isshinsha no kikanshi *Kōganroku* ni tsuite," *Takushoku Daikaku Hyakunenshi Kenkyū*, 11, December 2002, pp. 190–96.

39 Shimonaka Yasaburō-den Kankōkai, ed., *Shimonaka Yasaburō jiten*, Heibonsha, 1965, p. 1.

40 Ibid., pp. 10, 175–76 (quote, p. 176).

41 Ibid., p. 177.

42 *Sangoku*, 279. On Inoue Nisshō, see Stephen Large, "Nationalist Extremism in Early Shōwa Japan: Inoue Nisshō and the 'Blood-Pledge Corps' Incident, 1932," in *Modern Asian Studies*, 35:3, 2001, pp. 533–64.

43 "According to Tsurumi [Yūsuke], Gotō was impressed with Mitsukawa's article in the February 1924 issue of *Tōyō* entitled 'Taiheiyōjō no Nichi-Ei-Bei.'" Mitsukawa Kametarō nisshi, 27 February 1924. MKP.

44 Ayakawa Takeji, "Mitsukawa-san no sho-inshō," *Ishin*, 3:6, June 1936, p. 77.

45 Matsumoto Ken'ichi, "Dai-Ajia shugi no kyomō: Mitsukawa Kametarō to Shimonaka Yasaburō," in Takeuchi Yoshimi and Hashimoto Bunsō, eds, *Kindai Nihon to Chūgoku*, vol. 2, Asahi Shuppan, 1974, p. 312.

46 *Ubawaretaru Ajia*, pp. 30–31.

47 Ibid., p. 30. Unencumbered by sociological theory, Mitsukawa made no rigorous distinction between culture and civilization and often used the two terms interchangeably.

48 *Sekai gensei to Dai-Nihon*, Yūzonsha, 1926, pp. 64–65.

49 Ibid., p. 65.

50 *Ubawaretaru Ajia*, p. 32; "1930-nen ni okeru sekai no tenbō," *Tōyō*, 33:1, January 1930, MKC, II, p. 60.

51 *Ubawaretaru Ajia*, p. 32.

52 "Sekai no jinshu mondai," *Kinki*, 3:3, March 1934, pp. 93–94.

53 "1930-nen ni okeru sekai no tenbō," *Tōyō*, 33:1, January 1930, MKC, II, pp. 60–61.

54 *Ubawaretaru Ajia*, p. 32.

55 "1930-nen ni okeru sekai no tenbō," p. 62.

56 "Waga kokumin no junkasei to Ajia kaihatsu no shimei," (written January 1919) in *Ubawaretaru Ajia*, p. 38.

57 Mitsukawa, *Man-Mō tokushusei no kaibō*, Kō-A Kaku, 1931, p. 38.

58 Ibid., p. 38.

59 Ibid., pp. 32, 35–37.

60 Ibid., p. 38.

61 Ibid., p. 37.

62 *Tōzai jinshu tōsō shikan*, Tōyō Kyōkai Shuppanbu, 1924, p. 87.

63 "Taiyō no ko jidai kitaran," *Kokuhon*, 2:1, January 1922, p. 31.

64 "1930-nen ni okeru sekai no tenbō," p. 58.

65 Ibid., p. 58.

66 "Indo mondai o chūshin to seru Dai-Ei teikoku," *Tōyō*, 33:7, July 1930, MKC, II, p. 142.

67 "Ejiputo to Indo: Dai-Ei teikoku no unmei ikan," *Tōyō*, 33:2, February 1930, MKC, II, p. 77.
68 "Ajia fukkō undō no kichō," *Kokuhon*, 1:7, July 1921, 51. For references to Spengler and Demangeon see, for example, "Sekai no shinten to Nihon no shōrai," *Kōryō Gakuen*, January 1930, MKC, II, p. 49. For references to Richard, see *Sangoku*, p. 251.
69 *Ubawaretaru Ajia*, p. 45.
70 "1930-nen ni okeru sekai no tenbō," p. 60.
71 "20-seiki shotō ni okeru rekkoku sekai seisaku gaikan," *Takushoku Daigaku Ronshū*, 1:2, March 1931, p. 208.
72 "Hitō dokuritsu to Taiheiyō mondai," *Tōyō*, 35:5, May 1932, p. 270.
73 "1930-nen ni okeru sekai no tenbō," p. 60.
74 "20-seiki shotō ni okeru rekkoku sekai seisaku gaikan," p. 207.
75 "1930-nen ni okeru sekai no tenbō," p. 53.
76 "20-seiki shotō ni okeru rekkoku sekai seisaku gaikan," p. 208.
77 He held such views already in 1920. See, for example, "Kakumeiteki dai teikoku," p. 483.
78 "Eibei kankei no suii to sekai no shōrai," *Tōyō*, 32:11, November 1929, in MKC, II, p. 15.
79 "1930-nen ni okeru sekai no tenbō," p. 59.
80 Ibid., p. 60.
81 *Sekai gensei to Dai-Nihon*, Yūzonsha, 1926, p. 65.
82 Ibid.
83 *Ubawaretaru Ajia*, p. 355.
84 *Sekai gensei to Dai-Nihon*, pp. 156–57.
85 Mitsukawa criticized Japanese colonial policy in Korea and China and its application in his "Naisen akushu no konpon mondai," *Tōyō*, 27:8, August 1924, pp. 101–17.
86 Ibid., p. 106.
87 "Naisen akushu no konpon mondai," p. 104.
88 Ibid., p. 112.
89 Ibid.
90 Mitsukawa, *Gekihen kachū no sekai to Nihon*, Senshinsha, 1932, p. 188.
91 Ibid., p. 188.
92 Ibid., p. 194.
93 Ibid., p. 223.
94 Ibid., p. 220.
95 Ibid., pp. 194–95.
96 Ibid., p. 224.
97 "Watakushi wa Man-Mō shin-kokka ni kaku taibō su," 35:4, April 1932, MKC, II, p. 262. The concept of the "kingly way" is discussed in Roger Brown's article in this volume (the editors).
98 Mitsukawa, *Man-Mō tokushusei no kaibō*, Kō-A Kaku, 1931, pp. 1–6.
99 Ibid., pp. 24–25.
100 Ibid., p. 21.
101 Ibid., p. 23. But this advocacy of continental expansion was not new. As early as 1919 Mitsukawa had written that Japan was facing the stark choice, "expand or perish." See note 54 above.
102 *Man-Mō*, p. 23. Mitsukawa also took up this theme in *Gekihen kachū*, p. 248.
103 *Man-Mō*, p. 23.
104 "Taiyō no ko jidai kitaran," *Kokuhon*, 2:1, January 1922, p. 31.
105 "Sekai no shinten to Nihon no shōrai," *Kōryō gakuen*, January 1930, MKC, II, p. 51.
106 *Gekihen kachū*, p. 241. Mitsukawa insisted throughout the 1920s and 1930s that Japan (or the Pacific) had become the center of the world. See also his *Sekai no kōka*,

(1935, p. 11). A. Morgan Young probably had Mitsukawa in mind when he wrote: "the not very sapient remark of some picturesque journalist that the world's center of gravity had shifted from the Atlantic Ocean to the Pacific assisted in the process of attracting attention to the possibility of war between America and Japan." *Japan under Taisho Tenno*, Westport, CT: Greenwood, 1973, originally published in 1929, p. 198.

107 Mitsukawa, *Sekai no kōka*, Mitsukawa sensei nanashūnen tsuioku kinenkai, 1942; a lecture originally delivered to the Kannagara Kenshūkai [Society to Clarify the Divine Way] and first published in October 1935, pp. 7–14.

108 See, for example, James B. Crowley, *Japan's Quest for Autonomy*, Princeton, NJ: Princeton University Press, 1966, pp. 375–78.

109 Letter, Fukunaga Ken (1899–1991) to Mitsukawa, 10 November 1922. MKP.

7 Forgotten leaders of the interwar debate on regional integration: introducing Sugimori Kōjirō

1 Robert E. Ward and Dankwart A. Rustow, eds, *Political Modernization in Japan and Turkey*, Princeton, NJ: Princeton University Press, 1964.

2 Hamashita Takeshi and Kawakatsu Heita, eds, *Ajia kōekiken to Nihon no kōgyōka*, Riburopōto, 1991; Hamashita Takeshi, *Chōkō shisutemu to kindai Ajia*, Iwanami Shoten, 1997; Arano Yasunori, ed., *Ajia no naka no Nihonshi*, 6 vols., Tōkyō Daigaku Shuppankai, 1992–93.

3 Marukawa Tetsushi, *Shikō no furontia – Rījonarizumu*, Iwanami Shoten, 2003.

4 Two prominent examples are Kang Sang-jung, *Tōhoku Ajia kyōdō no ie o mezashite*, Heibonsha, 2001 and Wada Haruki, *Tōhoku Ajia kyōdō no ie: shin-chiikishugi sengen*, Heibonsha, 2003. The latter nevertheless envisions a "Greater East Asian Community" as the ultimate stage of regional cooperation in Asia, judging by his recent "From a 'Common House of Northeast Asia' to a 'Greater East Asian Community'," in *Social Science Japan* 28, 2004, pp. 19–21.

5 The article, whose less well-known original title is "Ajiashugi no tenbō," was published as an introductory essay to Takeuchi's compilation of prewar Asianist sources: *Ajiashugi* (Gendai Nihon shisō taikei, vol. 9), Chikuma Shobō, 1963.

6 Furuya Tetsuo, ed., *Kindai Nihon no Ajia ninshiki*, Kyōto Daigaku Jinbun Kagaku Kenkyūjo, 1994; Nihon Seiji Gakkai, ed., *Nenpō Seijigaku 1998 – Nihon gaikō ni okeru Ajiashugi*, Iwanami Shoten, 1999; Mitani Taichirō, "Nihon ni okeru [chiikishugi] no gainen," in Mitani Taichirō, *Kindai Nihon no sensō to seiji*, Iwanami Shoten, 1997, pp. 85–109; Inoue Toshikazu, "Kokusai kyōchō, chiikishugi, shinchitsujo," in Banno Junji *et al.*, eds, *Shirīzu Nihon kingendaishi – Kōzō to hendō 3: Gendai shakai e no tenkai*, Iwanami Shoten, 1993, pp. 269–303.

7 See my "Yoshino Sakuzō – The Isolated Figurehead of the Taishō Generation," in Dick Stegewerns, ed., *Nationalism and Internationalism in Imperial Japan*, London: Routledge-Curzon, 2003, pp. 114–32, and "The Japanese 'Civilization Critics' and the National Identity of their Asian Neighbours, 1918–32," in Li Narangoa and Robert Cribb, eds, *Imperial Japan and National Identities in Asia, 1895–1945*, London: RoutledgeCurzon, 2003, pp. 107–28.

8 The term "*bunmei hihyōka*" was introduced into the Japanese language around 1900 by the literary critic Takayama Chogyū as a translation of the German term *Kulturkritiker*. For an overview of the most representative "Kulturkritiker" of the Taishō period, see Iida Taizō, "Taishō-ki bunmei hihyōka chosaku ichiran," in *Hōgaku Shirin*, 80:3/4, 1983, pp. 179–211.

9 For Sugimori, see chapter 4 of my *Adjusting to the New World: Japanese Opinion Leaders of the Taishō Generation and the Outside World, 1918–1932*, forthcoming. For an analysis of the differences between internationalism and cosmopolitanism in the discourse on international relations in the post-First World War era, see my "The

Dilemma of Nationalism and Internationalism in Modern Japan: National Interest, Asian Brotherhood, International Cooperation or World Citizenship?," in Dick Stegewerns, ed., *Nationalism and Internationalism in Imperial Japan*, London: RoutledgeCurzon, 2003, pp. 9–13.

10 Waseda Daigaku Daigakushi Hensanjo, *Waseda Daigaku kōshi 1902–1920* (unpublished); Waseda Daigaku Daigakushi Hensanjo, *Waseda Daigaku hyakunenshi*, vol. 2, Waseda Daigaku Shuppanbu, 1981, pp. 19–20.

11 The full scope of Sugimori's output has only recently become clear through the good offices of Matsuda Yoshio who has been so kind as to make available a 71-page list of Sugimori's writings on his website: http://www1.cts.ne.jp/~ymatsuda (accessed on 5 October 2006).

12 Tsuchida Kyōson, "Junshin shisōka Sugimori-kun" and Shirayanagi Shūko, "Gakusei jidai no Sugimori-kun," in *Kaizō*, 1924.11, pp. 100–1, 107. Ii Gentarō, "Sugimori Kōjirō no Nihon bunka no kindaika e no kōken," in *Waseda Seiji Keizaigaku Zasshi* 177, 1963, p. 163.

13 Leslie Russell Oates, *Populist Nationalism in Prewar Japan: A Biography of Nakano Seigō*, George Allen & Unwin, 1985, p. 54.

14 Waseda Daigaku Daigakushi Hensanjo, *Waseda Daigaku hyakunenshi*, vols. 2–4, Waseda Daigaku Shuppanbu, 1981, 1987, 1992.

15 "Shinkokuminshugi," in *Tōhō Jiron*, 1919.10; "Kokuminshugi to sekaishugi," in *Taikan*, 1919.6, both reprinted in Sugimori Kōjirō, *Jinrui no saisei*, Tōhō Jironsha, 1919, pp. 63, 71, 86. Where I do not specify the author of an article in the following, the author is Sugimori Kōjirō.

16 Because in most of Sugimori's early articles he intermingles *kokuminshugi* with *minzokushugi*, and sometimes with *kokkashugi* and *aikokushugi*, I do not usually distinguish between these various terms and simply use "nationalism."

17 Sugimori Kōjirō, *The Principles of the Moral Empire*, London: University of London Press, 1917, p. 201; "Shinkokuminshugi," p. 63.

18 "Seiji no shinjōshiki," in *Tōhō Jiron*, 1920.4, p. 45; "Kokka tetsugaku no kōshin," in *Chūō Kōron*, 1920.1, pp. 162–64.

19 "Waga kuni no ichi," in *Tōhō Jiron*, 1921.9, pp. 27–28; "Shina no kokusai kanri-ron," in *Kaizō*, 1921.10, pp. 254–55; "Nihonjin no seizonken," in *Chūō Kōron*, 1921.9, p. 93.

20 "Nishi, Roshia, higashi, Beikoku to no kokkō zengosaku – Daini hōkensei kara no shinkateki yakudatsu," in *Chūō Kōron*, 1924.6, pp. 61–62; "Nihon no hozon ga hitsuyō to suru gensokuteki hōhō," in *Kaizō*, 1924.6, pp. 18–20.

21 "Waga kuni no ichi," pp. 27–28; "Shina no kokusai kanri-ron," pp. 254–55.

22 "Peruri sairai ka," in *Tōhō Jiron*, 1921.8, p. 1.

23 "Kōwakaigi to jinkakushugi nōryokushugi ni yoru sekai no kaizō," in *Kaizō*, 1919.6, pp. 22–23.

24 "Kokunaiteki oyobi kokusaiteki jichiku kaisei no junbi," in *Tōhō Jiron*, 1921.9, p. 1; "Amerika tai sekai mondai-kan," in *Chūō Kōron*, 1921.6, p. 83. Some of these "rational considerations" Sugimori borrowed from the writings of Nicholas Murray Butler – most likely *The International Mind*, dating from 1913.

25 "Nihonjin no seizonken," p. 94. Whether Russia belonged to Europe or not was not always clear from Sugimori's somewhat inconsistent writings; one also wonders what was to happen to such ignored entities as the Middle East, India, and Australia as a result of his classification.

26 "Bei shinkō! Ō saikō!! Sore kara?," in *Tōhō Jiron*, 1922.3, p. 1; "Kokuminshugi no Shina, Indo oyobi Amerika," p. 19; "Pan Amerikan Unyan o kotohogu," in *Tōhō Jiron*, 1923.4, p. 1.

27 "Uragaerubeki Nihon," in *Tōhō Jiron*, 1922.8, p. 1; "Nichi-Ro kankei no tōrai," in *Taiyō*, 1923.4, p. 64.

28 "Nihonjin no seizonken," p. 94.

29 "Waga kuni no ichi," p. 28; "Shukyakukan no Nihon to kokusai gensei," in *Tōhō Jiron*, 1922.3, pp. 16–17.

30 "Kokuryoku to kokui," in *Tōhō Jiron*, 1922.2, p. 14; "Bei shinkō! Ō saikō!! Sore kara?," p. 1; "Shukyakukan no Nihon to kokusai gensei," pp. 16–17; "Pan Amerikan Yunyan o kotohogu," p. 1.

31 "Nihonjin no seizonken," p. 92.

32 Ibid., pp. 91, 95.

33 "Kokunaiteki oyobi kokusaiteki jichiku kansei no junbi," p. 1; "Kafu kaigi shuppatsu no kōka," in *Tōhō Jiron*, 1921.10, pp. 20–21.

34 "Kafu kaigi shuppatsu no kōka," pp. 19–20; "Hakujin igai no jinrui no jijo o nozomu," in *Chūō Kōron*, 1922.5, pp. 19–20.

35 Sugimori, *The Principles of the Moral Empire*, p. 56; "Hakujin igai no jinrui no jijo o nozomu," pp. 10–11, 15, "Nihonjin no seizonken," p. 93.

36 "Waga kuni no ichi," p. 26; "Haku, ō, kokujin no honshitsuteki shakai gassaku," in *Kaizō*, 1921.11, pp. 20–21; "Bei shinkō! Ō saikō!! Sore kara?," p. 1; "Shukyakukan no Nihon to kokusai gensei," p. 15.

37 "Nihonjin no seizonken," pp. 92–93; "Haku, ō, kokujin no honshitsuteki shakai gassaku," pp. 20–21.

38 "Haku, ō, kokujin no honshitsuteki shakai gassaku," p. 26.

39 "Nihonjin no seizonken," p. 93; "Kafu kaigi shuppatsu no kōka," p. 20.

40 "Haku, ō, kokujin no honshitsuteki shakai gassaku," p. 21.

41 "Ajia jichi no sekaiteki hitsuyō," in *Tōyō*, 1922.3, p. 1; "Haku, ō, kokujin no honshitsuteki shakai gassaku," p. 22.

42 "Haku, ō, kokujin no honshitsuteki shakai gassaku," p. 22.

43 For a detailed explanation of the content of "utilizationism" and the effects of its implementation, see "Shoyūshugi kara shiyōshugi e no henka no fuhenteki kakuritsu," in Sugimori Kōjirō, *Shakaigaku*, Waseda Daigaku Shuppanbu, 1927, pp. 239–51 and "Shoyūshugi kara shiyōshugi e," in *Taiyō*, 1927.5, pp. 2–9.

44 "Shoyūshugi kara shiyōshugi e," p. 2.

45 See the two above-mentioned articles by Sugimori, respectively p. 241 and p. 2, and his "Ryōdo no rinrisei to Manshū mondai: Kokusai Renmei no kisoteki seigen," in *Teiyū Rinri*, 1931.12, reprinted in Ukita Kazutami, ed., *Manshūkoku dokuritsu to Kokusai Renmei*, Waseda Daigaku Shuppanbu, 1932, pp. 124–25, 132–34.

46 For an analysis of the similarities and differences between what I term the Taishō and Early Shōwa generations of opinion-leaders, see my "The End of World War One as a Turning Point in Modern Japanese History," in Bert Edström, ed., *Turning Points in Japanese History*, London: Japan Library, 2002, pp. 138–62.

47 "Nihon wa ika ni subeki ka," in *Kaizō*, 1932.4, pp. 30–32, 36.

48 Sugimori, *The Principles of the Moral Empire*, pp. 133–35; "Shingenshō to shinjin-butsu," in *Tōhō Jiron*, 1920.1, pp. 75–78; "Saikin sekai no kakumeiteki keikō," in *Tōhō Jiron*, 1920.3, pp. 60–61; "Kyōhei ijō no kokusaku," in *Tōhō Jiron*, 1921.3, p. 1; "Minzoku jiketsu no shingensoku hihyō," in *Tōhō Jiron*, 1921.4, p. 15.

49 "Shina bunkatsu no mondai," in *Kaizō*, 1932.11, pp. 75–76. The concept of a *civitas maxima*, "a great (European) republic," was introduced by the German scholar of international law Christian Wolff in the mid-eighteenth century.

50 See Yamamuro Shinichi, "Ajia ninshiki no kijiku," in Furuya Tetsuo, ed., *Kindai Nihon no Ajia ninshiki*, Kyōto Daigaku Jinbun Kagaku Kenkyūjo, 1994, pp. 3–45. In his recent *magnum opus*, Yamamuro has added the two elements of culture (*bunka*) and the ethnic nation (*minzoku*) to complete the quartet of his "pillars of thought" (*shisō kijiku*). Yamamuro Shinichi, *Shisō kadai toshite no Ajia: kijiku, rensa, tōki*, Iwanami Shoten, 2001, pp. 31–142.

51 Sharon H. Nolte, *Liberalism in Modern Japan*, Berkeley, CA: University of California Press, 1987, pp. 144, 146.

52 Rōyama Masamichi, "Sekai no saininshiki to chihōteki (rījonaru) kokusai renmei," in

Kokusai Chishiki, 1933.1, pp. 22–30. The term *"chihōshugi"* used in this article was changed to *"chiikishugi"* when it was included in Rōyama's *Sekai no henkyoku to Nihon no sekai seisaku*, Ganshōdō, 1938, pp. 91–103. On Rōyama, see J. Victor Koschmann's contribution in this volume (the editors).

53 Kobayashi Hiroharu, Sakai Tetsuya, Fujioka Kentarō, and Yamaguchi Hiroshi have all recently produced significant articles on Rōyama's ideas on foreign policy, a topic neglected before the mid-1990s. A revised English version of the article by Kobayashi is included in Dick Stegewerns, ed., *Nationalism and Internationalism in Imperial Japan*, London: RoutledgeCurzon, 2003, pp. 135–67.

54 For the term "developmental dictatorship" (*kaihatsu dokusai*), see Sakai Tetsuya, "[Tō-A kyōdōtai-ron] kara [kindaika-ron] e: Rōyama Masamichi ni okeru chiiki, kaihatsu, nashonarizumu-ron no isō," in Nihon Seiji Gakkai, ed., *Nenpō seijigaku 1998 – Nihon gaikō ni okeru Ajiashugi*, Iwanami Shoten, 1999, pp. 109–28, 119–20.

55 I discuss Takahashi's and Horie's versions of Sino-Japanese economic integration in "The End of World War One as a Turning Point in Modern Japanese History," pp. 154–55, and "How to Integrate a Region of 'Inferior Civilization': Japanese Concepts of Asian Regionalism in the Interwar Period," forthcoming.

56 Akazawa Shirō, "Dai-Nihon Genron Hōkokukai: hyōronkai to shisōsan," in Akazawa Shirō and Kitagawa Kenzō, eds, *Bunka to fashizumu – Senjiki Nihon ni okeru bunka no kōbō*, Nihon Keizai Hyōronsha, 1993, p. 164. For an overview of Sugimori's prolific output during the years 1937–45, see Fukushima Jūrō and Ōkubo Hisao, eds, *Senjika no genron*, Nichi-gai Asoshiētsu, 1995, pp. 414–15.

57 Family Mart, "Ajia wa kazoku da. Famirī da" campaign, February 2004. The campaign features the colour red and utilizes Japanese, Korean, Taiwanese, and Chinese female models, thus coincidentally replicating Japan's prewar (formal and informal) empire.

8 Were women pan-Asianists the worst? Internationalism and Pan-Asianism in the careers of Inoue Hideko and Inoue Masaji

1 I would like to thank Nakahara Michiko, John Dower, Sally Hastings, Andrea Germer, Hans Martin Krämer, Robin Leblanc, and two anonymous reviewers for their generous assistance at various stages of this project.

2 Inoue Hideko, *Fujin no me ni eijitaru shinchōryū* [New Currents as seen through the Eyes of Women], Jitsugyō no Nihon-sha, 1922, pp. 2–5. Inoue Masaji, *Kaizō tojō no sekai* [A World under Reconstruction], Min'yūsha, 1923, pp. 2–10. Inoue Hideko, "Sekai wa ugoku – 2," in *Katei Shūhō*, no. 1374 (1937.12.10), p. 5. Inoue Masaji, *Dainippon no susumu michi* [Japan's Path Forward], Jitsugyō no Nihon-sha, 1938, pp. 3–4.

3 Works on gender and international politics have understandably focused on war as the most prominent gendering device, as in pioneering works such as Jean Bethke Elshtain, *Women and War*, New York: Basic Books, 1987; and Margaret R. Higonnet *et al.*, eds, *Behind the Lines: Gender and the Two World Wars*, New Haven, CT: Yale University Press, 1998 looks more broadly at cultural and economic dimensions of gender. These have been followed by works examining specific aspects of war such as the gendered rhetoric of jingoism (Kristin Hoganson, *Fighting for American Manhood: How Gender Politics Provoked the Spanish–American and Philippine–American Wars*, New Haven, CT: Yale University Press, 1998) and homefront experiences of women as a neglected aspect of war (Belinda J. Davis, *Home Fires Burning: Food, Politics, and Everyday Life in World War I Berlin*, Chapel Hill, NC: University of North Carolina Press, 2000). General theoretical analysis of the gendered assumptions of international relations theory can be found in Rebecca Grant and Kathleen Newland, eds, *Gender and International Relations*, Bloomington, IN: Indiana University Press, 1991 and V. Spike Peterson, ed., *Gendered States: Feminist (Re)Visions of International Relations Theory*, Boulder, CO: Lynne Rienner, 1992. A broad-ranging approach is Cynthia Enloe,

Bananas, Beaches and Bases: Making Feminist Sense of International Politics, Berkeley, CA: University of California Press, 1989.

4 Neither Hideko nor Masaji is the subject of a recent biography. For details of their lives, see Inoue Hide-sensei Kinen Shuppan Iinkai, ed., *Inoue Hide sensei*, Ōfūkai Shuppan Henshūbu, 1973; Nagami Shichirō, *Kōa ichiro – Inoue Masaji*, Tōkō Shoin, 1942; Inoue Masaji, *Kensōroku*, Inoue Masaji, 1944.

5 Akira Iriye, *Power and Culture: The Japanese-American War, 1941–1945*, Cambridge, MA: Harvard University Press, 1984.

6 Klaus Theweleit, *Male Fantasies*, Minneapolis, MN: University of Minnesota Press, 1987–89 (2 vols); Barbara Spackman, *Fascist Virilities: Rhetoric, Ideology, and Social Fantasy in Italy*, Minneapolis, MN: University of Minnesota Press, 1996, chapters 1–2.

7 On the basic outline of this debate, see Adelheid von Saldern, "Victims or Perpetrators? Controversies about the Role of Women in the Nazi State," in *The Third Reich: The Essential Readings*, Christian Lentz, ed., Malden, MA: Blackwell, 1999; Atina Grossman, "Feminist Debates about Women and National Socialism," *Gender and History*, vol. 3, no. 3 (autumn 1991), pp. 350–58. This debate has generally not concentrated on foreign policy discourse but rather eugenic and racial policies. See also Renate Bridenthal, Atina Grossmann, and Marion Kaplan, eds, *When Biology Became Destiny: Women in Weimar and Nazi Germany*, New York: Monthly Review Press, 1984. "Forum: *When Biology Became Destiny: Women in Weimar and Nazi Germany* Twentieth Anniversary Retrospective," *German History*, vol. 22, no. 4 (2004), pp. 600–12.

8 Ueno Chizuko, *Nashonarizumu to jendaa* [Nationalism and Gender], Seidosha, 1998, pp. 38–39.

9 Prominent works include: Suzuki Yūko, *Shinban – Feminizumu to sensō – Fujin undōka no sensō kyōryoku* [New Edition: Feminism and War – The Women's Movement's Wartime Collaboration], Marujusha, 1997; Ueno Chizuko, *Nashonarizumu to jendaa*, pp. 31–51, 67–82; Narita Ryūichi, "Haha no kuni no onnatachi – Oku Mumeo no 'senji' to 'sengo'" [Women in a Nation of Mothers – Oku Mumeo's Pre- and Postwar], in Yamanouchi Yasushi *et al.*, eds, *Sōryokusen to gendaika*, Kashiwa Shobō, 1995; Kanō Mikiyo, *Onnatachi no 'Jūgo'* [The Female "Homefront"], Chikuma Shobō, 1987.

10 In addition to the Japanese works cited here, see the following works in English on the pragmatic concessions of Japanese feminists to wartime mobilization: Vera Mackie, *Feminism in Modern Japan: Citizenship, Embodiment, Sexuality*, New York: Cambridge University Press, 2003, ch. 5; Beth Sara Katzoff, "For the Sake of the Nation, For the Sake of Women: The Pragmatism of Japanese Feminisms in the Asia-Pacific War (1931–45)," PhD Thesis: Columbia University, 2000.

11 Fujino Yutaka, *Nihon fashizumu to yūseigaku* [Japanese Fascism and Eugenics], Kyōto: Kamogawa Shuppan, 1998.

12 Tsune Gauntlett, *Shichijūshichinen no omoide* [Recollections of Seventy-Seven Years], Uemura Shoten, 1949.

13 Oguma Eiji, *Tan'itsu minzoku shinwa no kigen – 'Nihonjin' jigazō no keifu* [Origins of the Myth of the Homogeneous Nation: A Genealogy of "Japanese" Self-images], Shin'yōsha, 1995, ch. 11.

14 "Petition Concerning the President of Japan Women's University" [1947], GHQ/SCAP Records, Box 5695, Folder 319.1 Nippon Joshi Daigaku. Japanese original not found. Special thanks to Hans Martin Krämer in finding these documents.

15 Sigrid Lillian Schultz, *Germany Will Try it Again*, New York, Reynal & Hitchcock, 1944, p. 121ff. For recent scholarship on the position of "women Nazis", see Elizabeth Harvey, "Visions of the Volk: German Women and the Far Right from Kaiserreich to Third Reich," in *Journal of Women's History*, vol. 16, no. 3 (2004), pp. 152–67.

16 Inoue Hideko, "Sekai wa ugoku – 4," in *Katei Shūhō*, no. 1378 (1938.1.21), p. 3. Inoue Hideko, "Sekai wa ugoku – 6," in *Katei Shūhō*, no. 1380 (1938.2.4), p. 3.

17 Nagami Shichirō, "Sodachiyuku hōsū," in *Shokumin*, vol. 10, no. 6 (6.1931), pp. 64–70.

18 Inoue Masaji, *Kankoku keiei shiryō – Eijiputo ni okeru Eikoku* [Korean Administration Documents; England in Egypt], Shimizu Shoten, 1906.

19 Inoue Masaji, *Kōa ichiro*, p. 52.

20 The author here refers to Toyotomi Hideyoshi (1536–98), a warlord who not only completed national unification, but also undertook military expeditions to Korea in the 1590s (the editors).

21 For a discussion of economic expansionism in this period, see Akira Iriye, "The Failure of Economic Expansionism," in Bernard S. Silberman and Harry D. Harootunian, eds, *Japan in Crisis: Essays on Taishō Democracy*, Princeton, NJ: Princeton University Press, 1974.

22 Inoue Masaji, *Kaizō tojō no sekai*, pp. 29–36.

23 Inoue Masaji, "Shokuminchi o sakushu suru zōmai keikaku wa waga kokusaku mujun nari," in *Shokumin* 6, no. 3 (March 1927), pp. 6–9; and "Kokusai-teki seishin undō toshite no kaigai ishokumin no daishimei," in *Shokumin* 6, no. 4 (April 1927), pp. 6–9.

A more widely available selection of Inoue's writings on emigration in this period is Inoue Masaji, *Ijū to kaitaku* [Emigration and Development], Nihon Shokumin Tsūshinsha, 1930.

24 Inoue Masaji, *Sekai o ie toshite* [The World as a Home], Hakubunkan, 1929, p. 4.

25 Inoue Masaji, "Shin Itari no bokō to Nihon no ikubeki michi" [The Rise of a New Italy and the Path Japan Should Follow], in *Gaikō Jihō*, no. 567 (1928.7.15), pp. 113–22.

26 Inoue Masaji, *Sekai o ie toshite*, pp. 36–38.

27 Inoue Hideko, *Saikin kaji teiyō* [Handbook of Contemporary Household Arts], Bunkōsha, 1925.

28 On eugenic thought and the so-called population problem, see Fujino Yutaka, *Nihon fashizumu to yūseigaku*, pp. 115–55.

29 Kobashi Miyoko, "Josei no te o motsu sekai bunka" [World culture in the hands of women], in *Shufu no Tomo*, vol. 6, no. 4 (1922.2.1), pp. 13–15; Kobashi, "Shinbunmei o umu shakai no botai no tame ni" [For the Womb of Society that Gave Birth to the New Civilization], in *Shufu no Tomo*, vol. 6, no. 5 (1922.3.1), pp. 46–49.

30 Inouye Hide, "Reasons for Submitting the Petition for Release from the Purge after the Expiration of the Prescribed Time for Protest" (7 May 1949), p. 8. GHQ/SCAP Records, Box 5695, Folder 319.1, Nippon Joshi Daigaku.

31 Inoue Hideko, in *Fujin no me ni*, pp. 2–33, 462–93.

32 Fujime Yuki, *Sei no rekishigaku: kōshō seido – dataizai taisei kara baishun bōshihō – yūsei hogohō taisei e*, Fuji Shuppan, 1997, pp. 245–377. See discussion of prostitution in Sheldon Garon, *Molding Japanese Minds: The State in Everyday Life*, Princeton, NJ: Princeton University Press, 1997.

33 See, for example, Inoue Masaji, "Manshū jihen o ittenki to suru seishinteki kaigai ijū no teishō" [A Promotion of Spiritual Overseas Emigration, seeing the Manchurian Incident as a Turning Point], in *Shokumin*, vol. 11, no. 1 (January 1932), pp. 46–52.

34 Nagami, *Kōa ichiro: Inoue Masaji*, p. 967.

35 This imagery appeared in almost every book he produced in this period, as in this book introducing young people to Pan-Asianism: Inoue Masaji, *Seishōnen bunkō 10 – Tōa kyōei ken to nanpō* [Youth Library 10 – The East Asian Co-Prosperity Sphere and Southward Advance], Nihon Seinenkan, 1940, p. 10.

36 The legendary first Tennō (Emperor) of Japan, who, according to ancient chronicles, ascended to the Throne in 660 BC (the editors).

37 Inoue Masaji, *Kōa gojūnen no saka o yojite* [Fifty Years Up the Hill of Asian Enlightenment], Inoue Masaji, 1944, pp. 121–22.

38 Inoue Masaji, *Dainippon no susumu michi*, p. 182.

39 Inoue Masaji, *Kōa gojūnen no saka*, pp. 139–40.
40 Sōma Hanji, "Kaikai no ji," pp. 1–2; Takahama Heihyōe, "Nihon ni okeru kashi tsuki Yamato minzoku no shikōmi," pp. 21–37; Inoue Hideko, "Okashi no kanmi," pp. 38–44, in *Kashi Kenkyū*, vol. 8 (1935).
41 Inoue Hideko, "Sekai wa ugoku – 2," in *Katei Shūhō*, no. 1374 (1937.12.10), p. 5.
42 Inoue Hideko, "Kokumin sōdōin jika ni warera o nasubeki koto," in *Katei Shūhō*, no. 1375 (1937.12.10), p. 3.
43 Inoue Hideko, "Kashi to bunka," in *Kashi Kenkyū*, vol. 11 (1938), pp. 304–16.
44 Inoue Hideko, "Kokumin sōdōin," p. 3.
45 Inoue Hideko, "Sokoku to josei: zadankai," in *Kōa Kyōiku*, vol. 1, no. 10 (Oct. 1942), p. 24.
46 Inoue Hideko, "Josei o takameyo, haha o takameyo" [Raise Up Women, Raise Up Mothers], in *Katei Shūhō*, no. 1376 (1938.1.1), p. 2.
47 Inoue Hideko, "Hijōji no katei kyōiku" [Home Education in Times of National Emergency], in *Katei Shūhō*, no. 1416 (1939.1.13), p. 3.
48 Katzoff, "For the Sake of the Nation," p. 227.
49 Inoue Hideko, "Joshi kyōiku no dōkō" [Trends in Women's Education], in *Kōa Kyōiku*, vol. 3, no. 3 (March 1944), p. 18.
50 Untitled report, September 1946, GHQ/SCAP Records, Box 5695, Folder 319.1 Nippon Joshi Daigaku.
51 Inoue Hideko, "Joshi kyōiku no dōkō," p. 19.
52 Inoue Hideko, "Kantōgen," in *Katei shūhō*, Shinnengō (January 1946), pp. 2–3.
53 Inouye Hide, "Reasons for Submitting the Petition for Release from the Purge after the Expiration of the Prescribed Time for Protest" (7 May 1949), p. 5. GHQ/SCAP Records, Box 5695, Folder 319.1 Nippon Joshi Daigaku.
54 Kamiyama Mitsuko to *Mainichi Shimbun* [letter], 27 September 1946. [Translated by Civil Censorship Detachment. Original Japanese not found.] GHQ/SCAP Records, Box 5695, Folder 319.1 Nippon Joshi Daigaku.
55 R.W. Arrowood, "Report of Conference," 17 September 1946. GHQ/SCAP Records, Box 5133, Folder 1, "Reports of Conferences – Civil Information and Education Section" CIE (A) 00679–2. The original says "light" instead of "right," apparently in error.

9 Visions of a virtuous manifest destiny: Yasuoka Masahiro and Japan's Kingly Way

1 Komagome Takeshi, "'Manshūkoku' ni okeru jukyō no isō: daidō, ōdō, kōdō," in *Shisō* 841, July 1994, p. 61. Cat's-paw is an idiomatic translation of "hunting dog" (*ryōken*). Other sources cite Sun as having said, "watchdog" (*banken*). For example, Takeuchi Yoshimi, "Ajiashugi no tenbō," in *Ajiashugi* (Gendai Nihon shisō taikei, vol. 9), Chikuma Shobō, 1963, p. 10.
2 Marius B. Jansen, *The Japanese and Sun Yat-sen*, Princeton, NJ: Princeton University Press, 1955, p. 212.
3 Takeuchi, "Ajiashugi no tenbō," p. 14.
4 For a review of Japanese scholarship on *ōdō*, see Komagome, "'Manshūkoku' ni okeru jukyō no isō," pp. 57–82. For discussions in English, see Joshua A. Fogel, *Politics and Sinology: The Case of Naitō Konan (1866–1934)*, Cambridge, MA: Harvard University Press, 1984, pp. 255–59, and Louise Young, *Japan's Total Empire: Manchuria and the Culture of Wartime Imperialism*, Berkeley, CA: University of California Press, 1998, pp. 200, 268–91. For accounts giving more credence to Kingly Way ideals, see John Hunter Boyle, *China and Japan at War, 1937–1945*, Stanford, CA: Stanford University Press, 1972, pp. 91–95, and Mark Peattie, *Ishiwara Kanji and Japan's Confrontation with the West*, Princeton, NJ: Princeton University Press, 1975, pp. 34, 141–81, who also points out the pre-Shōwa use of the term.

5 Young, *Japan's Total Empire*, p. 275. For another perspective on the ideals associated with Manchukuo – one that unfortunately appeared too late for consideration in preparing this paper – see Prasenjit Duara, *Sovereignty and Authenticity: Manchukuo and the East Asian Modern*, Lanham, MD: Rowman and Littlefield, 2003.

6 Michael H. Hunt, "Ideology," in Michael J. Hogan and Thomas G. Paterson, eds, *Explaining the History of American Foreign Relations*, Cambridge: Cambridge University Press, 1991, p. 194.

7 Ibid., pp. 194–95.

8 For a relevant study premised upon such radical discontinuity, see Stefan Tanaka, *Japan's Orient: Rendering Pasts into History*, Berkeley, CA: University of California Press, 1993. For a different perspective on the relationship between the Japanese and their past, as well as with other Asians, see Fogel, *Politics and Sinology*.

9 For years the most substantial English-language treatment of Yasuoka remained the three pages found in Richard Storry, *The Double Patriots: A Study of Japanese Nationalism*, Boston, MA: Houghton Mifflin, 1957, pp. 46–49. Similarly abbreviated mention has long been common in Japanese-language studies of the right wing. Otherwise, recognition of Yasuoka's historical significance has come primarily from those studying bureaucratic reformers and, to a lesser extent, court conservatives. See Itō Takashi, "Kyokoku itchi naikaku-ki no seikai saihensei mondai," in *Shakai Kagaku Kenkyū* 24:1, 1972, pp. 56–130, Kawashima Makoto, "Kokuikairon: Kokuikai to shinkanryō," in *Nihonshi Kenkyū* 360, August 1992, pp. 1–32, Otabe Yūji, "Tennōsei ideorogii to shin Ei-Bei-ha no keifu: Yasuoka Masahiro o chūshin ni," in *Shien* 43:1, May 1983, pp. 25–38, and Otabe Yūji, "Yasuoka Masahiro shokan: Kokuritsu kokkai toshokan kensei shiryō shozō," in *Shien* 40:2, November 1980, pp. 57–79.

10 "Shinken Manshūkoku no ōdō seiji ni tsuite," in *Shibun* 14:5, May 1932, pp. 1–84.

11 Peattie, *Ishiwara Kanji and Japan's Confrontation with the West*, pp. 33–34.

12 Ibid., p. 34.

13 Frederick R. Dickinson, *War and National Reinvention: Japan in the Great War, 1914–1919*, Cambridge, MA: Harvard University Press, 1999, pp. 162–64.

14 Uzawa Fusaaki, "Ōdō ni tsuite," (Part I) in *Shibun* 1:4, August 1919, pp. 313–37, "Ōdō ni tsuite," (Part II) in *Shibun* 1:5, October 1919, pp. 393–402.

15 Along with the 1925 essay on the Kingly Way discussed below, see Yasuoka Masahiro, *Nihon seikyō no konpon mondai: kokutai genron*, Kinkei Gakuin, 1927.

16 Yasuoka Masahiro, *Shina shisō oyobi jinbutsu kōwa*, Genkōsha, 1921, pp. 1–13.

17 Yasuoka Masahiro, *Fukkō Ajia no shisō-teki konkyo*, Yūzonsha shōsatsu no. 2 (November 1922), pp. 1–3.

18 Yasuoka Masahiro, "Ōdō ni tsuite," in *Tōyō Shisō Kenkyū* 20, January 1924, pp. 2–3.

19 Ibid., p. 3.

20 Yasuoka Masahiro, *Ō Yōmei kenkyū*, Genkōsha, 1922.

21 *Ō Yōmei kenkyū*, p. 153.

22 Ibid., pp. 154–55.

23 "Ōdō ni tsuite," pp. 4–5.

24 Ibid., p. 6.

25 Ibid., p. 7.

26 Ibid., pp. 7–15.

27 Ibid., pp. 15–16.

28 Ibid., pp. 16–18. Yasuoka elaborates on the relationship between ruler and official in "Tenshiron oyobi Kanriron," in *Tōyō Shisō Kenkyū* 8, June 1923, pp. 1–31, and "Kokumu daijinron: fu Kō Yūbo," in *Tōyō Shisō Kenkyū* 13, March 1924, pp. 1–20.

29 "Ōdō ni tsuite," pp. 18–19, emphasis in the original.

30 Ibid., pp. 19–20.

31 Ibid., pp. 20–21.

32 Ibid., pp. 22–23.

33 Ibid., p. 23.

34 Ibid., p. 29. The formula of the Three Mainstays and Five Constant Virtues is found in the *Discourses in the White Tiger Hall* (*Bohu tong*) compiled by the historian Ban Gu (32–92 CE). The Three Mainstays are the mutual bonds connecting ruler to minister, parent to child, and husband to wife. The Five Constant Virtues are humaneness, rightness, ritual decorum, wisdom, and trustworthiness. See *Sources of Chinese Tradition: From Earliest Times to 1600*, Volume One, compiled by Wm. Theodore de Bary and Irene Bloom, second edition, Columbia University Press, 1999, pp. 344–46, 735.

35 See Kawashima, "Kokuikairon" and Ozeki Motoaki, "'Seitō seiji' to kakusei to shinkanryō," in *Kokuritsu Rekishi Minzoku Hakubutsukan Kenkyū Hōkoku* 39, March 1992, pp. 121–41.

36 Yoshida Hiroshi, "Kokuikai no seiritsu to shisō katsudō," in Nakamura Katsunori, ed., *Manshū jihen no shōgeki*, Keisō Shobō, 1996, pp. 159–80.

37 Ibid., pp. 174–75.

38 Ibid., pp. 159–80. Fogel, *Politics and Sinology*, p. 259.

39 Yoshida, "Kokuikai no seiritsu to shisō katsudō," pp. 175–78.

40 Yasuoka Masahiro, "Ikanaru jinbutsu ga tenka o sukū ka," in *Kokui* 2, July 1932, p. 1.

41 Yasuoka Masahiro, *Tōyō seiji tetsugaku: ōdō no kenkyū*, Genkōsha, 1933.

42 Ibid., pp. 3–4.

43 Ibid., p. 4.

44 Ibid., pp. 99–181.

45 Ibid., pp. 183–88.

46 Satomi Kishio, "Ōdō wa hatashite kōdō ni hizaru ka," in Tōa Renmei Kyōkai, ed., *Tōa renmei kensetsu yōkō*, second expanded edition, Tōa Renmei Kyōkai, 1940, pp. 125–47. Unlike Yasuoka, however, Satomi also shared Ishiwara's vision of an apocalyptic war between Japan and the United States. Peattie, *Ishiwara Kanji and Japan's Confrontation with the West*, pp. 47–48, 136, 339–40.

47 Nakayama Hitoshi, "Ōdō shisō no gendai-teki tenkai," in *Tōyō Shisō Kenkyū* 1, October 1939, pp. 14–15. In contrast, the well-known Sinologist Tsuda Sōkichi responded to the burgeoning interest in the Kingly Way by arguing such ideals were the unique product of ancient China and not applicable outside of China or in the modern era. Tsuda Sōkichi, *Ōdō seiji shisō*, Iwanami Shoten, 1934.

48 On Minoda's attacks, see Kamei Toshirō, *Kinkei gakuin no fūkei*, Saitama: Yūshin Bunko, 2003, pp. 182–91. For a defense of the imperial Way as utterly distinct from the Kingly Way, see the three-part essay in Minoda's magazine by Tazakai Masayoshi, "Kōdō to ōdō to wa genbetsu suru o yōsu," in *Genri Nihon*, March, May and October 1929, pp. 15–19, 20–24 and 21–23.

49 "Seiji tetsugaku yori kantaru gendai Nihon," in *Kōen* 234, October 1933, p. 18.

50 Ibid., pp. 18–19. As part of an effort to make Japan's case overseas, some of Yasuoka's ideas on the Kingly Way appeared in English translation through the efforts of the Nippon Bunka Renmei (Japan Cultural League), a new organization headed by Yasuoka associate and "new bureaucrat" Matsumoto Gaku. Yasuoka Masaatsu [sic], "The Principle of Ōdō," in *Cultural Nippon* 2:3, October 1934, pp. 189–202.

51 Yasuoka Masahiro, *Manshū tōchi no ōdō-teki genri*, 1932. Reprint. Kinkei Gakuin, 1941, pp. 1–2.

52 Ibid., p. 2.

53 Ibid., pp. 2–3.

54 Ibid., pp. 13–15.

55 Ibid., pp. 13–16.

56 Yasuoka Masahiro, "Hokuhei no hen," in *Shūkan Taiyō* 9, 26 July 1937, p. 1.

57 Ibid.

58 Yasuoka Masahiro, "Jimu jūsaku," in *Shūkan Taiyō* 10, 2 August 1937, pp. 2–3.

59 Yasuoka Masahiro, "Nihon-bare," in *Shūkan Taiyō* 20, 1 November 1937, p. 1.

60 Yasuoka Masahiro, "Shina jihen no taigi to sochi," in *Kinkei Gakuhō*, tokusatsu,

September 1937, pp. 1–16. Also, see "Shina o sukū mono," in *Chūō Kōron*, Winter 1937, pp. 4–17.

61 Yasuoka Masahiro, "Shina bunka no ichi kōsatsu," in *Kinkei Gakuhō* 6, November 1937, p. 1.

62 "Shina jihen no taigi to sochi," pp. 5–8.

63 Yasuoka Masahiro, "Shin no metsubō," in *Kinkei Gakuhō* 5, October 1937, pp. 1–16.

64 Ibid., pp. 1–3.

65 Ibid., pp. 15–16.

66 Yasuoka Masahiro, *Shina kōbō dangi*, Nihon Gaikō Kyōkai 269 (August 1938). The speech also appears in *Shina tōchi ni kansuru ronshō*, Gaimushō, 1939, pp. 37–65.

67 Yasuoka Masahiro, "Ika ni iku-beki ka," in *Shūkan Taiyō* 27, December 20, 1937, p. 1.

68 Yasuoka Masahiro, "Shina jihen no shisa-suru kongo no kyōyō mondai," in *Kinkei Gakuhō* 12, August 1938, pp. 1–22.

69 Ibid., pp. 1–6.

70 Ibid., p. 22.

71 Yasuoka Masahiro, *Daitōa kyōeiken no shidōsha-taru beki Nihonjin no kyōiku*, Keimeikai, 1943.

72 Ibid., pp. 7–15.

73 Ibid., pp. 40–43.

74 Ibid., p. 44.

75 Liu Jie, *Nitchū sensō-ka no gaikō*, Yoshikawa Kōbunkan, 1995, pp. 315–32.

76 Ibid., p. 318. Also, see Liu Jie, *Kankan saiban: tainichi kyōryokusha o osowatta unmei*, Chūō Kōronsha, 2000, pp. 9–17.

77 "Shina jihen no taigi to sochi," pp. 8–10, "Shina o sukū mono," p. 17, and "Chiang Kai-shek," in *Zoku keisei sagen*, Tōe Shoin, 1942, pp. 130–35.

78 Liu, *Nitchū sensō-ka no gaikō*, pp. 315–32. Boyle, *China and Japan at War, 1937–1945*, pp. 167–77.

79 Liu, *Kankan saiban*, pp. 14–17.

80 Letter from Yasuoka Masahiro to Sekiya Teizaburō (date not fully legible, but probably September 1944). Sekiya Teizaburō Monjo no. 804.19. Kensei shiryō shitsu, National Diet Library.

81 Yasuoka Masahiro, "Sekai no ideorogii-ka to Nihon." in *Tōyō Shisō Kenkyū* 1, October 1939, pp. 1–12. Although clearly an advocate of Japanese leadership in Asia and not without sympathy for some of the philosophical ideals championed by the regimes governing Germany and Italy, Yasuoka counseled neutrality in Europe and believed Japan could achieve its objectives in Asia without going to war with the British and Americans.

82 Ibid., pp. 1–6.

83 Ibid., p. 6.

84 Ibid., pp. 9–12.

85 Ibid., pp. 13–14.

86 Yasuoka Masahiro, "Seisen to seisei." *Keisei Sagen*, 1940. Revised Edition. Tōe Shoin, 1942, pp. 244–49.

87 Fogel, *Politics and Sinology*, p. 258.

10 The temporality of empire: the imperial cosmopolitanism of Miki Kiyoshi and Tanabe Hajime

1 Robert J. C. Young, *Postcolonialism: An Historical Introduction*, London: Blackwell, 2001, p. 27.

2 Yasushi Yamanouchi, "Total-War and System Integration: A Methodological Introduction," in Yasushi Yamanouchi, J. Victor Koschmann, and Narita Ryūichi, eds, *Total War and "Modernization"* (Cornell East Asia Series, vol. 100), Ithaca, NY: Cornell University Press, 1998, p. 3.

3 Miki died in prison one month after the end of the War in 1945. David A. Dilworth, V. H. Viglielmo, and Agustin Jacinto Zavala, eds, *Sourcebook for Modern Japanese Philosophy: Selected Documents, Resources in Asian Philosophy and Religion*, Westport, CT: Greenwood Press, 1998, pp. 289–92; Michiko Yusa, "Philosophy and Inflation: Miki Kiyoshi in Weimar Germany, 1922–24," *Monumenta Nipponica* 53:1.

4 Immanuel Kant, *Zum Ewigen Frieden: Ein philosophischer Entwurf*, in Königlich Preußische Akademie der Wissenschaften, ed., *Gesammelte Schriften* (quoted as AK), vol. VIII, Berlin: Georg Reimer, 1912.

5 Seyla Benhabib, "Political Geographies in a Global World: Arendtian Reflections," *Social Research* 69:2, 2002.

6 AK8, p. 357 (Kant's emphasis).

7 AK 8, p. 358.

8 AK 8, p. 359. However, at Kant's time, there was no one way to refer either to "China" or "Japan" in the areas today known as China and Japan.

9 AK 8, p. 358.

10 AK 8, p. 343.

11 AK 8, pp. 343–57.

12 AK 8, p. 386.

13 Miki Kiyoshi, *Miki Kiyoshi Zenshū [The Complete Works of Miki Kiyoshi]* (quoted as MKZ), Tōkyō: Iwanami Shoten, 1966–68, vol. 17, p. 508. I thank Lewis Harrington for allowing me to consult his translation of "Principles of Thought for a New Japan." My understanding of the nuances of Miki's argument was greatly enhanced by Harrington's elaborate and philosophically meticulous annotations.

14 MKZ 17, p. 516.

15 MKZ 17, p. 513. Here, Miki clearly follows the neo-Romantic interpretation of Ferdinand Tönnies' 1887 work *Gemeinschaft und Gesellschaft: Grundbegriffe der reinen Soziologie*, Darmstadt: Wissenschaftliche Buchgesellschaft, 1979. This interpretation, widespread in Europe during Miki's time, criticized modern society (*Gesellschaft*) and advocated a return to pre-modern community (*Gemeinschaft*). However, Tönnies himself does not argue for a "return" in his work. Instead, he views the *Gemeinschaft/Gesellschaft* distinction as analytic markers for understanding various modes of collective social being in a world in which the putatively modern and the premodern exist in simultaneity.

16 MKZ 7, p. 476.

17 J. Victor Koschmann, *Revolution and Subjectivity in Postwar Japan*, Chicago, IL: University of Chicago Press, 1996, p. 2.

18 Ibid.

19 Hereafter, all instance of the English word "subject" throughout this essay will specifically mean *shutai* in the sense described above. The epistemological subject, or *shukan*, was principally used as a point of (negative) contrast to embodied practical subject, or *shutai*, within philosophical discourse at the time of Miki's writing.

20 MKZ 18, p. 147.

21 Harry D. Harootunian, *Overcome by Modernity: History, Culture, and Community in Interwar Japan*, Princeton, NJ: Princeton University Press, 2000, pp. 364–66.

22 Minoru Iwasaki, "Desire for a Poietic Metasubject: Miki Kiyoshi's Technology Theory," in Yasushi Yamanouchi, J. Victor Koschmann, and Narita Ryūichi, eds, *Total War and "Modernization"* (Cornell East Asia Series, vol. 100), Ithaca, NY: Cornell University Press, 1998, p. 176.

23 MKZ 17, p. 538.

24 MKZ 17, pp. 516–17.

25 MKZ 17, p. 561.

26 MKZ 17, p. 508.

27 MKZ 17, p. 515.

28 MKZ 17, pp. 512–13.

29 MKZ 17, pp. 508–9.
30 MKZ 17, p. 147.
31 MKZ 17, pp. 530–31.
32 MKZ 17, p. 531.
33 MKZ 17, pp. 579–80.
34 MKZ 17, p. 535.
35 MKZ 17, p. 510.
36 Dilworth, Viglielmo, and Jacinto Zavala, eds, *Sourcebook*, pp. 97–98.
37 Hajime Tanabe, *Tanabe Hajime Zenshū* [*The Complete Works of Tanabe Hajime*] (quoted as THZ), Tōkyō: Chikuma Shobō, 1963.
38 THZ 6, pp. 481–82.
39 THZ 6, p. 474.
40 THZ 6, p. 484.
41 THZ 6, p. 483.
42 THZ 6, p. 484.
43 THZ 6, p. 474.
44 "Being-at-home-with-oneself [Beisichsein]" and "being-outside-of-oneself [Außersichsein]" are technical terms that Tanabe adopts from Hegel and translates into Japanese. Tanabe uses the German word "Beisichsein" as an apposition to his translation "jikashijū." He however does not use the word "Außersichsein" as a gloss for "jikarijū." The latter is my addition.
45 THZ 6, p. 484.
46 THZ 6, p. 486.
47 THZ 6, p. 361.
48 Naoki Sakai, "Ethnicity and Species: On the Philosophy of the Multi-Ethnic State in Japanese Imperialism," in *Radical Philosophy* 95, 1999, p. 39.
49 THZ 7, p. 41.
50 "The National Security Strategy of the United States of America," Washington, DC: The White House, 2002, p. iv.

11 The concept of ethnic nationality and its role in Pan-Asianism in imperial Japan

1 In fact, the *Gemeinschaft* concept of an East Asia Community (*Tōa kyōdōtai*) coexisted with another concept of East Asia as a League (*Tōa renmei*), which in theory members were free to join or leave at any time. For my purposes here, the key point is that both regional concepts relied on the notion of *minzoku* as their core elements of local identity within the region. See Peter Duus' introduction "Sōzō no teikoku: higashi Ajia ni okeru Nihon" (Empire of Imagination: Japan in East Asia) (pp. 13–40) and Kobayashi Hideo's chapter "Tōa renmei undō" (The East Asian League Movement) (pp. 203–50), both in Peter Duus and Kobayashi Hideo, eds, *Teikoku to iu gensō: 'dai tōa kyōeiken' no shisō to genjitsu* (The Illusion of Empire: Ideology and Practice in the Greater East Asia Co-Prosperity Sphere), Aoki Shoten, 1998.
2 On the contrast between Nazi ideology and Japanese regionalism, see Miwa Kimitada, ed., *Nihon no 1930 nendai: kuni no uchi to soto kara* (Japan in the 1930s: Domestic and Foreign Perspectives), Sairyūsha, 1981.
3 Kamei Kan'ichirō was one of the first to note that "the word *minzoku* first appeared in print in actual world politics after the Versailles Treaty." Kamei Kan'ichirō, *Dai tōa minzoku no michi* (The Way to a Greater East Asian Nationality), Seiki Shobō, 1941, p. 301. Habu Nagaho and Kawai Tsuneo suggest that the problem of *minzoku* is best understood in the context of the rise of ethnic nationalism that accompanied the First World War. See Habu Nagaho and Kawai Tsuneo, "Minzokushugi shisō" (Ethnic Nationalist Thought), in Tamura Hideo and Tanaka Hiroshi, eds, *Shakai shisō jiten* (A Dictionary of Social Thought), Chūō Daigaku Shuppanbu, 1982, pp. 326–46.

4 On the methods and means by which *minzoku* consciousness provided a new conceptual foundation for populist, Japanese discourse on East Asia during the interwar period, see my "Narrating China, Ordering East Asia: The Discourse on Nation and Ethnicity in Imperial Japan," in Kai-wing Chow, Kevin M. Doak, and Poshek Fu, eds, *Constructing Nationhood in Modern East Asia*, Ann Arbor, MI: University of Michigan Press, 2001, pp. 85–113.

5 Yamauchi Masayuki, "Nihon ni oite wa *minzoku* to wa" (What Does Japan Consider a Nation?), in Yamauchi Masayuki, *Bummei no shōtotsu kara taiwa e* (From a Clash of Civilizations to Dialogue), Iwanami Shoten, 2000 (Iwanami gendai bunko, vol. 1100), pp. 217–41, 223.

6 On Mitsukawa Kametarō and the Yūzonsha, see the contribution of Christopher W. A. Szpilman in this volume (the editors).

7 Ōkawa Shūmei, *Fukkō Ajia no sho-mondai* (Various Problems in the Asian Renaissance), Chūō Kōronsha, 1993 (original published in 1922), p. 23.

8 Ōkawa's terms are "Anguro-sakison" and "Hakujin." Ōkawa, *Fukkō Ajia no sho-mondai*, pp. 33, 37.

9 Ibid., p. 26.

10 On the Meiji discourse on race (*jinshu*) and its legacy during the wartime, see the exhaustive chapter by Yamamuro Shin'ichi, "Shisō kijiku to shite no jinshu" (Race as an Intellectual Polarity), in his *Shisō kadai to shite no Ajia: kijiku, renso, tōki* (Asia as an Intellectual Problem: Axis, Chains, and Entwurf), Iwanami Shoten, 2001, pp. 54–77.

11 Ōkawa, *Fukkō Ajia no sho-mondai*, p. 25.

12 Ibid., pp. 25–26.

13 Tōyama Shigeki, "Futatsu no nashonarizumu no taikō: sono rekishi-teki kōsatsu," Chūō Kōron (June 1951), reprinted in Rekishi Kagaku Kyōgikai, ed., *Minzoku no mondai*, Kōsō Shobō, 1976 (Rekishi kagaku taikei, vol. 15), pp. 119–35.

14 The rivalry between this mono-ethnic nationalism and a more complex model of assimilation nationalism is the subject of Oguma Eiji, *Tan'itsu minzoku shinwa no kigen: 'Nihonjin' no jigazō no kigen*, Shin'yōsha, 1995. The English translation by David Askew, *A Genealogy of Japanese Self-Images*, Canberra: TransPacific Press, 2002, is useful, but it renders the central concept *minzoku* in a variety of ways, weakening its connection to the nationalism that Oguma analyzes.

15 See, for example, the collection of essays on the problem of nationality in *Nihon shakai-gakkai nenpō: shakaigaku* (Annals of the Japan Sociological Association: Sociology), Iwanami Shoten, 1934, which summarizes the state-of-the-field of Japanese sociology in the mid 1930s. Of particular significance is Seki Eikichi, "Kiso shakai to shite no *minzoku*" (Ethnic Nationality as the Basic Society), pp. 217–41. Seki adopts the "composite nation" theory that Oguma Eiji has made famous, noting that "the Japanese ethnic nation is, just like other ethnic nations, a composite of many different races" (p. 226).

16 Nakano Seiichi, "Tōa ni okeru minzoku genri no kaiken" (An Unfolding of the Principle of Ethnic Nationality in East Asia), in *Minzoku Kenkyūsho Kiyō*, September 1944, pp. 21–69, 64.

17 Akitoshi Shimizu, "Colonialism and the Development of Modern Anthropology in Japan," in Akitoshi Shimizu and Jan van Bremen, eds, *Anthropology and Colonialism in Asia and Oceania*, Surrey: Curzon Press, 1999, pp. 115–71.

18 Hatano Sumio, "'Tōa shinchitsujo' to chiseigaku" (Geopolitics and 'the New Order in East Asia'), in Miwa Kimitada, ed., *Nihon no 1930 nendai*, p. 39.

19 Noguchi Hoichirō, "Dai tōa kyōeiken no *minzoku*" (Nationalities of the Greater East Asia Co-Prosperity Sphere), in Maehara Mitsuo, Noguchi Hoichirō, and Kobayashi Hajime, *Dai tōa kyōeiken no minzoku* (Nationalities of the Greater East Asia Co-Prosperity Sphere), Rokumeikan, 1943 (Minzoku sōsho, vol. 2), p. 1.

20 Maehara Mitsuo, "Riron," in Maehara, Noguchi, and Kobayashi, *Dai tōa kyōeiken no minzoku*, p. 99.

21 Noguchi, "Dai tōa kyōeiken no minzoku," p. 1.

22 Ibid., pp. 11–13.

23 Ibid., p. 16.

24 Ibid., p. 209.

25 Ibid., pp. 210–11.

26 Yasuda Toshiaki, *Teikoku nihon no gengo hensei* (Language Organization in Imperial Japan), Yokohama: Seori Shobō, 1997, p. 293.

27 Komatsu Kentarō, "Dai Tōa *minzoku* no keisei" (The Formation of an East Asian Nationality), in Ogawa Yatarō, ed., *Nihon minzoku to shin sekaikan* (The New Weltanschauung of the Japanese Ethnic Nationality), Ōsaka: Kazuragi Shoten, 1943, pp. 101–02. Noguchi even cites Komatsu's theories on ethnic nationality, but only to share Komatsu's distinction between ethnicity and race, not to espouse a single East Asian nationality. See Noguchi, "Dai tōa kyōeiken no minzoku," pp. 32–33.

28 Ogawa, *Nihon minzoku to shin sekaikan*, p. 2.

29 Usui was a professor at Kyōto Imperial University, Komatsu was a professor at Kansai Gakuin University, Nakano, a former student of Takata and his colleague in the wartime Ethnology Institute, taught for a while at Foundation University in Manshūkoku, and Shimmei was a professor at Tōhoku Imperial University. Takata explicitly locates his work within the discourse of these other social theorists in his *Minzoku-ron* (On Ethnic Nationality), Iwanami Shoten, 1942, p. 2. It is unfortunate that the writings of these social theorists remain relatively unknown outside of Japan, since a more intimate familiarity with this discourse would temper the tendency to interpret wartime *minzoku* discourse as a "racial discourse." As their texts make explicit, the overwhelming interest in *minzoku* during the 1930s was directly connected to the contemporary European discourse on nationality. Tessa Morris-Suzuki has discussed Shimmei's theories on *minzoku* ("ethnic group") in *Re-inventing Japan: Time Space Nation*, London: M.E. Sharpe, 1998, pp. 96–102. The tag "ethnic group" seems to be Morris-Suzuki's own interpretation, however, rather than Shimmei's equivalent for what he means by *minzoku*, which he discusses within the context of theories on "the nation."

30 Kada Tetsuji, *Taiheiyō keizai sensō ron* (On the Economic War in the Pacific), 1941; cited in Miwa Kimitada, "Joron: Nihon ni totte no 1930 nendai: sono seishin-shi jō no tokuchō," in Miwa Kimitada, ed., *Nihon no 1930 nendai*.

31 See my "Building National Identity through Ethnicity: Ethnology in Wartime Japan and After," in *The Journal of Japanese Studies*, 27:1, 2001, pp. 1–39; also "Nakano Seiichi and Colonial Ethnic Studies," in Akitoshi Shimizu and Jan van Bremen, eds, *Wartime Japanese Anthropology in Asia and the Pacific*, Senri Ethnological Studies no. 65, Ōsaka: National Museum of Ethnology, 2003, pp. 109–29.

32 Takata Yasuma, *Minzoku no mondai* (The Problem of Nationality), Nihon Hyōronsha, 1935, p. 260.

33 Takata Yasuma, *Minzoku ron* (On Ethnities), Iwanami Shoten, 1942, p.18. See also Nakao Michio, *Nihon senji shisō no kenkyū: Nihon seishin to Tōa kyōdōtai* (Studies in Wartime Japanese Thought: Japanese Spirit and the East Asian Community), Kanseisha Koseikaku, 2001, pp. 84–96.

34 Nakano Seiichi, "Tōa ni okeru *minzoku* genri no kaiken" (An Unfolding of the Nationality Principle in East Asia), in *Minzoku Kenkyūsho Kiyō*, September 1944, p. 45.

35 Ibid., p. 54.

36 Kōseishō Jinkō Mondai Kenkyūsho, *Yamato minzoku o chūkaku to suru sekai seisaku no kentō* (A Study of Global Policy with the Yamato Volk as the Core), 6 vols, 1943; reprinted by Bunsei Shoin, 1981 (Kōseishō Kenkyūbu Jinkō Minzokubu, Minzoku jinkō seisaku kenkyū shiryō 3). In English, see John Dower, *War without Mercy: Race and Power in the Pacific War*, New York: Pantheon Books, 1986; Tessa Morris-Suzuki, "Ethnic Engineering: Scientific Racism and Public Opinion Surveys in Midcentury Japan," in *positions*, 8:2 (2000), pp. 499–529.

37 *Yamato minzoku o chūkaku to suru sekai seisaku no kentō* 3, p. 27. This rendering of *minzoku* is also justified by the gloss in the text for *minzoku chūshin shugi* as "ethno-centrism." *Yamato minzoku o chūkaku to suru sekai seisaku no kentō* 6, p. 2165.

38 *Yamato minzoku o chūkaku to suru sekai seisaku no kentō* 3, p. 20.

39 Ibid., p. 26.

40 Indeed, one section of the report urges cultural assimilation of other East Asian *Völker* by Japan, *Yamato minzoku o chūkaku to suru sekai seisaku no kentō* 7, p. 2351; another section argues against any single policy for all the *Völker* of Asia, and particularly warns that assimilation efforts would merely cause a backlash against the Japanese (ibid., pp. 2364–65). On the public debate between proponents of a single *Tōa minzoku* and those who insisted on a plural interpretation of *Tōa (sho-)minzoku*, see my "Narrating China, Ordering East Asia," pp. 102–5, 112, 157. It is easy to suspect Kamei's hand behind the anti-assimilation sections of the report, due to his influence in governmental circles, familiarity and support for Nazi nationality theories, and the parallels in the report's arguments and in Kamei's published works.

41 *Yamato minzoku o chūkaku to suru sekai seisaku no kentō* 7, pp. 2182–83.

42 Ibid., p. 2197.

43 Yamamuro Shin'ichi, "'Ta ni shite ichi' no chitsujo genri to Nihon no sentaku" (The Principle of Order through E Pluribus Unum and Japan's Choice), in Aoki Tamotsu and Saeki Keishi, eds, *'Ajia-teki kachi' to wa nani ka* (What are these so-called "Asian Values"?), TBS-Britannica, 1998, pp. 43–64.

44 Aoki Kazuo, cited in Yamamuro, *Shisō kadai to shite no Ajia*, p. 573

45 *Yamato minzoku o chūkaku to suru sekai seisaku no kentō* 6, pp. 2151–52.

12 Constructing destiny: Rōyama Masamichi and Asian regionalism in wartime Japan

1 Tetsuo Najita, *Japan: The Intellectual Foundations of Modern Japanese Politics*, Chicago, IL: University of Chicago Press, 1974, pp. 1–16.

2 For the connection between restorationism and Pan-Asianism, see Tetsuo Najita and Harry Harootunian, "Japanese Revolt against the West: Political and Cultural Criticism in the Twentieth Century," in Peter Duus, ed., *The Cambridge History of Japan, vol. 6*, Cambridge: Cambridge University Press, 1988, pp. 713–71.

3 Masao Maruyama, *Thought and Behavior in Modern Japanese Politics*, expanded edition, Ivan Morris, ed., Tokyo, Oxford and New York: Oxford University Press, 1969, p. 227.

4 Maruyama, *Thought and Behavior*, p. 229.

5 Ibid., p. 234.

6 Ibid., pp. 236–37.

7 This argument is also made by Mitani Taichirō, with somewhat different objectives in mind. See Mitani, "Nihon seijigaku no aidentitii o motomete – Rōyma seijigaku ni miru dai'ichiji sekai sensō no Nihon no seijigaku to sono hen'yō," in *Seikei Hōgaku* 49, 1999, especially pp. 79–84. As Mitani points out, Rōyama's own response to Maruyama's critique took the form of a full-scale defense of prewar Japanese political science, entitled *Nihon ni okeru kindai seijigaku no hattatsu* (1949). Maruyama ack-nowledges this work in his "Postscript" to the 1963 English translation of his essay, noting that his critique "brought forth a brilliant work by Professor Rōyama." See Maruyama, *Thought and Behavior*, p. 241.

8 Mitani, "Nihon seijigaku," p. 93. Also see Sakai Tetsuya, "Sengo shisō to kokusai seijiron no kōsaku," in *Kokusai Seiji* 117, 1998, p. 128, and Sakai Tetsuya, "'Tōa kyōdōtairon' kara 'kindaikaron' e: Rōyama Masamichi ni okeru chiiki-kaihatsu-nashonarizumuron no isō," in Nihon Seiji Gakkai, ed., *Nenpō Seijigaku 1998 – Nihon gaikō ni okeru Ajiashugi*, Iwanami Shoten, 1999, p. 111. Sakai points out that Rōyama was influenced in respect to his functionalism by the work of the Fabian international

relations specialist, Leonard Woolf. On this point, also see Kobayashi Hiroharu, "Royama Masamichi's perception of international order from the 1920s to 1930s and the concept of the East Asian Community," in Dick Stegewerns, ed., *Nationalism and Internationalism in Imperial Japan*, London: RoutledgeCurzon, 2003, pp. 136–38.

9 Mitani, "Nihon seijigaku," p. 94.

10 Ibid., pp. 96–98.

11 Rōyama, "Kokumin kyōdōtai no keisei", in *Kaizō*, May 1939.

12 Mitani, "Nihon seijigaku," pp. 100–02.

13 Ibid., pp. 104–5; Sakai, "'Tōa kyōdōtairon'," pp. 117–18.

14 Rōyama Masamichi, "Tōa kyōdōtai no rironteki kōzō," (1939), in Rōyama, *Tōa to sekai: shin chitsujo e no ronsaku*, Kaizōsha, 1941, p. 158.

15 Rōyama Masamichi, "Tōa kyōdōtai no riron," in *Kaizō*, November 1938, p. 21 (emphasis added).

16 On Miki see also the contribution of John Kim in this volume.

17 *Miki Kiyoshi zenshū VIII*, 7; quoted in Iwasaki Minoru, "Desire for a Poietic Meta-subject: Miki Kiyoshi's Technology Theory," in Yamanouchi Yasushi, J. Victor Koschmann, and Ryūichi Narita, eds, *Total War and 'Modernization'* (Cornell East Asia Series, vol. 100), Ithaca, NY: Cornell University Press, 1998, p. 163. Miki, in turn, had studied with and was heavily influenced by the German philosopher Martin Heidegger, for whom, "what man truly needs is to know the destining to which he belongs. ... A destining of Being is never a blind fate that simply compels man from beyond himself. It is, rather, an opening way in which man is called upon to move to bring about that which is taking place." William Lovitt, "Introduction," to Martin Heidegger, *The Question Concerning Technology and Other Essays*, translated and with an Introduction by William Lovitt, New York: Harper and Row, 1977, p. xxxiii.

18 Rōyama, "Tōa kyōdōtai no rironteki kōzō," pp. 21–23.

19 Rōyama, "Tōa kyōdōtai no riron," p. 29.

20 Rōyama, "Tōa kyōdōtai no rironteki kōzō," p. 167.

21 Ibid., p. 163.

22 Rōyama Masamichi, "Sekai shinchitsujo no tenbō" (1939), in Rōyama, *Tōa to sekai*, p. 77.

23 Ibid., pp. 78–79.

24 Rōyama, "Tōa kyōdōtai no riron," p. 6.

25 Rōyama, "Sekai shinchitsujo no tenbō," pp. 82–83.

26 Rōyama, "Kokumin kyōdōtai no keisei," in *Kaizō*, May 1939, p. 6. For further discussion of this text, see William Miles Fletcher III, *The Search for a New Order: Intellectual and Fascism in Prewar Japan*, Chapel Hill, NC: University of North Carolina Press, 1982, pp. 136–39. As Fletcher points out, in this text and others Rōyama presents the main ideas – "the need for occupational representation, administrative efficiency, centralized planning, and the ideal of the cooperative body" (p. 142) – that soon were to inform the official reports of the Shōwa Kenkyūkai which, in turn, provided the theoretical basis for Konoe's New Order.

27 Rōyama, "Sekai shinchitsujo no tenbō," pp. 82–83.

28 Sakai, "Sengo shisō," pp. 127–31. Noting that a negative evaluation of nationalism was not unusual among international relations scholars in the interwar period, Sakai points out that in the early 1930s Japanese intellectuals often criticized the Nazis for their "narrow nationalism" and claimed that Japan's conceptions of East Asian Community and the Greater East Asia Co-Prosperity Sphere were superior to Nazi equivalents in this regard. See Sakai Tetsuya, "Sengo gaikōron no keisei," in Kitaoka Shin'ichi and Mikuriya Takashi, eds, *Sensō, fukkō, hatten – Shōwa seijishi ni okeru kenryoku to kōsō*, Tōkyō Daigaku Shuppankai, 2000, p. 127.

29 Rōyama, "Tōa kyōdōtai no riron," pp. 16–17.

30 Ibid., pp. 19–20.

31 Sakai, "Sengo shisō," pp. 129–30; and Sakai, "'Tōa kyōdōtairon'," pp. 119–20.

32 A convincing account of the centrality of rationalization and economic development to Rōyama's conception of East Asian Community is Han Jung Sun, "Rationalizing the Orient: The 'East Asia Cooperative Community' in Prewar Japan," in *Monumenta Nipponica* 60.4, Winter 2005, pp. 481–514.

33 Rōyama, "Tōa kyōdōtai no riron," pp. 23–24.

34 Rōyama, "Daitōa kyōeiken no chiseigakuteki kōsatsu" (1941), in Rōyama, *Tōa to sekai*, p. 362.

35 Ibid., pp. 369–70.

36 Ibid., pp. 369–72.

37 Ibid., pp. 364–68. On Karl Haushofer's influence in prewar Japan, see Christian W. Spang, "Nichi-Doku kankei ni okeru Kaaru Hausuhōfā no gakusetsu to jinmyaku, 1909–45," in *Gendaishi Kenkyū* 46, 2000, pp. 35–52.

38 Rōyama, "Daitōa kyōeiken," p. 373.

39 Ibid., pp. 377–78.

40 Ibid., p. 378.

41 See, for example, his contribution to a round-table discussion in a major daily newspaper in 1942, "Daitōa kensetsu zadankai 5," in *Asahi Shinbun*, 23 March 1942.

42 Peace Problems Discussion Circle, "On Peace: Our Third Statement," in *Journal of Social and Political Ideas in Japan* 1.1, April 1963, p. 13.

13   The postwar intellectuals' view of "Asia"

1 Shimizu Ikutarō, "Nihonjin," first published in *Chūō Kōron*, January 1951, reprinted in *Shimizu Ikutarō chosakushū*, vol. 10, Kōdansha, 1992–93, p. 10.

2 The symposium, "Overcoming Modernity" was first carried in the October 1942 edition of the literary journal, *Bungakkai* (Literary World) and then in paperback form by Sōgensha in July 1943. This roundtable discussion included some 13 well-known Japanese philosophers, literary critics, poets, scientists, historians, musicians, movie critics, and others, including a number of apostate Marxists (*tenkō marukusushigisha*). While the content of the symposium was not really considered to be that substantial, it came to be widely known by intellectuals of the day as a discourse symbolizing wartime intellectual trends.

3 *Maruyama Masao shū* no. 3, vol. 3, Iwanami Shoten, 1995–97, p. 4.

4 Hotta Yoshie, Itō Hiroshi, Takeuchi Yoshimi, Hirano Ken, Hanada Kiyoteru, "Nihon no kindai to kokumin bungaku," in *Shin-Nihon Bungaku*, December 1953, p. 152.

5 The August 1948 edition of the Communist Party organ *Zen'ei* carried a special issue titled *Kindaishugi hihan* (A Critique of Modernism), criticizing the magazine *Kindai Bungaku* and individuals such as Ōtsuka Hisao.

6 Cited in *Uchida Yoshihiko chosakushū* vol. 10, Iwanami Shoten, 1988–89, p. 22.

7 *Ōtsuka Hisao chosakushū* vol. 8, Iwanami Shoten, 1969–70, p. 171.

8 See the essays in *Maruyama Masao shū*, vol. 2.

9 Ishimoda Shō, *Zoku rekishi to minzoku no hakken*, Tōkyō Daigaku Shuppankai, 1953, p. 411.

10 *Maruyama Masao shū*, vol. 2, pp. 289–90.

11 Representative of the line of argument attaching great importance to limited rearmament, the US Security Treaty, and economic growth is Yoshida Shigeru, the prime minister at the time the peace treaty was concluded (of course, being a politician, Yoshida's statements are anything but consistent). Yoshida's ties to "progressives" were subtle. In January 1951, for example, in order to resist increased American pressure to rearm, Yoshida secretly requested of the left-wing faction of the Socialist Party that they start an anti-rearmament movement. He then used the strength of domestic opposition as a reason to try and blunt American demands.

12 Etō Jun and Ōe Kenzaburō, "Gendai o dō ikiru ka," in *Gunzō*, January 1968, p. 176.

13 *Takeuchi Yoshimi zenshū*, vol. 4, Chikuma Shobō, 1980–82.

14 *Maruyama Masao shū* no. 5, vol. 8, p. 3.
15 Ōuchi Hyōe, Arisawa Hiromi, Minobe Ryōkichi, Inaba Shūzō, "Tandoku kōwa to Nihon keizai," in *Sekai*, October 1950.
16 Yamamoto Akira, *Sengo fūzoku shi*, Ōsaka: Ōsaka Shoseki, 1986, p. 97.
17 NHK Hōsō Yoron Chōsajo, ed., *Zusetsu: sengo yoron shi*, Nihon Hōsō Shuppan Kyōkai, 1975, p. 14.
18 Umesao Tadao, "Bunmei no seitai shikan yosetsu," in *Chūō Kōron*, February 1957.
19 Honda Katsuichi, *Chūgoku no tabi*, Asahi Shinbunsha, 1972.
20 International Military Tribunal for the Far East (IMTFE), 1946–48.
21 *Tsurumi Shunsuke chosakushū* vol. 5, no. 1, Chikuma Shobō, 1975, p. 131.
22 Howard Zinn, "Sakana to gyōshi", first published in *Sekai heiwa undō shiryō*, July 1967, reprinted in *Shiryō "Beheiren" undo*, Chikuma Shobō, 1974, p. 89.
23 *Hannichi kakumei sengen*, Higashi Ajia Hannichi Busō Sensen, 1979.
24 Mahathir bin Mohamad and Ishihara Shintarō, *"No" to ieru Ajia*, Kōbunsha, 1984.

14 Overcoming colonialism at Bandung, 1955

1 The Conference of Asian Nations (Ajia shokoku kaigi) in New Delhi, India, 6–10 April 1955, also reinforced this attention to Japan's relations with other Asian countries, especially India and China. For contemporary commentaries on these conferences, see the following articles in the June 1955 issue (no. 801) of *Chūō Kōron*: Nishino Shōtarō, "Ajia, Afurika kaigi no sekaishiteki igi" (The global historical significance of the Asia-Africa Conference), pp. 105–13; Sakamoto Tokumatsu, "Ajia shokoku kaigi no hito to inshō" (People and impressions at the conference of Asian countries), pp. 114–17. Kinoshita Junji, "Indo nōson no nokishita ni nete" (Sleeping under the eaves in an Indian farm village), pp. 118–24. Kinoshita was one of the Japanese representatives at the conference in India.
2 Shigemitsu Mamoru was one of 139 candidates elected to the Diet in 1952 who had previously been purged during the Occupation because of their prewar record. Hatoyama Ichirō, prime minister in 1955, was also elected to the Diet in the 1 October 1952 Lower House general election. Satō Seizaburō *et al.*, *Postwar Politician: The Life of Former Prime Minister Masayoshi Ōhira*, Kōdansha, 1990, p. 144. As Barbara Brooks notes in her study of China experts in the Ministry of Foreign Affairs, Shigemitsu maintained contact with wartime bureaucrats after 1945. Barbara Brooks, "The Gaimusho's China Experts," in Peter Duus *et al.*, eds, *The Japanese Informal Empire in China, 1895–1937*, Princeton, NJ: Princeton University Press, 1989, p. 378.
3 E. Bruce Reynolds, "Anomaly or Model? Independent Thailand's Role in Japan's Asian Strategy, 1941–43," in Peter Duus *et al.*, eds, *The Japanese Wartime Empire, 1931–1945*, Princeton, NJ: Princeton University Press, 1996, p. 267.
4 For a synopsis of Japan's delegation, see Miyagi Taizō, *Bandon kaigi to Nihon no Ajia fukki* (The Bandung Conference and Japan's Return to Asia), Sōshisha, 2001, p. 122.
5 Before 1945 Tani Masayuki had served as "chief of the Foreign Ministry's East Asia Bureau." Y. Tak Matsusaka, "Managing Occupied Manchuria, 1931–34," in Peter Duus *et al.*, eds, *The Japanese Wartime Empire, 1931–1945*, p. 118. Kase Toshikazu was an aide to Shigemitsu at the time of his change in strategy to establish "a moral basis for the war effort [that] would permit the Japanese to rationalize it as a noble one." See Reynolds, "Anomaly or Model?," p. 267.
6 Masumi Junnosuke, *Contemporary Politics in Japan*. Translated by Lonny E. Carlile, Berkeley, CA: University of California Press, 1995, p. 408.
7 Wakamiya Yoshibumi, *The Postwar Conservative View of Asia: How the Political Right Has Delayed Japan's Coming to Terms With its History of Aggression in Asia*, LTCB International Library Foundation, 1998, pp. 133, 138. Sheldon M. Garon, "The Imperial Bureaucracy and Labor Policy in Postwar Japan," in *The Journal of Asian Studies* 43:3, 1984, pp. 446, 452.

8 Benjamin C. Duke, *Japan's Militant Teachers: A History of the Left-Wing Teachers' Movement*, Honolulu, HI: The University Press of Hawaii, 1973, pp. 136, 174.

9 Such directives can be found in the proceedings of this group's annual meeting in 1952. Rekishi Kagaku Kyōgikai, ed., *Rekishi kagaku taikei dai-33 maki: Minka rekishi bukai shiryōshū*, Kōso Shobō, 1999, p. 73.

10 Miyoshi and Harootunian discuss several of the ambiguities of Japan's postwar position in the world in their introductory essay, "Japan in the World" in Masao Miyoshi and Harry D. Harootunian, eds, *Japan in the World*, Durham, NC: Duke University Press, 1993, pp. 1–9.

11 I use this phrase, "coming to terms with the past" along the lines of Dominick LaCapra's conception of "working through" the past, as discussed in his work, *Representing the Holocaust: History, Theory, Trauma*, Ithaca, NY: Cornell University Press, pp. 45–46. In this regard, LaCapra also cites Theodor W. Adorno's essay "What Does Coming to Terms with [*Aufarbeitung*] the Past Mean?" trans. Timothy Bahti and Geoffrey Hartman, in G. Hartman, ed., *Bitburg in Moral and Political Perspective*, Bloomington, IN: University of Indiana Press, 1986, pp. 114–29.

12 Kase Toshikazu, "Japan's New Role in Asia," in *Foreign Affairs* 34:1, October 1955, pp. 47–48.

13 Indonesian leader Ali Sastroamijoyo notes that Wajima's mission to normalize relations and trade in Southeast Asia in 1953 stemmed from Japan having outgrown "the demands of home market" after the end of the Korean War, when there was less demand in Korea, exports to the United States were limited, and there was no trade with mainland China. C. L. M. Penders, ed., *Milestones on my Journey: The Memoirs of Ali Sastroamijoyo, Indonesian Patriot and Political Leader*, Queensland: University of Queensland Press, 1979, p. 262.

14 Cf. Curtis Anderson Gayle, *Marxist History and Postwar Japanese Nationalism*, New York: RoutledgeCurzon, 2003, p. 75.

15 The Japanese term "*minzoku*" is used here because the English translation varies, depending on the context. Sometimes it connotes nationality or ethnicity, but generally the most apt translation is "people."

16 These points are culled from Chitta Biswas, *The Relevance of Bandung: Thirtieth Anniversary of the Bandung Conference*, Cairo: AAPSO, 1985, pp. 12–13. See also Nishino, "Ajia, Afurika kaigi no sekaishiteki igi," p. 111.

17 For a detailed account of the anti-colonial aspects of Asian-African movements, especially with regard to international law and connections to the United Nations, see Ochiai Kiyotaka, *Gendai kokusai hōsei yoron: Ajia, Afurika o chūshin toshite* (An outline of contemporary international laws and governments: centered on Asia and Africa), Keibundō Shuppanbu, 1970, pp. 14–30.

18 George McTurnan Kahin, *The Asian-African Conference*, Ithaca, NY: Cornell University Press, 1956, p. 2. C. L. M. Penders, ed., *Milestones on My Journey*, p. 293.

19 Biswas, *The Relevance of Bandung*, p. 14.

20 Ibid.

21 Ibid.

22 With regard to postwar pacifism, as John Dower has stated, "What matters is what the Japanese themselves made of their experience of defeat, then and thereafter; and, for a half century now, most of them have consistently made it the touchstone for affirming a commitment to 'peace and democracy.' This is the great mantra of postwar Japan." *Embracing Defeat: Japan in the Wake of World War II*, New York: W.W. Norton & Co., 1999, p. 30.

23 Carol Gluck, "The Past in the Present," in Andrew Gordon, ed., *Postwar Japan as History*, Berkeley, CA: University of California Press, 1993, p. 70.

24 J. A. A. Stockwin, *The Japanese Socialist Party and Neutralism: A Study of a Political Party and its Foreign Policy*, London and New York: Cambridge University Press, 1968, p. 83. Regarding the stance of postwar Socialist parties on neutralism and

related issues see Allan B. Cole, George O. Totten, and Cecil H. Uyehara, *Socialist Parties in Postwar Japan*, New Haven, CT: Yale University Press, 1966. Of particular note is the stance of the Heiwa Dōshikai faction leader, Matsumoto Jiichirō, who is described as follows: "In postwar Japan he has voiced pan-Asian views, has had good words for Communist China and the Soviet Union, and has roundly denounced Japan's ruling classes and Western imperialism" (p. 288).

25 On the Communist party's anti-imperialist stance, see Nihon Kyōsantō Chūō Iinkai Kyōikubu, ed., *Nihon Kyōsantō shokyū kyōkasho* (Japan Communist Party Beginner Textbook), Nihon Kyōsantō Chūō Iinkai Shuppankyoku, 1968. In part one, the authors attribute Japan's postwar high-speed growth to a combination of Japanese monopoly capitalism and its alliance with American imperialism. They criticize US imperialism for subjugating Japan politically, economically, and militarily (pp. 29–30).

26 Kweku Ampiah, "Japan at the Bandung Conference: The Cat Goes to the Mice's Convention," in *Japan Forum* 7:1, Spring 1995, p. 22, fn 2.

27 Kase, "Japan's New Role in East Asia," pp. 40–49.

28 Ibid., p. 42.

29 Ibid., p. 45. Emphasis added.

30 Ibid., p. 45.

31 In the 1974 edition of Hilary Conroy's 1960 study of Japanese expansionism in Korea, the author addresses the problems raised by the use of the term "realism" in his analysis of Japanese national security concern in the Meiji era. Hilary Conroy, *The Japanese Seizure of Korea: 1868–1910, A Study of Realism and Idealism in International Relations*, Philadelphia, PA: University of Pennsylvania Press, 1974, pp. 7–10.

32 As cited in Masumi, *Contemporary Politics in Japan*, p. 23.

33 Ibid. Masumi also describes the economic pitfalls of Fujiyama's involvement in LDP politics by the 1960s and 1970s, including the sale of "¥5 billion worth of assets for the sake of politics" (p. 226).

34 Satō *et al.*, *Postwar Politician*, p. 194.

35 Wakamiya, *The Postwar Conservative View of Asia*, p. 151.

36 Cited in Miyagi, *Bandon kaigi to Nihon no Ajia fukki*, p. 127.

37 Tanaka Hiroshi, "Nihon no sengo sekinin to Ajia: sengo hoshō to rekishi ninshiki" (Japan's postwar responsibility and Asia: postwar reparations and acknowledging history), in Ōe Shinobu *et al.*, eds, *Kindai Nihon to shokuminchi, vol. 8: Ajia no reisen to datsushokuminchika* (Modern Japan and its colonies, vol. 8: The Cold War in Asia and decolonization), Iwanami Shoten, p. 186.

38 Carlos P. Romulo, *The Meaning of Bandung*, Chapel Hill, NC: University of North Carolina Press, 1956, p. 3. Romulo was the leader of the delegation from the Philippines.

39 B. P. Dalal, "Bandung Conference – Triumph of Afro-Asian Identity," in *The Oracle* 9:4, October 1987, p. 52.

40 Biswas, *The Relevance of Bandung*, p. 3.

41 David Kimche, *The Afro-Asian Movement: Ideology and Foreign Policy of the Third World*, Jerusalem: Israel Universities Press, 1973, p. 1.

42 Ibid.

43 Ibid., p. 11.

44 Baba Kimihiko, "Japan and East Asia: Shifting Images on an Imagined Map," translated by Kristine Dennehy and Anne Phillips, in *Japanese Studies* 21:3, 2001, p. 244.

45 Biswas, *The Relevance of Bandung*, p. 5.

46 Romulo, *The Meaning of Bandung*, p. 2.

47 Curtis Gayle argues that leading members of *Rekishigaku Kenkyūkai* such as Eguchi Bokurō and Ishimoda Shō succeeded in separating "the idea of *minzoku* from any associations with pre-war *minzokushugi*, and they also offered up a mordant and compelling critique of American imperialism and global capitalism against the backdrop of

post-war nationalism in Asia." See his "Progressive Representations of the Nation: Early Post-war Japan and Beyond," in *Social Science Japan Journal* 4:1, 2001, p. 10.

48 Biswas, *The Relevance of Bandung*, pp. 16–17.

49 See James Orr, *The Victim as Hero: Ideologies of Peace and National Identity in Postwar Japan*, Honolulu, HI: University of Hawaii Press, 2001, p. 73. The position of the Japan Communist Party regarding its unique role in "an international united front against nuclear weapons" (p. 37) is outlined in The International Commission, Central Committee, Japan Communist Party, *Japanese Politics and the Communist Party*, Japan Press Service, 1985, pp. 36–38, 60–63.

50 Dower, *Embracing Defeat*, p. 29.

51 Orr, *The Victim as Hero*, p. 6.

52 Ibid., p. 7.

53 Cf. ibid., p. 67.

54 Japan Communist Party, *Japanese Politics and the Communist Party*, p. 60.

55 Orr, *The Victim as Hero*, pp. 47–48.

56 The literature on the connection between historical research and contemporary political activism is extensive. See, for example, Nakatsuka Akira's discussion of Hani Gorō and the importance of using historical criticism as a basis for a critical understanding of contemporary events, and vice versa. Nakatsuka Akira, *Rekishika no shigoto: hito wa naze rekishi o kenkyū suru no ka* (The work of a historian: why do people research history?), Kōbunken, 2000, p. 237.

57 See the description of the view of Left Socialists in 1952 and their "struggle against Japan's 'subordinate' position" *vis-à-vis* the United States as a result of the peace and security treaties, in Cole, *et al.*, *Socialist Parties in Postwar Japan*, p. 41. See also Miyoshi and Harootunian, "Japan in the World," p. 2. In the January 1955 issue (no. 179) of *Rekishigaku Kenkyū*, Tōyama Shigeki referred to the "semi-occupied status" (*han-hisenryō no jōtai*) of the Japanese people and tied their suffering to that of the masses (*minshū*) in Asia and Europe. Tōyama Shigeki, "1955-nen o koete kokuminteki rekishigaku o hiyakuteki ni hatten saseyō" (Let's make rapid progress in developing nationalist historiography and overcoming 1955), *Tōyama Shigeki chosakushū, dai-9-kan*, Iwanami Shoten, 1992, p. 152.

58 Regarding the particularly harsh conditions of the Okinawans under US military authority, see Takamae Eiji, *Inside GHQ: The Allied Occupation of Japan and its Legacy*, trans. Robert Ricketts and Sebastian Swann, New York: Continuum, 2002, pp. 441–44.

59 Kimche, *The Afro-Asian Movement*, p. 89.

60 Ibid., p. 82.

61 Kumakura Hiroyasu, *Sengo heiwa undōshi* (A history of the postwar peace movement), Ōtsuki Shoten, 1959, pp. 77–78. Tōyama Shigeki, "'Ajiateki seisan yōshiki' ronsō ni tsuite" (On the debate over the "Asiatic mode of production"), *Tōyama Shigeki chosakushū, dai-8-kan, Nihon kindai shigakushi*, Iwanami Shoten, 1992, p. 311.

15 Pan-Asianism in international relations: prewar, postwar, and present

1 The author thanks the Research Subsidy Fund (2004) of Kyoto Women's University for subsidizing his research on "Pan-Asianism in Globalization," from which this text derives.

2 Hatsuse Ryūhei, "International System," UNESCO, *Encyclopedia of Life Support System (EOLSS)*, http://www.eolss.net (accessed on 15 May 2006).

3 See the contribution of Kristine Dennehy in this volume (the editors).

4 Mohammad Mahathir and Ishihara Shintarō, *"No" to ieru Ajia*, Kōbunsha, 1984, pp. 94–126.

5 Marius B. Jansen, *The Japanese and Sun Yat-sen*, Cambridge, MA: Harvard University

Press, 1954; Hatsuse Ryūhei, *Dentōteki uyoku Uchida Ryōhei no kenkyū*, Fukuoka: Kyūshū Daigaku Shuppankai, 1980.

6 Uchida Ryōhei, *Kōseki 50 nenpu*, Fukuoka: Ashi Shobō, 1978, p. 77.

7 *Miyazaki Tōten zenshū, vol. 1*, Heibonsha, 1971, p. 263.

8 Japan's yen loans to Asian countries started when it lent to India in 1957, whereas its ODA started substantially with payment of reparations to Burma, the Philippines, Indonesia, and South Vietnam in the mid-1950s. The ODA policy became articulated in the mid-1960s. (Watanabe Akio, ed., *Sengo Nihon no taigai seisaku*, Yūhikaku, 1985, pp. 136–40, 286–28).

9 Tsūshō-sangyō-shō Bōeki-shinkō-kyoku, ed., *Keizai-kyōryoku-no genjō to mondaiten (1969)*, Tsūshō-sangyō Chōsakai, 1970, p. 79.

10 Kamei Shizuka, "Haikaisuru Tokyo-saiban shikan," in *Shokun*, July 1988, p. 141.

11 Round Table Talk, "Ajia to no kankei o kangeru," in *Keidanren Geppō*, vol. 34, no. 5, May 1986, pp. 11–12.

12 Ono Satoyo, "Kanbojia Nanmin Kyūen to Ajia no Shōrai," in *Hateshinaki ueno naka-de*, no. 1, October 1980, p. 6.

13 Iwamura Noboru, *Tomoni ikiru tame ni*, Shinkyō Shuppansha, 1982, p. 237.

14 Hatsuse Ryuhei, "Japanese responses to globalization: nationalism and transnationalism," in Glenn D. Hook and Hasegawa Haruhiko, eds, *The Political Economy of Japanese Globalization*, London: Routledge, 2001, pp. 179–80.

15 For the activities of Dr. Nakamura and Peshawar-kai, see Nakamura Tetsu, *Peshawar nite*, enlarged edition, Fukuoka: Sekifūsha, 1992; *Afghanistan no shinryōsho kara*, Chikuma Shobō, 1993; *Dara-e-Noor e no michi*, Fukuoka: Sekifūsha, 1993; *I wa kokkyō o koete*, Fukuoka: Sekifūsha, 1999; *Isha ido o horu*, Fukuoka: Sekifūsha, 2001; *Hontō no Afghanistan*, Kōbunsha, 2002; *Nakamura Tetsu-san kōenroku*, Kyōto: Peace Walk Kyoto, 2002; *Henkyō de miru, henkyō kara miru*, Fukuoka: Sekifūsha, 2003; *Isha-yo, shinnen wa iranai, mazu inochi o sukue*, Yōdosha, 2003; Nakamura Tetsu and Peshawarkai, eds, *Kūbaku to "fukkō,"* Fukuoka: Sekifūsha, 2004. Peshawar-kai Jimukyoku, ed., *Peshawar-kaihō, Gappon*, no. 1, December 1983–no. 79, April 2004, Fukuoka: Sekifūsha, 2004.

16 Maruyama Naoki, *Doctor Sābu*, Fukuoka: Sekifūsha, 2001, pp. 84–87.

17 http://www.yu-cho.japanpost.jp/volunteer-post (accessed on 1 September 2004).

18 Nakamura, *I wa kokkyō o koete*, pp. 164–65. The slogan originated from headlines in a newspaper that reported the worsening health situation in the region and Peshawar-kai's medical assistance to the suffering.

19 In January 2005, when two clinics in Dara-e-Paich and Dara-e-wama were handed over to the local authority by the order of the central government in Kabul, they were actually abandoned and closed.

20 Nakamura, *Isha-yo, shinnen wa iranai, mazu inochi o sukue*, p. 37.

21 "Point of View/Tetsu Nakamura: Military action against Afghan backlash," in *International Tribune/The Asahi Shinbun*, 13 December 2003, http://www1a.biglobe. ne.jp/peshawar/eg/naka13dec03.html (accessed on 27 December 2003).

22 *Magsaysay Awardees 2003*, http://www.rmaf.org.ph (accessed on 1 March 2004).

23 Peshawar-kai, *About Us*, http://www1a.biglobe.ne.jp/peshawar/ (accessed on 1 September 2004).

24 Nakamura, *Hontō no Afghanistan*, p. 121.

25 Nakamura, *Peshawar nite*, p. 251.

26 Nakamura, *Henkyō de miru, henkyō kara miru*, p. 68.

27 Nakamura, *Kūbaku to "fukkō"*, p. 44.

28 Nakamura, *Henkyō de miru, henkyō kara miru*, p. 22.

29 Fukumoto Manji, *Fukuryū no shikō*, Fukuoka: Sekifūsha, 2004, pp. 16–17.

30 Nakamura, *Afghanistan no shinryōsho kara*, p. 193.

31 Nakamura, *Peshawar nite*, pp. 252–53.

Index